VAN WYCK BROOKS

JAMES HOOPES

VAN WYCK BROOKS

In Search of American Culture

The University of Massachusetts Press   Amherst 1977

Copyright © 1977 by

The University of Massachusetts Press

All rights reserved

Library of Congress Catalog Card Number 76-8754

ISBN 0-87023-212-6

Printed in the United States of America

Designed by Mary Mendell

Cataloging in Publication data appears on the

last printed page of the book.

For my father, Edgar,
and my mother, Ruth

CONTENTS

ILLUSTRATIONS

PREFACE

IN this book I have used the word "culture" synonymously with high culture, the sense in which Van Wyck Brooks used it. But he would have disagreed with the current assumption that such usage necessarily excludes popular culture. In fact he came to believe that for a high culture to have significance in the United States it must also be popular, meaning not that it must be majoritarian but that it must work to a democratic purpose. Culture can work to a democratic purpose, he might have said, as a bringer of light, as an enhancer of our common understanding of social reality. In order to play its revealing light over the darker aspects of American experience, culture must be critical, detached, idealistic, or in a word, high.

I doubt that we can have such a culture in this country without a measure of the self-consciousness which Brooks deplored in the modern temperament. Neither do I agree with him that nationalism is the force best suited to promote American high culture. The danger there is the temptation, to which Brooks sometimes succumbed, to facilely turn much that is ambiguous in American history to good account. I have not hesitated to criticize him on these issues in the text that follows. Therefore, I here state my agreement with Brooks on two fundamental points: (1) that the United States did not have in his time (and still lacks in ours) a culture adequate to its needs and (2) that such a culture must not be genteely removed from, or merely reflective of social reality, but rather, critically engaged with it.

My treatment of Brooks as a cultural reformer has been influenced to some degree by most of the major interpretations of his reformist generation. These interpretations, which usually focus on the social situation, easily stand the test of being measured against the specific case of Brooks. Certainly his family suffered from status anxiety. Certainly his was a case of the alienated intellectual seeking an accommodation with American society. And certainly his life might be read as a search after vanished community and order. These interpretations may be found in many recent books and articles, but they have their by now almost classic expressions in, respectively, Richard Hofstadter, *The Age of Reform* (1955); Christopher Lasch, *The New Radicalism in America* (1965); and Robert Wiebe, *The Search for Order* (1967).

I believe, then, that whatever is original in this book stems not from my account of Brooks's social origins but rather from my examination of his cultural situation. Previous historians, notably Henry May in *The End of American Innocence* (1959), have suggested that culture was a principal issue in the ferment and strife of the pre-World War I years. Yet even May's admirable account is focused mainly on the politics and sociology of the struggle between genteel and modern culture. Our cultural historians have largely ignored the question of the relationship between the content of the two cultures, ignored the possibility that the old culture may have contained elements which provoked the new, ignored the possibility that culture may be a causative force in cultural history. The anthropological definition of culture as "the knowledge people use to generate and interpret social behavior" may serve the historian of high as well as of any other sort of culture.[1] But it requires that the historian take knowledge seriously.

I have tried to take seriously the knowledge about "art" which led Brooks to transform himself from a Harvard esthete into a spokesman for cultural radicalism. That knowledge had its origins in genteel culture, and insofar as it was shared by his fellow reformers it may suggest sources of radicalism that have been hitherto overlooked. If so, then further research is justified on questions like the following. How prevalent among the college-educated upper and middle classes was the sense of being a frustrated and thwarted personality? Did that sense of frustration have a source in any of the articles of genteel culture — that is, were there other symbols in the culture that functioned as "art" did for Brooks? For him the idea of the artist, with its connotations then of a free, robust, spontaneous, and individual personality, was a symbol of what human life should properly be. How widespread was the idea of American society as an infertile ground for the artistic spirit, an idea that located the sources of personality's frustration in society? Were any of Brooks's fellow reformers moved by these notions about art and America? In other words, how common a response to the frustration of "artistic instinct" was the idea of making social reform itself an art in America, the "art of society," as I have called it in this book?

The frequency with which the word "America" occurs in these pages is itself a reflection of Brooks's belief that art was social in nature and purpose. For him, "America" had a complex sense and was symbolic not only of a nation or geographical area but of the "world" or reality itself, the matter in which the artist expressed himself. For that reason no synonym exists for what Brooks meant by "America," and I have used the word often in this book. But for me it is not an incantation.

The responses of several readers of the manuscript indicate that one final caveat is in order. As with most of Brooks's personal attitudes, his ideas on women were conservative and reflected his turn-of-the-century, upper-middle-class origins. I would have felt heavy handed criticizing him on issues that are no longer debatable, and I have refrained from doing so. But my disagreement with Brooks on this score does not extend to his attacks on the "feminization" of culture and literature. Perhaps his image of genteel culture as feminine had connotations demeaning to women as well as to the culture. But his most basic objection to the genteel tradition was not that it was feminine in quality or essence. Rather, he objected to its having come to be seen as primarily the possession of middle-class women, a social group which was not directly related to the business and economic processes which he believed most needed enlightenment. Here his attitude was rightly shared by many cultural radicals, female as well as male. Thus, Christopher Lasch has argued that the sense of alienation from life of women like Jane Addams, Charlotte Perkins Gilman, and Margaret Sanger can be traced to their assigned social role as attendants of a meaningless culture while practical occupations were reserved for men; ". . . in no other country in the world was the distinction between the two, in the popular mind, so rigid."[2] Such a sexual division of labor not only created problems for women who desired practical pursuits but also caused difficulties for men with cultural interests, as has often been pointed out with reference to Henry Adams, Henry James, George Santayana, and numerous others. Brooks's revolt, therefore, was not against the restrictions of woman's "place" as a keeper of culture but against the limitations of man's role as a mere money earner. It was his resentment of the idea that culture had no meaning for men which led him to protest its "feminization." In this sense, his revolt was complementary rather than antagonistic to feminism.

ACKNOWLEDGMENTS

I N researching and writing this book I have incurred, in retrospect, an astonishing number of obligations. The discovery of so
much generosity and good will has been one of my principal rewards
in undertaking this project. It is a pleasure to express my gratitude,
inadequate as it must be, to the following people.

My largest intellectual debt is to Kenneth S. Lynn, who served as
my graduate advisor at Johns Hopkins, who responded to my initial
expression of interest in Brooks with the suggestion that he would
be a good subject for a Ph.D. dissertation, and who directed the
dissertation with the best possible combination of rigorous criticism
and friendly interest. David Donald was the dissertation's second
reader and provided a detailed, thorough, and immensely useful
reading. Two fellow graduate students, Robert Brugger and
Richard Kent, not only read the manuscript but constituted a forum
for the discussion of problems in biography and American culture.
Among numerous friends from Johns Hopkins, Lenard R. Berlan-
stein and Jack R. Censer have been particularly close and sustaining.

Parts or all of the manuscript profited from being read by
Daniel Aaron, Paul Buhle, Nancy Chudacoff, David Hirsch, William
McLoughlin, and John Thomas. Professors Hirsch, McLoughlin,
and Howard Chudacoff have served as co-chairpersons of the
American Civilization Program at Brown University during the

three years that I have taught in and helped administer the program, and they have been extremely sympathetic to the need of a young faculty member for time to write. It would also be accurate to say that the time to write this book was given to me by students at Brown. I am grateful to them for that, for their apparent lack of resentment of that, and for the friendship and interest of many of them in this book.

To Van Wyck Brooks's widow, Gladys, a gracious and spirited lady, I am grateful for warm friendship and support. She generously shared her acute insights into her husband's character with me, and she made it possible for me to spend three months in Brooks's last home in Bridgewater, Connecticut. There I was able to take advantage of resources in the house and area which would not otherwise have been available. This book, however, is in no sense an authorized or official biography. I was fortunate enough to receive Mrs. Brooks's aid and encouragement only after the project was well underway. She has read the manuscripts, saved me several factual errors, and suggested some changes in interpretation while insisting on none. The result of this, for me, particularly happy relationship is that I have had complete cooperation from the family while every judgment in the book is entirely my own.

Charles Van Wyck Brooks and Oliver Kenyon Brooks have been equally unstinting whenever their cooperation was essential in helping me get at the facts of their father's life. They too have provided information and materials, and they too have read the manuscript, saving me errors of omission as well as commission. Their authorization enabled me to see the medical records at Four Winds on which chapter seven is largely based.

Dr. John Lambert, the medical director of Four Winds, was kind and cooperative during my visit there. Dr. Lambert has checked chapter seven for factual accuracy and corrected my usage of medical terminology in the few passages where I have had to resort to it.

I am indebted to the following friends and acquaintances of Van Wyck Brooks for submitting to interviews: Mrs. Hamilton Basso, Malcolm Cowley, Henry A. Murray, Charles Seeger, the late Elizabeth Seeger, Joan Terrall, Louis Untermeyer, and John Hall Wheelock. My thanks also to Lewis Mumford, who answered several questions by mail.

For permission to quote from unpublished letters and manuscripts I am grateful to the following persons: Daniel Aaron for Newton Arvin's letters to Brooks; the Brooks family for the letters and manuscripts of their relatives and ancestors; Jean K. Frank for Waldo Frank's letters to Brooks; Judith Zinsser Lippmann for Hans Zinsser's letters to Lewis Mumford; Lewis Mumford for his letters to Eleanor Brooks; Margaret Sandburg for Carl Sandburg's letter to Brooks; Charles Scribner for letters in the Charles Scribner's Sons Archives at Princeton; and Dorothy G. Whyte for her letters to Brooks.

These and other letters on which this book is based are housed in the various manuscript collections listed in the Note on Sources. The libraries which made these collections available are also listed there, and I am grateful to all of them. I would be derelict, however, if I did not single out for special thanks Neda Westlake, Curator of Rare Books and Manuscripts at the C. P. Van Pelt Library of the University of Pennsylvania where the Brooks Papers are held. The professional competence of Mrs. Westlake and members of her staff, especially Eileen Garafano, eased the task of research.

Some letters and other materials were in the possession of private individuals and institutions other than libraries. My thanks, then, to the Brooks family, to Henry A. Murray, and to Dorothy G. Whyte, who all made available personal letters from Brooks. Mrs. Whyte had loaned her letters to Raymond Nelson, himself at work on a biography of Brooks, and he generously allowed me to see them. The Plainfield Public High School made available a complete file of the *Oracle,* to which the young Brooks was a prolific contributor. The Office of the Registrar at Harvard University permitted me to see Brooks's undergraduate transcript. The American Academy of Arts and Letters allowed me to see the correspondence relating to Brooks's service as secretary and, later, chancellor of that institution.

I am grateful to the Brooks family for supplying me with most of the photographs that appear in this book. I am also grateful to Mrs. John Frothingham for the photo of Maxwell Perkins, to the Archives of Smith College for the photo of Newton Arvin, to Charles A. Scribner for the photo of Mollie Colum, to the Newberry Library for the photo of Sherwood Anderson, to Malcolm Cowley for the photo of himself, and to the Libraries of the University of Pennsylvania for several photos of Brooks and of Waldo Frank and Lewis Mumford.

Malcolm Call and Janis Bolster of the University of Massachusetts Press have shown a gratifying interest in the book and improved it greatly with their editorial suggestions.

During the last two years Carol Aberbach Hoopes has willingly discussed various aspects of this book with me almost daily, has read the manuscript for errors in style and typography, and has been in all ways a constant source of encouragement.

The dedication expresses some small part of the gratitude I feel to my parents, who have always been supportive without demanding explanations or questioning any right thing I wished to do.

PLAINFIELD, 1886–1904

ONE August day in London in 1908, Van Wyck Brooks, age twenty-two, signed the contract for publication of his first book and returned to his room, not in jubilation at this early success, but in despair and worry about the book and "of the possibility of its hurting mama."[1] His concern was understandable, for his mother was a cultured and patriotic American woman, and the book, *The Wine of the Puritans,* was the opening salvo of Brooks's continuing attack on American culture for its excessive femininity. He would make the point often and more clearly in later books — *America's Coming-of-Age* (1915), *The Ordeal of Mark Twain* (1920), and *The Pilgrimage of Henry James* (1925) — books on which he eventually focused many of the feelings of guilt and inadequacy that troubled him all his life. But the personal note, the fact that his attacks on American culture were also attacks on those he loved, was never more evident than in this first book.

Van Wyck cast *The Wine of the Puritans* in the form of a dialogue on art between two young Americans in Italy. He had described one of them, "Graeling," in an essay he had written more than a year before, while still an undergraduate at Harvard. Charles Graeling bore a striking resemblance to Van Wyck and was in fact an imagined *alter ego.* Like Van Wyck, Graeling had been born in 1886 into a New York family "of American ancestry, mixed considerably on the father's side with Irish blood," a saving touch of Celtic warmth in an otherwise cold and Calvinistic heritage. Both Graeling and Van Wyck had been taken abroad for a year at the age of twelve and had been awestruck by their youthful exposure to European art and culture. Physically and emotionally, too, there were great similarities, both of them being shy and small but "perfectly proportioned," with "pure and fresh" complexions, "rather flowing black hair and bright blue eyes" — handsome youths of exquisite sensitivity in search of the grail of art.

The differences, however, were as significant as the similarities. Van Wyck, an acutely self-conscious young writer who felt frustrated in his ambition to be an artist, had written a book blaming his disappointment on the family and country in which he had been raised. But the happy Graeling had been reared in "the surroundings that were most perfectly suited to [his] development," thanks to his "fortunate circumstance" of being an orphan. Brought up by an unusually sympathetic aunt, Graeling experienced a "frequent feeling of satisfaction that his father and mother had died too soon to bring to bear the force of close personal influence upon the development of his own personality."[2] No wonder, then, that Van Wyck feared *The Wine of the Puritans* would hurt his mother: through the fictitious character of Charles Graeling, Van Wyck's idealized second self, he was attacking not only his mother's culture but his mother herself.

II

Sallie Brooks never questioned her own qualifications as an arbiter of American taste and culture, and it would have been surprising if she had done so, with her secure upper-class childhood and ancestry that was, as she understood the word, impeccably American. Consciously proud of her Dutch and English forebears, she was quick to join the Daughters of the American Revolution when the organization was founded in the 1890's. She impressed her family pride on her children, and Van Wyck, in both youth and old age, would take a far greater interest in his mother's ancestral line than in his father's.

Sallie could count back seven generations before reaching her first American ancestor, Cornelius Barente Van Wyck, who had emigrated to New Amsterdam in 1659. His descendants were mostly prosperous Long Island and, later, upstate farmer-gentry. But two of Cornelius Van Wyck's great-grandsons distinguished themselves as generals in the American army during the Revolution. Their sister, Altje Van Wyck, married a colonel, John Bailey, thus producing the mixture of Dutch and English blood from which Sallie was descended. One of Altje Bailey's sons, Theodorus, became a United States senator; another, William, became a large landholder by marrying into the Platt family (the founders of Plattsburgh). Sallie was especially interested in two of William's children. Theodorus Bailey entered the Navy, rose to the rank of rear admiral, and, second in command under Farragut at New Orleans, was the Union officer who accepted that city's surrender. John Bailey, brother of the admiral, was Sallie's grandfather. A successful businessman and farmer in Plattsburgh, he married a poet, Emily Thurber, who bore him three sons (two of whom perished in the Civil War) and in 1832 a daughter, Phebe, who became Sallie's mother.[3]

Phebe was a thorough New Yorker, raised in Plattsburgh and educated in a select Manhattan boarding school. One of her best friends there was a relative of James Fenimore Cooper's, and she visited the novelist's family in Cooperstown. Phebe was to live in the Brookses' house, or rather they in hers, all through Van Wyck's childhood, and she aided Sallie in vivifying all these ancestral memories of New York for Van Wyck, as when she told him of how she as a girl had met Washington Irving. It was also in New York that Phebe met her husband, Charles Ames, and gave birth to Sallie, her only child, in 1858.[4]

Charles Ames was a descendant of the family of Fisher Ames; he had been born and raised in Vermont but had moved to New York and gone into marine insurance. By 1869 he had succeeded well enough to move his family twenty-five miles out of New York to Plainfield, New Jersey. The town was originally a quiet Quaker village, but the advent of the commuter train had made it a wealthy "Wall Street suburb," as Van Wyck later called it. Charles Ames, florid and stoutish, was not, except for his business career, an active man. When he died in 1894, the newspaper obituary cited only his service as a vestryman in the Episcopal Church. He found his pleasure at home with his wife and daughter, whom he doted on and spoiled.[5]

Sallie was to develop into a woman who did not bear frustration easily. Believing whole-heartedly in the correctness of her own ideas and desires, she tended to see the resistance of others to her wishes as mere recalcitrance. As Van Wyck's stepsister put it to him many years later, "Your mother . . . *knows* that God is always beckoning her up." Most of the time Sallie was a gay companion for those around her, but when her wishes were denied, as they rarely were, she compensated herself by denying pleasure to others.[6] She had narrow but high expectations of men: they were to earn money and provide leisure for women, as her father had done. Perhaps the two largest frustrations of her life were that one of her husbands failed to make money and one of her sons refused even to try.

Pretty and wealthy, Sallie was a popular girl in Plainfield, elected "most popular," in fact, at ten cents a vote at an 1880 party for charity. She in turn was devoted to Plainfield and the small society in which she was raised to a life of cultured leisure, taking an interest in literature, painting, drama, and music. In many of the arts she was a dilettante and occasionally a prig, but she had a genuine gift for music and became an accomplished pianist. She was witty and vivacious, and Plainfield gossip may have been right that she had just missed a brilliant match before she married Charles Brooks on the first of June 1882, when she was twenty-four. A local paper reported that after the ceremony in Grace Episcopal Church, for which Sallie wore a gown trimmed in pearls and diamonds, a "*déjeuner*" was served, "and the subsequent reception was a display of representative wealth and tone." Then the couple departed for a three-month European honeymoon.[7]

After returning to America they lived in New York for a few months and then moved to Plainfield, to a house not far from the home of Sallie's parents. Perhaps they moved because Charles Brooks was already experiencing the financial problems which would eventually make him a burden to his in-laws. Or it may have been that in New York Sallie had become homesick for the small society of Plainfield in which she could take a large role.

Her first son, Charles Ames Brooks, was born in Plainfield in April 1883; he was known all his life as "Ames," Sallie's father's surname. Van Wyck, who was also given his name from Sallie's side of the family, was born on February 16, 1886. By then the Brookses had moved in with the Ameses, and Van Wyck would grow up in the house of his maternal grandparents.

Sallie Brooks continued her active social life after becoming a Plainfield matron. Though the Brooks family was not wealthy by Plainfield standards, Sallie mixed in the best of local society and maintained a close friendship with Elizabeth Perkins, the daughter of Senator Evarts of New York. Elizabeth was the mother of Maxwell Perkins, a close childhood friend of Van Wyck's, who would play his own large role in American literature as editor of Ernest Hemingway, Scott Fitzgerald, and Thomas Wolfe. Elizabeth Perkins and Sallie were both members of Plainfield's Monday Afternoon Club, which, according to its handbook, was an organization of one hundred "women of the highest standing in the city, associated together for intellectual and social culture." During the social season of 1888–89, Sallie addressed the club on "Roman, Byzantine, Arabian, Turkish and Moorish Ornament," while at another meeting Elizabeth Perkins explicated Matthew Arnold's "Dramatic Poetry." Sallie also threw herself into the work of charities, bringing in donations and subscriptions by serving as patron of innumerable cotillions, acting in amateur theatricals, and giving piano concerts in her home.[8]

Sallie did not, however, limit herself to fund raising. She involved herself personally in charitable activities and in the cause of moral uplift. For several years she was secretary of the Plainfield Relief Association, which, according to her 1895 report, aided poor women "in the only helpful way, by supplying them with work . . . which is paid for in groceries, — never in money." The ladies of the Relief Association visited the homes of the poor women once a week to see that the house was clean and the children cared for, and to ascertain whether the "inefficient and often dissipated man" of the house might "be found work and kept at it by some faithful visitor." Sallie's visits reflected some courage; many ladies would not visit the homes of the poor for fear of infectious disease.[9]

On the basis of a blueberry pie long since consumed, Sallie enjoyed the reputation of a good cook. The truth was that except for sewing she had forgotten or never acquired domestic skills. Her social life left no time for housework, and servants were cheap and plentiful in Plainfield in the 1890's. Sallie had a gardener, a chambermaid, a cook, and a nurse for her children, and she was efficient in the direction of this establishment.[10] Neither her activities nor her servants made Sallie remote from her children — far from it: she devoted long hours to their training. But she was also the chief example to Van Wyck of an active life beyond the home, for Van Wyck's father was a semi-invalid and business failure.

Sallie owed it only to her father's business success that her style of life was not lowered by her marriage to Charles Brooks. She tried to deal gracefully with this fact, and once in Van Wyck's hearing disdainfully exclaimed, "What's money!" It would be easy to mock her attempt at nonchalance, for she seldom had to do without the things money could buy — servants, fine furniture, stylish clothes and furs, and four trips abroad during Van Wyck's youth. But though Sallie had the appearance of wealth and strove not to care for the substance, the economic insecurity of her marriage to

Charles Brooks troubled her greatly. She early impressed on Van Wyck that the Brooks family was "poor" by Plainfield standards. A town of only twelve thousand people in 1890, Plainfield counted more than a hundred millionaires among its inhabitants, while Charles Brooks was a clerk in a brokerage house.[11]

The Brooks family was in the peculiarly American dilemma of having, on the one hand, an upper class lifestyle and social status, and, on the other hand, middle class anxieties and economic insecurity. Class and social status in fact depended on lifestyle, which in turn depended on income; economic anxiety therefore increased as one rose in class. European nobility were more secure because, unlike the American aristocracy, they could be impoverished without being declassed. Van Wyck would enviously point the contrast in *The Wine of the Puritans:* ". . . many a reduced baron and threadbare count have I seen standing up in the steerage of an ocean steamer, graciously accepting oranges and apples tossed down from the upper decks, and lifting their hats in an exquisite spirit of condescension." In America, however, it was "a social necessity to maintain the appearance of prosperity when we have not the reality."[12] Van Wyck came easily to understand such tensions, not only because of his youthful visits to Europe but also because of his birth into an American family of declining economic status.

Charles Brooks came from a business family. His immigrant grandfather, who was responsible for the Irish blood Van Wyck would mention in his essay on Charles Graeling, had settled in New York, made a successful career as an importer of woolens, and married into an old Dutch family. A daughter of this Irish wool merchant married Mitchell C. Brooks, who, like Van Wyck's Grandfather Ames, was a Vermonter who had come to New York and made his mark in business. Beginning as a cotton broker, Mitchell Brooks had been bankrupted by the Civil War but had made a second, more successful career as manager of a department store before he died of pneumonia at the age of forty-four. Charles Brooks, the youngest of Mitchell's four sons, was independent of the family when he graduated from the College of the City of New York in 1870. No doubt Charles could have profited from the support of his older, more established brothers, but he broke off relations with them in a quarrel over inheritance.[13]

Charles, following his family's tradition, chose a business career; he was taken into partnership as an agent for mining stocks by an older man named Leighton. Van Wyck was later possessed by an image of this Leighton as Lucifer, casting Charles Brooks into the

"Wall Street inferno." But Charles must have considered himself fortunate in being sent to Europe to represent the firm and spending ten years in Brussels, The Hague, London, and Paris. In the intervals at home he travelled in the West, dealing in mines. The frontier was not yet closed, and Charles would later conjure up images for his children of the wild West he had known, as when he crossed Arizona by stage coach in 1873. Leighton eventually lost his fortune and his business and left Charles Brooks on his own as a speculator in mines.[14]

When Charles returned to America to go into business for himself, he was still a relatively young man, a good tennis player and dancer, cheerful and witty. With his European polish he must have made an attractive suitor to Sallie Ames, whom he married when he was thirty-one. Within a decade, by the time Van Wyck's memory of him was established, he was a sick man and a failure. On a trip to San Francisco in 1880, Charles had acquired an Arizona copper mine for $15 thousand. Dissatisfied with his copper mine, he soon traded it for a nickel mine in Nevada. He had made a colossal mistake. The mine he traded away eventually supplied $68 million worth of copper to the United States mint, while his nickel mine, too far from the nearest railroad to be worked profitably, was worthless. Charles spent the rest of his life in Plainfield, living with his in-laws, trying first to work his mine and, failing there, ending his days as a clerk for Harvey Fisk and Sons, a New York brokerage house. For this last position he was supposed to have been poorly paid, though it is difficult to establish what Plainfield would have judged a small wage.[15]

Charles's business failure made him dependent socially as well as economically on his wife's family in Plainfield. He participated in a small way in the social and charitable activities in which Sallie was deeply involved, acting minor roles in her amateur theatricals or reading aloud in the men's ward at the hospital. But, as he implied once in a letter to Van Wyck in 1899 (when all of the Brooks family except Charles were in Europe), his social status in Plainfield was entirely dependent on his marriage into the Ames family: "I am very proud of my little family and I think the Plainfield people are very fond of them all — else they would not be so polite to me all the time — asking me to dinners and card parties."[16] In sum, he was as much an outsider in Plainfield as he was everywhere else — relations with his brothers had been broken off, the friends of his youth were in Europe, and above all he had failed in business.

If not a cheerful man, Charles remained a gentle and kindly

one, and he exercised some influence on his sons. A conservative in dress and manner, as both Ames and Van Wyck would be, he was fond of maxims and advised his sons never to "be the first by whom the new is tried."[17] Unlike many of his fellow businessmen in Plainfield, Charles loved art and music, especially opera, and he helped stimulate the strong cultural interests of both his sons. But the most important lesson that Charles taught Van Wyck was an unintentional one; business was a dangerous career, especially for a sensitive and cultured man. Business, in fact, could kill. The "morbid excitements,"[18] as Van Wyck later called them, of the business life had provoked gout, rheumatism, angina, and neuralgia in Charles. His headaches lasted for days, and during them he could hardly sleep or walk. During Van Wyck's adolescence his father grew ever weaker until finally, in the summer before Van Wyck's last year at Harvard, Charles died of a heart attack at the age of fifty-six.

III

Most of his life Van Wyck disappointed his family, and the tendency began at birth. Sallie had hoped for a daughter, but she noted in Van Wyck's baby book that he had "compensated" by being a "very sweet, lovely boy." The presence of the new baby in the home was probably a shock for the older brother, Ames, who was not quite three, and Sallie noticed that he gave Van Wyck "sly pokes and punches." A rivalry developed between the brothers, but in childhood they were also friends and played happily together. In 1892, when Van Wyck was six, he and Ames showed that they had learned the Republican bias of Plainfield politics by setting fire to a pillow which they called "Grover Cleveland."[19] They were also learning about culture and where it might be found; a crudely lettered handbill survives:

UNION ART GALLERY now open
Messrs Brooks Bro's invite your attention to
their elegant collection of paintings and
drawings, tickets only
2 CENTS

Both boys, like their father, were small, but Van Wyck was sturdier and healthier than Ames, who suffered from hay fever, frequent colds, tonsilitis, and appendicitis. Ames had the reputation of a reader in childhood while Van Wyck was more inclined to the outdoors, joining Max Perkins in searching for bird nests and turtle shells. Because he was stronger and perhaps also because Ames was Sallie's favorite, Van Wyck very early became the more independent from their mother. Once while they were still small children playing in their yard, an older boy threatened them with a brick, and Ames ran inside for Sallie. She emerged to find Van Wyck swaggering back and forth in front of the bully, shouting, "Throw your old brick and be damned."[20]

When Van Wyck was eight, his family moved into a new house that his Grandfather Ames had built just before he died in 1894. The large, three-story, yellow brick house stood on a corner lot on West Eighth Street, then one of Plainfield's most exclusive neighborhoods. Life was happy and secure there for the young boys, and Van Wyck was aware of but not touched by events whose meaning he pondered later. He had to tiptoe through a wealthy neighbor's house because the wife, like many upper-class women of the time, was prostrate and neurasthenic. But when financial reverses reduced the neighbor to a clerk, depriving his wife of nurse and servants, she was soon on her feet, cheerfully engaged in housework. Some neighbors, financial buccaneers, disappeared into prison, while others were bankrupted. Van Wyck saw such ruined men, who had been arrogant in their wealth and power, end pathetically on park benches, feeding squirrels.[21]

Sallie taught Ames and Van Wyck to sing, dance, act, play the piano, and worship God. Van Wyck was singing in the choir of Grace Episcopal Church when he was eleven, and he would walk home from services with Grandmother Phebe Ames on his arm. Sallie read *Pilgrim's Progress* aloud to the boys and on Sunday afternoons took them on nature walks, even though she was uncomfortable in the woods. She instructed them also in morality and theology, answering any question by saying that the matter was "so considered."[22]

Sallie brought another cultured woman into Van Wyck's life through her friendship with the remarkable Miss Eliza Elvira Kenyon. Miss Kenyon presided over a school for girls, which Sallie had attended, in a large building called the "Seminary." A woman of large interests, Miss Kenyon had made her school into the center of Plainfield's cultural life. Van Wyck's house on West Eighth Street was only a few blocks from the Seminary on West Seventh, and he was often in the building. On winter evenings he observed the town "gentlemen" gathered round a samovar in the library to discuss Lafcadio Hearn or Kipling, and summer afternoons he would see Miss Kenyon herself on a verandah, reading Browning or Goethe in the shade of wisteria vines. The Seminary was a rambling building of several wings that could accommodate numerous guests, sometimes including Julia Ward Howe, Thomas Nelson Page, and John Fiske. These and other eminences came to address the Seminary students and so enjoyed their stay that they became Miss Kenyon's friends and returned on annual visits. With H. G. O. Blake, Thoreau's literary executor, she had a special friendship, a twenty-year romance that never resulted in marriage. Miss Kenyon had met Blake while studying at the School of Philosophy in Concord in the 1870's. Her training there had prompted her to give her own school a Transcendental tone. The Seminary was where Van Wyck first became acquainted with the lofty Emersonian idealism which he would scorn as a young man but later greatly admire.[23]

During the summers, Sallie and Phebe took the boys to New England, and Van Wyck's visual sense developed rapidly there. He would later have colorful memories of the resort hotels where they usually spent these summers, memories of costumed Indians selling souvenirs and elegantly dressed ladies going into the woods to sit on rocks and read nature books aloud. More than fifty years after visiting the Perkins family's summer home in Vermont in 1897, Van Wyck could still vividly remember the house with little girls in pigtails, white dimity and sashes, playing croquet on the lawn "in the golden afternoon." That same summer, the Brookses visited Newport, and Van Wyck, age eleven, wrote a scenic description of the yacht illumination which was published in *Saint Nicholas Magazine.*[24]

Van Wyck was fascinated by ships, perhaps because they were the means of contact with the world's heavenly realm, culture's citadel, Europe. In the Brooks family, Europe was a frequent topic of conversation, and the conversation itself was sometimes conducted in French. Sallie Brooks thought of Europe as the source of all that was elevating, and travel there helped to mark her upper-class status in Plainfield. Charles Brooks looked wistfully back to his happy, healthy youth in Europe. More than thirty Baedekers reposed on the family bookshelves along with French novels, lithographs of Paris, and countless other memorabilia from Charles's European years. All through Van Wyck's childhood his imagination was stimulated by the idea of Europe until it came to seem a wonderful place. Later, in his Harvard essay on Charles Graeling, he described his own early conception of Europe as a wide shore under a shining sun with "very high spires and domes that gleamed like the City in *Revelations.*"[25]

European travel was also the requisite of a good education and proper cultural training, so in October of 1898 the entire Brooks family and Grandmother Phebe Ames boarded the steamship *Friesland* of the Red Star Line and sailed for Europe. On board were two other passengers from Plainfield, the recently divorced Mrs. John Ward Stimson, a friend of Sallie's, and her thirteen-year-old daughter, Eleanor, whom Van Wyck would marry in 1911 (there is no indication, however, that Eleanor and Van Wyck were particularly close at this time). The *Friesland* reached Antwerp on October 16, and the Plainfield party stayed together there for a week, touring the city. Van Wyck, Ames, and Eleanor climbed the cathedral tower, counting its 622 steps. Then the Stimsons departed for Switzerland, and Charles Brooks reboarded the *Friesland* for the return voyage to America.[26]

The absence of Van Wyck's father from this most important of his formative years was not an anomaly. During the hot summers when the rest of the family had sought respite in New England, Charles had remained tied to his desk in New York. Somehow it had been decided that now too Charles would remain at home and continue to act the farce of his role of breadwinner, though his salary must have been a pittance in comparison to the family's expenditures that year. Grandmother Phebe Ames, who had been left some money when her husband died four years earlier, was probably paying for the family's European wander year, and perhaps she had not included her son-in-law in the invitation. Charles would spend a lonely year in Plainfield, missing his family greatly and growing especially despondent as Christmas approached. Dreading the holiday, when there would be no room in other families for outsiders, he nevertheless hoped, as he wrote to Van Wyck, that "someone will take pity on me perhaps."[27]

Van Wyck recorded the events of this year in eight pocketbook diaries, "Dedicated to Grandma," numbering together over a thousand pages. It is tiring merely to read the record of the Brookses' journey; they lived at a level of intensity and activity sustainable only in the unusually stimulating atmosphere that Europe, for them, possessed. Van Wyck was put through a whirl of sensations, and a few years later he would write of his imagined second self, Charles Graeling, that "Everything he saw during these first European months was too wonderful for him to find any selection, to recognize distinction and degree in his vivid impressions."[28]

On October 22, Van Wyck, Ames, Sallie, and Phebe travelled from Antwerp to Rotterdam, spent an hour driving about that city in a hired carriage, and then went on to Delft. The Hague and Amsterdam were absorbed on succeeding days. During the next two weeks they visited Cologne, Heidelberg, Munich, Nuremberg, and several other German towns, arriving finally in Dresden on November 7, 1898.

They spent the winter in Dresden, recuperating for the southern campaign that awaited them in the spring. While Sallie and Phebe shopped for clothes and furs, Van Wyck and Ames continued their education. Tuesday, Thursday, and Saturday mornings they had German lessons with their landlady, and on alternate days they studied mathematics with Miss Mary Lewis, a recent graduate of Smith College travelling in Europe, whom Sallie had befriended. Sallie often took the boys to the opera, and Miss Lewis sometimes accompanied them to the museum.

The pictures at the Zwinger, the Dresden art gallery, fascinated Van Wyck. He already had a strong visual sense before the trip to Europe, but that visual sense was first greatly stimulated in European museums. The Renaissance painters especially interested him, and he admired Fra Angelico's hagiographs with their soft skin tones set off by yellows and golds. The biblical scenes of the Renaissance painters were familiar to him from Sunday School lessons in Plainfield. And, in turn, Van Wyck's later and most fearful images, while often drawing on Bible history for their symbols, owed their strength and color to the burly forms and livid violence of Renaissance paintings. When he came to hate the idea of a business career it was a strong and frightening picture, his vision of his father's first employer as Lucifer, snatching up Charles Brooks and casting him into the "Wall Street inferno."

Van Wyck began going to the gallery alone while Sallie and the others were shopping or just resting, and the intensity of his interest astonished his family. They treated it, however, as a sequel to the childish passion with which he had previously collected bird nests. Van Wyck was, as Sallie said, a "one-idead little chappie."[29] But in fact he was forming the desire to be an artist that would dominate his adult life.

The question was, what kind of artist could he be? By attempting sketches he would learn that he could not draw, and apparently for that reason he seems to have scarcely even toyed with the idea of becoming a painter. But his interest in painting led him toward an interest in art criticism and then toward literature. That winter and spring he read Anna Jameson's *Italian Painters* and Ruskin's *Mornings in Florence,* books which helped direct his hopes for a career in art toward criticism and writing. He began to keep a notebook on artists whose work he had viewed, entering their names according to schools and nationalities, and he soon had several hundred listed. Sallie had inadvertently helped turn him toward writing by insisting that both he and Ames keep diaries during their European tour. Van Wyck's diary was full of phrases borrowed from Sallie, like "perfectly delightful," but he was also learning to express his own opinions, as when, after a visit to the Potsdam apartments where Frederick the Great had kept a famous guest, he observed that "Voltaire looked like a monkey."

Finally, on the first of March, the Brookses headed south to meet the spring, leaving Dresden for Prague and then going on to Vienna, Venice, Bologna, Florence, and Rome, where they spent Easter. They passed much of March and all of April in Italy, travelling for a week around the Bay of Naples to Amalfi and Capri, places that Van Wyck loved all his life. Nine years later, writing *The Wine of the Puritans,* he would choose a hillside looking out over the Bay of Naples as the scene for Charles Graeling's effusions on art.

In Italy Van Wyck met a Graeling-like figure — Arthur Ryder, then a student at Leipzig and later a famous scholar of Sanskrit. Ryder crossed the Brookses' path in Venice and recrossed it at hotels and in railroad cars in Bologna, Florence, and Rome. The re-encounters were probably not accidental, as Ryder was infatuated with Sallie Brooks. Perhaps in order to ingratiate himself with Sallie, Ryder struck up a friendship with Ames and Van Wyck, taking the boys to Michelangelo's house and other famous sights. Fifty years later Van Wyck could "scarcely think of Italy" without also thinking of Ryder, who in less than a month had come to seem "as a youthful uncle or older brother." Part of the secret of Ryder's spell was probably that, in their father's absence, both Ames and Van Wyck would have been eager for the companionship of an older male. But more especially, Ryder fascinated Van Wyck as an example of a masculine figure committed totally to culture rather than to the business of earning a living.

The rest of the Brookses' journey in the spring and summer, through Switzerland, France, and England, resembled the earlier part of their tour. Everywhere they saw the sights and visited such monuments of culture as the Castle of Chillon in Switzerland and the Louvre in Paris. There was also a visit to the Paris morgue which the then jaded boys thought "not very horrible." They spent most of the summer in England, settling in London for July and visiting the Tower with its torture implements. Van Wyck passed much time in the British Museum and the National Gallery looking at yet more Fra Angelicos and a new discovery — Ucello. In August they travelled north to Scotland, stopping to see Wordsworth's grave in Grasmere and paying homage to Shakespeare by returning through Stratford.

Perhaps Van Wyck drew a lesson from the fact that even in Europe culture was not found everywhere but was sought in the relics of the past, ferreted out in the places of the dead. Cathedrals and churches, castles, museums, dungeons and instruments of torture, cemeteries and tombs of famous artists had been the Brookses' quarry in every European city. All his life Van Wyck would not only feel that American culture was inadequate judged against the standard of Europe but also that contemporary culture was inadequate against the standard of the past. If European culture had seemed otherworldly to Van Wyck in America, it remained so, to a degree, in Europe. Culture was the achievement of the dead, and the American boy was separated from it not only by the sea but also by life.

August twenty-ninth, back in London, the others packed while Van Wyck went alone to the National Gallery "to say good-bye to the pictures." Two days later they embarked at Liverpool, and after a stormy ten-day passage arrived safely in New York. Charles Brooks met the ship, and the boys "nearly tumbled over the rail" in their ecstasy at the family's reunion.

IV

The year before the trip to Europe, Sallie had taken Van Wyck out of the private school he had been attending and enrolled him in the sixth grade of the Plainfield public schools, "as the best place for a thorough education at present." He entered the eighth grade upon his return, and there is no indication that any teacher struck a spark in him during the next five years. Having decided that he wanted to be a writer, he was forced to conduct his own education for a literary career, and he did so through an intensive reading program. His list of "Books Read" shows that during his last two years in high school he read, in addition to school assignments, about two hundred books. His authors were mostly British — Carlyle, Johnson, Dickens, Thackeray, Shakespeare, Macaulay, Scott, Keats, Shelley, Burke, George Eliot, Coleridge, Byron, Milton, Ruskin, and Lamb. The

Americans listed were few — Emerson, Hawthorne, Irving, Mark Twain, Henry James, and John Fiske.[30] Van Wyck's favorite writer was Ruskin, but his favorite stylist was Thomas De Quincey, the "opium eater." He found De Quincey's mystical style irresistibly suggestive of some other world, and he sought another world because he was unhappy in Plainfield.

Van Wyck's tendency toward depressions and feelings of guilt first appeared while he was in high school. Textbook descriptions of the manic-depressive illness that was later diagnosed in him usually put the onset of the disease in the years fifteen to twenty, so it is possible that he suffered already from mental illness. The depressions, however, were not disabling in his youth. While his family considered him unusually moody, they did not think of him as sick. And it would be wrong to take his unhappiness entirely at face value, for he was trying to bring his personality into line with his ethereal idea of an artist's character. His self-consciousness was apparent in, for instance, "An Opium Dream," an essay imitating De Quincey's style, which he entered in a school contest in English composition and which ended in a paean to melancholy: ". . . thou, clad in the vestments of the grave, art no less the herald of imperishable day — inevitable Melancholy! Daughter of Solitude, Mother of Despair, Melancholy, huddling and inexorable!" (The judges did the safe thing and gave him second prize.) Van Wyck's unhappiness was real but not as great as he sometimes liked to think. The melancholia was not intense enough to affect his perception of reality, except perhaps to heighten it, for he sought an explanation for his unhappiness in his environment. If he was sick, it was in part a productive experience, leading him to think critically about his surroundings.[31]

One of the main sources of Van Wyck's unhappiness was the necessity of justifying his aspiration to be a writer when business, the monster which had ruined his father's life, was the most fashionable career choice for a young man in Plainfield. In the diary he kept during his senior year in high school he wrote: ". . . we are passing through an avaricious phase. . . . Business, it seems to me, is the one profession which is wholly sordid. . . . It is the one profession where the subject does not give his own personal service to some high cause." He went on to suggest that the businessman was in the lowest possible human state, that of a "savage" concerned only with food and shelter, knowing nothing of "higher things."[32]

Van Wyck's unhappiness with his surroundings also showed in his essay "Taste," published in the *Oracle*, the high school magazine he edited. Americans lacked taste, he said; otherwise there would have been "no light operas, nor coon-songs. . . . As to ragtime there may be a psychological reason for that connected with the American character." Van Wyck especially hated football and in "Athletic vs. Intellectual," another *Oracle* essay, he recommended more "thoughtful recreation" which could be provided by "formation of dramatic, debating and literary societies." He seems not to have taken part in games, and he later pictured Charles Graeling standing by the field, not playing, but watching with a good humor that "prevented the other boys from thinking any the less of him." But when Van Wyck was struck "a most undignified blow" by a foul ball, he angrily editorialized in the *Oracle* against playing baseball in the school yard: ". . . let peaceful, law-abiding citizens . . . take their airing in quiet." Such opinions would not have endeared him to his fellow students, and it is doubtful also that they properly appreciated his essay on Hazlitt or the English verse he translated into Latin when he needed a filler for the *Oracle.* He protested bitterly in his diary against having "to manage a school paper, edit football notes and live in such a town as this."[33]

Mortified by the drabness of the very name "Plainfield," Van Wyck was also disturbed by the town's lack of high culture of the sort he had experienced in Europe. Plainfield had pretensions to culture, a small art gallery, for instance, but Van Wyck was bored by its mediocre pictures. The gallery was evidence that Plainfield cared more for the appearance than the substance of culture, and Van Wyck later gave credence to the idea that its pictures had been purchased by the square yard. In school, American history was taught *à la* James Ford Rhodes, and it seemed dominated, like everything else in Plainfield, by money questions, the tariff and "the resumption of specie payment." It was coarse material compared to the romance of European history as Van Wyck encountered it in Carlyle, Macaulay, and Scott. Still resentful of the contrast when he wrote *The Wine of the Puritans,* he would exclaim, "American history is so unlovable!"[34]

Van Wyck's ideas alienated him from family and friends. His classmates evidently respected him, since they elected him president of his junior class, but they were also amused at the earnestness with which he had decided on a literary career. The class prophecy commented on his "mournful" appearance and foresaw his future as "Hawthorne the greater." His Grandmother Ames, the person to whom he felt closest in the family, regarded his bookishness with a "faint touch of scorn," as he later recalled. Increasingly, Van Wyck grew reluctant to participate in the Plainfield social life that meant everything to his mother and brother. Sallie and Ames, who were very close, quarreled with him and called him selfish. In all of Plainfield, Van Wyck felt, there was no one who understood or sympathized with him.[35]

But Van Wyck found understanding in Eleanor Kenyon Stimson, then a Wellesley undergraduate and later his wife. She was well equipped to understand him, for she was an aspiring artist from a family of artists. Her father, John Ward Stimson, had rebelled against his father, a Wall Street financier, and had gone to Paris to study art and, as his family believed, squander his patrimony on brushes and oils. Later he became a well-known art educator and founded the art school of the Metropolitan Museum. Eleanor's mother, Eleanor Manson Stimson, was a native of Plainfield and a niece of the Miss Kenyon who directed the Seminary. Mrs. Stimson, like her husband, was a painter who had studied in Europe, and their marriage must have seemed a good match at the time. But in fact their union was bitter, ending in divorce after a dozen years. The unhappy marriage produced two unhappy children who in adult life would deal with the world by withdrawing from it. John Francis (Frank) Stimson went to Yale and then studied architecture at the *Beaux Arts*, his father's school, in Paris. Briefly connected with McKim, Mead, and White, he later drifted off to Tahiti and Moorea to spend his life working at meaningless jobs while carrying on his important studies of Polynesian language and religion.[36] Eleanor, Frank's sister, was a feminist who hoped to become a writer and perhaps even a socialist activist; instead she would eventually marry Van Wyck and devote her life to caring for him and their children.

Eleanor's upbringing was not enviable. She had enjoyed her studies as a small child in her Great-Aunt Eliza Kenyon's Seminary in Plainfield. But when she was eight, her father hemorrhaged in the lungs and was diagnosed as tubercular. Eleanor, too, was found to have a "spot," so the family spent three lonely years at Saranac, high in the Adirondacks, seeking relief in the clean dry air. Because of her lung spot, because the doctors wanted her outdoors, and because she would be especially endangered by communicable diseases like measles, Eleanor was not sent to school at Saranac. She was as a result unusually shy and developed a lasting distaste for social life. After the divorce of her parents, Eleanor spent another lonely year with her mother in Europe — 1898-99, the same year that the Brookses were there — and like Van Wyck she fell in love with Europe and dated her cultural awakening from her visit there. Unlike Van Wyck, Eleanor developed a knack for managing practical affairs, partly because her divorced mother depended heavily upon her.[37]

Eleanor, a feminist from an early age, distrusted and disliked men. Her father had an uncontrollable temper, and often burst into rages and attacked those nearest at hand. As a child Eleanor participated in violent family quarrels, siding passionately with her mother against her father. On two occasions she saw her mother knocked to the floor and kicked, and she too, apparently, was attacked by her father. Her early shame at the public scenes her father created helped bring on her discomfort in society. Except for her father, Eleanor had little early experience with men, because when she and her mother returned from Europe, they went to Plainfield and took up residence in the Seminary, where the population was largely feminine. Studious and shy, she was not often invited to participate in Plainfield's snobbish whirl of parties, dances, and Sunday calls. Though she claimed not to want a social life, it was cruel to be excluded, and she suffered from her feeling that she was "marked out and different from my friends." Compensating with pride in her good mind and high marks in school, she decided that rather than marry and raise a family she would become a writer and work for the causes of feminism and socialism.[38]

Eleanor, in short, was the antithesis of Sallie Brooks and just the kind of girl to attract the attention of an unhappy and alienated youth like Van Wyck. Here was a girl who could understand why one would wish to be an artist rather than a businessman. His pursuit of Eleanor was to be difficult, since, as Eleanor wrote when she was almost sixty, her early experiences with her father had "warped" her and made her "terribly afraid of love, which seemed like a traitor that stabbed you in the back." Van Wyck, however, was nothing if not assiduous, and he ignored her rebuffs when, at fourteen, he first began to seek her out at the Seminary. Because he wanted to discuss books and writing, Eleanor gradually found him interesting, and they began to spend evenings and Sunday afternoons together. When he was sixteen he first asked her to marry him, but it required four more years before she consented even to engagement.[39]

Fifteen months older than Van Wyck, Eleanor was also two years ahead of him in her education. When she left Plainfield for her sophomore year at Wellesley in September 1903, he was only beginning his senior year in high school. On the eve of her departure he wrote in his diary, "Life will be almost unbearable here without her."

However, he was to have the solace of correspondence with her, and in their letters they exchanged not only expressions of affection but also comments on their reading. She asked about Henry James, and Van Wyck replied that he was the "reprobate who wrote Daisy Miller."[40]

Van Wyck also sent her the poems he was writing, strange poems on the face of it for a youth in love to send to his girlfriend; they dealt with death. In imagery of the sea and of Europe, he evoked a longing for escape from an unhappy world into a heavenly afterlife. The idea of Europe as heaven was strong, for instance, in a poem in which he spoke of death as the "shore" where, after the "storm" of life, a dying man was given a "tour." Eleanor was often present in Van Wyck's heavenly visions of Europe, as in the following sonnet:

> (1) Once in the visioned fancy of a dream
>   Willed from a cello-ecstasy, I came
>   Beyond the shores where men have named a Name
>   And stood the millionth of a lightning-gleam
>   Within that house where are the things that seem —
>   No more on earth;
>
>   .   .   .   .   .
>
> (13) A thousand times I died in visioned prayer,
>   A thousand times, and always she was there.[41]

So the poems of death he sent to Eleanor were love poems also. They would share their love in a happier afterlife.

Meanwhile, Van Wyck was speculating on the nature of that afterlife, for though he was intensely interested in religion, he had begun to doubt the Christian doctrines in which he had been trained. In part his doubt was a reaction against unusually strong piety in adolescence. He had hung a crucifix on his bedroom wall, erected an altar under it, and dreamed vaguely of becoming a Catholic priest — an aspiration that must have shocked Sallie Brooks. In part also his doubt was due to his observation of the role of Grace Episcopal Church in the lives of Plainfield businessmen: "Six days they worship Mammon of the seven,/Then pray for arm-chairs in a tinsel Heaven." He began to attend different churches in Plainfield, afterwards writing critiques of the sermons. Not yet having outgrown his mother's anti-Semitism, he argued against any authority for the Bible because it was only "a chronicle of the Jews, a semi-barbarous race who lived before Christ and exist degenerate still." Objecting to the idea of damnation, he came to believe in a succession of lives, each life "one moral plane higher" until the soul reached heaven "as all souls must."[42]

He did not tell these ideas to his family because ". . . they do not understand me at all" and because they would think him a "faddist." Instead, he discussed them with Frank Stimson during the Christmas holidays of 1903. Eleanor's brother was home on vacation from Yale, where he had learned a "theory of curves" which he now expounded to Van Wyck. According to this theory, no human soul could rejoin the Infinite Soul until it had achieved a finite unity by mating with another soul possessing complementary "brain curves" so as to form a perfect circle. Accordingly, male sought its female complement. Greatly pleased by this theological explanation for his attraction to Eleanor, Van Wyck became an ardent believer in the "theory of curves" for some time. It led him to some wonderful ideas, including an androgynous conception of the perfect soul that caused him to wonder, "Is it preposterous to think that Jesus Christ was half-woman?" But beneath the comic quality of his adolescent theology there was genuine alienation. He wanted to escape from this life to a better one, taking with him only one person, Eleanor Stimson.[43]

Van Wyck was unhappy not only with Plainfield but also with himself. For instance, despite his strenuous extracurricular program of reading and writing, he believed that "beyond all others, my faults are indolence downright, and half-heartedness in everything."[44] He was developing a large capacity for guilt, the most important symptom of the suicidal depression he later suffered.

He was well trained in guilt, thanks partly to his relations with his mother and brother. Neither Ames nor Sallie hid their disappointment with the self-centered, withdrawn moodiness that often overcame him. In the summer of 1901 when Sallie and Charles Brooks went abroad, Ames wrote to his mother: "Van Wyck talks of getting off a letter to 'Father and Mother' but he has taken very little interest so far. I'm afraid I don't quite understand the 'unselfish' part of his character I hear so much of." Perhaps it was Charles who defended Van Wyck's "unselfish" character, but he would have made a poor ally, broken by business failure and heart trouble, and weaker in any state than Sallie. In the autumn of Van Wyck's senior year in high school, he went to Princeton for a weekend visit with Ames, then an undergraduate and a social success there. Apparently chagrined at having to show his unsociable brother around the campus, Ames criticized Van Wyck for having nothing to say except about books and for acting "almost like an old man, too thoughtful to be enjoyable." Van Wyck, who was getting used to being a disappointment, wrote in his diary that his talk with Ames had made him "rather unhappy. . . . I suppose it was all true enough. . . ."[45]

Beneath the disappointment of Van Wyck's family that he did not fit smoothly into social life there must also have been resentment that he refused to consider a career in business. For all her genteel culture, what Sallie Brooks admired in men was the ability to make money and, as Van Wyck's stepsister said years later, "preferably in business. She thinks businessmen are so nice."[46] To Sallie, business must have seemed the best occupational choice for her sons if they were to restore the family's economic status, which had apparently declined considerably. The expense of educating Ames at Princeton and the anticipated cost of sending Van Wyck to Harvard may have accounted for the decision of the Brooks family to take up residence in the Seminary during Van Wyck's last year in high school. Apparently they sold the large house on West Eighth Street, for Van Wyck later wrote that it "fell at last into more affluent hands."[47] Giving up their home made it possible for the Brookses to maintain most of the other trappings of upper-class life as well as to educate their sons. Sallie was still able to afford stylish clothes, but she could ill afford an aspiring literatus. That was why she resented it when Van Wyck took so seriously to the cultural training she had provided. For a boy, that training was meant only as polish to smooth the way in a business career.

The sexual division of labor in upper-class Plainfield must have given Van Wyck the sense that as a male he was condemned to the brutal world of business which had ruined his father. Woman's work seemed far superior to man's; it was his mother, after all, who had accompanied him in the celestial realm of Europe while his father stayed in the brokerage office. Even in America there was a heavenly quality to a woman's life. While Charles Brooks worked at the killing pace of the New York commuter, Sallie read, sewed, or played the piano. As Van Wyck read of a summer afternoon, while his mother was upstairs practicing the feminine ritual of "lying down," he heard the distant sounds of servants beating rugs and mowing the lawn. His mother's house was a peaceful one of "endless time," he recalled in old age, and he would always believe it was the "woman" in Whitman who gave *Leaves of Grass* "the sense of an endless present."[48] A girl from an upper-class family like Van Wyck's could have counted on spending her life in such a timeless, genteel idyll, first in the same kind of cultural training which Van Wyck had received and then in the education of her own children. A male, however, once embarked upon adult life, would have little time for culture, since the responsibility of earning a living would fall on him. In his diary Van Wyck protested: "A boy is born. The first thought is what will he be? . . . (not how good or how great) but how much salary will he be able to draw?" Instead of heaven, a hellish fiery fate awaited a man child. In the same paragraph of his memoirs where he described the boyhood vision of his father being cast into the "Wall Street inferno," Brooks also wrote that he had thought of business as "Moloch," the god of the Ammonites to whom children were sacrificed in fire.[49]

Unlike many of the rebels against sexual roles in the pre-World War I era, Van Wyck would revolt less against woman's place as a keeper of culture than against man's place as a mere money-earner — a distinction that had large consequences for his life and writing. It led to an insecurity about his sexual identity that accounted in part for the depth of the guilt feelings that plagued him in later years. By hoping in youth to become an artist, he had opened himself to the charge, in a business-oriented society, that he was taking up woman's work. Thus, when he eventually turned against his own writing, his impelling guilt came not only from the fact that he had attacked his family but also from the belief that he had "ploughed the sea,"[50] had engaged in work that was effete. His strident, life-long insistence that literature should have practical consequences was in some part a defense of his masculinity. This defensiveness regarding his sexuality, combined with the consequent belief that a great writer was "whole-souled," robust, and manly, made it difficult for him to admit homosexuality in writers he admired, like Symonds and Whitman. Similarly, he was never comfortable dealing with writers whose direct impact on practical affairs was hard to trace — Henry James, for instance. The writer he most admired was Ruskin, who had wrathfully denounced the evils of industrialism: to throw a wrench in the works was to have practical consequences of a sort.

However, in adolescence Van Wyck's thinking about the function of art was inconsistent, to say the least, for he also looked to art for "abstraction," for escape from the materiality of American business life. One night when he was still a small child, after Sallie had left for one of her dinner parties, he had a dream that he was being chased by a Hindu with a knife, and just as the Hindu was about to catch him, "I soared into the air and floated away, free, aloft and safe." Although the dream recurred frequently during his childhood and intermittently all his life (sometimes with a minotaur in place of the Hindu), it soon lost its terror, "for I knew I possessed the power to float away." As he grew into adolescence he attributed "the power to float away" to his artistic gift. Art and literature had become associated, for him, with an ethereal, otherworldly life. Therefore he fervently approved "Emerson's idea that matter is *dead third,*" and objected to the Christian idea of the resurrection of the body, ". . . for the highest happpiness we can know is never associated with the body. . . . our future is abstract."[51]

Death was a powerful symbol of escape for Van Wyck. His family, understandably, thought him morbid. He wrote about death not only in his poetry but also in his letters, describing an elaborate funeral to his mother or telling Eleanor that he was reading Chatterton: ". . . he committed suicide when he was seventeen years old — just my age plus another month." He associated art with unworldliness, with death, and forty years later he reflected this early idea when he castigated some of the great artists of his time as death lovers.[52]

Van Wyck would try to reconcile his interest in the ethereal with his belief in the practical and this-worldly consequences of art through his assertion that the artist's spirit was that of a prophet in the Old Testament sense, a denouncer of worldly evil. He reflected that the word *poet* was not in the Bible because "the word *prophet* . . . was the Bible word for *poet.*" An artist was both Isaiah and Jeremiah, exhorting a people to greatness and warning them of the folly of their sins. Van Wyck took a stab at the task in the high school *Oracle* just before his graduation. His article, "The Mission of American Art," was a portent of his later critical position as well as an attempt at a prophetic response to the evil which he had observed in Plainfield — a decultured idea of manhood in an over-commercialized society. He wrote of the development of the ideal soul, composed of masculine and feminine complements:

> It becomes our responsibility as a composite people to unite the virtues of all races. . . . And this blending — this building up of ideal manhood — is the Mission of American Art.
> . . . Then must come the genuine expression of our national life — harmonized, softened, idealized. We shall combine a Lincoln and a Raphael. We shall have eloquent Beauty and sturdy Manhood.
> . . . It is art only which can purify our national failings. We have a mighty slough of commercialism that only Art can reconcile with the Ideal.[53]

V

It was Ames rather than Van Wyck who imitated their father and pleased their mother by trying to make money, but this decision did not come easily: in youth Ames was perhaps as deeply interested in art as Van Wyck. In Italy in the spring of 1899 the cultured young Arthur Ryder had chosen Ames as his special friend rather than Van Wyck. The boys had not then seen their father in six months, and it is a fair supposition that there was some competition between them for the companionship of this older male friend. There was also probably some jealousy on Van Wyck's part when Ryder found the more mature Ames the more interesting companion. Half a century later, when Van Wyck told in his memoirs the story of his encounter with Ryder in Italy, he left Ames entirely out of the picture, just as he no doubt wished to exclude him in 1899.[54]

But in real life Van Wyck could not exclude Ames, who was their mother's favorite son. Ames tried to conform to Sallie's idea of what a man should be — cultured surely, but first of all a money-maker. He went to Princeton and studied classical languages, perhaps on the model of Arthur Ryder. A serious student as well as a social success in college, Ames, like Van Wyck, wrote poetry as a young man. Van Wyck later thought he should have been a profes-sor, but in 1905 when Ames graduated from Princeton, Charles Brooks was becoming weaker and more of an invalid. Though the family could not have known Charles had only a year to live, it must have seemed imperative to them to have another breadwinner. So Ames went to law school at Harvard for a year and then, after Charles Brooks's death, stayed in Plainfield and finished his legal education at New York University. Then he practiced in New York, commuting from Plainfield as his father had done. Van Wyck may have had his brother in mind when he wrote in *The Wine of the Puritans,* which was dedicated to Ames, that too many college men, upon graduation, put aside their artistic and intellectual interests and "regard life with the idea that making a living is more impor-tant than making something of themselves." [55]

If Ames chose a worldly career out of solicitude for his mother, it was probably unnecessary. Sallie, who remained an attractive woman, married again, this time to an engineer as successful as Van Wyck's father had been the opposite. She settled once again into an upper-class life style in Plainfield, and Ames moved in with her and his stepfather.

Ames did not entirely abandon his scholarly and artistic interests. He wrote a novel, and Princeton awarded him the master of arts degree for a thesis on "The Egyptian Lake of Moeris: The Accounts of Herodotus, Strabo and Diodorus as Verified by Modern Discovery and Research." In 1922 Princeton University Press published a collection of his poetry, *Mauna Roa,* which he dedicated "To my mother in her own spirit of eternal youth." Ames's poems, like Van Wyck's, were concerned with death and the sea, with heaven a golden realm beyond the ocean of life.

There was another theme, however, in Ames's poetry, the theme of an artistic spirit misplaced in the business world. In "To Gather and to Spend" he spoke of his "bitterness of heart," and in another poem he hoped for deliverance:

> Will there no prophet rise, no bard to school us,
> No singer of the splendor of our race?
> How long, how long shall priests of mammon rule us,
> The Jew and swineherd of the market-place?

Ames wished to marry, but his several engagements were all broken. Van Wyck later thought Ames's failures in love might be attributed to Sallie, who perhaps did not want him to marry. If so, then Ames may have unconsciously made a plea in his "Hymn to Persephone":

> The fates at length shall bear us
> Through thy consuming fire;
> But now, oh mother, spare us
> Life and our love's desire.

Travelling restlessly and perhaps engaging in homosexual love affairs, Ames disappeared from Plainfield for months at a time. One of his chief pleasures was visiting friends with ranches in the West, living in the open air and working with cattle. A Republican in the old tradition, he was, for a time, executive secretary of the Kowaliga School for Negroes in Alabama. When America entered the First World War, Ames, age thirty-four, tried to enlist but failed the physical examination. He served instead as an ambulance driver in France. After the war, he roamed Europe and the South Seas. When he was in Plainfield, he relieved his tedium with nostalgic returns to Princeton to recall, he said, his "old buried life of the poet and dreamer."[56]

Such restlessness could not make for success in the business world. Ames had been unable to resist the lure of Wall Street, and his stock holdings were lost in the depression. Just a few days before Christmas of 1931, when he was waiting at the Plainfield station for the commuter train to New York, instead of boarding the train Ames jumped in front of it and ended forty-eight years of frustration.[57]

2

HARVARD, 1904–1907

V AN WYCK was seldom comfortable at Harvard, though he was largely accepted in its social and literary circles — how largely is indicated by his having achieved on two occasions the ultimate cachet of being invited to Dante evenings at Shady Hill. Sitting in the small, hushed circle with the text open before him, he listened as if in a sacred rite while Charles Eliot Norton read the *Paradiso* aloud beneath the picture of "Dante Meeting Beatrice" that Rosetti had painted especially for him. But on one of these occasions, just as the sherry and the silver basket of caraway cakes were being passed, Norton remarked that the bejewelled image of heaven in *Revelation* was worthy of a "New York woman."[1] Van Wyck no doubt shared the superior feeling implied in the remark, but he must also have been disconcerted. For what were his mother Sallie and his Grandmother Ames but New York women? And Van Wyck himself, like Charles Graeling, had been possessed by a heavenly vision of Europe with "very high spires and domes that gleamed like the City in *Revelations.*" New England's sensibility was different from New York's, and while that was its chief attraction for Van Wyck, it meant also that the discontented youth from Plainfield was, however amenable, a foreigner at Harvard.

New England had attracted Van Wyck almost as strongly as Europe while he was in high school and only partly because Eleanor Stimpson was at Wellesley. To him the Perkins family, with its strong

New England roots, had seemed an oasis of culture in Plainfield, and the impression was only reinforced by the Plainfield view of New Englanders as dry and bookish.[2] Both of Van Wyck's grandfathers had been born and raised in New England before coming to New York and going into business. As Van Wyck turned away from his mother and her New York roots, he turned toward the New England heritage his grandfathers had abandoned.

Van Wyck had been drawn to New England most of all, however, by his belief that Harvard was *the* school for writers. He seemed to find confirmation of this idea on his second evening at Harvard when he attended a punch given by the *Harvard Monthly*. There he met another new student, John Hall Wheelock, who remembered the meeting many years later: "I noticed standing near me a stranger who seemed equally alone. He was of medium height and delicately made, with a face sensitive and youthful yet with a certain austerity and resolution in its expression that attracted me. The eyes, particularly, had a withdrawn concentration. . . ."[3] The two new friends left the punch and spent the evening together discussing Swinburne, whom Van Wyck considered the greatest living poet. Soon they had another friend, Ned Sheldon, also a freshman, who would begin his successful career as a Broadway playwright while still in college. Max Perkins, a sophomore, was also in this circle of literary friends. The group went about Boston and Cambridge together, and Van Wyck may have been in their company when he heard Henry James lecture on Balzac during James's 1904 visit to Harvard.

The young literary men at Harvard adopted a Wertheresque pose, *triste* and vulnerable, with nerves too highly strung for the strenuous. The archetype of Harvard esthetes was Pierre de Chaignon la Rose of the class of 1896. Lazy, snobbish, and, according to one observer, a "little brother" of rich students, de la Rose had stayed in Cambridge to write an occasional piece for the *Atlantic,* design books, and study heraldry. He was friendly with Santayana, had a fashionable interest in Catholicism, and mixed with undergraduates. For a time Van Wyck admired de la Rose and the Harvard esthetes and modeled his behavior on theirs. Early in his freshman year he pictured himself in a diary, rising late and remaining in his dressing gown to read before finally breakfasting at noon on maraschino cherries.[4]

Most of Van Wyck's friends manifested the esthete in some degree. His favorite club was the Stylus, a literary club as its name suggests, and he found many fellow spirits there — Wheelock,

Sheldon, George Foote, Hermann Hagedorn, George and Francis Biddle, and Alfred Kidder. Wheelock was probably closest to Van Wyck in his love of melancholy idealizing, and he memorialized their deep conversations in his poem "Sunday Evening on the Common";

> Van Wyck — how often have we been together,
>   When this same moment made all mysteries clear.

But Van Wyck's "Sunday Evening by the Fireside" expressed the opposite feeling:

> Ah, Jack, is this the end of all,
>   The base that friendship has to show,
> No certain truth however small. . . .[5]

Like his literary friends Van Wyck hoped for an artist's life, made a romance of Bohemian poverty, and dreamed of crossing to Europe in steerage. In 1905 he and Wheelock paid for the printing of ten of each of their poems in a pamphlet, *Verses by Two Undergraduates,* and sold a few copies, six at most, on the street in Boston. But lack of appreciation may have been as satisfying as any other result to the romantic young poets.[6]

Of Van Wyck's friends, Max Perkins probably had fewest of the qualities of the esthete. Van Wyck and Max roomed together at the Stylus Club during their last year at Harvard, by which time Van Wyck also had come to doubt the virtue of the esthetic stance. The roommates vehemently discussed religion, politics, and literature, and they quarreled occasionally and stopped speaking. But usually they were on good terms, and Max, who admired the Spartans, would rise at six and drag Van Wyck from bed to read aloud Herbert Spencer or some other difficult writer. During the day, if they felt like it, they attended classes and then returned to the Stylus for tea with their friends.[7]

At least in part because of his friendship with Max, Van Wyck experienced little of the isolation and loneliness that Harvard afforded to other outlanders, such as John Reed and John Gould Fletcher, at about the same time. Only one-third of Harvard students had, like Van Wyck, attended public high schools, and such a background was usually an insurmountable social handicap. But Max had met the "right" people at St. Paul's, and thanks to him Van Wyck met the "right" people at Harvard and made the Fox Club. Admission to a final club like the Fox indicated the highest degree of social acceptance, and less than a fifth of the undergraduates passed the test. Although he had Max's help and though the Fox was one of the poorer clubs, Van Wyck's election to membership was still something of a social triumph in view of his handicaps. In 1907 Van Wyck was librarian of the Fox Club, an office held three years later by T. S. Eliot. However, Van Wyck's last year at Harvard was Eliot's first, and the two men never met, either in college or later.[8]

Van Wyck did not enjoy his social success. In fact, he was extremely uncomfortable in Harvard society, finding it no more meaningful and a great deal less delicate than the one he had fled in Plainfield. In his freshman year when Max Perkins had introduced him in select circles, Van Wyck had been "tongue-tied and thin-skinned" among the "young barbarians at play," as he acidly called them even fifty years later. When he suffered a harassing initiation into the Fox Club with oarsmen and football players, he was, in the terms which Theodore Roosevelt had made popular, the "molly coddle" among the "red bloods." His discomfort in this side of Harvard life should have been prefigured for him at a punch he attended on his very first evening at Harvard. He had been handed a glass of whiskey, neat, and at the cry of "Bottoms up!" had drained it and fainted.[9] With his literary aspirations it was inconsistent of him to become so involved in Harvard society — an early indication of a factor in his character which would later make life difficult for him as a cultural radical. For all his scorn of genteel culture and business society, he would never be free from an intense longing for acceptance by that society and possession of its symbols of success, especially money.

But he also strove for and achieved literary success at Harvard, a fact recognized by the Signet Club when it chose him as one of the twenty-eight outstanding men it took from each class. Van Wyck became an editor of the *Harvard Advocate*, which had begun to publish his poems even while he was a freshman. His Harvard poems showed little advance over his high school work; they were written in the manner of Browning and dealt with death and a heavenly afterlife, which Van Wyck still hoped to share with Eleanor Stimson. Heaven was often symbolized in European images, as in "Amalfi":

> When we come where long years ago
>   Eden I built for thee,
> There where hot noons with humming low
>   Beguile the sleeping sea,
> All the sweet dreams thy soul shall know
>   That seemed too sweet to be.

There we shall lie in the warm sand
   Together lost in dreams,
By orange-laden breezes fanned
   And perfume from cool streams,
And shall not care while hand in hand
   What is and what but seems.

That haze of childhood-born Romance
   Shall fetter us no more,
And every load of circumstance
   Our lives aforetime bore,
Shall melt within that silver trance
   Beside that silver shore.

Thy soul from mine among the spheres
   No longer far shall be,
Nor sightless fears nor useless tears
   Shall part thy love from me,
When we come where in distant years
   Eden I built for thee.[10]

Still another triumph of Van Wyck's Harvard years was his engagement to Eleanor in 1906. Even though he had been able to see Eleanor often because she was nearby at Wellesley, the courtship had not been easy. Eleanor had continued to fear men and distrust love, and she only consented to engagement, she later said, "after a truly terrible struggle on my part, which almost gave me a nervous breakdown. . . ." She finally gave in because she was so much in love "that I decided that, though I certainly should not be happy [with Van Wyck] I could not be unhappier than if I lost him."[11] Since Van Wyck was so young, with no immediate prospect of earning a living, they kept their engagement secret, especially from their mothers. Mrs. Stimson disapproved of Van Wyck because he hoped to be an artist, and she feared that Eleanor would be as unhappy with him as she had been in her marriage to John Ward Stimson. She suspected the engagement, and because it coincided with Eleanor's graduation from Wellesley in 1906, she was able to separate them by taking Eleanor abroad while Van Wyck remained at Harvard. From Europe, Eleanor wrote to Van Wyck that she loved *his* mother but was "dreadfully afraid of her and quite sure she doesn't approve of me." Eleanor, with her feminist beliefs and her hopes for a career of her own, would not have been a good wife for the businessman or banker that Sallie may still have hoped Van Wyck would become.

Eleanor must have known, however, that his mother's disapproval would only make her more attractive to Van Wyck. She probably meant to contrast herself favorably with Sallie Brooks when she told him not to become preoccupied with earning a living because of their engagement: "I *cannot* have you slighted, dear, or hurried or forced into a position that might ruin your whole life."[12]

II

During his last unhappy year in high school, Van Wyck had had high expectations of New England, comforting himself in his diary that "next year will be better" and hoping that New England's rich cultural history would stimulate him as greatly as Europe's had done six years before. Early in his freshman year at Harvard he had made excursions to Concord and Walden, visiting the Manse and the graves of Emerson and Thoreau, and he had self-consciously insisted that he was happy in this contact with an American literary past: "You feel it irreverent to talk loud on these country roads which haven't changed since Thoreau walked them." In fact, however, the New England scene provoked nothing like the feelings he had experienced in Europe. Disappointed, he soon despised the historical placards he saw in New England: ". . . the flaunting of wholesale history is much like talking of your ancestors — very American and very cheap." By December of his freshman year he had decided that Boston was "narrow, conceited and provincial," and only by virtue of education less despicable than Plainfield.[13]

Harvard, which had begun to take on its modern character, was as much of a disappointment as New England. Van Wyck had been attracted by Harvard's literary tradition, and he had gone there hoping to find a sort of artists' community. Instead, he found the large modern university that President Charles Eliot had created, and the hectic, worldly life of the place disturbed him. He told Eleanor that he was "on the ragged edge from one year's-end to another. I dread Cambridge when away and hate it when here." Francis Biddle recalled in his autobiography how Brooks had seemed "shy and young and fresh, as if anything in this strange world of Harvard outside of letters was a startling phenomenon." And there was much at Harvard outside of letters. In 1904 Henry James returned to Cambridge after an absence of a quarter of a century and was astonished at the change: ". . . nothing is more striking than the recent drop in her [Harvard] of any outward sign of literary curiosity."[14]

Portrait of Van Wyck Brooks by John Butler Yeats, 1909

Van Wyck's parents, Sarah Ames and Charles Edward Brooks

Van Wyck at the Plainfield Mardi gras in 1899. The costume was probably acquired during the family's tour of Europe in 1898.

Far left, Eleanor Stimson at her graduation from the Plainfield
Seminary; near left, above, Charles Ames Brooks, Van Wyck's
brother; near left, below, Van Wyck in Carmel on his honeymoon,
1911; right, Van Wyck, Eleanor, and Charles in California, 1912 or
1913

To some extent the Harvard that Van Wyck had sought still existed, and it was symbolized for him in the person of Charles Eliot Norton, editor of Donne and student of Dante. But he had not expected to find another and more powerful Harvard, personified by Norton's cousin, President Eliot, scientist and believer in efficiency. Eliot had diversified the curriculum, expanding from the older theological and literary offerings to bring in laboratory sciences and other courses of practical utility. To Van Wyck, Eliot's Harvard seemed a mere training school for industrial society. Between Norton's Harvard and Eliot's there was no more community of culture and worldly life than there had been in Plainfield, where Van Wyck's mother had trained him in a genteel culture irrelevant to the business world she had hoped he would enter. The year after his graduation from Harvard, Van Wyck would complain in *The Wine of the Puritans* that New England culture was related in no vital way to New England life.

At the same time that Eliot had broadened the curriculum away from literature, he had introduced the elective system to permit students to specialize their educations if they chose to do so. Van Wyck chose to specialize, but in literature, in the older Harvard tradition. There were almost no required courses in Eliot's last years as president, so Van Wyck was able to go through Harvard without taking a single course in mathematics or science.[15] This choice was personally satisfying to him, but most of the students did not share his interests, and under Eliot's system they could go through Harvard without receiving the literary education that had once characterized the college. So Harvard was not the kind of literary community Van Wyck had hoped to find. He had his literary friends, but they were only a clique, isolated from the rest of the university.

He would attempt to solve the problem of literature at Harvard, as he would later attempt to solve it in America, by urging that literature not be too strictly literary. Literature must comment upon life. The *Harvard Advocate* was in financial straits, and Van Wyck argued that the source of the problem was the *Advocate*'s failure to respond to Harvard's transition from a small, homogeneous college to a large, diversified university. Of course the subscription list was small when the *Advocate* depended for its humor on jingles about literature professors of whom most students had not even heard. The *Advocate* could retain its position as *the* Harvard magazine only if in addition to being literary it became a wide-ranging forum for discussion of university affairs.[16] At his urging the magazine began a guest column, "Varied Outlooks," in which students could speak out on diverse aspects of Harvard life.

The *Advocate* would have to take a stand on the realities of Harvard life, even upon so sordid a reality as football — "if not a diversion of the lower animals, at least a little disturbing to the sensibilities of gentlemen," as Van Wyck later said. Football, which was considerably more brutal then than now, had become so dominant a concern that the perennially hapless Harvard teams, instead of deadening interest, only raised discontent among undergraduates. During Van Wyck's freshman year President Eliot had ignited a controversy by publicly doubting that football developed the best moral qualities or even the most desirable physique. Yet Van Wyck held Eliot partly responsible. His elective system allowed the "typical athlete" to get through college by taking the "easiest available" courses. At a meeting held to discuss *Advocate* finances, Van Wyck argued that the magazine should take a public stand: "This time is a real crisis in university affairs. . . . If football is knocked on the head, the entire standpoint of the undergraduate will change."[17]

There was also the problem of business at Harvard. Many of Van Wyck's classmates were planning careers as employees of the new giant corporations, and they kept him focused on the evils of business. In a poem he pictured a boy watching the birds and the sky but unhappily distracted by "The World," which urged, "Come in, come in, the stool is set,/Life give up and living get." And he noticed that his father was not the only one destroyed by business; seven of his college friends had dead fathers, most of them "killed by the business life," he said years later. Yet Harvard encouraged his classmates to enter that fatal business world, and President Eliot proudly trumpeted the usefulness of a liberal education in a business career.[18]

Still more troubling was Eliot's idea that culture was, by definition, useless. He designated as "culture courses" those whose practical utility he could not comprehend. Van Wyck protested in his notebook that culture had "vitally practical results," and one of his main objections to Eliot's elective system was that it produced large numbers of men with a dilettantish "pseudo-culture." In an *Advocate* essay, he warned his fellow students that every man had need of beauty in his life, even if he impractically refused to recognize that fact out of deference to a false ideal of masculinity: "The truth is that we deliberately acquire our ungraceful ways in an effort to be manly."[19] Thus, even at Harvard it was necessary to show that literature was not an effeminate interest. By actively trying to change the nature of things at Harvard, Van Wyck believed, the *Advocate* would not only enlarge its readership but would affirm that literature was a practical and manly endeavor.

Yet there was also the danger that by trying to get in touch with life, literature might simply accept it or merge with it. Such a literature would be an effete echo of the *status quo* rather than proof that culture had consequences. The problem was one of critical distance. When literature seemed unable to effect Brooks's desire, he would often resort to the hope that history would do so, and then he tended to follow the course of events uncritically. The tendency was early evident, for his urging that the *Advocate* take a prophetic and denunciatory stance toward modern college life had little more impact on Harvard literati than his later exhortations would have on American writers. The year after his graduation Van Wyck wrote his article "Harvard and American Life," in which he observed that "old-fashioned undergraduate life, with all its human significance, is giving way before the increasingly intellectual modern idea of effective specialization." Arguing that resistance to this trend was futile, Van Wyck took comfort in the larger hope that the onrushing modernization of Harvard might eradicate its provincialism and bring Harvard culture into touch with American life. The cost, which he did not mention, would be a loss of critical capacity, so he concluded in a paragraph of mixed emotions that ". . . inevitable and inexorable is that intellectualism which, in the coming generation, will sweep away the gentle sentiments of Puritan tradition, and make of Harvard the factory of American imperialism. Year after year the Harvard type grows less and less distinct as the American type more and more defines itself: with the College the old-fashioned humanist fades away, with the University the efficient practitioner of the future emerges."[20]

III

Van Wyck was dissatisfied not only with the general direction of the university but also with literary instruction at Harvard, and as a result his grades were mediocre. Having received mostly Ds and Es on his entrance examinations, which had included mathematics and physics, he had been admitted on probation. During his freshman year he got off probation, but only barely, by earning all Cs and Ds except for a lonely A in the survey of English literature taught by

Professors Briggs, Kittredge, and Perry. His sophomore year was little better — Bs, Cs, Ds, and again a solitary A, this time in Latin — and he was "admonished" for poor scholarship. Only in his third and final year, when he was stimulated by Irving Babbitt's teaching, did he do well, earning all As and Bs. During the summer before that last Harvard year, he had become engaged to Eleanor and then his father had died — events which might have helped make him a more serious student. For the entire three years, however, his average was only a little better than C. There is no reason to doubt his statement that he owed his Phi Beta Kappa key to the influence of friends.[21]

His dissatisfaction with Harvard literary instruction showed also in his decision to take his degree in three years. President Eliot had gradually reduced graduation requirements, and it did not require much extra effort to finish a year early. About a third of Van Wyck's class probably did so.[22] In addition to his dissatisfaction with Harvard, there were other obvious reasons for finishing early. Eleanor, who had been two years ahead of him in her education, had gone to Europe with her mother, and Van Wyck wished to pursue her there. Then, too, he saved his family the seven or eight hundred dollars which a year at Harvard cost when combined with an expensive social and club life. Nevertheless, in later years Van Wyck never showed extreme concern for the family treasury or let his affection for Eleanor displace his ambitions: if he had thought a fourth year at Harvard useful, he would have stayed.

Harvard, Van Wyck had decided, was an inappropriate place to prepare for a literary career. The Harvard esthetes had gradually palled on him, and he objected to the "select dilettantes" among whom Oscar Wilde was more popular than Keats. He also disliked the opposite extreme, the cult-belief in "seeing life" as a preparation for literature. Representative of this position at Harvard was Charles Townsend Copeland, who prepared a generation of students to see life in the glamorous profession of journalism. Van Wyck took Copeland's course in composition, but he and Copey had irreconcilable ideas about writing. When Van Wyck refused to write in an emphatic, journalistic style, Copeland called him "willful and stubborn." Van Wyck angrily wrote in his notebook:

> ... composition courses succeed in keeping their members to an almost even average of mediocre excellence.
>
> Now Mr. Copeland does not know me: therefore Q.E.D. he does not know my style.

I ... lack self-confidence to the extent of being afraid of Hermann Hagedorn and [second name illegible] and when I hear their poems praised and mine never are, to agree perfectly with the judgment that they are perfectly splendid, and that my poor trash is after all hopeless. But when I come back to my own room my own conceit (if you will) returns and I am quite sure in myself that nothing they write could equal what I can write, because my whole soul seems emersed [*sic*] for good or ill in this trick or art of literature and I cannot believe theirs is.

So the young man who was to hurry through Harvard in three years decided that *"the university is the very worst place possible for a man with literary ideals."*[23]

Most of Van Wyck's other courses were happier, but many of them had no more impact on him than did his course with Copeland. He was bored by his courses in government, history, and philosophy and even by his courses in classical literature. His real interest was in modern literature, and the serious influences on him were Professors Lyman Kittredge, Barrett Wendell, and above all, Irving Babbitt.[24]

Babbitt was intolerant and dogmatic, and Van Wyck later remembered him "tossing and goring the writers he disliked," all "grunts, blowings and gurgitations, roaring his opponents down."[25] Add to his harsh personality his animus against romanticism, to which Van Wyck was continuously faithful, and the question must be asked, why was Babbitt of all Van Wyck's teachers the greatest influence on him? Why not someone like Edward Kennard Rand, whose course he enjoyed and who impressed him as a good man? The answer is that Babbitt of all his teachers took literature most seriously. Like Van Wyck, Babbitt resented Eliot's elective system for destroying Harvard's literary tradition. For Babbitt literature was not a gentlemanly accomplishment but a real force in life with moral responsibility. Van Wyck's conception of the artist as prophet put him in fundamental agreement with Babbitt even while he disagreed about where the artist's moral responsibility lay.

Comparative Literature 22, Babbitt's course in the history of literary criticism, was where Van Wyck first read Renan, Taine, and Sainte-Beuve, on whose careers he would model his own. Though he disliked Babbitt, Van Wyck would be grateful all his life for this introduction to the great nineteenth-century critics, especially Sainte-Beuve. He would always admire and often emulate Sainte-Beuve, and in later years he would be proud of the many re-

semblances between his own career and that of the French critic.
However, Van Wyck did not have to wait until the end of his life to
recognize similarities between himself and Sainte-Beuve: he must
have stirred with sympathy as he learned how the great critic had
been born to a bourgeois mother with false pretensions to culture,
who hoped her son would make money rather than write.[26]

Babbitt seldom missed a chance to denounce romanticism and
he was critical of Sainte-Beuve, who had begun his career as a
militant romantic and then tempered his convictions after 1848. In
his lecture notes, Van Wyck recorded Babbitt speaking of Sainte-
Beuve's "point of view as moving along at random, of his ship having
no anchor." Van Wyck, however, was no more moved by Babbitt's
criticism of Sainte-Beuve or by his vehement attacks on romanticism
than he had been by Copeland's criticisms of his writing style. In a
few years Brooks would be a leader of the attack on Babbitt's New
Humanism. In the meantime, in the middle of the year when he
studied under Babbitt, he registered his dissent in a *Harvard Monthly*
essay, "The Quality of Romance": ". . . all truly beautiful things are
joined with the current of eternal life, that cannot have part in the
reason or dialect of any particular age or world, because it has part
in all ages and in all worlds. So it is with art. It is evolved from the
infinite, and to the infinite it returns, happy indeed to bring men
glimpses of what they may never understand."[27]

Thus Van Wyck maintained not only his attachment to romanticism but also his spiritual conception of art. Art was the medium of
communication with that better, heavenly afterlife, the timeless
world of the "infinite," on which his thoughts had dwelt since
adolescence. The only problem was that at Harvard he had begun to
doubt that he himself could personally glimpse the infinite. Did he
or did he not have the soul of an artist?

IV

Van Wyck made his second voyage to Europe, to Italy, in the
summer of 1905 after his freshman year at Harvard, and while the
seven week pilgrimage was in part a joyous encounter with what had
become an idealized other world for him, the journey was also an
unhappy experience. It came at a time when he was full of doubt,
guilt, and self-criticism, and he made it in the company of his
mother and his sick father. Grandmother Phebe Ames had died the
previous March, and Van Wyck's brother Ames was spending the
summer as an amateur cowboy in the West.

Perhaps this voyage was undertaken for Charles Brooks's benefit, since, as Van Wyck later wrote, European travel was regarded in Plainfield as the "panacea for all illnesses." But it was not a panacea for Charles, who contracted dysentery in Sorrento a week after their landing. Van Wyck, going out only briefly for medicine, stayed indoors with his parents. He ate alone in the great dining room of their hotel while his mother spent the dinner hour upstairs with his ailing father. Thus, in Europe where Charles Brooks had been happy as a young man, he now entered the last year of his disappointed life. His neuralgia returned and on the voyage home he would have a headache that lasted twelve days.[28]

Van Wyck soon escaped from the hotel and roamed for a few days alone along the Italian coast. On Capri he made friends with G. E. Marshall, an Englishman employed as a tutor by a family of Neapolitan nobility. Marshall was a liberal spirit who, though a Catholic, used the Index as a guide to good reading. With his blue blazer and Cambridge boater, he seemed to Van Wyck like one of Max Beerbohm's *Yellow Book* characters sprung to life. The two new friends made an overnight excursion to the island of Ischia, where they came upon a secluded beach and bathed nude: "Italy breaks away many useless barriers to comfort and freedom." Van Wyck was impressed also by the way Marshall washed his linen before retiring and hung it up to dry in his hotel room during the night. Donning his clean shirt in the morning, he remained "impeccably fresh" while travelling without encumbering baggage.[29] The happy and healthy Marshall understood that material life must be simplified, and he was a strong contrast to Van Wyck's businessman father, languishing in an Italian hotel room.

Marshall served as the kind of model for Van Wyck that Arthur Ryder had provided in Italy in 1899 — a masculine figure in pursuit of culture rather than money. Marshall had abandoned all thought of worldly success and earned a living as a tutor because it enabled him to follow his interests and live in Italy. This was at least part of the reason that Marshall made, as Ryder had, a great impression on Van Wyck, and in an acquaintance that was even briefer than the one with Ryder. In all, Van Wyck spent only thirty-six hours with Marshall, but he corresponded with him for years and recalled him half a century later as a "many-sided man, delightful on all sides."[30]

On another solitary excursion one Sunday, Van Wyck glimpsed the infinite and the ideal. He hired a donkey and rode alone out of Naples to a monastery situated several miles west of the city on the high volcanic rise at Camaldoli. In the monastery, approached through an avenue of cypresses, the silence was broken only by the rustling of lizards and the humming of bees in the flowers. An elderly monk guided Van Wyck to a parapet where he gazed south, across fields, villages, and sea, to Capri, twenty miles away. Another parapet overlooked Naples, and from there he scanned the eastern horizon till Vesuvius loomed up and interrupted the vista. Haze gave the great landmarks an indistinct, unreal appearance. Van Wyck was glad it was Sunday, ". . . for there is always a peculiar quality in the air Sundays; and what a place that is to spend them! It seemed to me the very essence of Italy, in the hot still afternoon, no one within hearing except that old monk and I, crumbling walls falling into decay, the history of that place, the very name — Camaldoli!"[31]

Unfortunately, Van Wyck was not often experiencing the thrills which he believed should have accompanied such glimmering visions, and he was disappointed, not in Italy but in his own lack of poetic sensibility. He had believed that this trip to the heavenly realm of Europe would inspire "the grandest poem in the world. . . ." Yet, ". . . now that the time has come it is nothing and I yawn." The problem, he believed, was his self-consciousness. In Naples he had been struck by the unplanned effect of the beautiful furnishings of an ordinary Italian hotel room, in contrast to its American counterpart: "We Americans are the only people who *know* how to be artistic but seldom are. Over here they know nothing at all about it, they simply are." He saw that he was as self-consciously artistic as most Americans, and occasionally he admitted what one feels in reading his journal, that it was written with an eye on posterity. He did not bother to describe some sights because he remembered them well: "If you are reading this — well it's your fault. . . . Should I call this journal self-conscious?"[32]

Thus, even as he visited the otherworldly paradise of Italy, he was beginning to doubt that it was a fit habitation for an American artist. Yet it did not seem possible to be an artist in America either, so perhaps it was best to give up his plans. On the day he returned to America after the voyage home from Italy, he wrote to Eleanor:

There are some sorts of personal poetry which I think it best to give up writing altogether.

I have been morbid and mawkish . . . and much of this state of mind has been fostered by ideas and ambitions that have been in a sense unmanly. . . .

I have developed a sudden thirst for institutions, for races rather than individuals, for the people rather than the classes, almost for economics — and along with this prose is appealing to me almost more than poetry. I don't know but that to write socialist pamphlets is the most precious desire I have. But in them would be thoughts on art, and really aiming at a general system of culture. . . . This sounds very ordinary and perhaps is, but if it had a few powerful preachers, what a short cut it would be to everything we have hoped for.[33]

Actually, he was not so much giving up hope for an artistic career as working out a stratagem for the seemingly impossible task of being an artist in America. By deciding to become a "preacher" of art and culture, he was only stepping back one pace from the role of the artist-priest who gave men glimpses of the infinite. If he could not play the primary role of "realizing" the ideal in art, he could play the secondary role of making it possible for others to do so; he could become a critic. However, he was not genuinely reconciled to a secondary role, as was evident ten years later when he argued in *America's Coming-of-Age* that criticism was also an art, a method of bringing the ideal down to earth. More and more he was to believe that the artist, while still a prophet, was also a worldly man, and that idea turned him against the concept of the esthete. To understand how his thinking changed it is necessary to examine the ideal of the artist which he learned at Harvard.

To begin, he learned, not only from Babbitt and Sainte-Beuve but also from friends and other teachers, that the great writer was produced by a great national tradition. The case seemed clearly proved by examples like Turgenev and Tolstoy or, better still, Yeats and Synge, for Van Wyck and his Harvard set were fascinated by the Irish literary revival. In one sense the nationalism of the artist was an easy lesson for Van Wyck, who had written "The Mission of American Art" for his high school magazine. But the real lesson of this nationalism was the sad fate of the American artist who, because of the sterile and narrow tradition from which he came, could not hope to accomplish anything significant.

Barrett Wendell, more than any other Harvard teacher, reinforced Van Wyck's conviction that the American artist was rooted in an infertile soil. Although Wendell was primarily interested in the Elizabethans, he taught the one course in American literature offered at Harvard, and he reflected the tone of that course in his *Literary History of America* (1900), which was written to "discern what, if anything, America has so far contributed to the literature of our ancestral language."[34] Little or nothing was the answer. Van Wyck received the feeling from Wendell's course that of all the regions only New England had produced anything resembling literature and even this was hardly worthy of critical attention. The scorn with which Brooks would dismiss Emerson, Hawthorne, and Lowell in *America's Coming-of-Age* was directly attributable to Wendell's influence.

Wendell abhorred the time and place in which fate had unkindly placed him, and he communicated his disdain to Harvard students, not only in his lectures but in his person. With his affected English accent, his goatee, and the cane which he carried on his little finger, he was a cartoon of the esthete, and he shared the weary languor and mild *fin-de-siècle* pessimism that was fashionable at Harvard. Even so, he thought of himself as a "man of letters" and in his writing attempted a graciousness of style that was pomposity itself. Henry James, reading him in 1895, said sickly that Wendell did not write "as the Professor of English of Harvard should write. It has made me unhappy." To whatever degree Wendell understood his own failings, he attributed them to living in a region past its prime. He wrote to Robert Herrick in 1900 that New England had half a century before experienced its "flowering of ripe national character. And now the region is virtually extinct." A Tory in politics as well as in literature, Wendell complained to another correspondent of "the racial agony in which we are being strangled by invading aliens . . . as the end of me — and of ours — comes nearer. . . ." This agony justified despair for one like Wendell who believed that literature was significant "as the unconscious expression of a national temper."[35]

Although Van Wyck was not always in complete agreement with Wendell, he got on well with him and found that Wendell's teachings reinforced some of his own ideas. The appeal of the idea of America's artistic sterility lay in its consistency with Van Wyck's continuing hatred of business life: ". . . we are too vulgar, too commercial, too narrow to appreciate the meaning of art." Wendell believed that the best possible society was one of class based on merit, "each in his place, none unworthily secure, . . . none undeservedly oppressed." Van Wyck, while favoring a clear class structure, found Wendell's ideas too bourgeois and leaned more strongly toward inherited privilege, the basis of European aristocracy, as became evident in *The Wine of the Puritans* when he objected to the "curious democratic assumption . . . that all men are equal who have the money." Like Wendell, however, Van Wyck would often be disturbed by the immigration question and the fact that, as Graeling would say, "Nations of foreigners came to our ports desiring to be called American."[36]

The idea that great art was nationalistic, to which most Harvard literati subscribed, was related to a still more significant idea about the great artist's personality — he was passionately absorbed in the everyday life of the world around him. Van Wyck learned from Lyman Kittredge that "Chaucer was a man of the world," and from George P. Baker that Shakespeare worked "in the busy world and in the human heart of his time." In his journal Van Wyck noted that great writers like Dante and Goethe were "philistine almost," and he suggested in an essay that Pascal could have been a still greater writer if he had been a more worldly man.[37]

The idea of the artist's absorption in the worldly life around him suggested another lesson: the true artist was not introspective or self-conscious, an idea consistent with the romantic belief that great art was spontaneously produced. Van Wyck's essay on "Dante and the Literary Temperament" argued that second-rate writers were destroyed by self-consciousness: "The mind in becoming an observer . . . and a translator of things observed into the vehicle that conveys them to other minds, incidentally ceases to *live*." In other words, concern for the audience adds an element of self-consciousness to expression. However, a few men "of great nobility" are not affected by their audience: ". . . unable to divorce experiences and emotions from the literary expression . . . that is instinctive in them, [they] may yet unconsciously crystallize the two: so that literature becomes their life and life literature." For such nobly unself-conscious men, artistic expression would be "a loving repetition of the original experience, and emotions would not grow dependent upon expression. . . ." Rather, "Life itself *becomes* expression." This was the achievement of Dante and "of all supreme literature."[38]

Even during his freshman year, while he was aping the Harvard esthetes, Van Wyck had begun to learn this new ideal of the artist's personality, and the learning helped make genuine the despair that was only a fashionable pose for many of his friends. As his never absent feelings of guilt played on these new ideas, he decided that his family had been correct in criticizing him for his morbidness. When he had undertaken his own training for art as a youth in Plainfield, he had cultivated in himself a desire for abstraction from life. Therefore, he now concluded, he did not have the soul of an artist.

With characteristic intensity, he compared his own personality to his new worldly and unself-conscious ideal of the artist, and the result was a change in the attitude as well as the style of his poetry. For instance, "Misconceptions":

> (Walt Whitman's manner, for the moment mine and
>   vitally sincere.)
> No longer I exalted to self-believed supremacy —
> .   .   .   .
> But I a mere morbid boy —
> Having had just enough acquaintance with men's ways
>   to appoint myself a warning to you,
> Now believe these words which shall be everlasting
>   truth:
> There is but one unpardonable sin —
> The permitting, fostering, cultivating of life
>   without a passionate heart. . . .

About the same time he wrote: "All for the sake of his imagined art/He found that he had cast away his heart." Believing now that great art was the expression of a large, expansive soul, conscious of experience, not of itself, he had to question the *soulfulness* of the personality he had self-consciously attempted to develop in himself:

> VOX CLAMANTIS (July 7, 1905)
>
>   Sometimes there comes to me
> The piercing vision of an intellect
> That without soul took flesh, that in the growth
> The body requires conceived a soul of brain,
> The counterfeit of spirit, counterfeit
> In all soul-attributes, ideals, loves
> And half-beliefs in God, yet which concerned
> No phase of life, although in mock of life,
> And conquering through cleverness, it won
> Affection, and the goal of some desires
> It never longed for.[39]

He meditated in his notebooks about his self-consciousness, and his "whole soul blushed" when he reflected that he had "written no letter in five years which I did not write tacitly assuming that it would be eventually published." There were exceptions, however, like his carelessly written letters to his mother which he knew she did not save: "I never read *these* through after writing to gloat over the great thoughts I have committed to posterity." Then finally he stepped off the page, as it were, and spoke directly to the reader, admitting that even as he meditated on his self-consciousness in his journal, he was posturing for posterity.[40]

In this way, Van Wyck's own poetic development ended in the mood of effete sophistication that characterized the *fin de siècle*. The subjectivity in which he had romantically indulged had been purchased at the expense of his ability to express himself objectively in art. He was trapped in a web of thought, examining first his self-consciousness, then his awareness of his self-consciousness, his awareness of that awareness, and so on. Gradually, painfully, he resigned himself to a career as a critic.

Brooks later said that he "never wished to be anything but a critic," but this was the older man depreciating the desire of the younger. Self-disgust accompanied his growing conviction that he did not have the soul of a poet. His ambivalent attitude toward himself showed clearly in the series of "Imaginary Letters" which he wrote in the summer of 1906. Sometimes he spoke in the guise of a personality he admired, as in the letter "From a Young Irish Poet to a Gentleman of Fashion," but in other letters he adopted a mask he disliked, as in "From a Dilettante to a Student of Art."[41]

"From a Critic to a Poet" is the only one of Van Wyck's imaginary letters in which it is difficult to tell whether he most admired the addressor or the addressee. He consciously tried to place his sympathy with the critic by saying that midway between the worldly vocation of the scientist and the priestly calling of the poet, ". . . the opportunity is given me [the critic] of the sanest life, . . . the most balanced." But when the letter "From a Critic to a Poet" is read carefully, it is clear that Van Wyck preferred the inspired vision of the poet to the balanced sanity of the critic. For instance, he compared the critic's surroundings unfavorably to the poet's — the critic, needing his papers and books, was restricted to the indoors, while the poet might work at the seashore and leave his "clothes around the point." Worse still, the critic was not even as good a critic as the poet, for as Matthew Arnold had said, all literature was a criticism of life. And the poet, who was a "passive or unconscious critic," had an advantage: "The opportunities of poetry make it the greatest form of criticism, since it employs more varied and subtle vehicles of expression and can treat more directly of higher themes."[42]

Clearly, Van Wyck would have preferred to be a poet, and he believed that he could have been if only things had been a little different. In the Harvard essay in which he created the character of Charles Graeling, he outlined the kind of person he believed he could have become if he had grown up, like Graeling, in the "fortunate circumstance" of having dead parents. Graeling was "one of those rare souls that are able to enjoy and understand life for its own sake." While absorbed in worldly life, Graeling was nevertheless an idealist who had written that he would endeavor "to give men, so far as I am able, an interpretation of the world we *will* by means of the symbolic world we *perceive*. To this end, I have become a literary man." In Italy, Charles Graeling saw a vision of the ideal world. He dreamed of old frescoes and ruined colonnades, of incense and eyes full of sorrow. Van Wyck rhapsodized: "Yes that is the youth of which Charles Graeling was capable, the youth that in finding earth as beautiful as heaven, finds heaven very beautiful. . . . Feeling thus in his heart . . . he went forth at fifteen to 'a world' — as he describes it — of neat and careful streets, scrubbed curb-stones and well-cut lawns, where the lovely wind blows to and fro, and the gray sun looks out upon neat and positive excellence."[43] An insipid world like that needed a poet like Charles Graeling, but it was not to have him. The essay was a "Memorial," for Charles Graeling, like the poet in Van Wyck, was dead at twenty-one.

3

THE LIMITATIONS OF LIFE

JUST after Harvard's Christmas recess of 1906-07, Van Wyck wrote to Eleanor, "Really, dear heart, you never saw such a *Gothic horde*. . . ." During the holidays, he had made the rounds of New York editorial offices, unsuccessfully attempting to find employment to follow his forthcoming graduation in June, and he had not been impressed by the men he had met. They seemed so unliterary, these men like Paul Elmer More from Missouri and William Dean Howells from Ohio. How "very strange" to find that ". . . the literary editors of New York were all born in the Middle West!" Having admired More's graceful essays in the *Evening Post* and hoping to form a connection with the *Post* himself, he had obtained a letter of introduction from Irving Babbitt. But More had merely given him a book to review anonymously for the *Nation* and then passed him along to F. M. Colby of the *Bookman*. And there was a disenchanting tone in More's letter to Colby, which spoke of Van Wyck's "intention of taking up literary work" as if literary aspirations implied the same sordid motives with which one "took up" stocks and bonds![1]

Howells, whom Van Wyck managed to see because he was related to the Mead family into which Howells had married, was still less helpful, absolutely void of suggestions as to how to begin a literary career. He also seemed careless of literary ideals; Van Wyck did not think he should stoop to newspaper work unless he could write editorials, but Howells had replied that one could not join an army as a general. The old novelist had tried to make up in kindness and geniality for what he lacked in advice, but Van Wyck found him an unimpressive figure: ". . . such a funny little round-shouldered *bunch* of a man! — He almost rolled about the floor rather than walked. . . ."[2]

"If I were to be in business, I suppose it would be straight sailing indeed," he reflected, but literature was another matter.[3] In the spring of 1907, just before graduation, he made one last effort, attempting to place his "Imaginary Letters," but he was again unsuccessful. America seemed a barren field for the aspiring writer.

The path to Europe was opened by Frederick Moore, an established American political correspondent in London who had written a well-known book on politics in southeastern Europe, *The Balkan Trail* (1906). Dissatisfied with his writing, he had come to Harvard for a year with Copeland. Attractive, masculine, and romantic, he reinforced the fashionableness of journalism as a beginning career for Harvard's young men of letters. Moore took a paternal interest in Van Wyck, nine years his junior, and offered to find him a newspaper job in London. If the position had been in America, Van Wyck would have been torn by his mixed feelings about journalism. On the one hand, he believed now that the artist was a worldly man, and journalism offered the opportunity of "seeing life." On the other hand, from his bad experience in Copeland's course, he already doubted his fitness for journalism. Then too, as he had tried to tell Howells, the coarseness of newspaper work might be repugnant to his high literary ideals. But Moore offered him a chance in Europe and that was reason enough to put aside his qualms about journalism. The same Harvard which had taught Van Wyck that the great writer was a nationalist had nevertheless also taught him that America was a literary dependency of England. So, as he wrote in his memoirs, he "supposed that the only chance an American had to succeed as a writer was to betake himself [to England] with all possible speed."[4]

After graduation in June of 1907 Van Wyck spent a month in Plainfield with his mother, who agreed to support his plans, happy perhaps that he was taking up work with at least a possibility of worldly profit. Then he embarked for England, crossing in steerage partly to save money but mostly to indulge his romantic thirst for poverty. Steerage turned out to be a bore, with edible food and a clean place to sleep, but he consoled himself with thoughts of Europe ahead. From the deck he saw Ireland and "felt the Irish blood glowing in my veins," as he wrote to Eleanor, whose presence in Paris was another compelling reason for this European venture. On the first of August he landed in Liverpool, treated himself to a room in a good hotel, and rather prematurely wrote to Eleanor that he felt guilty at taking "so easily to England — as indeed I knew I should. . . . England is the home of *gentlemen:* the quiet, the simplicity, the distinctly graded class-system all contribute."[5]

The next day he entrained for London, where he was to find literary ideals not very superior to those of New York. With letters of introduction from Moore, he unsuccessfully appealed to the editors of several magazines for employment, offering among other things his "Imaginary Letter from a Critic to a Poet" as a sample of his writing. Even an editor of the *Spectator* found this a bit lofty for his readers, and he analyzed Van Wyck acutely, telling him that while he seemed to have a genuine interest in literature he was unlikely to be a successful journalist. Another editor cheerfully said that he turned away half the pieces he received because they were too good and that a writer was most likely to succeed by turning out work he despised. Van Wyck decided not to use his letter to the wife of a man in the Harmsworth organization lest he be exposed to the lucrative temptations of yellow journalism. Still, he had to work, so he finally accepted a position at thirty shillings a week in the American literary agency of Curtis Brown, a former employer of Frederick Moore. Van Wyck's duties consisted of clipping stories and jokes from English papers to be reprinted in the United States, sometimes rewriting and making them more "breezy" for the American audience. He worked in the office from ten to six, and in addition he had to write stories on his own time on subjects like dogs trained to collect for charity, a recently discovered boot of Cromwell's, and the Prince of Wales's tattoo artist.[6]

He accepted such menial writing chores in spite of his high literary ideals because, thanks in part to his engagement to Eleanor, he was anxious for worldly success. Moore, who returned to London not long after Van Wyck went to work for Curtis Brown, told him that within six months, if he worked hard, he would be making twenty pounds or a hundred dollars a month. Van Wyck breathlessly reported to Eleanor that, thanks to Moore, "I have stumbled into a kind of El Dorado." But he was to continue at a low wage, a reflection no doubt of the agency's assessment of his skills as a reporter. And he was soon making loans to Moore, his supposed benefactor, who needed money to get married on. Moore also acted as an agent for him, commissioning articles like "Harvard and

American Life." Yet even with this extra work, Van Wyck was earning little more than his expenses.[7]

Neither was he gaining entry into English literary circles, for while he had literary friends in London, they were mostly Americans. Friendliest of all was Eleanor, who persuaded her mother to bring her to London for three months. After work Van Wyck had tea with her, and on weekends they made excursions into the country together. Many old acquaintances passed through the city, including Irving Babbitt, "tamed and kind," whom Van Wyck encountered in the British Museum. Half a dozen Harvard friends visited Van Wyck in London, among them Lee Simonson and Ned Sheldon. Thomas H. Thomas, who had just finished writing his notable book *French Portrait Engraving of the XVIIth and XVIIIth Centuries* (1910), roomed with Van Wyck for two months in Pimlico.[8]

Because of Thomas, Van Wyck witnessed an incident which reinforced his conviction of the superiority of English culture over American. He had gone with Thomas to the National Gallery, where they saw a portrait which was attributed, Thomas thought, to the wrong artist. They found the director, Sir Charles Holroyd, who stood in front of the painting and listened carefully while Thomas made his case. Convinced, Holroyd tore the label from the picture, and the name of the other painter soon appeared in its place. Van Wyck marveled over the incident, which illustrated "how swift and sure is the response to [intellectual] authority in England," while in America, he was certain, such a challenge from an unknown youth would have provoked only defensive bluster.[9] It was exactly such quick and certain recognition as Holroyd's, and the belief that such acuteness was only possible in an organic high culture, that had brought Brooks to Europe. It was only against such a fine background as this that the authentic artist could be drawn out of himself and so experience his finest and fullest development.

Van Wyck, however, had found nothing in England to draw him out, and he must have been especially disappointed by his failure to achieve the entrance into English literary life for which he had made the compromise of trying his hand at London journalism. He made a few English friends, but he was too shy to push himself into literary circles with the boldness of some of his youthful contemporaries, whom he enviously heard describe lunches with Shaw and tennis matches with H. G. Wells. He had to be content with mere glimpses of these greats and such others as Chesterton, Swinburne, J. M. Barrie, and Havelock Ellis, whom he saw in the street and at the British Museum. Dumbstruck in their presence and too diffident to think of introducing himself, he looked at them almost as if they were sights or monuments, and his touristic attitude made them as distant as the deceased De Quincey, whose squalid attic he searched out in York Street. He remained an outsider in literary London.[10]

He had hoped that even as a journalist he would profit from English culture, from the Fleet Street tradition which "draws us all together from the ends of the earth," as he would write in *The Wine of the Puritans*. But he was disenchanted by his dreary assignments from Curtis Brown, and he concluded now that "Fleet Street is dead and gone." More than that, he was beginning to think that such conscious pursuit of tradition was futile; it was impossible for an American to master European culture. One could acquire a surface knowledge and a "few memories," but one could not deeply feel an alien tradition: "One can really *secure* nothing in Europe of the life that must lie behind artistic expression. . . ." Instead, "We only destroy ourselves by wandering up and down the world."[11] Alienated and alone in London, his thoughts turned toward home.

America as a subject was also provoked by the problem he had outlined in his article "Harvard and American Life." There he had written that the immigrant population and the addition of new states — the fact, in short, that America was a young country — "has made it almost impossible as yet to define the common point of view of America." Defining a national "point of view" was a problem more worthy of a young literary man's attention than writing about the Prince of Wales's tattoo artist. Brooks's work clipping jokes at the agency had focused his attention on humor, and he considered writing an American counterpart to Thackeray's *English Humourists*. Then he thought of writing a humorous book himself, or rather, a book "satirical: crushing of idealism in America: a picture of what happens to the American artist forced to leave his country: a satire & an appeal — the barrenness of American life."[12]

To write his book he needed peace and quiet away from the busy, worried life he had been leading in London. Fred Moore, who still owed him money, helped him search out a suitable haven and agreed to make regular payments on the debt, so that Van Wyck would have a small income. In February 1908, in West Chiltington, a village in Sussex, they found a farmer who would supply meals and a room with a fire for a pound a week, and Van Wyck spent the next few months there writing *The Wine of the Puritans*. The farmhouse, called "The Friars," had once been part of a monastery and must have been an appealing setting for the young prophet at work. He fell into a productive routine, writing every morning and going for ten-mile walks in the afternoon, accompanied sometimes by the village parson. He had seldom been happier, and while the logic of his book would indicate a return to America, it is understandable that at least consciously he planned a future in England. He probably felt some guilt toward his mother as he worked out his criticisms of American genteel culture, and he assuaged such feelings by planning to bring her to England to live with him the next year.[13] Thus he would have separated her from his brother Ames and also from the culture he was criticizing.

Under the working title "What Is America?" Brooks wrote three drafts of his short book, the first in the form of an exchange of letters and the second as an essay. He soon found that he had no gift for satire, and the final draft was a subdued conversational dialogue, modeled after a book that had greatly impressed him in college, G. Lowes Dickinson's *Modern Symposium*. He finished the manuscript at the end of May and resolved to try the various London publishers till there were none left. If no one would take it, he would himself pay to print the book and bind it in paper, for ". . . my book is a comment which absolutely demands being said." However, the final draft was accepted by the first publisher he tried, Sisley's.[14]

Meanwhile, he had fallen into what was probably the worst depression of his life thus far. Returning to London for the summer of 1908 to see his book into print, he was thrown back into the harried life of a journalist. Again he was financially insecure and, worse, doing work he hated. Moore secured freelance assignments for him from a Manchester newspaper, which requested an article on William Jennings Bryan: "Dear God! Bryan! I must however remember that I am a journalist." Still, he was troubled that the quality which he hoped would make him a superior writer, his care for the ideal, seemed to make him an inferior journalist. But then he was brought up short by guilt; it was morbid to long only for the ideal. Journalism was at least a wordly career: "There are nobler types than Amiel."[15]

It was in this period that he lived the impoverished life he later described in the *Opinions of Oliver Allston*. For shelter he could afford only an unfurnished artist's studio in Chelsea, where he slept on the model's stand and covered himself with a moth-eaten bearskin rug. He lived the entire summer on buns and tea, and fainted once from hunger. Eleanor, whom he visited briefly on the continent, found him thin and ashen. She put him to bed and fed him till he recovered his strength. But he was never really in desperate straits. He was receiving an allowance from his mother and somehow he found the money to publish *The Wine of the Puritans*: Sisley's had accepted the book provided that he would risk half the initial investment himself, a not unusual practice at the time.[16]

Although he was certain that he could have done better, he had accepted Sisley's offer because he was tired with worry about the book and about "the possibility of its hurting mama." Sometimes he believed the book was "nothing" and lacking in both "construction" and "vigour." He was "not an artist, a poet, a writer at all — that is the truth: and because I try to be and imagine myself to be I bring all this terrible misery upon myself and others." He had begun to borrow money, and his debts together with "the sense that I am not acting fairly toward my family [cause] . . . often for days together suffering which I seem hardly able to bear." Instead of writing, it would be better to retreat to a monastery where he might work with his hands in the garden and, if he felt regrets, "go back into the chapel and pray to some power which is able to stifle the eternal heart-ache."[17]

All through the summer he had meditated in his notebooks on the source of his feeling of guilt, his fear of being alone with his thoughts, his inability to apply and concentrate himself. He wondered if his melancholy was a romantic pose, an attempt to convince himself and others that he had an artist's depth. No, he decided, his feelings were only too real. He compared himself to the always exuberant Frederick Moore, whom he had just seen off in slouch hat and unstarched collar for an adventurous assignment in Constantinople, and he concluded that the contrast was due to Moore's not possessing "the dreadful responsibility of an art." The real problem was that there was nothing sublime or mysterious in life on which he could exercise his artistic spirit. In the modern world, "We see all sides of all questions," and the result was that ". . . the soul loses form and outline and becomes a vague shadow." Other times he worried that his mind was "falling away" and described it as "a piece of machinery which whirls and whirls without being oiled and without producing anything." As so often in the past, he decided that the origin of his problems lay in his self-consciousness, his tendency to self-analysis, the very activity he was engaged in as he sought the source of his troubles. He was trapped in a circle of thought that laid his nerves "bare to the wind, . . . we are not protected even by an instant of stupidity, of callousness — the power to suspend our consciousness at moments and to rest from life."[18]

To find surcease of consciousness and rest from life — how did one accomplish that? There was one obvious and permanent solution, and Van Wyck was impressed that "A French psychologist [Durkheim?] establishes the fact that suicide is always the result of thought and imagination." It would be years yet before he would seriously contemplate such a measure, but if he was not ready to hasten death, he took pleasure from its ultimate certainty: "There is only one thing which I enjoy, — the sense that all these things must fade, die. . . . How it consoles one's futility to look on and smile and remember the futility of anything else! Oh, we can hate God and curse God and God has not the power to take this away! God has not the power to make one beautiful thing endure. God has not the power to defeat our craving for non-existence."[19]

II

T. S. Eliot, still an undergraduate in 1909 when he reviewed *The Wine of the Puritans* for the *Harvard Advocate,* found it an impressive book, unusually acute and refined, he said, but also chilling: "The reasons for the failure of American life . . . are surgically exposed; . . . and the more sensitive of us may find ourselves shivering under the operation. For the book is a confession of national weakness." Eliot's shivers were understandable, for Van Wyck's book was an intensely personal effort, addressed primarily to Americans like himself and Eliot who aspired to be artists but felt frustrated by an infertile soil. *The Wine of the Puritans* made no general impression, but among the Harvard literati it was considered profound.[20]

The book's acclaim at Harvard was due in part to its being a pastiche of ideas which Brooks had acquired as an undergraduate there. Accepting as a given the sterility of American culture, he found an explanation for that unfruitfulness in the concept of national character, or "race," that Wendell and Babbitt (through Sainte-Beuve) and other of his teachers had propagated. America's problem was that "unlike any other great race we were founded by full-grown, modern, self-conscious men." The Germans, French, and English had occupied their respective territories before they were civilized, and so, "moulded by the special traits of the lands of their choice," each developed a distinct culture harmonious with its particular environment. Their cultures would always be "relevant" because they were organic; they grew "out of an antiquity which held in embryo all the later problems of the race." America, unlike these great European peoples, "had had no childhood," no half-conscious era before the dawn of civilization in which to shape a primitive culture adequate to its environment. Instead, America was founded by civilized Englishmen whose culture, developed in England, could not be adapted to the American wilderness. The "particularly vivid reality of pioneering could hardly find its ideal reflection in the genial traditions" which the Puritans had brought from England. At the very outset, American culture was inadequate to the harshness of American life.[21]

The inadequacy of the Puritans' culture to their situation accounted for both their rapacious materialism and their vapid idealism. As pioneers the Puritans were forced to emphasize the virtues of thrift and industry. And, with no meaningful culture or ideals to restrain them, they surrendered to the real and came "to believe that whatever was not in some way economically necessary was in some way wrong." The "New England idea" had nothing to do with the ideal, and this materialistic outlook remained a habit long after the need for it had passed. Whittier and Holmes, for instance, with their "note of shrewdness and homely comfort" showed that the New England mind was trapped in a strictly economic viewpoint though, by then, "there were peace and plenty for more gracious purposes." The economic viewpoint could not tell the New Englander what to do with the gold of California or what to make of less economically inclined cultures now that he could afford ancestral pilgrimages to Europe. The New Englander, finding that his intellectual heritage offered no explanation or interpretation for much that confronted him, assumed that culture bore no organic relation to life and turned to "arbitrary and purely spiritual" explanations. The result was Transcendentalism: "Emerson is a lofty and inspired sophist who begs the whole question of life, and whose sophism is the direct result of a provincial training, . . . inadequate to explain life in the wider sense." Brooks summed up the complex argument in the book's central metaphor: "You put the old wine into new bottles, . . . and when the explosion results, one may say, the aroma passes into the air and the wine spills on the floor. The aroma, or the ideal, turns into transcendentalism, and the wine, or the real, becomes commercialism."[22]

Robert Spiller, representing a common opinion, later criticized Brooks for creating a "Puritan bogy," a "straw man." With "little regard for historical facts," Brooks "warped" the word Puritan in order "to make it convey all the traits and none but the traits" which he disliked. Actually, Brooks was not so harsh. Once the Puritans had provided an historical explanation for the contemporary situation, they played no very large role in any of Brooks's books, and he blamed circumstances as much as the Puritans for their narrow ways. "Pioneers," he wrote, "cannot allow themselves the virtue of breadth."[23] Another problem with Spiller's criticism was that it was based on the achievement of New England historians like Perry Miller and Kenneth Murdock who wrote *after* Brooks. Thus Spiller betrayed the same lack of historical insight for which he criticized Brooks: Spiller had not thought himself into Brooks's intellectual situation in 1908. While Brooks attributed traits he disliked to the Puritans, so did many other writers in his time. Unitarian Boston had long since ceased defending the Puritans, and if one seeks the creator of the "Puritan bogy" one must look back at least as far as Brooks Adams's *Emancipation of Massachusetts* (1882). Brooks was engaged in cultural analysis rather than historical research. What he had done was to take the received history of New England, which he had learned at Harvard, and hold it to the ideal of cultural integration, which he had learned from European critics. And he found the Puritans wanting because the received history described a fractured New England mind.

Brooks's major source on New England history was, of course, Barrett Wendell. In his *Literary History of America* (1900) Wendell called Emerson a "Yankee preacher of unfettered idealism," adding, "Idealism, of course, is ancestrally familiar to any race of Puritan origin." What was the character of the idealism with which, thanks to his Puritan ancestry, Emerson was familiar? Despite the "vagaries of his ideal philosophy," he remained a "shrewd sensible Yankee." Aware of the Over-Soul, Emerson "was equally aware that a dollar is a dollar, and a cent a cent. . . . [Emerson] hitched his waggon to star after star, but never really confused the star with the waggon."[24] What a meaningless idealism it must have seemed to Van Wyck, full of his scorn for business, an idealism "aware that a dollar is a dollar"! No wonder he called Emerson a "lofty and inspired sophist."

Another likely source on New England history was Santayana. Although Brooks had not taken any courses with Santayana, who was on leave during the first two of his three years at Harvard, he could not have mixed as he did in literary circles and not at least have heard of Santayana and his ideas. As early as 1900 in his poem "Young Sammy's First Wild Oats," Santayana had asked what had happened to culture in colonial New England, a culture founded, as Brooks was to say, by "full-grown, modern, self-conscious men." Santayana wrote:

> I am old, and you are old, sir:
>   old the thoughts we live among.
> If the truth were to be told, sir,
>   none of us was ever young.

Like Brooks, Santayana saw a devaluation of culture in favor of economics to the point where Young Sammy, "Trained by sordid inventories/to scorn all he couldn't buy," made commercialism into a chimerical god. Yet, to whatever degree Brooks may have been indebted to Santayana, it seems likely that he repaid the debt: *The Wine of the Puritans* made a splash in the Harvard pond that probably drew the philosopher's attention, and Santayana's famous address "The Genteel Tradition," delivered just three years after publication of Brooks's book, contained several echoes of it. For instance: "The country was new, but the race was tried, chastened, and full of solemn memories. It was an old wine in new bottles."[25]

Having offered an historical explanation certain to ring true to Harvard readers, Brooks turned to an examination of contemporary American culture, and here too his sources guaranteed a line of argument familiar to American anglophiles like Wendell and T. S. Eliot. The English had long been interested observers and commentators on American life, and Brooks's book was clearly influenced by Matthew Arnold's *Civilization in the United States* (1888), G. Lowes Dickinson's *Modern Symposium* (1905), H. G. Wells's *Future in America* (1906), and expatriate Henry James's *American Scene* (1907). All of these writers had deplored America's materialistic excesses and rampant commercialism. Wells had taken Rockefeller as a symbol and said just what Brooks would say — that Rockefeller had lived a tragic life of gargantuan meaninglessness, not through evil intentions, for he was not moral enough to be evil, but simply through living as mindlessly, Brooks said, "as all American business men live, only a little more so." Similarly, all of these English observers had harped, like Brooks, on America's lack of achievement in matters spiritual and cultural. Dickinson and Arnold had both found American religion irreligious. Arnold and Wells were disappointed by the quality of education and politics in the United States. Wells had mocked the "genteel remoteness" of New England and insisted that "culture, as it is conceived in Boston, is no contribution to the future of America." Arnold, perhaps the severest critic, deplored

American humor as a "national misfortune," concluding, "In truth, everything is against distinction in America, and against the sense of elevation to be gained through admiring and respecting it."[26]

Brooks's own criticism of American culture was that it consisted of a series of incidents, none of them related to each other or to the material base of life. Instead of being an extraction from life of the "best that has been thought and said" (Arnold's definition of culture), American culture was a distraction, an escape from life. Businessmen took no genuine interest in politics because they knew that the important events of their lives occurred in Wall Street, not in Washington. Young men passed through college sincerely interested in art and thought but also accepting their education as an enjoyable idyll before getting on with the real life of business. American religion was cast in forms that appealed to the mind rather than the heart. Politics, education, and religion were all "absolutely separate. And being incidents they do not mix together to form a background from which we may look out upon life in general." American culture was passive and, though he did not explicitly say it in this book, effeminate.[27]

Literature, too, was an irrelevant incident in America. To make his point Brooks quoted from a burlesque of a publisher's blurb he had written for *Punch*. *The Call of the Lungs* by Jack Paris is the story of John Sprod, an Indian fighter, and of Lady Gwendolyn, who, tired of effete society, "has disguised herself as an old Indian war-chief, and single-handed has held at bay, through the interminable Arctic-like winter, seven regiments of United States troops. . . . she hears [John's] voice calling to her from across the boundless prairie hundreds of miles away. . . . It is a clash of races, and her deep, vivid, passionate nature responds. . . . The book is big: it burns hot with harsh but hopeful truth." Brooks had an explanation for the prevalence in America of this "Literature of Apoplexy." The grammar schools "deliberately abet the New England provinciality" by teaching Bryant and Whittier. Offered second-rate literature instead of, say, Wordsworth and Shelley, Americans grew up "unaccustomed to the literature of great forces." Then, in adult life, they cast about for more powerful voices and believed they found them in apoplectic writers. Brooks predicted that a doctor would come and "insert his knife somewhere to lower our temperature. That strange doctor is going to be the first great American satirist." America had many humorous writers, but they "don't carry on the great tradition of humour." Thackeray had said that the humorist should be a "week-day preacher," but American humorists were not preachers, not prophets: "In our humour we seek not life itself but a refuge from life. . . ." No wonder American humorists wrote under assumed names, as if they were ashamed of their scurrilous literature. And "Mark Twain is the apotheosis of all these traditions."[28]

Although Brooks did not use the word "culture" exceptionally often in this book, it was his main concern. His conception of culture was high, critical, idealistic, and organic. When he said that America had no integrated system of values for getting a perspective on life, he was saying that America had no meaningful culture. America had only a system for escaping from life and "perpetually spurning the present moment." That escapism was the condition of success in a cultureless society accounted for a man like Barnum, whose stature resulted, not from the "fulfilling of a national need" which had developed force in his ancestors and burst forth in him, but only from a circus *tour de force*. Barnum was a colossal absurdity and only incidental to national life because he had "no connection with race or any reality." Thus Brooks's thought returned full circle to the problem of a nation that "had had no childhood." He was an organicist, and he could not believe it possible to have a high culture in a country that had had no opportunity to develop "racial instincts."[29]

The lack of an organic culture was a doubly serious problem in a society faced by problems of race, immigration, and imperialism, Brooks said, ticking off the issues that had fascinated observers from afar, such as H. G. Wells and Henry James. These problems of a "cosmopolitan civilization" required a "preparation in kind," which America did not have.[30] American culture, developed from the "Puritan idea," faced problems that were distinctly un-Puritan.

Commercialism was the problem that most interested Brooks. As pioneers the Puritans had every reason to associate material wealth with virtue and happiness, but for their descendants the problem was too much rather than too little prosperity. There was "less happiness in America than in any other country in the civilized world. And it is because we associate happiness with spending money." Thus Brooks put himself in the tradition not only of Matthew Arnold but also of Ruskin. Americans were caught in a vicious circle of joyless prosperity, for with no meaningful culture to stop them they would continue, ever more successfully, to concentrate upon getting a living rather than upon the things that make life worth living. One of the primary joys lost was association with other people; in an echo of H. G. Wells's criticism of Americans as "state-blind," Brooks asserted that competition deprived Americans of a sense of community and its possible satisfactions. Brooks echoed

Wells again in saying that mere legal reform, the solution of the muckrakers, would accomplish nothing, "For what law can correct a point of view?" America's problem was cultural, and the solution was "the cultivation of some sort of inner national life."[31]

Like Arnold, Wells, and James before him, Brooks focused on the subjective life of Americans and found it wanting. Americans were noetic and rational to the point of being "morbid." They always had explanations for their political and religious beliefs and were able "to discuss these questions intellectually." More "mellow" civilizations, however, had "learned to assume that many things capable of logical explanation depend for their value upon not being explained, that the potential explanation must be taken for granted, and one's attention devoted to the emotions built upon it."[32] Thus Brooks continued, as he had done in college, to place himself in the Romantic tradition of Ruskin, Wordsworth, and Keats. He maintained that the artist, in order to record experience accurately, had to be capable of passively submitting to it. But Americans were too rational and intellectual, too self-reflexive for such submission. The problem that he had diagnosed in himself as an undergraduate — that he was too self-conscious to be an artist — turned out to be a national illness.

The implication was that art was impossible for Americans, and this, surely, was what left T. S. Eliot and the Harvard literati "shivering." Although they had felt their artistic impulses thwarted by America's cultural poverty, they had still had hopes till Brooks, with no apparent remorse, dashed them. Brooks did not even leave open to them the possibility that they could survive as artists by fleeing to Europe, as he and at least ten of his Harvard friends had done upon graduation. In the opening pages of *The Wine of the Puritans* he suggested the danger of the Harvard sensibility and its love of things Italian and Catholic by setting the scene on an Italian hilltop with a view much like the one he had enjoyed in the monastery at Camaldoli in 1905. One could look down on the ruins of twenty centuries and see yellow columns standing out from the foliage "like rich candles among the silks of a splendid altar." Though Brooks had been thrilled by Camaldoli in 1905, he now pictured an American artist overwhelmed by the lushness of the scene and feeling "as if a great many things had suddenly come together to brush [him] out of existence. . . ."[33] Thus spoke "Graeling," the same name Brooks had used in his Harvard essay for the artist he might have been if only he had been born in a different family. Now he felt that the molding of himself into an artist would have required his being born

in a different country as well. For the time being he had given up
hope, and he no longer identified with Graeling, the aspiring
American artist. Instead, his sympathies were with the other
speaker, the un-named "I" who carried on the dialogue with
Graeling.

It has been possible to discuss the book thus far without mentioning its dialogue form because there are few differences between
the speakers during the first four chapters. Although Brooks chose
the dialogue form partly out of admiration for the brilliance with
which G. Lowes Dickinson had created different personalities as well
as different ideas for the thirteen speakers of *A Modern Symposium,*
Brooks was unable to achieve similar distinctions between his two
speakers. The reason was that the two represented different aspects
of one personality, Van Wyck's own. *The Wine of the Puritans* was a
dialogue between Van Wyck's artistic spirit (Graeling), from which
he now expected nothing, and his critical spirit, from which he now
hoped for a career.

The book's two interlocutors were in agreement for four chapters as they analyzed the reasons for America's impoverished cultural history, but in the fifth and final chapter they disagreed on the
appropriate individual response to that unfortunate circumstance.
Brooks the critic asked, ". . . why are *we* abroad?" Perhaps they too
were only incidental: ". . . are we not cultivating our distraction
from American life rather than our extraction from it?" Graeling
the artist replied that it made sense to be in Europe where one "finds
the premises of an artistic life really taken for granted." But the
organic logic of the book was on Brooks's side as he answered that
great art could only be produced out of "racial fibre, the accretion of
countless generations of ancestors, trained to one deep, local indigenous attitude toward life." Without racial fiber, an American could
not be an artist whether or not he lived where the premises of art
were taken for granted. To prove his point Brooks analyzed the
work of two American artists abroad, Whistler and Sargent, and
condemned their work as "merely a series of incidents," however
superior technically. Well then, Graeling said, at least in Europe one
could master technique. But Brooks answered that that was like
"cultivating a brilliant complexion without cultivating health."[34] Like
Ruskin, Brooks scorned Whistler and the notion of "art pour l'art";
better to sternly face the truth that the artist was the voice of the
people, and if they had nothing to say, the artist could speak no art.

If America was not ready for art, it was ripe for criticism.
Matthew Arnold, in "The Function of Criticism," had pointed out

that art was "not at all epochs and under all conditions possible; and that therefore labour may be vainly spent in attempting it, which might with more fruit be used in preparing for it. . . ." Similarly, Brooks the critic told Graeling the artist that they should "act in such a way that this generation will have its romance and its tradition for those who come after." In other words they must found a tradition. But they must not attempt it self-consciously. Americans had nothing to do with tradition, and even to think of it was to think of Europe and thus to "cut ourselves away from vital contact with American life." Rather, they should "teach our pulses to beat with American ideas and ideals, absorb American life, until we are able to see that in all its vulgarities and distractions and boastings there lie the elements of a gigantic art." But that achievement was far in the future, Brooks implied, as he urged Graeling to give up attempting to create art. The best that the contemporary American artist could do was to "sacrifice" himself in order to help create that far future when ". . . the names of Denver and Sioux City will have a traditional and antique dignity like Damascus and Perugia — and when it will not seem to us grotesque that they have."[35]

In this closing sentence of the book, Van Wyck underlined the point on which he parted company with the English critics — Arnold, Dickinson, and Wells — from whom he had drawn so many ideas. Their attention had been drawn to America as a portent of Europe's future. America, without any obscuring vestiges of feudalism, was supposed to offer the clearest glass in which to read the future of the modern, middle-class, industrial state. Wells had argued that England's future was "dependent" on America's, and Dickinson had called America the "civilization of the future." All of them, even the optimistic Wells, had shuddered somewhat at the prospect. Brooks, however, rather than expecting Europe to become like America, expected America to become like Europe. He was almost complacently certain that America would duplicate the pattern of European history by gradually developing a high culture and then standing still in time. There were occasional intimations in *The Wine of the Puritans* that Europe's place in history was not totally static — for instance, Brooks's remark that industrialism was stripping the European peasantry of their sense of beauty.[36] But the remark was only an echo of Ruskin rather than Brooks's own perception, and he did not follow it up. The starting point of many of his ideas — Arnold, Ruskin, and the romantic literature of nineteenth-century Europe — might have indicated to him that many of the problems he saw in American life were common to modern societies which had experienced the industrial revolution. But instead of seeing these problems as modern, Brooks saw them as exclusively American and therefore thought that the solution was to emulate the heavenly model of Europe. That was the basic weakness of his position as an American prophet in the early years of the twentieth century, a century in which it would soon be clear that there were chaotic forces in modern society too powerful for even European culture to resist.

In any case, Van Wyck's course was charted for rough water. Perhaps it had not been difficult to persuade the artist Graeling to "sacrifice" himself to the need for criticism. It took courage for a struggling artist to live in America, but for the defeated artist America offered a blameless death. It was only one side of Van Wyck's personality, this side of him subject already to overwhelming despair. There was also the critic in him for whom it was an act of courage rather than a suicidal gesture to live in his own country. But in his book he had succeeded for a moment in unifying the disparate elements of his personality, for whichever side had the upper hand — the defeated and death-seeking artist or the courageous young critic with a program for the future — the logical thing for him to do was to return to America.

III

He returned on the saloon deck, as if to signal that he had accomplished much in the year since he had crossed to England in steerage. But on the practical side his literary career was probably no more advanced than it would have been if he had stayed at Harvard for a fourth year. For help in finding a job in New York he had to turn to Max Perkins, now working there as a reporter, who told him that Walter Hines Page needed help on his magazine, the *World's Work*. So, despite Van Wyck's bad experience in London, he was to try his hand again at journalism. The *World's Work* featured articles on science and technology and only occasionally used literary subjects. Page liked articles quick after the event and brightly written. In short, it was the kind of magazine Van Wyck was certain to dislike, and most of his assignments, whether editing President Taft's speeches or writing on technological "improvements," were drudgery for him.[37]

He had only a few interesting assignments during his year with the *World's Work*, one of them an interview with Howells that showed Van Wyck still scornful and somewhat ignorant of American literature. His first meeting with Howells two years earlier had left him unimpressed, and now, in his interview, he was a little contemptuous. Believing art the result of unself-conscious spontaneity, he asked if Howells ever "lost himself" in his work and thought it of "deep significance" that Howells answered negatively. Was such dispassion also characteristic, Van Wyck asked, "of novelists who dealt with crude and powerful emotions, with moments of tragedy which, after all, do occur in life?" Surely Dickens was not so objective? Howells, who had been a major force for realism in the novel, had reason to be irritated, and he answered that there was an "element of claptrap" in Dickens. Unconvinced, Brooks wrote in the *World's Work* that Howells suffered from a "lack of force." His novels were a true reflection of the common things of life but one "rebels against them [the novels] as one rebels against the common things themselves." This was a bold opinion from one who had at the time, as he later guiltily admitted, read only one Howells novel.[38]

By so unfairly and unfeelingly dismissing Howells, Brooks vented some of his own frustration and disappointment. He was making little advance with his own literary career, even though in June of 1909, not long after the Howells interview, he found an American publisher, Mitchell Kennerley, for *The Wine of the Puritans*. Kennerley was willing to bring the book out in America not because of any success in the English edition, however, but rather because of its failure to sell. Sisley's had hundreds of sets of unbound sheets on hand in London, so Kennerley purchased the sheets from Sisley's — surely not an expensive proposition, since Van Wyck had borne half of Sisley's expense in printing them — and bound two hundred copies for the American edition. The argument of the book had been that the best thing an American artist could do was to sacrifice himself in America, and that seemed an accurate description of what Van Wyck was doing on the *World's Work*. He had written little in which he could take pride, and the magazine's emphasis on material progress only confirmed the ideas about the quality of American life which he had expressed in *The Wine of the Puritans*. He told Eleanor that he wished himself an "ancient" or "hermit" or "seraph" — anything but an American — and he also complained bitterly to her of the "sublime modern logic by which industry is proved to be the same as joy, love the same as industry, life the same as art — everything the same as everything else." Art was born of "confusion, waste, prodigality," not the calculated efficiency of modern life. "I *hate* and distrust the trend of things. . . . You cannot imagine how commercial the very fabric of this nation is."[39]

He revolted in small ways, dressing a bit dandyishly and stretching his lunch hour to two in order finish his Balzac or visit a Catholic church, where the incense wafted him away to Italy. (The next year, 1910, he was attracted to a church by a large crowd in front of it, and climbing up to the gallery, he looked down and saw Mark Twain, with his white flannels and whiter hair, lying in his coffin.) He hated the routine of office work which fit one to be "an efficient member of society: but damn members of society!" He could not take his job seriously, and Page in turn, though he liked Brooks personally, grew dissatisfied with him as an employee. Sheldon and other friends urged Van Wyck to leave the magazine, and he was beginning to think them right: "Are there not in me a certain feeling for art, and especially a knowledge of much which should grow and be exercised?" He began working on some "imaginary sayings" to submit to the *Evening Post* or the *Nation,* and he still hoped, as he had in college, that Paul Elmer More would take him on. In October of 1909 he quit the *World's Work* without notice. [40]

Unfortunately, his "imaginary sayings" were not "topical" enough for the *Nation,* and he had to accept a job writing definitions for Funk and Wagnall's *Standard Dictionary.* Working in his room with several other dictionaries, he wrote entries that were not exact copies of anyone else's. At five cents a definition, he could earn a dollar an hour by working at the incredible pace of a word every three minutes. Usually he limited himself to thirty dollars a week — six daily stints of five hours — because he was warned that the rate would be lowered if the work seemed too easy. [41]

Thirty dollars a week was the largest income he had yet enjoyed, and he reflected that it would have been enough to get married on if he was living in Europe, if he was not five hundred dollars in debt, and if the work was steadier. But work on the dictionary was sometimes stopped, leaving him with time on his hands and no income. And his accounting system was hardly adequate to making inroads on his debts, though he tried to pay them. His method was to collect his week's pay and immediately disburse it among his nearest, most troublesome creditors. But then he needed money in the week ahead for food and rent and also for drink in the cafés where he liked to sit and write, so he acquired new debts. He wrote to Eleanor that she would have to manage their money after they were married, and so it was to be. In fact, one of his debts in 1909 was to her, and it cost him "nights of shame and misery." [42]

But as 1910 began he was encouraged by signs that he was gaining respect in the literary world. He refused an offer of five hundred dollars to write the official biography of Heinrich Conreid, the theater manager who had scandalized New York with his production of Oscar Wilde's *Salome.* Instead, he worked on his "imaginary sayings" for an unpaid weekly newspaper column given him by Francis Hackett, literary editor of the *Chicago Evening Sun,* whom he had met through a friend on the *World's Work.* The unpaid column was preferable to producing the desired eulogy of "the old scoundrel" Conreid, because in the column he would not have to write "to order." And he hoped to syndicate the column, believing that it would earn forty dollars a week within six months. That, he told Eleanor, would mean escape for them both to Italy or at least to a farmhouse in Vermont where there would be only "long, cold, snowy days, with plenty of firewood, and you, and me, and immortal dreams."[43]

With new hope and cheer, he felt confident enough to begin a book which he had wanted to write for some time on the English critic Vernon Lee, and he set himself an ambitious schedule for the new year: four hours in the morning reading and taking notes for the book, five hours in the afternoon writing definitions, and most of the evening to be spent on miscellaneous work including his column. Characteristically, he put the column, which he regarded as his largest worldly opportunity, last on the day's agenda. Happy for the moment, he even hoped that he might yet find a prophetic calling in America: "Sometimes I have a glimmering that in me — somewhere — a something is stirring, the first breath of a view of life that is not mere literature — but a statement of something absent in American life. . . . And that is not a fine art, it is to have in some vague and minor degree, a mission, a significance, a personality. It is that which gives me a genuine hope. . . . "[44]

To heighten his spirits he had good company, for New York had become the locus of his Harvard circle. Ned Sheldon, writing hit plays, was in New York, and so were two new acquaintances, also Harvard graduates, Conrad Aiken and Alan Seeger. Brooks never knew Aiken well, but he became friendly with the romantic poet Seeger who shortly departed for France to be killed in the World War. Jack Wheelock, returning soon from Göttingen with duelling scars but without his Ph.D., would get a job at Scribner's, where Max Perkins had already started to work.

Van Wyck made older and less cheerful friends in his rooming house and among his fellow workers on the dictionary — nameless and broken hacks who drifted about New York from dictionary to encyclopedia to business manual. One of them, unable to face his sixty-fifth birthday, turned on but did not light the gas lamp in his room, and Van Wyck later heard an editor pronounce his epitaph: "What a pity, when he had got our style so well!" Van Wyck's bug-infested rooming house was in a bleak slum on West Twenty-third Street near Tenth or "Death Avenue," as the people in the neighborhood called it. There he made friends with R. W. Sneddon, a forlorn and impoverished Scot who aspired to write plays but who earned a meager living writing jokes for *Judge* and *Puck*. Van Wyck had not outgrown his knack for mitigating the dreariness of such surroundings by romanticizing them, and he thought of the hacks and Sneddon and himself as living in the tradition of Grub Street.[45]

With Seeger, Sneddon and other friends, Van Wyck often dined at Petitpas' Restaurant on West Twenty-ninth Street where the chief attraction was an elderly Irish portrait painter, John Butler Yeats. In 1908, at the age of seventy, Yeats had come to New York for what was to have been a visit of two weeks; he stayed for thirteen years and died there at eighty-three. The penurious but vital old artist thought New York was a "huge fair" where he might yet make his fortune. Van Wyck, always interested in the Irish, could not help but be drawn to Petitpas', where Yeats presided in an autocratic manner over a table of young artists and admirers. They were attracted to him at least in part, and somewhat to his irritation, by his being the father of the poet W. B. Yeats. When referred to as the father of the great Yeats, he replied, "*I* am the great Yeats." But once assured that his audience was his own he was glad to speak of the Irish renaissance, telling stories of Synge and Moore and Dunsany, and mystically chanting his son's poems while Van Wyck and the others at Petitpas' sat still in rapt attention.[46]

Yeats in turn liked Van Wyck, as is clear from Conrad Aiken's story, "The Orange Moth." Aiken pictured Yeats as "Butler," an old portraitist eager to have Brooks, or "Cooke," sit for him because he was taken with the idealistic young writer's "honest blue eyes" and "lovely face . . . of an innocence indescribable." In real life Brooks did sit for Yeats, who depicted a delicate but handsome young man with straight dark hair, blue eyes, good features, and red cheeks, over one of the tall stiff collars of the day. Van Wyck had unsuccessfully urged the old man, who was living precariously in New York, to spend his time on a profitable sitter. But Yeats, who said that he preferred a congenial subject to one who paid well, enjoyed the attention with which Van Wyck not only held his pose but listened reverently as the bewhiskered painter expounded, out of his accumulated wisdom, some basic principles of art and life.[47] Thus began a close friendship which Yeats continued, after Van Wyck left New York, in dozens of long, involved, and instructive letters. Yeats succeeded and surpassed Ryder and Marshall as masculine exemplars of culture, and Van Wyck's next piece of writing, *The Soul*, was dedicated to Yeats with a quotation from Dante: *"Tu se'lo mio maestro."*

Yeats was prepared to teach many things. He distrusted abstractions and strove for concrete knowledge — a position Van Wyck would not reach for many years. Yeats disliked cubism and the other non-mimetic forms of the new century, as Van Wyck would distrust many of the new forms in literature. Having once been a correspondent of Whitman's, Yeats had more than a passing acquaintance with American literature. He encouraged Van Wyck to write in his own preferred style, a more elaborate one than the journalistic style Copey had advocated. Yeats was impressed with the potential of the younger artists whom he had met at Petitpas' and elsewhere in New York, and when he spoke hopefully of the American prospect, he spoke with the authority of a man who had not only lived through the artistic renaissance of a nation but had also fathered its leading figure. Van Wyck had reason to be impressed when he heard Yeats remark, "The fiddles are tuning all over America.[48]

In Yeats's circle at Petitpas' early in 1910 Van Wyck met John Sloan, Robert Henri, and Maurice Prendergast, all of whom had helped instigate an important revolt in American painting in 1908. Until then the National Academy of Design had dominated the hanging committees and juries at American exhibitions. Without the academy's approval it was difficult for a painter to get the attention and ultimately the sales on which his livelihood depended. The academy was traditional and derivative, favoring period costumes and "ideal nudes," and it looked askance at painters like Sloan and his friends who painted street scenes with a realistic attention to detail that won them the name "Ashcan School." In 1908 Sloan, Henri, and six others — the famous "Eight" — presented an independent exhibition in New York, and their innovative themes and treatments created a sensation. Their exhibition led to the formation of the Society of Independent Artists and helped prepare the way for the Armory Show of 1913. American painting was never the same again.[49]

How fine, Van Wyck wrote to Eleanor, that he was meeting men of "artistic conscience." As he talked with these new friends in their studios as well as at Petitpas', he heard much that reinforced his ideas about what constituted an artistic vocation. Sloan, for instance, was a prophet, a denouncer of evil; his interest in street scenes was related to his awareness of economic realities and socialist convictions. Similarly, Henri argued that the artist had a responsibility to society and should not forget his primary duty — "the presentation in art of ideas of value." Because this goal could best be attained by absorbing "the great ideas native to the country," Henri was a nationalist. Art, he said, required "deep roots, stretching far down into the soil of the nation." Van Wyck already believed that style involved not only technique but substance. He understood Sloan's remark that what had united the Eight, despite their apparently disparate styles, was that they all "loved life and people and tried to express that love of life." Sloan meant that they had all rejected the formalism and derivativeness of the academy because those things stood between the artist and life. Henri put it more succinctly when he said that the artist should paint "life, not art."[50]

If Sloan and Henri had been able to follow Van Wyck's inmost thoughts in 1910, they would have been surprised by the extreme to which he was carrying Henri's dictum. As he worked on his book on Vernon Lee, he began to develop the radical hope that a world might be possible in which there would be life without art, for art expresses the ideas of men who are not "normal," men who are "unable to live their ideas." Normal men, with normal ideas, express themselves simply in ordinary behavior. But abnormal men, possessed by ideas which society will not accept, cannot live their ideas and instead express them in art, or, more precisely, "sensuous forms." However, an idea should be lived; it properly "has neither beginning nor end." To express an idea in sensuous form is "to call a halt to its natural expansion, to urge upon it a temporary reckoning." In other words, the idea of art becomes trapped in the form of art: ". . . art has been a kind of Limbo in which all the ideas that have not been able to fit themselves for life have had a dim unearthly incarnation." Brooks asked, "How are the types of experience that have hitherto found expression only through art to be drawn into the service of life, to be given the chance of expressing themselves through conduct? Under what conditions, to be attained how, can the artist reach normality?"[51]

Actually, Brooks's somewhat confused ideas did not offer any solutions, nor for that matter did the work of Vernon Lee, but Van Wyck was intrigued by her "conception of the future." While Vernon Lee had not explained how this future was to be attained, one can understand the appeal of her vision to Van Wyck, for he interpreted it as a future without self-consciousness. Rather, there would be only "the achieved human soul in whom the serenity of perfect intuition has succeeded the battles of thought. . . ." By "perfect intuition" he meant a transparent "relation to the conscious universe." If human beings lived in a society founded on such transparent relationships, *all* ideas would be understood and accepted as human. In such a society ". . . the artist having regained his normality would cease to exist." Meanwhile, the tension that had previously been relieved through expression in the sensuous forms of art would spring forth in "unbodied joy." Such transparency had previously been thought possible only in heaven, but Vernon Lee's conception of the future "represents quite literally the idea of heaven expressing itself in human society." Thus the artist would be able to abandon art and live normally not only in heaven but also on earth; not only, Van Wyck might have added, in Europe but also in America.[52]

IV

To Van Wyck's disappointment his thoughts on Vernon Lee were not destined to appear in book form. Mitchell Kennerley, to whom he had offered the manuscript in the spring of 1910, said that not fifty copies of such a book could be sold, so Van Wyck pared it down to an article, "Notes on Vernon Lee," which Kennerley kindly printed in his *Forum.* An additional disappointment that spring was his failure to get his column in the *Chicago Evening Sun* syndicated. Entitled "Mortal Things," the column was too wistful and melancholy to have a broad appeal, and Van Wyck had expressed little that was new in it. As he had done in *The Wine of the Puritans,* he compared the American landscape unfavorably to the European, and he wrote critically of Whistler, regretting of course the self-consciousness which made him analyze the pictures rather than simply enjoy them as he had done in childhood. Hackett, the literary editor of the *Evening Sun,* liked the column but was unwilling to pay for it. So Van Wyck dropped "Mortal Things." These disappointments were all the more frustrating because he had counted on publishing the book on Vernon Lee and also a collection of his columns so that he would be well enough established by 1911 to marry Eleanor. The energy with which he had worked during the cheerful winter and spring of 1910 had been almost entirely wasted, and on a gloomy, drizzly day in June he wrote to Eleanor that he could "hardly speak for depression when it rains and all my life and hopes lie like ruins about me."[53]

Most distressing of all were Eleanor's fluctuating feelings toward Van Wyck. They had been separated for most of the last four years, and he had not made the rapid success on which they had counted. His mother had tried to interest him in other girls, and he took more than a passing interest in two of them. Eleanor, perceiving his diminishing interest, had broken the engagement by letter, but when she too returned to America they were happily reconciled. Then Eleanor's mother took her to California, separating them again. In Van Wyck's absence Eleanor had received three other proposals, including, in the summer of 1910, one she seriously considered from a man who had the advantage of being in California. However, in August she concluded that her allegiance must be to Van Wyck, and they decided to be married within a few months. Van Wyck's spirits were high when he gave the news to Sloan and Yeats (while Sloan worked on "Yeats at Petitpas," which depicted the old man at a crowded table with Van Wyck at his right hand). But Van Wyck's jubilation was premature, and Eleanor was soon writing that she was certain she did not love him. She apologized for putting him through the self-conscious analysis of feeling that they both hated, but such analysis revealed that there were too many differences between them, his gloom, for instance, on the outdoor walks she loved. Worst of all was her feeling that he cherished not her real self but an "ideal." This was true enough, for he did associate her with heaven or Europe or some other faraway place like "the beautiful garden I shall descend to before long, with you, darling one." Eleanor felt that this romantic idealization led to a lack of "frankness" which would be "fatal to real married happiness."[54]

She spoke better than she knew, for Van Wyck was casting not only Eleanor but also himself in an ideal role. He had thus far been too insecure about his masculinity to tell her of the depth of his depressions, fears, and anxieties. He had written in his diary that he could not "always be *manly.* And love depends upon woman being woman and man being man." Since he could not always be "frank" in "human love," he could not be satisfied merely with Eleanor but craved also "a Divine Heart to which I need not explain or justify myself, but which can understand me as I really am, and pity my weakness. . . ." In his essay on Vernon Lee he had defined the ideal relationship as one "in which our natures would be to someone so transparent that we should not have to explain anything."[55] He had feared that he and Eleanor could not fulfill his longing for this ideal. Now it appeared that she would not even try.

In the fall of 1910, full of fear that he was losing his only chance for happiness in this world, Van Wyck surveyed his dreary rooming house and the work on the dictionary in which he devilled his best self away, and he concluded that his life was a failure. All that remained to him was *The Soul,* as he would call the little book in which he was examining the part of himself that seemed unable to find expression in this world's life. There he insisted it was wrong to believe "that failure in life is the same as failure in us. . . ." Could it not be rather that life itself, as he had formerly said of art in "Notes on Vernon Lee," was too narrow to permit "the full expression of personality?"[56]

He drew back, almost in horror, from consciously stating any such extreme conclusions, yet in *The Soul* he was ambiguous about the meaningfulness of life, calling it only a "projection of all those thoughts that have the special kind of vitality required for visible existence." Such thoughts are few beside the many which are not expressed because they require circumstances different from those life offers. Life is too narrow to permit the complete realization of wide ideas like happiness, love, and truth. The best to be done is to "forget that we desire all, all, all." Death, then, is a "silent opening of the door" into eternity, for nature understands that the human heart is so deep "that the terms of life cannot express it. . . ." But he was "frozen" by the grimness of this logic, and willfully refused it validity: "To know that . . . life and time are nothing — surely this is not so true as to believe that all these things are a little something. . . ." The mistake, he said desperately, is not in life itself but in what is made of life by a middle-class society.[57]

In his state of depression that fall, he gave up the hope he had expressed the previous spring in "Notes on Vernon Lee" that the idea of heaven could be realized in human society. He decided instead that society limits life by requiring that men choose an occupation and thus gratify one part of themselves at the expense of other parts. Having put limitations upon themselves, they are happy at least to be greater gnats than others: "Life then turns into a competition." How much better to live without such alienation from other men and the universe of which they are a part. Instead of competition, life could be a gradual, peaceful realization of oneness with all things till ". . . we see in everything a connection with everything else, meaning within meaning. . . ." Brooks had a vision of humanity as an infinite ocean of possibilities. But the lives of individual men had all the limitations of ships at sea, steering for a distant shore, when in reality "this ocean had no shore." Wishing to experience life in all its diffuse variegation, he vowed not to place upon himself the limitations of any great full-rigged capitalist. Rather, "I will be this ocean: and if I have to be a ship I will be only a raft for the first wave to capsize and sink. . . ."[58]

Brooks blamed his own middle class for the narrowness of social life. The poor and the rich, without middle-class restraints, "have always been one in heart because abundant in human nature, while both have been feared and suspected by the conventional classes between." Responding negatively to progressive social movements, he scorned society's attempt "to bind itself together in a moral programme." Middle-class progessives could not offer true conceptions of justice precisely because their conceptions were social. For truth one should turn to the workers, the poor, and the blind who, heedless of social conventions, were "working out through suffering and weakness the mysterious destiny of the soul."[59]

Because he still idealized poverty and slum life, social injustice did not lead him, as it did John Sloan, into socialism but rather into social irresponsibility. "The social ideal is that of unselfishness," of responsibility to others. Van Wyck compared the human rewards of responsibility and irresponsibility by contrasting Martin Luther and Saint Francis on their deathbeds. Francis had lived selfishly in the sense that he had never been a reformer of society but had devoted himself to the spirit, achieving a mystical oneness with the universe. Death had been merely a dissolution into the universe of which he was already a part so that he could cry, "Welcome, Sister Death!" Luther, on the other hand, who had been a social reformer and "a master of the worldly situation," said wearily on his deathbed that he had "no love for the world. . . . I am well tired of it. God come soon and take me away." The reward of happiness had come to the self-absorbed Francis while it had been denied to the socially responsible Luther. Here was consolation for one like Van Wyck whose family considered him selfish and who was, from the social point of view, a failure who could neither make money nor marry. If one lived without responsibility, then ". . . there is no such thing as failure. . . ."[60]

How had the social point of view achieved its dominance? The history of poetry offered an explanation, or rather "a parallel of the soul's history in the midst of life." Primordial man, feeling himself composed of the same elements that composed the universe, was yet not as free as them. Wind and fire "came and went like a whim" while man "could only conjecture what lay beyond the mountains." To relieve his chagrin at being "hampered by the mortal dress in which he found himself," man cried "out of his heart." All true poetry springs from the same impulse. However, primordial man found that his shriek consoled not only himself but others. Words not only released the soul but offered power to "command others, unite with others, create organization. And from poetry he turned to rhetoric, which is the poetry of the social man." Likewise, he soon found in himself the power to command fire and wind and fell into the ceaseless social and economic activity that has ever since distracted men and spared them the necessity of remembering that the final destiny of the soul is one with the free and formless universe.[61]

Thus Van Wyck acknowledged his loss of faith in literature, which he had previously and mistakenly considered a "refuge" from society. He had thought of literature and art as a "vicarious life" which contained more latitude than life itself. But now he realized that even literary expression implied an audience, a social point of view. Certainly there was no satisfaction in contemporary Western literature with its "nervous and finite compactness," its insistence on a form which stifled the true cry of the heart. What of the almost formless Russian novel, which moved "across life with all the cumulative aimlessness of a human soul . . ."? The Russian people, the most inarticulate in the world, had no social rhetoric. Their writers were most likely to speak truth because they spoke from the sheer pressure of a previously silent race. Yet even their greatest artist, Tolstoy, had "felt the utter inadequacy of literature" and concluded that beside death, "Everything else was a lie."[62]

But Van Wyck would not consciously accept his argument's logical conclusion, which was that if the soul could not be satisfied with form it would be better to hurry on to some more disembodied existence by embracing death. So, to his little treatise on the meaninglessness of art and life, he appended a final page of affirmation, arguing that the inner life of the soul could after all be free in a world of form. He compared the experience of life to having a sculptor make a plaster mask of one's face. The mask's form would capture only one expression and miss innumerable others.

> Yet under the plaster as it grows gradually cold I am free all the time. . . . I give a strong impression to the mould. Then I leave it to perpetuate itself.
> I release my lips. I open my eyes. Oh, the silence! oh, the dark solitude! and all that whirls within me.[63]

But the weakness of this final affirmation was revealed in the imagery he chose, for the sculptor and plaster suggested one of his favorite art objects — a death mask.

Stil, the affirmation did show that some residue remained of the tension between his desire for death and his conscious belief that it was right to love life. The possibility remained that a person as intensely conscious as he might yet strike a compromise with society and find an art in which he could attempt to express himself.

4

THE ART OF SOCIETY

ELEANOR finally relented, and in February of 1911, after borrowing $2000 from Ned Sheldon to cover his wedding expenses, Van Wyck entrained for California. He had given journalism and hack writing three years, and they had led nowhere. It was time to try something else, something literary but secure enough to enable him to marry. Eleanor had been taking some courses at Berkeley, and that circumstance had suggested a teaching position. Van Wyck believed that his Harvard degree and Phi Beta Kappa key would count for more in the untutored West than in New York, so he resolved to go to California and present himself boldly as a "brilliant young scholar." How much better, he told Eleanor, to be doing "honorable work" like preparing lectures than to be "cribbing things out of dictionaries."[1]

As Van Wyck boarded the train for California, he must have felt that he was dropping into a void. To him the center of civilized life was Europe, beside which New England had a provincial quality and New Jersey the air of a raw wilderness. The West was a limbo and only Eleanor had the power to draw him into it. On her way to California in 1909, she had posted a letter to him from a train stop in Colorado, and he had replied with a description of his horror of such "godless" places: ". . . towns with no traditions, no myriad life behind them, lived in today only with the meagrest combination of thoughts and feelings. . . . How cold, bleak, far away the West is to me, — *dearest,* I feel as if I must rush now and bring you back, here, anywhere, where life is beautiful and where man has a mystery apart from the deserts and mountains. How shall I put into words this chilly fear of the West, this craving for the East, ever more Eastern!"[2]

Furthermore, he was already beginning to identify the West with the avant-garde sensibility that appalled him as immoral. Neither could he abide "advanced" sexual mores, and he blamed the West for them too. Early in 1911, before he left for California, he had written to Eleanor with an "anecdote characteristic of the *West* — which gives me the more reason for hating it." The story, related to him in New York, concerned a California couple, a professor and a "doctor-woman," who were "happily (agreeably) divorced."

> He & she both married again. The professor & his new wife went to live in Mexico — the old wife with her new "pal" stayed in California. The prosperous wife soon was to have a child. There was apparently no doctor in Mexico. So the first wife took the train, arrived on the spot, and nursed the second wife of her own husband. All this was told cooly — as an example of "what *strides* we have made." I at once got furiously angry — and I said it would revolt any decent woman's instincts as much as mine. A number of "advanced" individuals, the kind who live on nuts and discuss digestive processes at table, pooh-poohed me. . . . Now I lay it before you. It's a test case. . . . Is that hateful or is it not? Do tell me, dearest! Whenever one objects to "advanced people," one is called "Early Victorian" — there appears to be nothing between. And I have noticed that these people consider that if one doesn't talk about nasty things in a scientific way perpetually with women — it means that one perpetually talks about one [nasty subject] in a jocular way with men. Oh dear saints in heaven.[3]

For the moment, however, his largest antagonism was reserved not for "new thought" but simply for the West. His geographical preference was the result of one of the deepest lessons of his childhood, for the West was where Charles Brooks had failed with his adventures in mining. As Van Wyck crossed the continent in 1911 he imagined his father in the lizard-inhabited ghost towns where the train stopped for water, towns with furnaces and chimneys built to smelt ore that was never found or, as with Charles Brooks's mine, was too deep to be worked profitably.[4]

However, when Van Wyck arrived in San Francisco in 1911, he found a great deal more civilization than he had expected. The red-tiled Spanish roofs, the balmy air, and the summer greenery under a winter sun all suggested the otherworldly quality that had so appealed to him in Italy and which he associated with a "mellow" culture. He had letters from several friends which gained him admittance to clubs where he could read papers and magazines. There were motion picture theaters and a literary world that revolved around the local socialist club. Weekends he went to visit Eleanor in Carmel, the artist's colony to which Mrs. Stimson had naturally migrated.[5]

Van Wyck had promised Eleanor that he would "learn to love" the outdoors in California, so weekdays, when he was not looking for work, he tramped out of San Francisco to lie in the tall grass and read Robert Louis Stevenson. It bothered him, however, that there was no place to write in his rooming house, and he compensated by paying to have *The Soul* printed as a pamphlet. He sent copies to friends in the East and also to a professor at Berkeley — Arthur Ryder, the scholarly friend he had met in childhood in Italy in 1899.

He had turned to Ryder, who had fond memories of Sallie Brooks, for help in finding a job, and Ryder had inquired with apparent success about a place in the English Department at Berkeley. Van Wyck was offered a position, and impatient after their years of waiting, he and Eleanor planned to be married on April 22. But Berkeley's president, Benjamin Wheeler, had been in Europe when the offer was made, and finding the university financially overcommitted on his return, he withdrew it. Van Wyck cursed "that GOD-DAMNED Wheeler," and the wedding was delayed four days before they decided to go ahead with it, even without a position in hand.[6]

They made their vows on April 26 with only witnesses and Eleanor's mother present. Mrs. Stimson, who had opposed the marriage to the last, was ill, so to be near her they stayed for a month in a cabin in Carmel.[7] The job question was soon resolved by an offer from the English Department at Stanford. Then Van Wyck gave Eleanor a summer honeymoon of camping in Yosemite before they settled in Palo Alto. There, the next February, their first son, Charles Van Wyck Brooks, was born.

Eleanor looked hopefully to marriage as an escape from responsibility. She had felt guilty at relying on her mother's meager income after graduation from Wellesley, so now at least she had broken the maternal bond. She did not seem concerned that she had accomplished this independence from her mother by accepting a role as Van Wyck's wife which was certain to interfere with her hopes for a career of her own. After the wedding she threw herself into learning to cook and clean, and it did not occur either to her or to Van Wyck that he should help. He was taking on teaching responsibilities at Stanford, so traditional domestic arrangements seemed fair enough if he was to write also. Unlike Van Wyck, Eleanor did not demand a margin of time in which to write, so her literary career ended before it began. She was willing to exchange honor and obedience in return for freedom from the strain of helping her mother make ends meet. On her honeymoon she wrote glowingly to a Wellesley friend of her groom's previous worldly successes in London and New York, referring to Van Wyck, only partly in humor, as "himself," a fittingly distant and respectful title for her lord and protector.[8] The only drawback was that in the long run it was she who would protect Van Wyck from worldly cares.

Although Eleanor disagreed with many of Van Wyck's ideas, she submitted to them. Believing the church a refuge for moral "cowards and weaklings," she was troubled by his love of Roman Catholic imagery. But she excused this and other faults by attributing them to the artist in him; it was the vividness rather than the decadence which appealed to him in the Catholic ritual. Similarly, she accepted his instruction in the art of conversation, for he felt that she supported her radical ideas too vehemently. "Truly, dear," he counseled her, "a contentious woman is like a Scythian chariot, covered with knives: you are mangled if you come within a yard of her." He tried but could not genuinely sympathize with her feminist convictions, and here too he won his point. In 1907 when she had told him of her desire to join the struggle for woman's suffrage, "clear down to the public street speeches," she imagined him shivering with horror, for he felt that it made a girl "common" if she was "merely seen in the street a good deal." So Eleanor promised to be ladylike, though she viewed such conventions as only "useful machinery."[9] But whether her motives for behaving like a lady were decorous or utilitarian, the result was the same. Their difference over woman's place in public life did not threaten their relationship, because Eleanor did not question woman's place in private life.

For Van Wyck also, marriage was to be a mixed blessing, in part because he too accepted traditional roles. By freeing him from many of the practical details of daily living, Eleanor gave him peace and quiet and thus helped make him the prolific writer he became. But he also expected his wife to ease the loneliness of writing by providing him with the pleasures of a social life, much after the pattern of genteel women in Plainfield. Although he admired the shyness resulting from Eleanor's lonely childhood as a mark of sensitivity, he would be disappointed when it prevented her from being as socially active as he wanted. Further, he agreed with Eleanor that the largest worldly responsibility — earning a living — was his because he was male. He would therefore be forced into jobs which he hated and which interfered with his development as a writer and artist. His wife and children would sometimes seem a material incubus that denied him access to the ideal — a feeling which, upon reflection, would give him much cause for guilt.

Teaching was the first of the mundane jobs to which he turned in order to support his new family, and he soon knew that he was no more a teacher than a journalist. When he arrived at Stanford, his genuine interests were the medieval church and Italian painting rather than the surveys of American and English literature he was assigned to teach. Refusing to take his lectures seriously, he prepared them outdoors under an oak tree. He was always uncomfortable in the role of public speaker, and students found him shy. Too absorbed in his own ideas to take much interest in his students, he often turned their themes over to Eleanor to correct.[10] He viewed teaching as a distraction from his writing, which he was carrying forward with great intensity.

Happier after his marriage, Brooks was reconciled to life if not to art. He gradually abandoned the idealistic despair of *The Soul* and returned to the belief expressed in "Notes on Vernon Lee" that heaven might be realized in earthly society. Ideas would leave the "sensuous forms" of art behind and spring forth in "unbodied joy." During the Stanford years he wrote an essay with the significant title "The Twilight of the Arts," in which he said that literature endeavors "to render itself unnecessary, . . . to permit its forces to be absorbed by life." Art, then, "is tending toward the condition of silence." Until that event transpired, however, art and especially literature had much to say. He told his Stanford classes that ". . . literature maps out in advance what society wants & creates the enthusiasm to get it."[11] By creating in society the enthusiasm to realize the ideal, literature would not only fulfill its prophetic responsibility but would also render itself obsolete. The ultimate objective of even the most worldly literature turned out to be self-destruction.

If art was tending towards silence, politics were as noisy as ever. Van Wyck was becoming more sensitive to "what society wants" because of his exposure to radical politics in Palo Alto. At the socialist local he heard the word "intellectual" used as a noun for the first time and met those to whom the word was applied — alienated ex-miners and immigrant Germans and Russians with minds full of Bakunin and Marx. Even Stanford's president, David Starr Jordan, who took a friendly, paternalistic interest in Van Wyck, was a leader in the peace movement. And there were socialists and revolutionaries among Brooks's students and friends on the faculty. Max Lippitt, who taught economics, had been in the Russian Revolution of 1905 and afterwards had escaped from Siberia to California. Har Dayal, professor of Hindu philosophy, hopefully plotted against the British Empire and trained terrorists in Berkeley (one of whom threw a bomb at George V in Delhi in 1912, missing the king but killing the viceroy for India). Dayal once staged a clandestine meeting between himself and a Punjabi nationalist in Brooks's home. To Van Wyck, Lippitt and Dayal seemed types of the nineteenth-century revolutionary nationalists like Mazzini and Kossuth, who had gripped his imagination since adolescence.[12] They were not artists in the fine sense, but they were prophets possessed by an ideal vision which they were attempting to make real, not only on earth but in society.

Socialism seemed sympathetic to literature. The People's Literary League in Oakland invited Van Wyck to speak on Whitman, and socialist friends wanted him to edit a journal of radical thought. He declined the latter opportunity, telling Har Dayal that he would not make a good propagandist of the Emma Goldman type. But in this relatively cheerful time he engaged less in melancholy idealizing and was coming to agree with Dayal and other radicals that literature not only was but should be social. In the fall of 1912 he wrote to a Harvard friend that he would vote for neither Wilson nor Roosevelt. Presumably he voted for Eugene Debs, and he viewed his vote as a literary as well as a political act. Nothing, he told his friend, would prevent "the union of politics with sociology and with poetry."[13]

Thanks to what he was hearing of "scientific socialism" and to his growing fascination with and absorption in H. G. Wells, Brooks was also becoming more sympathetic to science, no longer believing it antipathetic to poetic vision. This change was due also to a new friendship with his next-door neighbor in Palo Alto, Hans Zinsser, who was not only a bacteriologist soon to be famous for his work on typhus but also a published poet. They spent days together, hiking in the hills around Palo Alto, and Zinsser, a rugged outdoorsman and aspiring Renaissance man who wished to live in the "whole," scolded Van Wyck for the narrow literary idealism that had previously made him unsympathetic to science.[14]

Although Zinsser was about the same age as Van Wyck, he became another in the series of father figures — Ryder, Marshall, and Yeats — who symbolized for Van Wyck the possibility of masculine culture. An artist as well as a scientist, Zinsser represented more directly than the others the possibility of relating culture to life. Van Wyck was impressed by the healthy quality of Zinsser's worldliness, his good spirits and "masculine physical charm." During the Stanford years Van Wyck sometimes dreamt of himself dying on an operating table, "But I felt sure that Hans would somehow snatch me out of the arms of death."[15] The vision approached reality fifteen years later when Brooks was in the throes of suicidal depression.

During his two brief years in California, Van Wyck had passed through an almost complete metamorphosis from the mood of despairing idealism which had led him in New York to write *The Soul*. In marriage he had found, at least for the present, reasons for happiness in this world. His growing belief in a social, even a scientific mission for literature also indicated an accommodation with the here and now. Similarly, he did not long quite so intensely for heavenly Europe but was a little reconciled to America, which turned out to be less mundane than he had thought. California's climate and landscape had Mediterranean qualities, and in the spring when the orchards were in bloom, Palo Alto smelled like Italy. At Stanford and Berkeley, in San Francisco and Carmel, he had met people who convinced him that the West, and therefore America, was not quite the cultural desert he had imagined.

II

Though all three books which Brooks wrote in California had European subjects and thus indicated that he still craved "the East, ever more Eastern," the books also reveal, when read carefully, a steady movement toward affirmation of the American prospect. None of the books were published till after he left Stanford, and the last one was completed in Europe. But they must be treated together because they form a trilogy with a symmetrical structure. In *The Malady of the Ideal* (1913), he treated unworldliness as an illness, considering its origins and symptoms. In *John Addington Symonds* (1914) he looked at the opposite disease, submission to the established fact, to the real.

And in *The World of H. G. Wells* (1915) he offered an example of a man sanely balanced between the real world and an ideal vision, a model for American personality to emulate.

In *The Malady of the Ideal,* Brooks seemed to be continuing the argument he had made in *The Soul;* worldly, social, and artistic forms interfered with the true life of the spirit. He dealt with three figures, Senancour's Obermann, Maurice de Guérin, and H. F. Amiel, who had been unable to express their visions of the ideal in coherent works of literature. Instead, they had achieved only fragmentary expression in letters and journals. The reason was that the intensity of their commitment to the ideal made them "superior to the compromise involved in expression." This compromise was "rhetoric," which Brooks defined as "a form of infidelity by which the writer conveys the impression that he has felt what he has not felt, in order to give his expression the form and consistency demanded by art." Most men were too weak to refrain from trying to express the ineffable in the "beautiful untruth" of art. But Amiel and the others understood that the truly free spirit "would become silent like the clouds."[16]

But beside the continuing distrust of art and worldly forms, Brooks also exhibited in *The Malady of the Ideal* a growing commitment to life, to literature, and to science. Literary criticism, if practiced scientifically, could cleanse life of its baseness, its "alloy." Even the first word of the title, *Malady,* suggested an approach to his subjects that was medical, psychological, scientific. Brooks was to be a critic in the tradition of Sainte-Beuve and Taine, who focused on writers as much as on literature, because, stunted in his own artistic growth, he wanted to remove the obstacles which had thwarted him. What interested him was "personality," and in a religious as well as a scientific sense. For him personality was a given, a soul, and what he wanted to know in his study of men and books was "How far do they . . . add to the number of ways in which personality can achieve itself?" Personality, or the soul, is innately good till it takes on flesh and passes through the world of form, where it encounters "obstructions." History is a moral science that offers the spectacle of the human race "rising *en masse* from nature." Criticism deals with the same process in individual men and works by watching "for each individual perfection." It is satisfying to know of Dante, Goethe, and Plato because "in their complete self-realization they are, so to speak, an earnest of the human faculty." But a scientific criticism is interested in imperfection also. By studying personalities unable to

realize themselves in this life, ". . . we can understand the obstructions that exist in the world and the methods of removing them."[17]

From this book and from the next in the trilogy, *John Addington
Symonds,* it is clear that the main obstruction to full realization of
personality for Brooks was the social order. Part of the reason that
the French subjects of *The Malady of the Ideal* were unable to express
their ideal visions was the resistance of their society to the life of the
spirit. In France religion was regarded as a mere "adjunct to the
social order." Similarly, John Addington Symonds' poetic tendency
had been stifled by a cold and Calvinistic heritage, a father with false
ideas of manhood, and an Oxford education that stressed the practical. Van Wyck had long been enthralled by Symonds' numerous
books on Italian art and literature, but he also believed them
"neither quite true to fact nor yet quite true to the poet's consciousness." Despite his twenty volumes, Symonds' life was a close parallel
to the laconic Amiel's. There was a profound Symonds which never
spoke, "never got itself on paper." Symonds also suffered from a
malady, for his massive works had been dragged out of him by social
circumstances and by the fact that, unlike Amiel, he was "capable of
compromise with the ideal." His work lacked the "unifying bond of
personality" because it was written not to express his inner self but
rather to satisfy a "sheer pathological necessity of turning out
words."[18]

Despite the authoritative tone with which Brooks analyzed his
subjects' psyches, he knew little about them beyond their published
writings. *John Addington Symonds* was the best researched of his early
books and yet it drew only on printed sources — various Victorian
memoirs, Symonds' books themselves, and the *Papers and Correspondence* compiled by Horatio F. Brown. Brooks was especially
dependent on the latter, just as his *Ordeal of Mark Twain* (1920)
would rest largely on Albert Bigelow Paine's massive biography.
Brooks considered his biographical method scientific because he
used his subject's life as a source of empirical data around which to
construct a psychological theory: ". . . the inner history of Symonds
could be detailed and charted scientifically." But he failed to gather
his data carefully, sometimes accepting spurious information almost
gullibly and at other times dismissing true accounts with no authority for doing so. Symonds, for instance, was suspected by his readers
and known by his friends to be a homosexual. Yet Van Wyck insisted
that Symonds' "passion for adolescent masculine beauty, conceived
in the true Greek spirit . . . led also to certain cross misunderstand-

ings that have hardly yet disconnected themselves from Symonds' name."[19] Thus Van Wyck revealed not only his own comparative innocence and possibly his own sexual insecurity, but also the predilection for abstract theory that would mar his later books on Twain and James. He was less interested in his subjects' lives than in establishing his own idea of the artist's right relation to the world. Even if he had understood Symonds' sexual adjustment it would have interested him less than the deep neurosis stemming from Symonds' submission to the real and the consequent repression of his desire for the ideal. Like Clemens in *The Ordeal of Mark Twain*, Symonds had killed the artist in himself.

To crown his trilogy, Brooks abandoned the study of incomplete personalities and wrote about a man who lived like an artist. H. G. Wells was involved in worldly life, but unlike Symonds he did not submit to the real. Wells had achieved a distance that allowed clear vision, but unlike Amiel he was not abstracted from the world. "And of all writers who have so immediately felt life," said Brooks, "I doubt if there has been one so detached as Wells." Wells was a prophet who was making real a visionary ideal — socialism. But he was not a doctrinaire. For him socialism was a creative response to the challenges of life: ". . . if socialism had not existed Wells would have invented it. It is, in his own formulation of it, the projection of his whole nature, the expression of his will, the very content of his art." Wells was an "artist of society . . . disturbed by the absence of right composition in human things."[20]

But before making this argument Brooks digressed into a comparison of Wells and Matthew Arnold which revealed how traditional his own ideas remained. Brooks argued that socialism was the natural outgrowth of "the best things that have been thought and said," and that therefore Wells had "played toward his own epoch a part very similar to that played by Matthew Arnold."[21] Brooks disliked Arnold, perhaps because he had heard his name invoked in defense of culture as it was conceived in Plainfield, and he probably enjoyed subverting Arnold by linking him to Wells. Yet even while committing himself to science and socialism, Brooks remained committed also to Arnold's idealistic conception of culture. Arnold had first formulated many of Brooks's ideas on Senancour and de Guérin and also on American culture. Arnold had treated the problem of the artist and the social order, despairing of poetic vision in an industrialized and self-conscious society. But Arnold never lost faith that there was such a thing as the ideal.

Neither did Brooks, and he was closer in temperament to Arnold than to many of his near contemporaries, who would lose all faith in the ideal on the battlefields of the First World War or in the struggle for survival in the bottom ranks of industrial society. Those events nearly destroyed the world of ideas Matthew Arnold helped create, the intellectual situation in which Brooks came of age. That explains much about why Brooks distrusted naturalistic writers like Dreiser and Hemingway, and why he came to seem old-fashioned before his time.

The main difference, Brooks believed, between Arnold and Wells was Arnold's failure to understand that science was not necessarily antagonistic to the life of the spirit. In his trilogy — *The Malady of the Ideal, John Addington Symonds,* and *The World of H. G. Wells* — Brooks found several opportunities to blast Arnold on this score. Arnold was wrong in saying that Senancour had lived stoically in a scientific age that did not respect his religious nature. Senancour's mysticism was "harmonious with modern science," and he would have looked forward to science's dethronement of man "from that base eminence, the false result of a lost link separating him from the rest of creation." By invoking the "lost link" Brooks was saying that Darwinism raised rather than lowered man's estimation of himself. Symonds, understanding science better than Arnold, would have recognized that "instead of debasing our view of the human soul, [science] glorifies our idea of the human body." In other words, science would fulfill what Brooks had earlier described as Vernon Lee's conception of the future — "a kind of quietism that has got rid of heaven and become sublunized . . . because we discovered that we could have all the really good things of heaven without waiting so long for them." Science, mixed with socialism, would bring heaven to earth.[22]

Brooks was himself practicing the science of criticism, the search for "obstructions that exist in the world and the methods of removing them." Taking Wells himself as a subject, Van Wyck had been led again to the idea he had first expressed at Harvard that the critic's task was to make scientific ideas "vital" by mixing them with poetic vision. Initially, Wells's personality had been typically scientific — cold, lifeless, and too purely intellectual. What redeemed Wells was that he had made his science vital by mixing it with a visionary ideal — socialism. Here then was Brooks's own critical discovery: Wells's coldness was an obstruction to the effectuation of his personality or soul, and what had removed the obstruction was the visionary ideal of socialism in behalf of which science, however cold and lifeless in itself, might find meaningful employment.

What socialism had done for Wells it would also do for America. Wells resembled the archetype of American personality which Brooks had constructed in *The Wine of the Puritans* — intellectual rather than emotional, self-conscious rather than spontaneous, adept at explanation and unwilling to allow for mystery in life. There was a "special sort of connection" between America and Wells: ". . . were the spirit of America suddenly to become critical of itself it would resemble nothing in the world so much as the spirit of Wells magnified by many diameters." Wells had found a new focus for culture, a "synthetic motive without which a secular and industrial race is as devoid of animating morality as a swarm of flies." In the socialist world envisaged by Wells, modern men, especially Americans, might rid themselves of their excessive self-consciousness through absorption in a large cause. Wells had established a new basis for values, a new source of instinct, a new subject for art — society itself. What Wordsworth had done for nature, Wells had done for the social organism. "In him [Wells] this new world of intelligence is already exuberant with instinct; the social machine has become a personality; that cold abstraction the world has become in his hands a throbbing, breathing, living thing. . . ."[23]

In this way Brooks arrived at the solution to the problem that had plagued him since adolescence, the problem of being an artist in America. He would subvert the barrier of the social order that stood between himself and art by making that barrier itself a new basis for art. As an American critic Brooks was well situated to practice this new art, for "If the future is anywhere going to follow the lines that Wells has suggested for it, . . . it will most likely be in America." As Wells had done in *The Future in America,* Brooks cited the large corporations, the charitable foundations, the universities and research institutes as evidence of how highly developed, albeit extra-governmentally, the social mechanism already was in America. What was needed was an "understanding of the right function of this mechanism." Creating that understanding and making it "exuberant with instinct" was the task for a critic, a prophet, an American artist of society. It is possible that Brooks wrote this part of his book on Wells after *America's Coming-of-Age* (also published in 1915) but even if so, these passages indicate the reason for the spirited tone of the latter book. Just as Brooks had predicted in *The Wine of the Puritans,* America did offer, and much sooner than he had dared hope, "the elements of a gigantic art," the art of society.[24]

III

Alfred Zimmern, later Sir Alfred and already a well-known historian, was touring the United States in 1912 and in New York fell in
with J. B. Yeats's circle at Petitpas', where he was given a letter of
introduction to Van Wyck in California. Arriving there, Zimmern
sought Brooks out on the Stanford campus, liked him, and offered
him a teaching post in England with the Workers' Educational
Association, of which Zimmern was a government inspector.[25] Although Brooks's experience in the West had been superior to his
expectations and were helping him to the conclusion that it was in
America that the vision of H. G. Wells would most likely be realized,
he leapt at the opportunity to return to England. His ambivalent
feelings about America versus Europe were far from resolved.

Thanks to Zimmern, Van Wyck would view English literary and
intellectual life in much closer perspective than he had been able to
do during his lonely year in London in 1907–08. What he saw in
closer range impressed and also appalled him in its implication of
America's cultural inferiority. His old feelings of inadequacy began
to return as soon as he visited London after settling Eleanor, her
mother, and his infant son Charles on the Isle of Wight for July and
August of 1913.

He saw a number of Americans in England that summer, and
some of them, luminous at home, were not so distinguished in the
European setting. For instance, David Starr Jordan, retired now
from Stanford's presidency, was beginning a European lecture tour
on behalf of pacifism of the Carnegie variety. Van Wyck was typically kind and respectful to the older Jordan but could not take him
seriously. After meeting the father of English Marxism, H. M.
Hyndman, in the London home of the American millionaire socialist
Gaylord Wilshire, Van Wyck wrote to Eleanor, "I put my foot in it
terribly by mentioning Dr. Jordan and appearing as if I agreed with
the Peace Movement — (which of course I think chiefly flub-
dub. . .)." Later, in the autumn, he served briefly as Jordan's secretary on a visit to Cambridge and was amused by the old man's
reaction: "He . . . says Carnegie should make a real university of
it."[26]

There were more noteworthy Americans in London, however,
men like Ezra Pound, whom Brooks met briefly, and John Cournos.
Brooks also began at this time his lifelong friendships with the
sculptor Jo Davidson and the poet John Gould Fletcher. But the
most immediately important of Brooks's new American friends in

London was the twenty-three-year-old Walter Lippmann, whom he met at D. J. Rider's bookshop (Rider arranged for English publication of Mitchell Kennerley's authors, Lippmann among them). Lippmann had recently published *A Preface to Politics* (1913), which would greatly influence Van Wyck as he wrote *America's Coming-of-Age* during the following year. Lippmann opposed mere reform, mere Good Government, because it was, in Van Wyck's phrase, highbrow, that is, out of touch with the real economic issues. Genuine revolutions, Lippmann said in apparent agreement with Van Wyck, were made "out of culture," and the real question in America was whether or not "the words of the intellect have anything to do with the facts of life?" Van Wyck, greatly impressed, thought that the mere existence of a precocious young writer like Lippmann was a good omen for the future of America. But Lippmann also made Van Wyck feel somewhat adolescent or retarded in his own development — a feeling confirmed by his inability to do much but blush and stammer when, at the National Liberal Club, Lippmann briefly introduced him to S. K. Ratcliffe and H. G. Wells. Van Wyck wrote to Eleanor that Lippmann was "the most satisfactory Harvard man I have met since I left. He is a man I know I should be great friends with, if I could see more of him." Lippmann also valued their meeting, and they would exchange a few letters during the next year, with Lippmann telling of his plans for the *New Republic*. But the two men would seldom meet in later years, once Lippmann had dropped his cultural radicalism and Van Wyck had developed his opposition to the pragmatism which came to characterize both Lippmann and the *New Republic*.[27]

As Van Wyck began to observe the English scene his ideas became more precise about the reasons for the superiority of England over America in drawing out and usefully employing men of talent. He was impressed when Zimmern told him that a friend had written a political tract whose ideas quickly became law, because he had a friend in the cabinet. Van Wyck could not imagine Lippmann's *Preface to Politics* provoking legislation in America, and he wrote to Eleanor that one could not help but see the advantages of a "social-intellectual hierarchy." Even the king, whom Brooks saw snarl traffic for two hours by merely appearing in the street, served a useful purpose: "Aside from the really disgusting elements in it," it was good for a country to be "thus centralized in a symbol. . . . Centralization is the secret of all thought & art here. . . . every act & thought has its place and affects every other act and thought — like the solar system. Standing in London you can put your fingers on every shade of opinion, and as in coherent organisms nothing is lost."[28] "Centralization" was the organic quality missing in American life, the quality to be created through socialism and the art of society.

But in London Van Wyck also revealed the vestiges of middle-class prejudice and fastidiousness that would always make participation in politics, especially socialist politics, difficult for him. He sympathized with the demonstrators in Hyde Park, but they "made my soul sick," and he complained to Eleanor: ". . . how palling these never-ending, shallow, ill-considered, shrill arguments, points made, oratorical claptrap, combat, rancourousness become!" To achieve the "calm, understanding, harmonious existence" he wanted, something "a whole lot better than socialism" would be required. He was disturbed also by socialist legislation already in effect: "The Insurance Act, etc. have created hordes of professional loafers." Social legislation in England had "lost sight of the ideal."[29]

He reversed this opinion the next week, the beginning of August, when he went to Oxford with Zimmern for a congress of the Workers' Educational Association. The congress overwhelmed him with its sense of spiritual and prophetic mission, and the very scene at Oxford was elysian. The university was on holiday, and the delegates wandered about the lawns and gardens with thoughts undisturbed except by an occasional chime. Thanks in part to his meeting at the congress the socialist Bishop of Oxford, Charles Gore, and also a future Archbishop of Canterbury, William Temple, Brooks concluded that the delegates were moved by a "truly apostolic feeling." Also in attendance were the librarian of the House of Commons and two Members of Parliament. The varied and well-articulated viewpoints reminded Van Wyck of Dickinson's *Modern Symposium*. To be so close to the center of English culture was an exercise in humility, and he wrote to Eleanor that he was "tremendously — truly — surprised — that they seem to think I will do — and that they don't regard knowledge as having anything whatever to do with the teaching of literature."[30]

His old feeling that he had lost everything by not being born European returned. He met some Rhodes scholars at Oxford who struck him as "wizened," the result of having been raised, he later said, in a barren culture, where they had "never known a day of good growing weather." Feeling equally puny, he tried to explain to Eleanor what he meant by saying that he had no "knowledge": "Where English educated minds have the advantage over me is not in quantity of reading, but in control of the mental instrument — in an instinctive synthetic, political, social sense. My mind is impulsive, fragmentary and by no means under the domination of will or mental discipline of any kind. . . ." Although teaching English working people would be a valuable experience, his lack of "mental discipline" made him certain that he was unqualified. English education was meant to give people "an intellectual instrument for looking at first principles." His students would want to know *"what poetry is"* and would not be satisfied, as the students at Stanford had been, with "epigrams about it." Furthermore, he was doubtful of being accepted as a teacher in a country where education meant mastery of Greek and Latin, subjects through which he had scraped at Harvard with minimal effort and then forgotten. At the Oxford congress he had been galled by working girls who lengthily quoted Horace: "Damn learning & teaching anyway!"[31]

For once, however, he had found a situation that agreed with his temperament, and the teaching went smoothly enough after he received his assignment in South Norwood, a working-class neighborhood in London. He avoided the classics by offering a course on the nineteenth-century essayists — Lamb, Carlyle, and Macaulay — whom he had read and known well since adolescence. Though he later wrote that his class of thirty working men and women "put me on my mettle," teaching required little of his time and energy.[32] His class met one evening a week, and his stipend of sixty pounds, or three hundred dollars, was adequate to support his family in a rented house in the suburb of Eltham. He was free to write.

Just as had happened during his year in England in 1907–08, his thoughts turned toward home, and by August of 1913 he decided to write a book on America. As in *The Wine of the Puritans,* he would address himself to the problem of discerning what it was that made Europe superior. And just as he had done in that book, he would dismiss Emerson and the other classic American writers as part of a meaningless, irrelevant culture. By the spring of 1914 he had completed a draft of the book and mailed it to Max Perkins in New York for submission to Scribner's. William Crary Brownell, still the senior editor there, rejected the manuscript because, as he told Perkins, Brooks had "swept these fellows into the dustbin of the past with a contemptuousness of gesture which was at least pre-mature." Brownell had added with an appreciative smile that Brooks was certainly a "live wire." The book would have to wait for a publisher until Van Wyck returned to America.[33]

Meanwhile, Brooks dallied again with the idea of a literary career in Europe, since he expected to be reappointed by the Workers' Educational Association for 1914-15. In 1913-14 he had both earned a living and written a book. He seemed in England to have resolved the unworldly exigencies of the literary life and the conflicting problem of a livelihood. In England he had found a publisher — the idealistic Tolstoyan, A. C. Fifield — for *The Malady of the Ideal*, while in America Mitchell Kennerley refused to do more than print two chapters in his *Forum*. And the European response to the book made it seem likely that he would find a receptive audience there rather than in America. The *Cambridge Review* found the book "charming" and faulty only in its brevity. The *Mercure de France* admired Brooks's treatment of his French subjects: "Ces pages permettent d'espérer de Mr. Brooks une oeuvre critique remarquable."[34]

For the summer of 1914 he found a heavenly scene in France, near the Breton coast, in the village of Saint-Jean-du-Doigt (the village church claimed as a relic the right index finger of John the Baptist). The village numbered only a few hundred inhabitants, but it was well known as an artist's colony. Early in July, Van Wyck rented rooms for himself, Eleanor, and Charles in one of the village homes and arranged to take meals in the Hotel Saint-Jean across the square.[35] He worked hard and well through July, putting the finishing touches on his *World of H. G. Wells*. It was an idyllic existence. There were other babies for Charles to play with, and Eleanor and Van Wyck could walk to the shore where fishermen's nets hung in the sun to dry. Along the way they would have passed artists at their easels and peasants in the field. It was the hundredth anniversary of the Congress of Vienna, and during all of Van Wyck's twenty-eight years Europe had seemed as permanently fixed and stable as the stars in the sky.

But while Brooks passed his blissful summer, the Europe he thought of as heaven prepared to turn itself into hell. Thanks to Har Dayal, Van Wyck may have already been involved in the coming struggle. In England he had forwarded a number of letters and parcels for Dayal, who either had formed or was about to form a connection with the Germans against the English.[36] But Van Wyck probably would not have thought it important, even if he had known that he had unwittingly served as a German agent. Like most people, he could not believe that events in the Balkans that summer counted for much. If he was shocked by the assassination of the Austrian heir apparent in Sarajevo on June 28, he was lulled by the month of relative calm while Germany made guaranties to Austria, who meditated her ultimatum to Serbia. On July 21 Van Wyck wrote to David

Starr Jordan, congratulating him on his "successful" year of lecturing Europe on the wisdom of peace and adding, "I can imagine how discouraging you must have found those incorrigible Balkans." Unaware of the threat which events in the Balkans posed to his own hopes for a career in Europe, he thanked Jordan for the kind thought, but no, he would not return to Stanford. He was committed to England for the coming year.[37]

In the week following Van Wyck's letter to Jordan, Austria delivered her ultimatum, rejected Serbia's reply, and on July 28 declared war. Russia mobilized during the next two days, then Germany, and finally, on the first of August, France. The people of Saint-Jean-du-Doigt wept; every able-bodied man under fifty was to leave the village on the second day of mobilization. Eleanor Brooks, socialist, wrote to her genteel mother-in-law in Plainfield: "War seems so madly *silly* that I cannot imagine how all Europe should be dragged into it against its will. A general strike alone would have averted it. . . ."[38]

The French trains were mobilized, so the visiting artists in Saint-Jean-du-Doigt were stranded there for two weeks after the war began. Eleanor was distressed; Charles had a cold, there was no doctor in the village, and the mails were disrupted. They missed a check on which they had been counting, and they had barely enough money for passage to England whenever that became possible. The Hotel Saint-Jean extended their credit though they were already behind on their board. Meanwhile, the tourists and artists in the hotel helped the women and children bring in the harvest which the village men had been forced to leave in the field — work which Eleanor found "great fun." She had already ceased to be neutral in heart and mind, and she hoped that "Germany gets the drubbing she deserves."[39]

Van Wyck, for his part, still planned a future in England, though he knew that the war would spell the end of the Workers' Educational Association, which depended on voluntary contributions. However, he expected a manpower shortage in England and was confident of finding a job that would enable him both to support his family and to write.[40]

When train service resumed, they departed for Rennes, arriving there at one in the morning. Two year old Charles woke in Eleanor's arms, demanding to "go home," and Eleanor and Van Wyck were stricken by the thought that they had no home. They went on to St. Malo, where they were stranded again, waiting a week or ten days for a boat to England. Standing on the beach, they looked across to Mont-Saint-Michel, but could not afford the fare out to the island. Van Wyck passed the time reading Chateaubriand's *Génie du Christianisme,* and moved by the lavish color and detail, he first conceived the idea of writing historical pageantry himself, though it would be seventeen years yet before he began *The Flowering of New England.* Finally, they got a boat to England and arrived there in late August with eight shillings.[41]

Van Wyck left Eleanor and Charles in Worthing and went up to London, where Eleanor's mother had been spending the summer. He found Mrs. Stimson frightened by the war news, and he too was growing worried. The Germans had advanced relentlessly and were within fifty miles of Paris on August 31, when Van Wyck wrote to Eleanor: "There is no doubt now about the danger of England." He abandoned his hopes for a career in Europe and proposed to Eleanor that they go to Liverpool as soon as possible. Though they could not book passage to America for at least two weeks, train service might be interrupted as it had been in France, and he felt that Mrs. Stimson would rest easier in Liverpool. If Eleanor wanted to come to London, she should wait until he was back in Worthing with Charles: *"Don't leave baby alone with Ada, I beg you."*[42]

Even as the possibility of a career in Europe seemed closed, there was a new possibility in America. In London, Van Wyck had had dinner with Jordan and Lippmann at the National Liberal Club, and Jordan recommended him for the *New Republic,* which would first be issued in November. Lippmann had replied, "We've got him already," and Van Wyck, certain that he would be offered a position, told Eleanor, "It's just what I have been looking for for years & makes me feel quite a 'man of destiny.' "[43] Although the decision to return to America had been made for him, he would return in a hopeful mood, carrying with him the manuscript that became *America's Coming-of-Age.*

IV

Culture, Brooks said in *America's Coming-of-Age,* should bear a critical relationship to social reality. Culture should express the ideal and exhort society to realize it. But in America culture was dissociated from social reality. There was no middle ground, no "centralization" — the quality that he had so admired in England. In most areas of American life there was no communication, only scorn, between idealist and realist, between theorist and practitioner, between " 'Highbrow' and 'Lowbrow' " — the title of the first chapter.

What side of American life is not touched by this antithesis? What explanation of American life is more central or more illuminating? In everything one finds this frank acceptance of twin values which are not expected to have anything in common: on the one hand a quite unclouded, quite unhypocritical assumption of transcendent theory ("high ideals"); on the other a simultaneous acceptance of catchpenny realities. Between university ethics and business ethics, between American culture and American humor, between Good Government and Tammany, between academic pedantry and pavement slang, there is no community, no genial middle ground.[44]

Brooks gave the same historical explanation as in *The Wine of the Puritans*. The fragmented character of American life was due to the dilemma of the Puritans, whose material life in the wilderness could not be illuminated by the domesticated culture they had brought with them from Europe. Hence opportunism, a necessity in the Puritans' practical life, eventually became a philosophy in Benjamin Franklin and resulted "in the atmosphere of contemporary business life." Meanwhile, Puritan piety found a spokesman in Jonathan Edwards and resulted in "the final unreality of most contemporary American culture."[45]

Believing that literature recorded the spirit of a people, Brooks searched in his second chapter, "Our Poets," for evidence that "Highbrow" and "Lowbrow" truly figured the American character. And he found that American literature was divided between a mindless realism and a meaningless idealism, between a commitment to society or a commitment to culture, but seldom to both. Bryant and Longfellow, for instance, lacked artistic instinct and they revealed this lack by becoming moralists, unable to let poetry speak for itself. But the misplaced moralism that betrayed their art was due precisely to their social instinct, to their understanding of the need in the new world for a civilized and domesticated warmth. Similarly, in the realm of thought and criticism, James Russell Lowell had a good social instinct but no philosophy, no ideas to inform and direct his astute social sense. On the other hand, Hawthorne and Poe, "the two principal artists in American literature, . . . were out of touch with society as few other artists in the world had been before." Therefore, they created and inhabited "worlds of their own, — diaphanous private worlds of mist and twilight."[46]

The special etherealness of American culture was best illustrated by Transcendentalism: "Emerson was not interested in human life; he cared nothing for experience or emotion, possessing so little himself." This unconcern accounted for the feebleness of Emersonian thought in restraining America's rampant materialism. The doctrine of self-reliance, brought down to the economic plane, merely sanctioned business: "And in fact it would be hard to say whether Emerson more keenly relished saintliness or shrewdness." Margaret Fuller also illustrated the futility of Transcendentalism as an instrument of social criticism until she went to Europe, where the revolutions of 1848–49 fulfilled her and made her "serene, capable, commanding." The moral of her story was the moral "of all unattached idealism: that the more deeply and urgently and organically you feel the pressure of society the more deeply and consciously and fruitfully you feel and you become yourself."[47]

Thus far, in its reading of American history and literature, *America's Coming-of-Age* had little to say that differed from what had been said in *The Wine of the Puritans*. Brooks still labored under Barrett Wendell's influence; long before Brooks said it, Wendell had called Franklin and Edwards the classic representatives of the two opposing aspects of the Yankee character. Wendell, however, had disliked Edwards and admired Franklin, while Brooks with his insistence on the need for a middle ground objected to both men, to both highbrow and lowbrow. Brooks also broke with Wendell on his gloomy reading of the future in America, for Wendell had remained convinced that he lived in an era of racial degeneration. Yet even in his own more hopeful expectations for the future, Brooks remained somewhat indebted to Wendell, who, albeit with great distaste, had said that the raucous Whitman was the one poet who had "thrown light on the future of America."[48]

Whitman was the one poet, Van Wyck said, who had given America "the rudiments of a middle tradition." The third chapter of *America's Coming-of-Age*, "The Precipitant," argued that Whitman had brought the national character out of solution and made it substantial and real. Whitman was the Antaeus who took the exquisite refinement of the Puritan tradition and "touched earth with it. . . . All those things which had been separate, self-sufficient, incoordinate — action, theory, idealism, business — he cast into a crucible; and they emerged, harmonious and molten, in a fresh democratic ideal, which is based upon the whole personality."[49]

But Whitman affirmed everything, and while that was correct on the emotional plane, it meant that on the plane of ideas he had uncritically accepted the *fait accompli*. Many of Whitman's disciples had failed to mark the distinction, and the result was the

"Apotheosis of the Lowbrow," as Brooks argued in his fourth chapter. He singled out one Whitmanian in particular, Gerald Stanley Lee. Lee's *Inspired Millionaires* (1908) had been called to Brooks's attention by Lippmann, who was angered not only by the book's impoverished thought but also by its large sale. Lee had argued that the ideal industrial system was not socialism but paternalistic capitalism. Making a fortune, Lee said, was a creative act, and therefore capitalists were men of vision who could be counted on to see what was needed in American life. Brooks easily destroyed Lee's argument by making a distinction between ownership and management as Lippmann had done in *Drift and Mastery*. The manager rather than the owner was well placed for creative innovation, provided that he could be freed from fulfilling the owner's selfish interests. Socialism was the best system for accomplishing that goal.[50]

Lee's obvious weaknesses as a social theorist led Brooks into a discussion of the state of critical thought in America. It was not entirely Lee's fault that he was a toady and a flatterer who illustrated the principle that "To be a prophet in America it is not enough to be totally uninformed; one must also have a bland smile." Lee had enough intelligence to see that something was wrong with the social system and enough courage to attempt to offer it a new ideal. But in the absence of a school of rigorous critical thought to force him to think straight and see that socialism was the logical conclusion of his premises, he was at the mercy of his sentimental Yankee individualism: "How much talent goes to waste every day, it seems, simply because there is no criticism, no standard, no authority to trip it up and shake it and make it think!" This was the absent quality that made American culture inferior to English culture and that in turn made the social situation less hopeful in America than in England. If, as Huxley had said, society's *raison d'être* was the creation of a garden in the cosmic wilderness, then society required cultivators who could tell flowers from weeds, and ". . . while England has at least a handful of trained gardeners, we have nothing but cowboys and a flag."[51]

According to Brooks's final chapter, American society resembled, not a garden, but the "Sargasso Sea": "All manner of living things are drifting in it, phosphorescent, gayly colored, gathered into knots and clotted masses, gelatinous, unformed, flimsy, tangled, rising and falling, floating and merging, here an immense distended belly, there a tiny rudimentary brain (the gross devouring the fine) — everywhere an unchecked, uncharted, unorganized vitality like that of the first chaos." America had not been cultivated, not been "worked into an organism," and so it lacked those "fruitful values and standards of humane economy" which "produce a fine temper in the human animal." The object of culture was, after all, as he had implied in *The Malady of the Ideal*, "perfect self-realization" or, as he said now, the full expression of "personality."[52]

"Personality" still meant "soul" or "self" to Brooks, and the question that still concerned him was how the ideal life of the soul could be made real in the world, in America. His conception of socialism was always a little vague, but it certainly included the subjection of business society to a criticism based on ideal standards: ". . . contemporary social thought is at bottom simply a restatement for the mass of commercialized men . . . of those personal instincts that have been the essence of art, religion, literature — the essence of personality itself — since the beginning of things." Personality could not live or express itself in a society devoted to "an impersonal end like the accumulation of money." Work performed for an ulterior purpose like making money rather than for the expression of self must inevitably result in alienation. America was not a well-cultivated garden but, rather, a jungle of economic competition where men were alientated not only from their work and themselves but also from each other — still another obstruction to the development of personality. No one could fulfill or express his best self without some "visible or invisible host about him, since the mind is a flower that has an organic connection with the soil it springs from." Lacking that sympathetic, cultured community, most Americans struggled as if only to survive economically, and as if they had no soul or "object in living."[53]

Thanks to Lippmann and Wells, Brooks had new confidence that the solution lay in cultural change rather than in traditional conceptions of political reform: "It is of no use to talk about Reform. Society will be very obedient when the myriad personalities that compose it . . . have an object in living." The "centre of gravity in American affairs" had shifted "to the plane of psychology and morals." Therefore, abstractions from political theory like "New Nationalism" or "New Freedom" were not as useful as catchwords like "Highbrow" and "Lowbrow," which had their roots in the actuality of the American psyche or soul. Catchwords should "really *catch* at the bottom of things," and for Brooks that meant that they must touch moral as well as social issues: "For generations the test of a living society, a living philosophy of art, will be whether or not the catchwords it flings forth really correspond with profound divisions of type, deeply felt issues, genuine convictions, in whichever field, between — I was going to say — some good and some evil. But these words are so unfashionable that if I use them I shall certainly alienate any Advanced Person who honors these pages with a glance."[54]

In this way Brooks illustrated, probably without entirely realizing it, how little he shared the premises of American social thought and its rapidly developing naturalism. It is true that like Lippmann and others, Brooks was engaged in a revolt against formalism, against, in Brooks's case, the peculiarly meaningless formalism of contemporary American culture. But even though *America's Coming-of-Age* was distinguished by its passion for social reality, an immense distinction for a book of American criticism in 1915, Brooks would never have argued that reality was everything. The purpose of criticism, in fact, was to change reality, to bring it to terms with the ideal. Many social thinkers, even Lippmann, who had tried to link his pragmatism to "human ends," had remained vague about the need for standards and values. For Brooks, however, there was never any doubt that while culture should be related in a meaningful way to the real, it had to depend for its values on contact with the ideal.

Brooks's quasi-religious conception of culture — that it should enhance and reflect the fruition of the soul "on a middle plane between vaporous idealism and self-interested practicality" — gave the vital, critical tension to *America's Coming-of-Age*. It permitted him to attempt to embrace America, as it were, without falling into the uncritical apotheosis of the lowbrow that had misled the Whitmanians. While Whitman's affirmations had laid the cornerstone of a national ideal capable of "releasing personality," they had been uninformed by critical ideals or values, and his followers had betrayed his vision by affirming the status quo. Brooks insisted that ". . . affirmation, in the most real sense, proceeds to a certain extent through rejection. . . ." Here was the critical program for Brooks's generation: "In some way — and primarily. . . by adding intellect to emotion — the social ideal the raw materials of which have been provided by Whitman must be formulated and driven home." The Whitmanian social ideal could only be purified of its dross by subjecting it to the scrutiny of ideas. In other words, the intellect of Wells must be added to the spirit of Whitman. The question was how this cultural revolution could be initiated by the stunted souls of America. "How can one speak of progress in a people like our own that so sends up to heaven the stench of atrophied personality?"[55]

The answer lay in the art of society: "Issues which really make the life of a society . . . have almost to be created like works of art." This was the first task for American thinkers, an incomparably difficult task, "Like standing on clouds and attempting to gain purchase for a lever," but once it was accomplished the other arts would have a "resisting background" to brace their feet against. Creating this resisting background was the work for a great man, an American artist, a prophet or messiah, and Van Wyck asked, ". . . how shall we know him when he comes?" He humbly advised his readers that he and they could only prepare their hearts by abandoning Yankee individualism, by working together, and by prostrating themselves before ideal standards.[56]

But despite the humble tone, Van Wyck's aspirations were becoming messianic. He was not certain that he was not the "man out of ninety million" who "can throw American life into relief." There was a personal significance to his saying that the greatest poets "see life as a fable," for the book's working title was *A Fable for Yankees.* He too was a fabulist, a great poet, and even when Ben Huebsch persuaded him the next year to change the title because there was nothing fabulous about the book, he still closed it like a fable: "THE END."[57] Van Wyck was practicing the art of society, creating the issues which revivify a people, by pointing out the schism in America between culture and reality, between highbrow and lowbrow.

His delight in the discovery and practice of a prophetic role for himself accounted for the triumphant tone of *America's Coming-of-Age,* which contrasted strongly with the despair of *The Wine of the Puritans.* However much the two books agreed in their dim view of the American past, *America's Coming-of-Age* offered a hopeful future, and that change explained not only the confident, flowing style but also the fact that, unlike the earlier book, this one found readers outside Harvard Yard. Men like Sherwood Anderson, Randolph Bourne, and Waldo Frank would look to Brooks for leadership because this book seemed to give evidence of a bold personality in touch with itself. *America's Coming-of-Age,* unlike *The Wine of the Puritans,* had no obscuring dialogue to blur Brooks's relationship to the narrative persona. The book's personal tone made it clear that this confident new artist of society was Van Wyck Brooks. The book was to be a liberating experience for its readers because writing it had been a liberating experience for Van Wyck. He had even managed an indirect attack upon his mother by associating America's irrelevant culture with women in the book's closing, prophetic passage:

When the women of America have gathered together all the culture in the world there is — who knows? — perhaps the dry old Yankee stock will begin to stir and send forth shoots and burst into a storm of blossoms. Strange things happen. I have heard of seeds which, either planted too deep or covered with accretions of rubble, have kept themselves alive for generations until by chance they have been turned up once more to the friendly sun. And after all humanity is older than Puritanism.[58]

Yet one must wonder if, beneath his delight in his newfound role of prophet, Van Wyck did not have doubts about the art of society. The object of this art was to make America come of age, to make it repeat the life history of European nations by creating a "national culture" in which "everything admirably characteristic of a people sums itself up, which creates everywhere a kind of spiritual teamwork, which radiates outward and articulates the entire living fabric of a race."[59] Was it possible to create such cohesion in America? Indeed, was it possible any longer in modern Europe? Thanks to H. G. Wells, Van Wyck had finally begun to recognize that industrialism threatened the life of the spirit, of instinct, even in Europe, and hence it was necessary everywhere to reconstitute life on the "plane of ideas." Brooks as self-conscious American critic seemed well situated for such a task, but precisely for that reason did it not constitute a surrender to the very intellectualism that had previously troubled him in American life? It had always been the emotiveness of art that had attracted him. He was not temperamentally suited for an art that required him to affirm through rejection and add "intellect to emotion." Was he not willfully convincing himself that he had found the art he wanted just as he suggested that socialists could recover a spiritual, instinctual basis for life by willfully, consciously submitting to the inevitable dominance of the social organism? "There is a free will within determinism by which, as it were, men can cheat nature, convincing themselves — and with a whole heart — that what nature wills is what they will: and if they will it enough, which is master of the situation?"[60]

Van Wyck would strongly exercise his will as he tried to muster the energy and intensity necessary for the task he had set himself. To attempt to embrace American society with a reach as broad as Whitman's was challenge enough, but to attempt also to give it direction with an intelligence as selective as Wells's was daring, prideful, and possibly tragic. Although Whitmanian expansion and Wellsian precision were supposed to work to the same ideal end, they were opposing principles in practice. A critic would have to bear great tension if he wished to implement both principles simultaneously and yet maintain a proper balance between them. Which way lay the immediate danger for Van Wyck? Toward an uncritical affirmation or toward too conscious a rejection of much in American life? Early in his book he had written of the importance of realizing that Lowbrow had as much to teach Highbrow as vice versa, or, as he had learned from Lippmann, "that Tammany has quite as much to teach Good Government as Good Government has to teach Tammany. . . ."[61] The question, then, was whether or not a critic of such high culture and conscious moral purpose as he would realize how much an artist with lowbrow origins — say, for instance, Mark Twain — could teach him about America.

5

BEGINNING LOW

IT had been almost four years since Van Wyck had been in the New York area for any substantial period of time, and he had missed much — the social and sexual experimentation in Greenwich Village, Mabel Dodge's evenings, John Reed's Patterson Pageant, the Armory Show, the opening of Stieglitz's gallery at 291 Fifth Avenue, the political insurgency of Max Eastman and the *Masses* — all, in fact, of the prewar "innocent" rebellion with its hopeful fervor. With his basically conservative nature, he would have been appalled by much of the New York cultural rebellion if he had been there to see it. But he had not been there, and upon his return in the fall of 1914 he settled for the coming winter not in New York but in Plainfield. From a distance, he too could take hope from the New York scene. Only gradually would he be drawn into the ferment and disabused of the illusion that his own aspirations were consistent with developments there.

The expected position with the *New Republic* failed to materialize, so he settled instead for a job reading and editing manuscripts for the Century Company. He ghostwrote the memoirs of Iliodor, the mad monk of Russia, and he met, as he told Eleanor, "another Har Dayal" — Miroslav Sichinsky, a political refugee who had assassinated the Polish governor of Galicia in 1908. Sichinsky became a good friend, and Van Wyck edited, "out of love for the cause," a book on the Galician struggle for independence. But these were highlights of his experience with the Century Company, which he generally found hopelessly becalmed in the genteel culture of the Gilded Age. Ancient, gentlemanly authors drifted in and out of the office, reminding him of his scorn for Howells and the generation Howells represented.[1]

Van Wyck himself seemed trapped in the Gilded Age, living in Plainfield and commuting by train to a job he detested in New York — an existence too much like his father's for comfort. His mind turned back fifteen years to his adolescence and the introversion into which he had withdrawn lest he too be sucked into the maelstrom of business that had killed his father. In Plainfield now he observed his father's friends in their retirement, happier as wood carvers and amateur photographers than in the businesses to which they had given their lives, and he felt that he could not escape fast enough to the practice of his own art, the art of society.[2]

He began by finding a publisher, Ben Huebsch, for *America's Coming-of-Age.* (Mitchell Kennerley had dealt shabbily with him and others, including Lippmann, in the matter of royalties, and Van Wyck would not receive fair treatment for his earlier books till he eventually had his brother Ames threaten a lawsuit.) During his spare time away from the Century Company, Van Wyck worked on the manuscript, trying at Huebsch's insistence to think of a more suitable title than *A Fable for Yankees* and softening somewhat, at Eleanor's suggestion, his treatment of Emerson and Gerald Stanley Lee.[3] Finally, he settled on the title *America's Coming-of-Age* and submitted the manuscript to Huebsch for publication in the fall of 1915.

Meanwhile, he escaped from Plainfield to a rented room in New York for July and August of 1915, while Eleanor took Charles, then three years old, to the Stimson family estate at East Hampton. Not wishing to return to Plainfield, Van Wyck began to look at houses for rent in the city but could not afford the required seventy dollars a month.[4] Eleanor was pregnant again, and they needed space. They finally settled that fall in a small apartment on 118th Street, near Columbia University. Their second son, Oliver Kenyon Brooks, was born there the next January.

Always, it seemed, there was not enough money. By May of 1916 when he received his first royalties from *America's Coming-of-Age,* the book had sold 478 copies at a dollar each. His ten per cent royalty had netted him thus far $47.80 for his year of hard work.[5]

If the book did not bring gold, it at least brought controversy. Though the reviews of his other books had been variously friendly or hostile, they had not divided along party lines. But *America's Coming-of-Age* offended precisely the two groups it attacked, the highbrows and lowbrows. Representative of high ideals was Stuart Sherman, who wrote in the *Nation* that Brooks had ignored "the great conflict of ideals with practice which made a new nation." By invoking the names of Emerson and Lowell "without evoking the historical circumstances in which they worked, [Brooks] creates frequently a false impression of their detachment and ineffectiveness." Meanwhile, Horace Traubel objected to Van Wyck's assertion that the Whitmanians had apotheosized the lowbrow by formulating "spurious social ideals" from Whitman's materials. Brooks feared "the crowd," said Traubel, but "America will come of age out of the crowd, . . . not as the gift of professors of colleges or of any of the cloistered influences of progress."[6]

Van Wyck was left with a small appreciative audience of "Young Intellectuals," as they would sometimes be called, who agreed with him that culture should be related critically to life. Carl Van Doren encountered *America's Coming-of-Age* on the shelf of new accessions at the Columbia University library, turned the pages tentatively at first, and then excitedly read the entire book, standing all the while beside the shelf where he had found it. Over the next few years *America's Coming-of-Age* would have a powerful effect of liberation on men like Sherwood Anderson, Lewis Mumford, Paul Rosenfeld, and Randolph Bourne. This small but intelligent audience admired and supported Brooks and with their large hopes drew from him some of his best writing. They too sought a new direction in American life and they looked to Brooks to help supply it, to be like H. G. Wells an artist of society seeking the right composition in things. When Waldo Frank wrote to enlist Brooks for the new magazine which he and James Oppenehim were planning, he called *America's Coming-of-Age* the "prologemena [*sic*] to our Future Seven Arts Magazine."[7]

Ben Huebsch had called Frank's and Oppenheim's attention to the book. After excitedly reading it, they called at the Century Company office, where they were surprised to find the creator of a book "luminous as flame" occupying a desk in a long room with an "amorphous mass" of humanity bent over typewriters. Neither did they find Brooks physically prepossessing when he had separated his compact frame from the crowd of office workers and "trotted" forward to meet them. But his eyes were "warm and shrewd," and the visitors liked his explanation of his humble position; having to work, he preferred a job without responsibilities so that he could reserve his thinking for his writing. They offered him a position on the advisory board of the *Seven Arts,* and he accepted.[8]

Oppenheim later wrote that Van Wyck soon had everyone on the *Seven Arts* "shadowing America," and indeed the magazine did seem inspired by Brooks's critical purpose. In the summer of 1916 Oppenheim and his associates had announced in a letter to American writers that they were founding a magazine because America was in a renascent period when the arts "become not only an expression of the national life but a means to its enhancement." The first issue, November 1916, carried a brief essay by Brooks and announced a larger piece the next month: "With Mr. Brooks, a creative power in criticism emerges: a wedge behind which the new forces in our arts may advance."[9] By March of 1917 Brooks had joined Frank as one of the magazine's two associate editors, just below Oppenheim on the masthead. Thanks to the *Seven Arts* he was able to quit the Century Company and devote himself almost full time to his writing.

Briefly liberated, Brooks began to practice the art of society and produced for the *Seven Arts* some of the finest cultural criticism ever written in America. Even the prospect of the magazine's appearance had exhilarated and convinced him that a "propitious"[10] moment was at hand, so from the outset his new mood was reflected in his writing. "Enterprise," published in the first issue, beautifully expressed his sense of the relation between the impoverished culture of modern, industrial America and the heritage of the pioneer by comparing a bleak Manhattan warehouse district to "the outskirts of some pioneer city on the plains of the Southwest, one of those half-built cities that sprawl out over the prairie, their long streets hectically alive in the centre but gradually shedding their population and the poor trees that mitigate the sun's glare till at last, all but obliterated in alkali dust and marked only by the chaotic litter of old out-buildings and broken-down fences that straggle beside them, they lose themselves in the sand and the silence." What a contrast to Europe, which was "alive in all its members"! But such scenes were only to be expected in a country where men, seeking only the main chance and conscious of the possibility of greater advantage elsewhere, invested no life in their surroundings. No wonder that old American things were old "as nothing else anywhere in the world is old," without majesty, mellowness, or pathos, "just shabby and bloodless and worn out." Americans had won a Pyrrhic victory over the wilderness, for nature "robbed and despoiled and wasted" would be left with no easy rewards to offer and would have her revenge on those who had not learned to cooperate with her. Meanwhile, the very barrenness of the American scene encouraged still more self-defeating enterprise: ". . . how all but irrevocably it commits us to a sharply individual, experimental existence!"[11]

The *Seven Arts* hoped to establish a common ground for artists, and with its first issue it seemed to have made a good start. In addition to articles by Brooks, Frank, and Oppenheim, there were contributions from Robert Frost, Amy Lowell, Paul Rosenfeld, Louise Driscoll, Romain Rolland, and Floyd Dell. Subsequent issues carried the work of Sherwood Anderson, Edna Kenton, Stephen Vincent Benét, Randolph Bourne, Leo Stein, Padraic Colum, Theodore Dreiser, D. H. Lawrence, Carl Sandburg, and Eugene O'Neill. As Brooks became acquainted with most of these writers and friendly with some, he had reason to feel that America was about to develop a literary community similar to the one he had admired in England.

His second *Seven Arts* essay, "Young America," expressed in typically organic metaphors his horror of not having such a community and of the consequent violence and chaos of American life, due primarily to competition and the law of the jungle, "the only mode of life our fathers knew." Americans were left

> cold and dumb in spirit, incoherent and uncohesive as between man and man, given to many devices, without community in aim or purpose.
>
> Thus it is that the fierce rudimentary mind of America, like that of some inchoate primeval monster, relentlessly concentrated in the appetite of the moment, knows nothing of its own vast, inert, nerveless body, encrusted with parasites and half indistinguishable from the slime in which it moves.

Yet he also felt that among the young, competition had lost the "leaven of spiritual conflict and adventure" that had once made it attractive. The young were experiencing a new sense of spiritual cooperation which indicated "some prodigious organism that lies undelivered in the midst of our society, an immense brotherhood of talents and capacities coming to a single birth."[12]

The time seemed right for cultural revolt, yet unlike many of his comrades on the magazine, Van Wyck was not sanguine of the outcome. His January 1917 essay "The Splinter of Ice" warned those who had taken hope from the mere coming into being of the *Seven Arts* to "recall how many are the lights that have misled our dawn."

Poe, Emerson, and Whitman had all been apostles of newness who appeared to have had no lasting impact on this side of the Atlantic. The American mind seemed proof against "incursions of [emotional] experience" as if, like the hero of Hans Anderson's "Snow Queen," it had a splinter of ice buried in it which "literature has never been able to melt." The reason proffered was that American writers had never been able to transcend their origins. Like their countrymen, they undervalued the life of the spirit and had "passively surrendered our human values at the demand of circumstances." American writers had gradually accepted their environment on its own terms, as in the realism of Howells where life was seen "not through the eyes of a free personality but of a certain social convention, at a certain epoch, in a certain place." It was apparent, then, that ". . . all the fresh enthusiasm in the world cannot produce an American literature." For a national literature to be created, America would have to be changed. Writers would have to practice the art of society and "create the life that literature springs from." Although he stridently called it "our categorical imperative" that they be able to do so, his confidence in American men of letters was never more than shaky.[13]

His lack of confidence in American writers may have arisen partly from his friendship with two of the *Seven Arts'* most prominent figures, Sherwood Anderson and Waldo Frank. Both men admired Brooks and wanted his respect, but there was an egoistic individualism in each of them which prevented Van Wyck from ever completely liking either man's fiction. Both became a little resentful of Brooks and his failure to appreciate what they considered their largest achievements. The problem was severest with Frank, who had a titanic ego and unconsciously adopted an air of superiority toward everyone. Van Wyck admired Frank's romantic insistence on a religion of the "whole" man but refused to acknowledge the regal claims of Frank's ego. He may have impaired their friendship as early as 1917, when he wrote an ostensibly friendly review of Frank's first novel, *The Unwelcome Man,* praising the novel's ideas but damning the experimental, subjective technique on which Frank prided himself.[14]

Van Wyck saw that Sherwood Anderson had larger gifts and admired some of his stories, but he viewed Anderson's career as an exercise in self-indulgence rather than an expression of a writer's proper sense of prophetic responsibility. His reaction may have been partly due to dislike of the sexual emphasis in Anderson's fiction, but he was silent on this point for the time being. Anderson had visited New York briefly in the winter of 1917 and been introduced in the *Seven Arts* office by Waldo Frank. Anxious to put down American roots, the alienated Eastern intellectuals of the *Seven Arts*, including even Brooks, felt "that the heart of America lay in the West; and Sherwood was the essence of his West." They flattered Anderson, who was glad of such attention even if it depended on his western specificity, and he returned the compliments in western lingo, writing to Frank that Brooks was "thundering along the right trail sure as hell" in his *Seven Arts* essays. Anderson liked Frank better but respected Brooks more, and he was hurt when Van Wyck catechized him about a writer's responsibilities. He wrote to Frank: "I see what Brooks meant when he suggested that I did not take letters seriously enough. I do not. He is right."[15]

In his March essay, "Toward a National Culture," Brooks returned to the problem of the "egocentric" individualism that made great American talents into mere cranks, albeit *"preëminent* cranks," like Thoreau or Henry George. Americans were especially prone to this crippling individualism because they lacked "a living culture, a complicated scheme of ideal objectives, upheld by society at large, enabling them to submerge their liberties in their loyalties and to unite in the task of building up a civilization." In the absence of such a culture, great artistic talents like Henry James were driven to seek it elsewhere, while those with lesser gifts of mind and spirit remained at home, palsied, sapless, and prematurely aged, as if in fact they had never been young. Men of action, on the other hand, never developed the wisdom of old men but simply became old boys, existing in later years on a mental and spiritual level "in no way deeper or richer than that of their own childhood. . . ." How monstrously impoverished American life was and how desperately in need of spiritual leadership! Yet individualism made those who needed leadership suspicious of it and those who could provide it reluctant to do so. Brooks hoped that the contemporary individualism of American writers was not born of a competitive spirit but was rather "only an inherited bad habit." If writers did not discover how much they had in common and also how much they commonly lacked, they would not lead the way in creating the necessary "program for the conservation of our spiritual resources," which was a national culture.[16]

In April Brooks argued that "The Culture of Industrialism" was no culture at all but merely the heritage of pioneer materialism. Lacking a culture to begin with, America offered the clearest view of the "externalizing," depersonalizing effects of industrialism. Not that Europe had been exempt from this process, but in Europe there had been resistance to industrialism because there "the great traditional culture, the culture that has ever held up the flame of the human spirit has never been gutted out." Meanwhile, the typical American plutocrat, having made his pile of money, faced a "blank within himself where a world of meanings ought to be." Searching for meaning, he naturally turned to culture, often to European culture, because he did not understand that culture must be organically related to the life it is to inform. His "industrial conception of culture" led him to assume that by the mechanical process of exposing himself to the best that has been thought and said, "the fact that life is a miraculous and beautiful thing can be somehow pumped into the middle of his soul." But the typical plutocrat was left restless and dissatisfied; highbrow culture in industrial America could reach no deeper than the upper level of the brain.[17]

Therefore, ". . . it is the real work of criticism in this country to begin *low*," to recognize the fact that the only organic literature being produced in America was being created by minds which, "artistically speaking, seem scarcely to have emerged from the protozoa." Brooks did not name names, but he may have meant Sherwood Anderson. In any case, a criticism that judged such writers by European standards only provided discouragement rather than, in Arnold's phrase, making a situation of which the creative power could profitably avail itself. While it was necessary to begin low, growth would quickly follow, for there was much in America so high it put heaven to shame and required nothing but a "center" around which to rally. "Then, and only then, shall we cease to be a blind, selfish, disorderly people; we shall become a luminous people, dwelling in the light and sharing our light."[18]

He continued to emphasize the need to begin low in his May essay, "Our Critics," in which he attacked Babbitt, More, Woodberry, Brownell, Spingarn, and Stuart Sherman for their "determination not to be practical," not to address themselves to the question of how literature could be related to life in America. How futile the "cosmopolitan eclecticism" that prompted Babbitt to try to import the principles of French criticism or Spingarn to bring in Croce. With their high classical standards they actually prevented literature from "coming into direct contact with a society whose acquisitive, non-creative programme it would immediately upset and destroy." They could only deplore the creative upsurge all about them, for, sharing the competitive, materialistic ethos of business society, they were not so much interested in fostering literature as in defending society from it. To prove the point Brooks had a damning quotation from Paul Elmer More: ". . . *the rights of property are more important than the right to life.*"[19]

But while it was necessary to begin low, one should not lose sight of the ideal, as had the sociologists, environmentalists, and "the pragmatic and realistic philosophers who stand behind them." Brooks's June essay, "Our Awakeners," attacked the pragmatists and social scientists who for twenty years had stood at the center of American life, claiming "that they alone apprehend reality," that they alone could do something with it. Properly, they should be judged by their fruits. What then was the nature of their creation? A society "sultry, flaccid, hesitant," acquisitive, restless, joyless, fearful, and hate-ridden. The problem was that pragmatism had tried to fill the vacancy created by the absence of meaningful culture and literature in America. Not content with remaining a method, pragmatism had attempted to fill the place of poetry, that is, "to formulate the aims of life and the values by which those aims are tested."[20] But pragmatism rested on intelligence, not on imagination, so while it had the merit of beginning low, it could not do what poetry should do — rise toward the ideal and drag mankind after. The great artist, Brooks had earlier written, measures reality not by its values but by the values that he has created out of the experience of his own "descent into the abyss of life." How weak by comparison the method of Dewey, who mistook efficiency for a stirring ideal when it was only an idea "in harmony with the existing fact."[21]

Again Brooks expressed his certainty that reform in America had to be cultural before it could be political. Without values to guide them, pragmatic social scientists would not attempt to formulate the conditions under which labor could be made a joyous activity but would continue instead to study methods of controlling fatigue. Unlike Wells and English liberals in general, American liberals did not wish to rationalize the place of machinery in life but only to make the machinery run smoothly. In the final analysis the pragmatists encouraged Americans to escape from reality, "to seek reality in anything else than their work — riding about the country in Ford cars, for example, with their mouths open. Such is the destiny of the working class, as our young pragmatic intellectuals see it. As to the middle class, they can in time, by consummating their freedom and capping it with control, attain the more discreet paradise that the Pierce-Arrow Company is at last able to place at their disposal." Pragmatism, rather than being an awakening or prophetic philosophy, was the dog in the manger of American creative life, the

traducing cur that "makes its bed where the winged horse of poetry
ought to lie."[22]

The thread running through all of Brooks's *Seven Arts* essays
was the need for cultural criticism so that American talent would not
be "seduced from its right path." Such criticism required the creation of a national culture or "objects of loyalty within the nation" to
serve as energizing, critical ideals.[23] Exactly what such objects of
loyalty would look like he had not been able to say; his work was
literally "toward" rather than suggestive of what would constitute a
national culture in America. He attributed his vagueness on the
point to the peculiar difficulty of the American problem; in Europe,
where literature was organically related to society, "a new movement
in order to get on its feet at all, has to overcome the inertia of the
established fact," so that by the time it reaches the point of articula-
tion it has passed through a "pre-natal" process of refinement and
emerges "fully conscious of itself."[24] In America, where there was no
"resistance," as he often said, new movements were not forced to
define themselves as they emerged: hence the vague "newness" of
the *Seven Arts* and hence also the importance of keeping the
magazine focused on the problem of culture until the new movement had established a sense of itself and its ideal goals. It was
precisely here that Brooks's lack of confidence in such American
literati as Frank and Oppenheim seemed justified, for before the
Seven Arts had come to stand for anything positive in American life,
they used the anti-war essays of Randolph Bourne to plunge the
magazine into politics, where it thrashed violently about and
drowned.

II

Few lives more significant can have had beginnings less auspicious
than the life of Randolph Bourne, who was born in Bloomfield, New
Jersey, in 1886 — the same state and year as Brooks. Forceps were
used in the delivery, and in the process one of the baby's ears was
mangled, the mouth torn, and the lower jaw permanently damaged.
Then, at four, Bourne contracted tuberculosis of the spine and was
left a hunchback and a dwarf for life. As a child his precocious
intelligence was recognized, but like Brooks he was left cold and
unmoved by his early education. Bourne's father, like Brooks's, was
a failure, and when Randolph graduated from high school there was
not enough money to send him to Princeton, where he had been
accepted.

While his contemporaries were at college, Bourne earned a living through his facility at the piano — giving lessons, playing at vaudeville shows and silent movies, and making perforated sheets for the player pianos which were coming into vogue. On this last job he mastered the rudiments of capitalism — for every twelve inches of perforations he earned a nickel until his speed improved and then his pay was cut to four and a half cents. It was no wonder that a few years later at Columbia he championed the cause of scrub-women against the university.

Incredibly, Bourne's spirit was not broken, and at twenty-three, with a vague desire to write, he had saved enough money to enter Columbia University. Life opened there for him, but not immediately. Like Brooks he was disappointed with his literary studies at college and especially by the assumption of his teachers that literature was a thing over and done with. Like Miro in his "History of a Literary Radical," Bourne turned to "the teachers of history and philosophy" in order "to put literature into its proper place, making all 'culture' serve its apprenticeship for him as interpretation of things larger than itself, of the course of individual lives and the great tides of society." Franz Boas, Charles Beard, Frederick Wood-bridge, and especially John Dewey became his favorite teachers.[25]

After class, Bourne delighted in the company of his fellow undergraduates. He loved the discussions about William James and H. G. Wells, about G. Lowes Dickinson and Henri Bergson, which wore on far into the night, and he found friendship of a depth he had not imagined in childhood. A brilliant student, he became a recognized figure in the university and an editor of *Columbia Monthly.* When Professor Woodbridge was irritated by an *Atlantic Monthly* article attacking the younger generation, he suggested that Bourne write a reply, which he did; Woodbridge sent it to Ellery Sedgwick, the *Atlantic* editor, who published it. Before Bourne left college, he had become a regular contributor to the *Atlantic,* his essays passionately defending the young adults at Columbia who formed the warmest environment he had known. He declared, "To keep one's reactions warm and true, is to have found the secret of perpetual youth, and perpetual youth is salvation."[26] In 1913 the essays were collected into his first book, *Youth and Life,* and Bourne found himself a recognized "Young Intellectual" and cultural rebel.

Then he departed for Europe on a postgraduate fellowship awarded him by Columbia. Like Brooks he was impressed by the felicities of European culture and scarcely conscious of any disturbances below the surface till in Germany in 1914 he stood beneath the Kaiser's balcony and heard war declared. Fleeing home, he settled in Greenwich Village, where he was to live frenziedly for the next four years, moving constantly from one apartment to another, conducting experimental friendships with women, searching always for a girl who would not be repelled by his crippled body, and supporting himself solely by his pen.

Thanks partly to the influence of Ellery Sedgwick and Charles Beard, Bourne became a contributing editor to the *New Republic*. But he was soon dissatisfied with his "ornamental" role there. He had hoped to write on politics and the arts but instead was assigned to education because of his interest in Dewey, his former teacher, whom he called "the most significant thinker in America."[27] In 1915 the *New Republic* sent him to Indiana to report on the progressive school system there, and the result was five favorable articles and his second book, *The Gary Schools* (1916).

To Brooks later, Bourne seemed to have achieved the proper balance between cultural revolt and respect for what was useful in his heritage. A literary nationalist who objected to "Our Cultural Humility" in his *Atlantic* essay of 1914, Bourne was also, Brooks said, "intensely Anglo-Saxon." While both men revolted against the tradition of genteel anglophilia in which they had been raised, they nevertheless hoped to salvage something useful from their origins. This attitude was consistent with their respect for other cultures, and they both objected strenuously to any Americanism that meant simple assimilation of immigrants. In the *Seven Arts* Brooks denounced the pragmatic sociologists who failed to see the richness of immigrant cultures and sought "to 'lift' to the level of some ordinary American neighborhood . . . men and women who are often immeasurably above it in the scale of the spirit." He hoped, in fact, that immigrants, with their experience of living "poetically and creatively" in a meaningful culture, would help vitalize America. Still, by "American culture" Brooks more often than not meant Anglo-Saxon culture in America. His revolt against "Puritanism" was meant to transform Anglo-Saxon culture and make it relevant to the American scene, rather than displace it from its predominance. He was always vague on the constituent elements of a national culture in America, but he apparently saw the final product as a hybrid with the Anglo-Saxon root providing a primary stem on which immigrant cultures could "engraft" themselves.[28]

Bourne went farther than Brooks and actually articulated a national ideal, or rather a "trans-national" ideal for America. He had observed during the first two years of the war in Europe that it was the most established Americans who were arousing interventionist sentiments on behalf of the English, even while they suspected the neutrality of immigrants and German-Americans. Angrily, Bourne wrote that the "English-Americans" more than any others were enslaved to the will of their old country. This was in "Trans-National America," Bourne's brilliant *Atlantic Monthly* essay of 1916 in which he questioned the American ideal of the melting pot. It was true, this fact which gave anguish to the establishment, that the immigrants were not assimilating into the Anglo-Saxon cultural tradition. Nor should they, said Bourne, as he urged on his readers "an investigation of what Americanism may rightly mean." To force an Anglo-Saxon tradition on people who did not value it would create anarchy rather than order: "Just so surely as we tend to disintegrate these nuclei of nationalistic culture do we tend to create hordes of men and women without a spiritual country, cultural outlaws, without taste, without standards but those of the mob." It was given to America to have not the narrow and intensely nationalistic spirit of a European culture but rather the "more adventurous ideal" of a cosmopolitanism that would make her "the first international nation." The question of the war in Europe was unmentioned but apparent as Bourne wrote that "America is already the world-federation in miniature, the continent where for the first time in history has been achieved that miracle of hope, the peaceful living side by side, with character substantially preserved, of the most heterogeneous peoples under the sun. Nowhere else has such contiguity been anything but the breeder of misery."[29]

Van Wyck had met Bourne in 1914, not long after both men had returned, dazed, from Europe at war, but the friendship developed slowly and was not of large importance to either of them until the summer of 1917, after Bourne had begun to write for the *Seven Arts*. While at the Century Company, Brooks had tried unsuccessfully to get Bourne to write for *Century Magazine,* and it was he who introduced Bourne to Oppenheim in the spring of 1917. Oppenheim and Frank had printed an editorial in the very first issue of the *Seven Arts* praising Romain Rolland for his stance above the battle in Europe, and their opposition to American entry into the conflict was predictable. What had not been predictable was that Oppenheim, who wrote most of the magazine's editorials in his posturing and sentimental prose, would find a writer more talented than himself to express his position. Thanks to Brooks he had, and the result was Bourne's now classic series of anti-war essays.

Bourne had been frustrated on the *New Republic;* the large national issues about which he would have liked to write were reserved for Croly, Lippmann, and Weyl, and he had no influence on editorial policy. Abhorring violence and having declared himself a pacifist at the outbreak of the war in 1914, he had watched helplessly in 1916 as the *New Republic* steered toward an anti-German, pro-war position. His disgust with the magazine mounted to rage after the American declaration of war. In April 1917, the *New Republic* attacked the pacifists' idea that the country had been led into war by munitions makers. Rather, "The effective and decisive work on behalf of the war has been accomplished by an entirely different class — . . . the 'intellectuals.' " The editorial contended that for the first time in history a nation had chosen to fight a war "under the influence of ideas rather than immediate interests."[30]

Hence the title of Bourne's ironic and mocking contribution to the June *Seven Arts,* "The War and the Intellectuals": "They [the intellectuals] are now complacently asserting that it was they who effectively willed it, against the hestitation and dim perceptions of the American democratic masses. A war made deliberately by the intellectuals! . . . An intellectual class gently guiding a nation through sheer force of ideas into what the other nations entered only through predatory craft or popular hysteria or militarist madness!" Objecting harshly to the idea of the "realists" that the war would necessitate a restructuring of society which might be influenced toward liberal ends, Bourne scored tellingly on Lippmann: ". . . how soon their 'mastery' becomes 'drift,' tangled in the fatal drive toward victory as its own end, how soon they become mere agents, and expositors of forces as they are."[31] Except for a few reviews the *New Republic* had no use for Bourne's services from the middle of 1917 on. But for five heroic months, through the summer and into the fall of 1917, Bourne poured his vitriolic opposition to the war into the pages of the *Seven Arts.*

Brooks opposed the magazine's anti-war position. He believed Germany a menacing force, and while America was still officially neutral, he had told Har Dayal that his own sympathies were with England and France. Eleanor was pro-war, writing to Van Wyck from California in July of 1917 that ". . . pacifists just now have something fatally wrong with either their intelligence or their natures." She added that David Starr Jordan was travelling all over the West urging young men to support the war effort. But added to all these reasons for his support of the war was Brooks's hope, much like that of the liberals whom Bourne criticized, that the war would accomplish a good purpose. Brooks's essay, "War's Heritage to Youth," would argue that cultural rebels should "take advantage of the present French alliance." Would not the average American be more easily reconciled to a restructuring of American life if he was shown "that the more closely he draws to any of the societies of Europe the more he will have to surrender the baser elements of his own Americanism?"[32]

Despite the violence and destruction of the war in Europe, Brooks still thought of European culture as the exemplary model for America, and he had cited it as such time after time in his *Seven Arts* essays. It was not that he wanted to imitate European art; it was the sterile derivativeness of American genteel culture which had made him a radical and a literary nationalist. He agreed with what Randolph Bourne had said in "Our Cultural Humility," that culture, like the kingdom of heaven, must be sought within. But for Brooks the result of that inner search was to be a national culture similar to those of Europe. Unlike Bourne, he could not envision a "trans-national" ideal, and for that reason, given America's ethnic pluralism, he had difficulty in getting down to specifics about what would constitute a national culture in America. Limited by the inapplicable model of Europe, he tried but could not imagine the actual shape of a relevant culture in America, however genuine and useful his insistence on the importance of having one. Beyond the cultural humility that made Americans imitative of European art, there was a subtler humility that made them think art could not live without a national culture corresponding to those of Europe. While Brooks had escaped the one humility, he had not escaped the other, as he would discover when he wrote of Henry James. In the complex of reason and emotion which led him finally to support the American war effort, there may have been the feeling, hidden even to himself, that if Europe was at war, America should be at war.

But in the *Seven Arts* office he argued more practically against Oppenheim and Frank, objecting to their anti-war position not because it was politically wrong but because it was political; they were turning the magazine away from cultural criticism, away from the art of society. Whether Bourne was right or not, opposing the war was as futile as opposing an earthquake — a meaningless gesture that would accomplish nothing but self-destruction. But he could never make these points forcefully enough. Except intellectually, Frank recalled in his memoirs, Brooks was a "timid" man who shrank from the loud arguments that characterized the *Seven Arts* office in its latter months. Van Wyck would close his door on the shouters and work on one of his essays, conscious perhaps that the days were numbered for the magazine where he had briefly found freedom to write. Frank would add in his memoirs that Brooks had been right and that he and Oppenheim had suffered from "the ego of the martyr" at a moment requiring "the shrewdness of the saint."[33]

While Brooks and Bourne were heading in opposite directions in their thinking on the war, they were becoming close friends. Although Bourne felt that Brooks had no head for politics, he found that Van Wyck had already known something which it had taken the war to demonstrate to him — the valuelessness and spiritual emptiness of pragmatism. Lippmann and the *New Republic* had gradually disappointed Brooks also, not by their pro-war position but by their emphasis on political realism rather than cultural reform. In a *Seven Arts* essay, he had scornfully insisted that the *New Republic*'s uncritical support of the war was no surpirse, for what could one expect from a realism in touch only with the "existing fact"?[34]

But Bourne had been surprised and stunned as Dewey, his admired former teacher, had moved toward a pro-war, anti-German position in a series of *New Republic* essays in 1916. When Dewey supported the American declaration of war, Bourne spoke bitterly in private of his mentor's "betrayal" and in the *Seven Arts* poignantly described his "sense of suddenly being left in the lurch, of suddenly finding that a philosophy upon which I had relied to carry us through no longer works." After Dewey had called the pacifists "opportunistic — breathlessly, frantically so" in the summer of 1917, Bourne tried to understand how a philosopher could be "so much more concerned over the excesses of the pacifists than over the excesses of military policy," and he found the answer in Brooks's essay, "Our Awakeners": "What is the matter with the philosophy? . . . Van Wyck Brooks has pointed out searchingly the lack of poetic vision in our pragmatist 'awakeners.' Is there something in these realistic attitudes that works actually against poetic vision, against concern for the quality of life as above the machinery of life? Apparently there is." Disagreement over the effect of the war was a minor issue between two men who agreed, as Brooks had said, that ". . . the really effective approach to life is the poetic approach."[35]

Van Wyck, disappointed at his loss of personal influence on the *Seven Arts*, began to consider resigning. He was certain that he could "advance" to a better job, having recently turned one down, in fact, with Ben Huebsch. And Max Perkins had implied that there might be a place for him at Scribner's. But these were office jobs and did not offer the freedom to write which he so enjoyed on the *Seven Arts.* He wrote to Eleanor that he wished he could earn a living solely by his pen so that he could join her in Carmel, where she had taken the children for a visit with her mother that summer. Sometimes, he said, he regretted having left Stanford. Eleanor, who believed that the *Seven Arts* had become a "baleful influence" because of its anti-war stance, urged him to quit, but he finally decided to give the magazine's anti-war policy a chance to die a "natural death." Bourne had told him that he had said his piece, and Van Wyck believed that Frank "will cool off when he finds that he is not drafted." The "volatile" Oppenheim was already working a different vein. Van Wyck was planning a vacation in New England with Bourne, and he decided to use the trip as a testing period. If his writing went well, "I may swing back into the magazine and the magazine may swing back to me."[36]

Although it did not result in the regaining of Brooks's lost influence on the *Seven Arts,* the visit to New England with Bourne was nevertheless profitable. The old houses and gracious expanses of Boston charmed Bourne, who in turn opened Van Wyck's eyes to the beauty of the city that had left him unimpressed as a Harvard undergraduate. He wrote to Eleanor that he was "amazed to find how enchanting the architecture was and what an air of grace and unity the city had," and he would eventually write glowingly of this American "culture city" in *The Flowering of New England.* He and Bourne continued their vacation by touring Cape Cod on foot, walking from Sandwich to Provincetown in three days. Here too Van Wyck profited from the intensity of Bourne's interest in every-thing along the way. Despite the constriction placed on his breathing by his humped back and narrow chest, Bourne kept up the pace with short quick steps and seemed, Van Wyck told Eleanor, "a triumph of mind over matter if there ever was one."[37]

They stayed in Provincetown for nine days, and Van Wyck, predictably, disliked the transplanted Greenwich Villagers there: "The men go about in corduroys & are good natured & futile. The women are all of an uncertain age & look as if they had been used by life. They have strange theatrical voices and are unnaturally natural. I never could get on with such people." He and Bourne stayed in the rooms they had rented, each trying to write an article for the *Seven Arts.* Van Wyck probably worked on "War's Heritage to Youth," which, after the collapse of the *Seven Arts,* would appear in the *Dial.* In the essay he took the opposite of Bourne's position, arguing that the war might be good for American culture, and he evidently found it hard going. Bourne wrote to Alyse Gregory that "Brooks is in the next room leading 'la vie litteraire' with many groans."[38]

Van Wyck did not recover his influence on the *Seven Arts*, and he suffered a deep depression in August after his return from New England. He moved out to Plainfield again, staying first with Max Perkins for two weeks, then a week at the Seminary, and finally moving in with his mother and step-father. Tormented by headaches and oppressed by the sense of failure and inadequacy which he usually experienced in times of transition and financial insecurity (and which was probably heightened by having to stay with his mother in Plainfield), he declared that he would never write again, and he finally decided to break with the *Seven Arts*. The decision made, he soon felt better, was ashamed of some letters he had written to Eleanor, and asked her to tear them up, as apparently she did.[39]

Brooks's resignation, along with quarrels and jealousy between Frank and Oppenheim, killed the *Seven Arts*. The wealthy woman who had provided Oppenheim with the money to found the magazine had announced that because of its opposition to the war she would not subsidize it beyond its first year. As the October issue, the twelfth number, went to press, there was a flurry of attempts to save the magazine, but no compromise could satisfy all parties. Scofield Thayer, Bourne's rich friend who later bought the *Dial*, was willing to provide financing if Oppenheim would give up his one-man rule in favor of an editorial board with Bourne on it. But Oppenheim was intent on retaining control, as Van Wyck explained to Eleanor:

> The last week at the *Seven Arts* has been a series of sensations. . . . James and Waldo quarrelled: and then, just as it was about to go under, each, separately, got enough money to continue it. But each insisted it could only go on without the other, and only if I would stay. . . . Bourne was quite willing to go on with it, but he refused to do so unless I did. . . . I should have preferred not to have the whole responsibility placed upon me. But really I had no confidence either in James or in Waldo, or at least in my capacity to work with them . . . and so I thought it best to refuse all round. Consequently, the *Seven Arts* passed out of existence. But Bourne and I now plan to start another magazine some time, which really will be what the *Seven Arts* ought to have been.[40]

In the final analysis it was the war which had destroyed the *Seven Arts,* where Brooks had found a livelihood and, for some months at least, the spiritual leadership of an intellectual community bent on giving direction and values to American life. The magazine's destruction was an omen of the lonely future which awaited Brooks in the intellectual climate of the postwar years, though he could not yet recognize that fact. In his essay, "War's Heritage to Youth," he implied that the war, by encouraging the development of a national (that is, organic) culture, might save the younger generation from "the creeping paralysis of the mechanistic view of life."[41] He could not have been more wrong. In the atmosphere of discouraged fatalism following the war there would be few who could share his belief that the artist's proper role was that of prophet and exemplar of the soul's free will.

III

Finding another position was not as easy as Van Wyck had expected, and at first he accepted work piecemeal, earning fifty dollars by editing a manuscript for Henry Holt. He soon regretted the casualness with which he had told Ben Huebsch in July not to save a place for him. Eleanor's mother suggested that he come to Carmel to live, but he refused just yet to depend on her. He wrote to Stanford, hoping that they would make an offer for the academic year which was just beginning. But nothing turned up except his old job at the Century Company, which he finally accepted at the end of September for twenty-five dollars a week, five dollars less than he had been earning there a year earlier.[42]

How "inept," he admitted to Eleanor, and how contradictory of his feeling that ". . . there must be some way of reaching out energetically & romantically and breaking this humdrum little circle of small things we have been living in." He had collected his *Seven Arts* essays for publication as a book, *Letters and Leadership* (1918), which would increase his reputation but bring in no money. Still, "I know that if I keep my writing steadily going the time will come when it will mean something practically as well as in other ways."[43] Such a time would come, and in 1917 it was only twenty years away.

He managed to write one more piece, "On Creating a Usable Past," which followed in the line of his *Seven Arts* essays by addressing itself to the problem of creating a national culture in America. How was this "travesty of a civilization" to achieve new ideals and finer attitudes except through its creative minds? Everything depended on encouraging them. Yet university professors wrote American literary history with a "pathological" desire to shame and subdue contemporary creative minds with the example of a superior, august past. The professors, with their institutional base, had an interest in the established fact which the new mood, with its anti-business bias, wished to destroy. The situation was different in Europe, where a "relatively free" criticism made a richer past readily available, not to shame but to encourage. What could be done with the American past to enrich and render it similarly useful? Brooks proposed: "If we need another past so badly, is it inconceivable that we might discover one, that we might even invent one? . . . The past is an inexhaustible storehouse of apt attitudes and adaptable ideals; it opens of itself at the touch of desire; it yields up now this treasure, now that, to anyone who comes to it armed with a capacity for personal choices."[44] This selective approach to the past was in keeping with the historical relativism then being argued by Beard and Robinson and also with the older examples of Carlyle, Michelet, and Motley, whom Brooks cited.

However, a selective treatment of the past implied that there were some good or useful things there to select, and Brooks could not actually see any bright spots in American history. The search which he proposed was not for previously hidden treasure — the few masterpieces, he said, were all too obvious — but for thwarted talents. A history of the creative impulse could only reveal "the appalling obstacles" to the life of the spirit in America. Criticism should search out and remove "obstructions" to the full realization of personality, as he had argued in *The Malady of the Ideal*. The real question for an American historian was "What became of Herman Melville?" or, though he did not say it, what had been the nature of Mark Twain's inner life? Brooks realized that this search for the negative forces in American life was not consistent with his plea for an exemplary, inspiring treatment of the past, and he answered weakly that the search he proposed would also reveal that ". . . time has begun to face these obstacles down."[45] In this way he revealed that he could not imagine anything useful to know about American history, and especially the Gilded Age in which he had his own origins, except that its evil was ending. The book which he had decided to write on Mark Twain could only be negative, a discouragement rather than an inspiration to American writers.

The year 1918 was a dreary and unproductive one for Brooks.

There had been much interest in Mark Twain in the *Seven Arts* office, stimulated in part by posthumous publication of *The Mysterious Stranger* in 1916, and Van Wyck had decided to write a book on Twain as the beginning of his search for a usable past. But he made little progress because of the demands of his job and family, who had returned from California in the fall of 1917. At the Century Company he edited a book of Louis Raemaeker's cartoons, *America in the War,* which caricatured German brutality, depicted the Kaiser being hung, and attacked the enemy within by showing a rat marked "Pacifism" tearing open a bag of "Soldiers' Food." When he finished laboring over such material, he went to lunch or tea with Randolph Bourne, who about this time told his mother, ". . . of all my men friends I like and admire him [Brooks] the most. . . ." Though they saw each other often, they had begun to write letters to each other on the subject of "creating a new literary leadership" with the idea of making a book of the correspondence.[46] But only a few letters got written.

Thanks to Bourne, Brooks had his first public skirmish with the avant-garde sensibility that was to dominate the postwar years. Bourne's 1918 *Dial* essay, "Traps for the Unwary," had deplored "the vogue of the little theatres and the little magazines" and had called for a "criticism that will discriminate between what is fresh, sincere, and creative and what is merely stagy and blatantly rebellious." Harriet Monroe replied angrily in a *Poetry* editorial that the little magazines published criticism as well as poetry; furthermore, by providing an audience and a sustenance for the poet, the little magazines were doing more to improve the quality of poetry than any critic could hope to do. Brooks and Bourne co-authored a reply saying that by "criticism" they meant "discussion of a larger scope" than the assessments of technical merit which *Poetry* usually printed. If poetry was not related to the social and intellectual movements of the day, it would be driven "into futility and empty verbalism." The artist could profit from the hospitality of the little magazines, but he required even more "the spur . . . of a criticism that aims at carrying the fresh and creative expression of the present towards a greater wisdom and clarity and ardor of life."[47]

Agreeing on the need to combine "ardor for life" with responsibility, the two men leaned in opposite directions — Bourne toward ardor, Brooks toward responsibility — and yet each was attracted by the lifestyle of the other. Van Wyck with his family responsibilities envied the freedom of the single Bourne, who once defended his Bohemian existence to his mother by telling her that Brooks "has been tied to a desk in the Century Co., and he looks on me as one who leads the ideal, free, dignified, leisurely life of a true man of letters, making my living by my pen with no sordid job to hold down. So, when you think I ought to have a job, remember that I am admired just because I haven't one." Bourne, on the other hand, was often lonely and envied Van Wyck his domesticity. He spent a few weeks in the summer of 1918 with the Brooks family in a rented house at Sound Beach, Connecticut, paying for his board by typing the manuscript of a French novel that Eleanor was translating. He had hardly left before he was dreading "melancholy" and hinting for another invitation: "I wonder if you have the place or desire for me again" closing his letter with the hope that he had not got on Eleanor's nerves. Eleanor probably sensed and resented Van Wyck's envy of Bourne's free-spirited existence, but she need not have worried. Beneath his craving for freedom from responsibility, Van Wyck desired the comforts of a bourgeois household at least as much as she did. In 1917 when Bourne had suggested living together with the Brookses in a California shack, Van Wyck had reassured Eleanor, ". . . the irresponsible life is not for us."[48]

Van Wyck finally purchased his freedom in the fall of 1918 by taking his family to Carmel to live, not in a shack , but in the house of his mother-in-law. Eleanor had begun to earn some money by translating French novels, so they would have an income while Van Wyck wrote his book on Mark Twain. Exhilarated by his freedom from the Century office and the frenetic pace of New York, Brooks told Waldo Frank just after arriving in California that he could not describe the "sense of simplification that has come over me here." He added, "I find myself more confident at once."[49]

His confidence rapidly evaporated as he worked fitfully on the book in late 1918 and early 1919, trying to decide on the best form and abandoning it for days at a time to help Eleanor with the five French novels she would translate during their first ten months in California. He had not planned to write a biography, but in February, after four months of casting about for the right form, he decided that it was his only choice. It was a shock, he told Frank, "and all my confidence deserted me." He wrote to his mother in March that he was "frightened to death for fear it isn't coming out right" and that he was having "ridiculous ups and downs."[50]

In fact, he was entering the cycle of depression and alternating mania which would characterize his life for the next decade. The severe depressions of his adolescence and frequent bad moods since then had not been disabling, but in middle life the depressions would increase gradually in depth and length till the late 1920's, when writing would become impossible rather than, as now, difficult.

Depressed by the "giddy" Bohemianism and futile atmosphere of Carmel, Van Wyck rapidly regained his old "chilly fear" of the West and his "craving for the East, ever more Eastern!" California still suggested another world, but Carmel, unlike San Francisco and Palo Alto, was a nether world. Madmen seemed to be all about, ranging in type from the harmless old journalist who spoke nightly with the people of Mars to the fantastic ethnologist, Jaime de Angulo, who boxed with his pet stallion and went about bearded and ragged with a great knife at his waist. At Point Lobos, where Nora French had leaped to her death, Brooks saw the poet George Sterling, also to be a suicide, "who had precisely the aspect of Dante in hell." In his memoirs Brooks described himself in Carmel feeling often "that I was immobilized, living as if in a fresco of Puvis de Chavannes. . . ." Hearing in the winter of 1919 that Waldo Frank was thinking of settling in the Middle West to farm and get close to the soil, Van Wyck wrote to warn him that the future of America would come out of "the slow and patient processes of a few minds" but never out of the West. By May he could be more specific as he explained to Frank why Carmel was not a fit place to live:

> People relapse here. . . . They talk about Kipling and Stevenson — you have no idea, or perhaps you have, how little the ideas of the last twenty years have penetrated across this continent. . . . all our will-to-live as writers comes to us, or rather stays with us, through our intercourse with Europe. Never believe people who talk to you about the West, Waldo; never forget that it is we New Yorkers and New Englanders who have the monopoly of whatever oxygen there is in the American continent! Art is a property of Asia, just as religion is a property of Asia: we shall have it here some day but we shall never interpret America except through a conception of the literary life we can only gain by our contact with Europe.[51]

Adding to Brooks's tension was the new experience of having a public, a demanding public as he was beginning to learn. He had been an obscure, almost anonymous figure while writing his previous books, but now, thanks to *America's Coming-of-Age* and the *Seven Arts,* there were readers waiting eagerly. What they sought was what he said he sought, not merely negative criticism of America but rather an art of society that offered a positive new direction toward the right composition of things. Waldo Frank described Brooks in *Our America* (1919) as not a scholar merely but a "brother to the poet," helping to create a new "consciousness of American life . . . in which all life shall enter, and which shall have no end save to bring all life to its fruition." Van Wyck answered in a letter, "Waldo, . . . you have spoken the truth — not the truth about what I am, what I have done, but the truth of my desire." Yet desire was one thing, accomplishment another, and Frank had expressed disappointment once already when he reviewed the collected *Seven Arts* essays, *Letters and Leadership,* in 1918, and called the volume "not so much a finished work as the preface to a book." Brooks himself had opened the book with the remark that it was "all too largely negative," hoping that his readers would find "between the lines certain suggestions of a programme for the future." His old friend Francis Hackett, finding nothing of the sort, wrote that although Brooks was distinguished and elevated by his "passion for a collective understanding of national life," he had "no definite program for a new life. . . . His book is not rounded. It is partial, inadequate, even harsh."[52]

There was an eager, expectant audience for the study of Mark Twain, but Van Wyck was not writing the book his audience wanted to read. Sherwood Anderson, who respected Brooks's mind "more than any other mind in America," as he told Hart Crane, looked forward eagerly to the book, in which he expected to find sordid "muck" and "ugliness" around Twain but above this ugliness a triumphant, positive portrait of the artist. But Van Wyck was finding only a negative use for Mark Twain, a cautionary warning of the pitfalls for the artist in America. Possibly sensing this tendency, Anderson had written to him in 1918 of "a growing desire I have to sell you Mark Twain." Similarly, Randolph Bourne, apparently aware of the distinction Brooks would make in criticizing Twain for having been a humorist rather than a satirist, had cautioned that parts of *The Mysterious Stranger* were "as blinding satire on the human comedy as anything Swift ever wrote. . . ." Like Anderson, Bourne also had expected a positive portrait of Twain and had written in his "History of a Literary Radical" that it was necessary "to do what Van Wyck Brooks calls 'inventing a usable past.' . . . the new classicist will yet rescue Thoreau and Whitman and Mark Twain and try to tap through them a certain eternal human tradition of abounding vitality and moral freedom, and so build out the future."[53] But Bourne was far ahead of Brooks in his "new classicism," and it would be years yet before Van Wyck would find anything in the American past on which the future could build.

Bourne, the one person who might have convinced Brooks to take a more positive attitude toward Mark Twain, died in the influenza epidemic of 1918, not long after Van Wyck left for California. Contrary to legend, he did not starve to death because of his opposition to the war; a few magazines continued to employ him as a reviewer, and he had eight hundred dollars in the bank when he died. In fact the last month of his life may have been his happiest time. The war he hated was over, and he had fallen in love with a woman who agreed to marry him. But then he contracted the dangerously strong new strain of influenza which was probably brought into the country by soldiers returning from the war. With his narrow chest he knew from the outset that he was in grave danger, and he had time to appoint Brooks his literary executor before he died at the age of thirty-two on December 22, 1918.

James Oppenheim packed Bourne's papers together and shipped them to Carmel, where Van Wyck, striking a snag in his writing on Mark Twain in the spring of 1919, edited the posthumous *History of a Literary Radical*, published by Huebsch the next year. To the astonishment of Oppenheim and others of Bourne's friends, Brooks left out of the collection several political essays, including the unfinished fragment "The State," where Bourne had called war "the health of the state." In protest, Oppenheim began to collect the anti-war pieces for publication as Bourne's *Untimely Papers* (1919). But Brooks told Waldo Frank that he had never been more certain of a critical decision. Bourne's primary function had been spiritual, and his political essays were "incredibly below the level of his best and quite ephemeral."[54]

Underlying this difference of opinion was Brooks's projection onto Bourne of his own desires, a projection encouraged by the responsibility of literary executorship — one of the great rituals of the nineteenth-century man of letters, the role that gripped Van Wyck's imagination. He had often before imagined himself as literary executor for his own dead self, or rather a surrogate self like Charles Graeling, so that without egotism he could explain himself to family, friends, and contemporaries. Now he did actually stand in that relationship to a deceased friend, and it was almost habit for him to make Bourne into an *alter ego*. What Bourne had really desired, Brooks wrote in his introduction to *The History of a Literary*

Radical, was to create "out of the blind chaos of American society, a fine, free, articulate cultural order." Bourne had opposed the war out of his conviction that it would check and thwart the cultural concerns "in which he had invested the whole passion of his life." In his political essays he had resembled a great medical specialist practicing general surgery on a battlefield, accomplishing much good but wasting his special powers. So Van Wyck liked to think that if Bourne had lived he would have returned after the war to his "more purely cultural interests" and helped to create the bright future of which he was a symbol, "the new America incarnate."[55]

Yet Bourne had had a different idea of the future than Brooks, as was evident from Van Wyck's misreading of "Trans-National America." He saw Bourne's essay as a plea for a "super-culture," an American national culture transcending ethnic loyalties, when in fact Bourne had asked for no more than cultural tolerance and co-existence. Bourne was prepared to live with a "cultural order" considerably less ordered than the one Brooks desired. Despite their common dislike of mechanistic attitudes and their agreement on the need for values, Brooks might have found Bourne a different sort of figure in the postwar world than he imagined. To Brooks the American future still included a coming-of-age into a national culture like those of nineteenth-century Europe, where a man like Bourne could have revived "the lapsed rôle of the man of letters."[56]

But beside this tendency to project his own hopes onto Bourne, Van Wyck did reveal also a friend's understanding. Bourne had been forced to develop a hard shell in order to live so full a life in a cripple's body, and Van Wyck insisted that those who had found him bitter and malicious had failed to realize "how instinctively we impute these qualities to the physically deformed who are so dauntless in spirit that they repel our pity." He saw also that Bourne's physical disability had made him as "detached as any young East Sider from the herd-unity of American life," and had given him freedom from concern for the money-oriented values of the dominant WASP culture toward which Van Wyck himself would always have ambivalent feelings. Hence Van Wyck's feeling that Bourne more than himself had been a dreamer, a prophet, a "spirit that creates out of the void the thing it contemplates." The essence of Bourne's personality was revealed in his frequent, half-conscious recurrence to the word "wistful," "that secret signature, sown like some beautiful wild flower over the meadow of his writing, which no man can counterfeit, which is indeed the token of their inviolable sincerity. He was a wanderer, the child of some nation yet unborn, smitten with an inappeasable nostalgia for the Beloved Community on the far side of socialism. . . ."[57]

Spurred on by ambiguous motives, on the one hand his inspiring farewell image of Bourne and on the other his hope that his book on Mark Twain would be a best seller and earn him some money for once, Van Wyck returned to his own work in the late spring with renewed energy. E. P. Dutton and Company, for whom he and Eleanor were doing a translation, offered a five hundred dollar advance when they heard of the Twain project, and Brooks accepted with alacrity, necessitating a painful letter of explanation to Ben Huebsch, who had done so much for him and who had expected to publish the book: "I think you know how exceedingly important the question of money has become with me. . . ." This difficulty resolved, he worked furiously through the summer and wrote to Waldo Frank at the beginning of the autumn: "I had an extraordinary rebirth after weeks of a vague insanity. 'The Ordeal of Mark Twain' — as I call it — began to come with a rush. . . . He was born like . . . Minerva out of the hand of Jove! fully formed. In short, I've written the book I dreamed of, a book more tragic than I had dreamed of: and for the first time I have put away a piece of work feeling that it is finished. . . ."[58]

IV

The Ordeal of Mark Twain began with the much-needed assertion that "Mark Twain's Despair" was deeply felt and not, as many liked to think, the amusing cantankerousness of a loveable and essentially happy old man. The assertion was a necessary prelude to the book, justifying Brooks's idea that Mark Twain had suffered an ordeal. Twain's tragedy had been that the dominant American values of success and pursuit of the cash nexus had frustrated his great gift, his "endowment more extraordinary than that of any other American writer." It was an unusual tribute to Mark Twain even to take him so seriously, more seriously than Stuart Sherman had with his faint praise that, against complaints "that our soil lacks the humanity essential to great literature, we are grateful even for the firing of a national joke heard round the world." Yet in emphasizing the tragedy of Mark Twain's frustrated talent, Brooks was led to estimate Twain's writing as a mere glimpse of an unfulfilled potential. *Huckleberry Finn* and *Tom Sawyer* were his finest works, but Brooks quoted, with approval, Arnold Bennett's judgment that while those books were "episodically magnificent, as complete works of art they are of quite inferior quality."[59]

Twain's ordeal was not due to any outward misfortune but was rather a spiritual difficulty: ". . . it was some deep malady of the soul that afflicted Mark Twain, a malady common to many Americans, perhaps." Here Brooks made his customary point as to the materialism of the Gilded Age being the heritage of life on the frontier, "the barrennest spot in all Christendom, surely, for the seed of genius to fall in." To a pioneer society, safety lay in numbers, in "the integrity of what is called the herd." Hence the "creative spirit" had to be "repressed," for its whole tendency was "skeptical, critical, realistic, disruptive." Therefore in the Gilded Age ". . . a vast unconscious conspiracy actuated all America against the creative spirit." All Americans, living in the materialistic society that the pioneers had built, knew something of Mark Twain's spiritual problem. But it was worse for Twain himself, who had a larger spirit than most and who was actually raised on the frontier.[60]

Yet his harsh environment did not absolve Mark Twain from personal responsibility for the betrayal of his creative instinct. Twain understood his great artistic power well enough to have faced up to its accompanying obligations if only he had mustered the courage. Otherwise, said Brooks in a passage that incidentally revealed how humorlessly and tendentiously he could read his evidence, one could not explain Twain's conundrum: "Why am I like the Pacific Ocean? I don't know. I was just asking for information." The joke would not have occurred to him if he "had not had a certain sense of colossal force." But on the other hand, if he had been "in control" of that force it would have resulted in more than a humorous remark: "Men who are not only great in energy but masters of themselves let their work speak for them." Thus, while Brooks criticized the Gilded Age which crippled Mark Twain, he condemned Twain also for not resisting the infectious money lust of the era. Twain was partly responsible for his "disintegration of the spirit" in the gold fields of Nevada, for acting "exactly as if his literary life were indeed a business enterprise," and for his "moral surrender."[61]

Brooks went on to interpret Twain's humor as a safety valve by which he had released his pent-up hatred of commercial society. It was for not having condemned that society in satire that Brooks in turn condemned Twain's art. Mark Twain had not fulfilled the role of the artist as prophet, had not denounced the evil society in which Brooks had spent his unhappy childhood. Twain had the qualities of a great satirist, "the kindest of hearts, the humanest of souls." If he had had a sense of artistic mission he would have avoided the compromise of being a humorist: ". . . his antagonism would have ultimately taken the form, not of humor, but of satire also." Mark Twain's humor subverted not only his own creative individualism but also the nation's. The humorous relief of psychic tension built up by the repression of individuality was as necessary to the businessman as to the pioneer. That was the secret of Mark Twain's popularity; his humor "contributed to the efficiency of the business régime."[62]

The repression of his creative spirit made Mark Twain angry, not only at others but at himself. His self-hatred was rooted in his sense of self-betrayal, which explained his opposition to the idea of free will, his analogies between men and machines, and his philosophizing about the "damned human race." Why would a creative mind have found satisfaction in denying the possibility of creation? Clearly, said Brooks, Twain had been searching for absolution of the sins he had committed against his creative spirit. If no one was free to create, then he had not been free to create: ". . . the poet, the artist in him, consequently, had withered into the cynic and the whole man had become a spiritual valetudinarian."[63]

None of this argument was dependent on the Freudian scheme in which it was couched. Yet one can see why Feudianism appealed to Brooks. He believed that criticism was the moral science of personality (even though by personality he meant the inner self or soul rather than the outward traits of behavior), and Freudianism was scientific. Furthermore, it could be applied to divided or split personalities — an attractive feature to Brooks, who had acquired a belief in the virtue of "wholeness" from the nineteenth-century romantics. Like most Americans in 1919, he did not know much of Freud, though he invoked the name along with those of Jung and Adler throughout the book. He had heard Freud discussed by the *Seven Arts* staff, especially by James Oppenheim, whose analyst, in fact, had first suggested the magazine's creation as a kind of therapy for Oppenheim. Brooks had at least seen Freud's name in print in Lippmann's *Preface to Politics,* and he had learned something of Freudianism from Bourne, who had read Adler in German as early as 1915. His main source, however, was Bernard Hart's eclectic book *The Psychology of Insanity* (1912), which accepted the idea of the unconscious but rejected Freud on sex.[64] Hart justified Brooks's substitution of the "creative instinct" for sex as the primal urge. Mark Twain's psyche was damaged by suppression of his desire to be an artist rather than by any sexual repression. What Brooks actually found useful in Freud and Hart was not so much method as moral support. They gave the prestige of science to discussion of the unconscious and thus licensed a critic like Brooks to speculate in an unprecedented way about the inner life of his subject.

But Brooks did take from Hart one piece of substantive information — the knowledge that "somnambulism" was a symptom of insanity and resulted sometimes in states of dissociation so extreme, Hart said, that they "are regarded as examples of 'Double Personality.'"[65] Using "somnambulism" to denote a state of waking autism rather than, literally, sleepwalking, Hart had given an example of a woman who had experienced traumatic shock at her mother's death and become a "somnambulist." Brooks, taking Hart's terminology literally, found what seemed to him a similar incident in Albert Bigelow Paine's authorized biography of Mark Twain. Paine recounted the story told by the aged Twain of how, as a boy, he had been grief-stricken at his father's death and of how his mother, seeing her refractory son so moved, led him into the room where his father's body lay and made him promise "to be a faithful and industrious man, and upright, like his father." Paine continued:

> That night — it was after the funeral — his tendency to somnambulism manifested itself. His mother and sister, who were sleeping together, saw the door open and a form in white enter. . . . They were terrified and covered their heads. . . . A thought struck Mrs. Clemens:
> "Sam!" she said.
> He answered, but he was sound asleep and fell to the floor. He had risen and thrown a sheet around him in his dreams. He walked in his sleep several nights in succession after that. Then he slept more soundly.[66]

Struck by the similarity of the cases Hart and Paine described where the death of a parent had resulted in "somnambulism," Brooks wrote:

> It is perfectly evident what happened to Mark Twain at this moment: He became, and his immediate manifestation of somnambulism is the proof of it, a dual personality. If I were sufficiently hardy, as I am not, I should say that that little sleepwalker who appeared at Jane Clemens's bedside on the night of her husband's funeral was the spirit of Tom Sawyer, come to demand again the possession of his own soul, to revoke that ruthless promise he had given. He came for several nights,

and then, we are told, the little boy slept more soundly, a sign, one might say, if one were a fortune-teller, that he had grown accustomed to the new and difficult rôle of being two people at once![67]

Sadly simplistic and faulty as it was, Brooks's psychoanalysis did no major damage to the book. The argument that Mark Twain had betrayed the artist in himself did not hang on so slender a thread as Brooks's interpretation of Hart. Twain did after all possess the destructive money lust that Brooks condemned. The damage that Brooks did do with his misreading of Hart was the discrediting of his book with future audiences who had a more sophisticated knowledge of Freud. In return, however, Hart's idea of dual personality, which reinforced Brooks's own ideas, enabled Brooks to make an important contribution to Mark Twain scholarship; he was the first to point out the personal significance of Twain's lifelong fascination with twins and doubleness of all kinds and the first to say that life on the Mississippi had appealed to the poet in Mark Twain. If Brooks did not recognize the absolute greatness of *Huckleberry Finn,* he at least saw that it was Mark Twain's freest and finest work. By returning to the river life of his youth, Mark Twain escaped the repressive surroundings of his adult life and was able to "let himself go."[68]

The villains of the piece, the agents of American repression, were women. First there was Mark Twain's mother, like Van Wyck's own mother, married to a failed businessman and eager to have her sons recoup the family's business losses. Later there was Mrs. Fairbanks of the *Quaker City* voyage, and after her Twain's wife, Olivia Langdon, the genteel daughter of an Elmira coal baron. The humorist's daughters had also been eager to aid in refining, editing, and bowdlerizing their father, whom they considered a buffoon. Then there was New England itself, where Twain had come to enjoy his success and where culture had "passed into the hands of women." William Dean Howells, Twain's close friend and advisor, was also a Westerner, "intimidated by the prestige of Boston," following the tastes of New England spinsters. Mark Twain's life was dominated by women, "And by virtue of this lovable weakness, too, he was the typical American male."[69]

Van Wyck was conscious to some degree at least that in attacking the restrictions placed on the creative spirit by the genteel, feminine culture of the Gilded Age, he was attacking his mother. Sallie Brooks and Olivia Langdon might almost have been related, both of them having roots in the "stagnant fresh-water aristocracy" of upstate New York and consequently certain of their capacities as arbiters of taste and culture. In dealing with Twain's courtship, Brooks wrote a passage full of resentment against the scenes of his own childhood: "Who does not know those august brick-and-stucco Mansard palaces of the Middle States, those fountains on the front lawn that have never played, those bronze animals with their permanent but economical suggestions of the baronial park? . . . They are the Vaticans of the coal-popes of yesteryear, and all the Elmiras with a single voice proclaimed them sacronsanct."[70]

What Van Wyck seemed not to be so conscious of was the extent to which his criticism of Twain for not prevailing over such a society could be applied to himself also. The poet in Van Wyck had also died young. Apparently he felt that Twain should have found the same solution he had found — the art of society, the only art Brooks could presently think possible for an American. Yet by abandoning art simple for the art of society, Brooks no less than Twain had compromised his own desires. His commitment to the art of society required a conscious act of will, quite a different thing from the lassitude he saw in Twain but not exactly similar either to the "whole souled" spontaneity which he still believed characteristic of the great artist.

That Brooks had to some degree depicted his own despair when he wrote of Mark Twain's is indicated by his emphasis on Twain's failure to develop from a humorist into a satirist. For Brooks also had once dreamt of becoming an American satirist and had found the challenge too great. *The Wine of the Pruitans* had possessed little of the satiric quality he had originally intended it to have. When Brooks wrote that Mark Twain's fatalism was a defense against his sense of self-betrayal, he was condemning himself also for the resigned fatalism with which he had given up his own artistic or satiric career. There had been an element of self-apology in *America's Coming-of-Age* when he observed that it was just as well that Cervantes had lived in Spain three hundred years before: "Had he been born an American of the twentieth century he might have found the task of satire an all too overwhelming one."[71] It had been so for both Brooks and Twain.

Yet, believing that life was better for the American artist in 1919 than in the Gilded Age, Brooks was prepared to be harder on himself than on Twain. He implied a negative answer when he asked in his peroration: "Has the American writer of to-day the same excuse for missing his vocation? Read, writers of America, the driven, disenchanted faces of your sensitive countrymen; remember the splendid parts your confrères have played in the human drama of other times and other peoples, and ask yourselves whether the hour has not come to put away childish things and walk the stage as poets do."[72] He could scarcely have been more accusatory and negative than he had been in his treatment of Twain, yet this passage suggested that he would be even more critical of himself and his contemporaries if, in riper times, they repeated the failures of the past. Like his audience of "Young Intellectuals," Brooks continued to have large, almost messianic expectations for his own career and therefore cause for guilt when failure followed.

Perhaps it was because Brooks was writing of his own ordeal as well as Mark Twain's that his book was humorless, joyless, with no apparent gratitude for the few good things which he believed Twain had written. In his memoirs Van Wyck would admit: "I had fallen short, — I should have sung the praises of *Huckleberry Finn*." Of all the reviewers of *The Ordeal of Mark Twain*, Carl Van Doren made the shrewdest observation. Brooks, he said, was too "rigorously monistic" in his conception of the creative process, regarding any dualism in the artist's nature as not only tragic but sinful. Van Doren believed that Brooks had made "the Mark Twain of his re-creation suffer more . . . than the originally created Mark Twain did by reason of the turbulent confusion of his career. Mr. Brooks, sparer, more clear-cut, more conscious, would thus have suffered if *he* had walked such a fraying path."[73] Thus did he suffer.

6

FAILURE

AFTER he had finished writing *The Ordeal of Mark Twain* in Carmel in the autumn of 1919, Van Wyck fell into a deep depression. He stayed indoors, brooding morbidly, smoking too much, and not writing because he could not. He was "out of focus," as he later described such periods in his life, and when he was out of focus he was "in hell." Except for the few final weeks when the book on Twain had come "with a rush," writing it had been agony, yet to be done was worse. He was finding that work, with all its frustrations, was the best way to stave off the worst depressions. For the next five years he would cling desperately to his work, exhausting himself, and then fall into the deepest depression of all.

Typically, Brooks blamed himself for his inability to work that autumn of 1919, writing to James Oppenheim that he alone was responsible in a free-willed world. Oppenheim replied that belief in free will was mindless American optimism and that Van Wyck's depression was a reasonable response to the realities of American life. He urged Van Wyck to come East, adding that Ben Huebsch was going to publish a new political weekly. The *Freeman* was to be literary as well as political, and Huebsch arranged for Brooks to be offered the literary editorship. Van Wyck accepted at the end of December, provided that the job would not occupy all his time and that they could agree on a salary. He told Huebsch that he was "restless," tired of California, and eager to be "in the current again."

Perhaps the *Freeman* would bring his mind "to a focus" as the *Seven Arts* had done.[1]

Unable to work, he waited listlessly in January and February of 1920 to hear how much the *Freeman* would pay. He hoped that his new book would be out before he returned to New York so that he could command a higher salary, but in the last week of February, with nothing settled definitely, he boarded a train for New York. Eleanor remained behind with the children, and Van Wyck wrote to her from Ogden, Utah, that he had found a better perspective and could see that except for the last few months it had been a "tremendously happy & successful" year.[2]

"So we're safe!" he wrote to Eleanor on the first of March. New York had given him a warm reception, and she should burn his "disgraceful" letters. He had taken a half-time position at the *Freeman* for forty dollars a week, five hundred dollars more a year than he had made with his full-time job at the Century Company. He had seen Alfred Harcourt, who was friendly and who expected to have translations for them, and he had stopped at the *Dial* office and found it full of Harvard graduates: "It was just like Cambridge and the *Advocate* twelve years ago. They treated me quite like an Old Master. . . ." The *Dial* had accepted two chapters of *Mark Twain* for lead articles in the March and April numbers, and Dutton had committed itself to heavy advertising of the book. He had begun to correct the proofs and was earning some extra money by editing a book of Houdini's tricks.[3]

Gloom quickly returned. Less than a week later he was urging Eleanor to help him "shake off this apathy, this fearful dread that I shan't be able to grasp what I can see is the opportunity of our life." He was supposed to be writing his first article for the *Freeman*, but he could not "coax a single impression, a fragment of an idea." After correcting the proofs of *Mark Twain* he had decided that it was "dull and characterless," and he thought that Dutton no longer hoped for a large sale.[4]

During this period he lived with friends in New York and sometimes, unfortunately, with his family in Plainfield. A missing letter must have described an unhappy family situation, for his next letter advised Eleanor not to believe "all that nonsense I wrote the other day about the family here." Ames, "*good* Ames," had taken him to dinner at the Princeton Club and to a Gilbert and Sullivan opera later: "I do feel so sorry for Ames. His life is so empty and repressed. All his savageness comes from that." Nevertheless, a week later Van Wyck had moved to New York, complaining that Plainfield "acts on me like a slow and deadly poison." He dreaded another week there, "though really I am treated angelically. Mama and Ames are endlessly forbearing with me." Meanwhile, weekly *Freeman* deadlines disturbed him, and he could not write "even a book review without wanting to weep."[5]

Eleanor and the children returned from California in May of 1920 after Van Wyck found a temporary residence for them in Peekskill. Then they began looking for a house of their own which, thanks to the *Freeman,* they finally felt secure enough to buy. They looked in Connecticut because, as Van Wyck explained to his mother, it was less suburbanized than New Jersey. He did not say, but surely it was another of the advantages of Connecticut that it was on the other side of New York from Plainfield.[6]

He finally found a permanent home in Westport, Connecticut, where he settled with his family in 1921. It was a small white house perched on a high, rocky corner of the old post road, the King's Highway, but shut off from the road by a row of Lombardy poplars. Two poets in succession had lived there before Brooks, and the second, Florence Evans, had decorated the house in the new light colors that were coming into fashion — canary yellow, apple green, Chinese blue, and terra cotta. Van Wyck would write downstairs in the back of the house in his book-lined study, warmed in winter by a Franklin stove. On summer mornings the children could play in the tree house and Eleanor work in the garden, and then Van Wyck would meet them for lunch outdoors at a table in the shade of an old apple tree. The house was a "Künstlerheim," as a friend remarked, and so was Westport. Paul Rosenfeld and Hendrik Van Loon, friends from the *Seven Arts,* lived there, as did Arthur Dove, John Stuart Curry, Maurice and Charles Prendergast, Lillian Wald, and Ray and Karl Anderson, Sherwood's brothers. Brooks would remark later that in the twenties many had sought tradition and many had flouted it; among the latter in Westport were Rose O'Neill and, for a summer, F. Scott Fitzgerald, who summoned the local fire department to a party because he was "lit."[7]

Van Wyck, however, was one of those who sought tradition, and he kept aloof from the adventurous part of Westport society. What he valued in Westport, apart from his artist friends, was that it was a "long settled region" where one could find "at least a rill of tradition." Two or three days a week he commuted by train to New York to work in the *Freeman* office, and the rest of the time he could live like a man of letters in the country. He rose early and sustained himself through the morning's work on powdered coffee, and in the afternoon took six and seven mile walks along Westport's wooded roads. Van Wyck was not a close observer of nature, but such a walk appealed to his visual sense, and he composed scenes in his imagination as a painter might have done. He enjoyed conversation as much as ever, and his walks were a time for talk with his family, with his neighbor, Hendrik van Loon, or with guests. For he found in this new house that he enjoyed the role of host. In the evening there was reading, and if a *Freeman* deadline was near, there might be labored writing far into the night.[8]

Occasionally he stayed in New York for the evening when he was done at the *Freeman* office, so he could attend the meetings at Harold Stearns's house which led to the publication of *Civilization in the United States* (1922). The idea for a book of essays attacking American life had occurred to Stearns and some friends while they were drinking bootleg and complaining about the eighteenth amendment. Soon the various writers were elbowing through swarms of Italian children to climb the stoop of Stearns's rickety house on Jones Street in Greenwich Village. Upon admittance they descended to the basement, which was also the dining room and kitchen, and sat around the table. Burton Rascoe later recalled some of the contributors, supposedly presided over by the untidy and distracted Harold Stearns: Lewis Mumford, "a hulking fellow dressed like a mining prospector in the movies"; Paul Rosenfeld, "rosy and globular"; J. E. Spingarn, "a tall, darkish man, like the hero of a novel by E. P. Roe"; Hendrik Van Loon, "huge, fattish, urbane and with a monocle"; and Van Wyck Brooks, "neat, sharp-nosed, nervously diffident, bowing from the waist with a mechanical stiffness and precision." The meetings were called "seminars" but were actually parties. There was always a jug of sherry and except for the question of a title and who should write the unassigned essays, the book was hardly discussed. Occasionally, part of an essay which had just come in was read aloud amid cheerful speculation as to how *that* would be received in certain quarters.[9]

Stearns, who had gone to Harvard a few years after Brooks and had mixed in the same delicate and world-weary atmosphere of the *Harvard Advocate,* wrote a piece deploring American "Intellectual Life," and Brooks attacked "The Literary Life." Lewis Mumford condemned the American city, H. L. Mencken attacked the venality of American politicians, and John Macy called the American press corrupt. Other essays vilified marriage, the universities, and the business ethic. Six months before *Civilization in the United States* was published, Stearns anticipated the love-it-or-leave-it response by embarking for Europe, where he spent the rest of the decade.

Brooks, however, could not resolve the dilemma so easily. He had long since rejected the Harvard dilettantes' *triste* longing for Europe as the proper stance for an American artist, for he was committed to America as the raw material of his art, the art of society. Thus there was a difference between Brooks and many of the other essayists in *Civilization in the United States*. Like them, he compared American life unfavorably to European life, but he also compared American writers unfavorably to their European counterparts. He did not agree with Dreiser's statement that the "iron hand of convention" destroyed American writers: " . . . what is significant is that the American writer *does* show less resistance; and as literature is nothing but the expression of power, of the creative will, of 'free will,' in short, is it not more accurate to say . . . that our writers yield to the 'iron hand of convention'?" At the end of the article, however, Brooks argued in a circle, contradicting his emphasis on free will by saying that Howells and Mark Twain, as Westerners, had been "obliged to compromise, consciously or unconsciously, to gain a foothold in the one corner of the country where men were able to exist as writers at all." Therefore, the relatively recent closing of the frontier might mark the turning point in American literature, the beginning of the end of the pioneering mentality, which alone would make possible a national culture.[10] For the moment Brooks seemed to be hoping that if the failure of Howells and Mark Twain had been determined, so was his own success.

Meanwhile, his experience with the *Freeman* was coming to resemble that with the *Seven Arts*. The *Freeman* also owed its existence to a wealthy woman with little genuine interest in the magazine, and the results were similar — quarrels and jealousy among those on the masthead. Mrs. Francis Neilson, *née* Swift and first married to a Morris, could tap the resources of two of Chicago's largest meat-packing fortunes. Later widowed, she married an Englishman, Francis Neilson, an act which gave grief to her family, who considered the impecunious Neilson unrespectable. Van Wyck had hardly met Mrs. Neilson in the spring of 1920 before she gave him the love letters Neilson had written to her and asked him to edit them for publication. Obviously, Van Wyck concluded, hers was a pathetic case of emotional starvation after a lifetime among Chicago businessmen. She needed the stimulus provided by her new husband, a former Liberal Member of Parliament and a Henry Georgite single taxer. Casting about for an occupation in America, Neilson had decided to finance a political journal with his wife's money. He had called on his friends, Albert Jay Nock and Benjamin Huebsch, to edit and publish the magazine. Neilson had chosen the title, the *Freeman*, to suggest economic emancipation, and he was probably also responsible for modeling the format after the *Spectator* and for the use of English spelling throughout the paper. But Neilson's influence ended there. He was fond of fishing and golf, and the paper was largely directed by Albert Jay Nock. Later, when the magazine came to be known as Nock's creation, Neilson called him a usurper, but if the assertion was justified, the situation was due as much to Neilson's lethargy as to Nock's ambition. Nock, however, could have eased the situation with tact, of which he unfortunately knew little. When Mrs. Neilson sent in some essays under her maiden name, she received no encouragement from Nock.[11]

Forty-seven years old in 1920, Nock seems to have had previous careers as a semi-professional baseball player, an Episcopal clergyman, and a muckraker for *American Magazine*. He was secretive, and not much else is known about him. The *Freeman* staff did not even know where he lived, and they joked that he could be reached by leaving a note under a certain rock in Central Park. Many interpreted Nock's reticence as a passion for privacy, but it might also have been the conscious mysteriousness of the man who wishes to be a legend in his own time. He had a preternaturally large ego, a fact apparent in his otherwise unrevealing and overestimated *Memoirs of a Superfluous Man*, and his mainspring may have been an incapacity for intimacy and human warmth. After two years of association on the *Freeman*, his letters to his literary editor still began, "My dear Mr. Brooks."[12]

Nock wore the air of an eccentric man of principle, perversely consistent, but in fact he found it difficult to practice his often contradictory ideas. The *Freeman*, mirroring his confusion, was committed to tax reform on the one hand and to philosophical anarchism on the other. In his *Memoirs* Nock pictured himself running the *Freeman* in an anarchic spirit, bored and having nothing to do because he had no editorial policies to enforce and because he gave so much freedom to his subordinates. While it is true that he permitted Brooks to argue for socialism rather than anarchism in his weekly column, it is not true that Nock was bored and had nothing to do. In fact, he was jealous of his authority and so reluctant to share responsibility that by the end of 1922 he had exhausted himself and was, in the opinion of Ben Huebsch, on the verge of nervous collapse. And Brooks, disgusted with his own lack of editorial authority, offered to resign. So Nock apparently exercised a more stringent authority over his subordinates than a consistent anarchist would have.[13]

As Brooks had done on the *Seven Arts,* he tried to ignore the office tensions and get on with his work. As literary editor he was in charge of getting reviewers, a chore which gave him a considerable amount of patronage to dispense. The *Freeman* printed three or four reviews of more than a thousand words and several shorter notices every issue. During the two days a week when Brooks was in his office, a simply furnished room in the rear of the brick house which sheltered the *Freeman* on West Thirteenth Street, writers would stop in, hoping that he would supplement their incomes that week. Passing through the outer office, Llewelyn Powys later recalled, they would see Nock in a corner "expatiating to three or four trig maidens on some abstruse point," before finding Brooks, who greeted them with "nervous reserved affability" and scanned his shelves, matching the reviewer to a book.[14]

Powys, a Welshman, was one of several European intellectuals living in New York whom Brooks helped keep afloat. Another was old John Butler Yeats, who wrote several essays for the *Freeman* before dying in 1922. Yeats had introduced Van Wyck to Padraic and Mollie Colum several years before, and both Colums, Mollie on a regular basis, were soon working for the magazine. Alyse Gregory, editor of the *Dial,* and Ernest Boyd, author of *Ireland's Literary Renaissance,* wrote for the *Freeman.* Brooks also solicited contributions from the Irish who had stayed at home, especially George Russell, whom he never met but with whom he carried on a friendly corrsepondence long after the *Freeman* ceased publication. From England Bertrand Russell and Arthur Symons sent contributions, and the essays of the Scottish Edwin Muir, with their religious note, were among Van Wyck's favorites. His preference for foreign writers reflected not only his continuing personal taste for things European but also his distaste for editorial work. It seemed to him that the Europeans were more competent and that he could usually send their work straight to the printer, but he had to spend whole afternoons ironing out the essays of his countrymen.[15]

Still, he meant to use his patronage power to develop native talent. He turned first to old friends like John Gould Fletcher and Carl Sandburg, both of whom reviewed poetry, and he printed essays by Constance Rourke and V. L. Parrington, who were em-

barking upon their ambitious studies of American culture. But it was
the new writers coming of age just after the war whom Brooks most
wished to aid. He saw into print some of the earliest writing of John
Dos Passos, Malcolm Cowley, and Matthew Josephson, and with the
encouragement he provided to Newton Arvin and Lewis Mumford,
he made two lifelong friends who would aid him in the search for
America's usable past.

Mumford, a New Yorker and nine years younger than Van
Wyck, was large, handsome, and robust, a strong contrast to Randolph Bourne, whose place he eventually filled in Brooks's life. Yet
Mumford had something of Bourne's spiritual intensity, irritable
sometimes but usually generous. And like Bourne, whom Mumford
admired, his interest as a critic went beyond the work of art; criticism should have the largest possible scope. Mumford had not been
a bookish youth, and he brought a worldly knowledge to literature.
He had studied at Stuyvesant High School with the hope of becoming an electrical engineer, and then turned to biology and sociology
with enough intensity to lead him to Sir Patrick Geddes, the largest
single influence in his life. Studying evenings at the City College of
New York, Columbia, New York University, and the New School for
Social Research, Mumford earned enough credits for a degree but
never took one. Such independence from academic convention was
typical of him. His real university was the city of New York itself and
its diverse cultural resources, museums, libraries, and theaters. In
1917 he worked in a laboratory in Pittsburgh, where he became an
admirer of Brooks and Bourne by reading the *Seven Arts,* and then,
after serving in the Navy during the war, he returned to New York
as an editor of the *Dial.*[16]

Walter Fuller, another *Freeman* editor, introduced Brooks to
Mumford in the spring of 1920, just before Mumford departed for
England to serve as acting editor of Geddes' *Sociological Review.* He
could have continued permanently in this post, and he faced a
difficult decision — whether to return to America or to stay in
England and thus follow Harold Stearns's injunction that a young
man should "Get out!" But Brooks had begun to use his *Freeman*
column to expand his master essay on the duties of the American
writer, and his exhortations helped Mumford decide to return after
only six months abroad: "That quiet but vibrant voice of his called
me home."[17]

Once home, Mumford settled down to his varied career as
free-lance writer, critic, philosopher, and social thinker. Like
Bourne, he seemed easily to surmount any worldly cares which

might have stood between him and the literary life. Brooks printed Mumford's early work in the *Freeman* and suggested the subject of his first book, *The Story of Utopias,* a study of prophetic vision. Their friendship blossomed rapidly, and they were soon meeting often in New York. Just as he had done with Bourne, Van Wyck planned more projects with Mumford than they could ever hope to carry out, though one of these ideas — a subscription list to guarantee support for new work — was the germ of the Literary Guild. Again like Bourne, Mumford as a young man had a more positive attitude than Brooks toward the American past, and he observed in his *Golden Day* (1926) that "If the disintegration [of traditional culture] went farthest in America, the processes of renewal have, at intervals, been most active in the new country; and it is for the beginnings of a genuine culture, rather than for its relentless exploitation of materials, that the American adventure has been significant."[18]

Unlike Bourne, Mumford wrote prose which carried a freight of sociological and scientific terms and which eventually led to trouble with Nock, who liked his English more Saxon than Latin. Brooks insisted that Mumford's style was necessary for his subject matter and that there would always be room for Mumford in his department, adding in a letter to Mumford that he did not understand how Nock tolerated his own work. But with the exception of a few Freudian terms, Brooks's English was more conservative than Mumford's — a difference which reflected Mumford's greater willingness to oppose the machine age on its own ground, and one that perhaps explains why Mumford was never quite as intimate with Brooks as Bourne had been.[19]

With Newton Arvin, Brooks's other *Freeman* protégé, there was never any problem of style. His interests, resembling Van Wyck's, were more narrowly literary than Mumford's and hence more easily expressed in traditional English. Having grown up as an unusually bookish child in an Indiana town, Arvin wrote in a clear, forceful, graceful style that resembled Brooks's. In his senior year at Harvard he wrote to the literary editors of New York, asking for work, just as Van Wyck had done in undergraduate days. And as Paul Elmer More had done in his own case, Van Wyck now offered Arvin a chance to review something for the *Freeman.* Impressed with Arvin's first effort, Brooks sent him more books to review.[20]

By the time Arvin graduated from Harvard in 1921, Brooks had begun to count on him as an ally and was consciously conducting his critical education. He sent Arvin some biographies, pointing out that they had nothing in common and suggesting their dissimilarity as a theme for an essay: ". . . they reveal the lack of a *centre* in American thought and feeling." Reviewing a volume of More's *Shelburne Essays,* Arvin wrote that the once gentlemanly More had become a "quarrelsome, one might almost say a febrile reactionary," and Brooks congratulated him: "You have got him in the heart." In others reviews Arvin called Stuart Sherman "a warrior tilting at windmills" and outdid even Harold Stearns in his dislike for American life.[21]

Brooks guided Arvin in more mundane ways also, first by trying but failing to get him a job on the *Freeman* and then by telling him not to be afraid to take a teaching position. Practical matters counted for little: "Nothing will prevent you from writing. . . ." The important thing, said Brooks, who believed that criticism was a moral science, was the kind of man Arvin became: "Your ultimate authority as a critic will depend as much upon this as upon your knowledge of books." The next year he assured Arvin, "You are a born critic and you will be a distinguished one."[22]

For all the force and distinction with which he wrote, Arvin needed the encouragement. He was insecure, both economically and psychologically, and he had difficulty following Van Wyck's advice of beginning a book in order to focus himself. A similar suggestion to Mumford had resulted promptly in *The Story of Utopias,* but with Arvin it seemed to have little effect. At first he was occupied with the teaching position he found at Smith College in 1922, a position which he would keep all his life, and when he finally did decide to write a book he vacillated on a subject. Not till 1930, ten years after Van Wyck had first suggested such a project, did Arvin's fine *Hawthorne* emerge from the press, carrying with it an epigraph from *America's Coming-of-Age:* ". . . this most deeply planted of American writers, who indicates more than any other the subterranean history of the American character."

II

Van Wyck's job on the *Freeman* was supposed to be half-time, requiring him to spend two days at the office and to write a column, "A Reviewer's Notebook," at home. But the column took most of his time at home, as he recalled in his memoirs: "What misery to spend five nights sitting up till three o'clock to find oneself represented in print by a wretched composition." The rest of the *Freeman* staff did not agree with his harsh judgment of his work, and the woman who composed the paper refused to cut a line of his writing. Since

Brooks's "Notebook" was the last feature of every issue, she had to make up the dummy from the back.[23] Yet it was true that his *Freeman* pieces never acquired the consistent high quality of his *Seven Arts* essays. The *Freeman*, a weekly, forced him to write too much, too fast. Almost every week for two years and with less frequency thereafter, he filled the "Notebook" with a two- or three-thousand-word essay.

Pressed to fill space, he resorted even to gossip, as when, in reviewing a Mary Austin novel, he praised her understanding of the artist's role as "priestess" by telling a story he had heard about her in Carmel. During a forest fire near the town, she had "conceived of herself in the role of a Joan of Arc" and, dressed "in a long white robe, riding on a white horse and with her hair streaming over her shoulders," led the townspeople "forth to stem the flames." He added that in New York she went to the Indian rooms at the Museum of Natural History to commune with the Great Spirit and once, taking some relics from an open case, put them "into her bosom and fell into a state of silent ecstasy." Unfortunately, none of the incidents were true and Mary Austin threatened a lawsuit. She had a sense of humor, however, and settled for having Brooks do penance by reading all of her novels and then meeting her at the Museum of Natural History. For the next few months she bombarded him with querulous letters about his *Freeman* essays, and she forced him to admit that he was "ill equipped" in esthetics. As he told her in his letter of apology, he was used to dealing with the careers of dead writers but not of the "living."[24]

The admission was significant, suggesting the feeling already indicated in his essay "On Creating a Usable Past" that history did not require the same respect for its objectivity as the present. From this time on he largely limited his column to the dead, who were less likely to rise up in rebuke. Often he reviewed a biography of an American writer, using the book as an illustration of some large tendency of American life. The result was a series of "ordeal" essays on men like Joel Barlow, Melville, Hamlin Garland, Poe, O'Henry, Jack London, the elder Henry James, Joaquin Miller, and Bret Harte. Like Mark Twain these men had suffered because their artistic spirits had been confined and destroyed by the materialism of American life.

Reviewing Americana made Brooks critical not only of American history but also of American historians and biographers. One would never guess from their work that any writer had "lived consciously in this American world that drives the sensitive man almost to despair." Never questioning the *status quo,* historians were partly responsible for the absence of conscious values which encouraged businessmen to live "on the land like locusts." Historians had not understood that Henry Thoreau was more interesting than Daniel Boone. Consequently, American history lay untouched, awaiting a historian like Michelet with the soul of a poet. Yet the fault was not entirely that of the historians and biographers. Brooks argued in his review of Gamaliel Bradford's *American Portraits* (1922) that there was a dearth of interesting subjects in America: ". . . the American character, during the last half-century has simply failed to undergo any distinct individual development." One found interesting characters like Whistler or Henry Adams on "the periphery of our civilization" but none of interest in the center. Therefore, an American Sainte-Beuve or Lytton Strachey was "quite impossible."[25]

But Brooks was gradually narrowing down his dislike of the American past to the post-Civil War era and developing ever greater respect for the ante-bellum period and especially New England, which contained more "than meets the casual eye." When Stuart Sherman cited Emerson as a constructive social critic from whose example the "Young Intellectuals" could profit, Brooks answered that Emerson was "a dangerous ally for Professor Sherman." Emerson had proclaimed the only truly American tradition — trampling on tradition. Brooks's growing respect for the pre-Civil War era also caused him to give a more generous review to Gamaliel Bradford's next book, *Damaged Souls* (1923). Bradford's earlier book, *American Portraits,* had dealt with figures of the Gilded Age, while *Damaged Souls* treated such earlier subjects as Aaron Burr, John Randolph, and John Brown, whom Brooks found not only interesting but close to the center of American life. The Civil War, Van Wyck wrote in the "Notebook," had destroyed "the living fabric of a small, provisional but none the less homogeneous 'national culture.' The homing instinct of these earlier writers — even Poe — proves how tough it was; they wandered all over the world, but it never occurred to any of them not to bring his spoils back to America. . . . With the chaos of the war everything changed. American life had ceased to be a fabric and it had lost its own centre; London became the centre again as it had been before the revolution."[26]

Hence Brooks's continuing opposition to the colonial mentality which "prevents a people from frankly accepting its own life." It was not wrong to travel in Europe as Emerson, Cooper, Hawthorne, and Ticknor had done. Brooks could even defend Ezra Pound for "living in England and sticking out his tongue at his native land" as long as he at least kept his native land on his mind. What was wrong was to attempt a European career as Henry James had done. To American writers before the Civil War "a 'career in England' would have seemed . . . almost as fantastic a notion as a career in the island of Guam."[27]

Although in retrospect the rising star of Henry James's reputation in the twenties would seem to have made him the logical subject for Brooks's next book, it was two years after Brooks finished *Mark Twain* before he decided to write *The Pilgrimage of Henry James.* If Twain symbolized the danger of surrender to American life, James was the perfect subject through which to explore the consequences of flight. Furthermore, James was the precursor of the postwar sensibility which Brooks was already beginning to detest, a sensibility skeptical of moral standards, skeptical of traditional syntax, skeptical of its own perceptions. But Van Wyck had difficulty settling on a subject and suffered, as he told Newton Arvin, from a "sort of spiritual malaise between books." As late as the summer of 1921 he was still only thinking of a book, perhaps on Howells, perhaps on James.[28]

But as Brooks reviewed new books in the early twenties, James was often brought to his attention. He had hardly begun to work for the *Freeman* before he was reviewing Percy Lubbock's edition of *The Letters of Henry James* and telling Eleanor, even before its appearance, that the review was "unprintably bad" — a portent of the guilt which James as a subject would always provoke in him.[29] During the next two years he reviewed Ezra Pound's *Instigations,* with its sixty-page essay on James; a collection of the novelist's writings by Pierre de la Rose; and Gamaliel Bradford's *American Portraits,* which included a chapter on James.

In these reviews and a few other *Freeman* essays, he frankly explored his own thoughts and created the broad outlines of *The Pilgrimage of Henry James.* James's career bore witness to the dangers of expatriation for Americans because, in contrast with European expatriates like Ibsen or Turgenev, James's youth was as "unanchored" as his adulthood. The evasion of America implied also an evasion of life, committing James "to a pursuit of his gift almost monstrously disproportionate with any pursuit possible to him of the facts upon which a great gift is adequately nourished." Unlike Whitman, for whom the national fact had been a gateway to the universal, for James it was a wall "against which the powerful current of his genius broke into spray, losing itself ultimately in a thousand circuitous rivulets." Hence the obscure late manner, spreading "like an impenetrable fog behind which James himself more and more escapes into an inviolable privacy." Yet Brooks believed that there was a positive point to be made also, which was, as he explained to Gamaliel Bradford, the relative superiority of James's early work: ". . . the reputation of James rests, to his great detriment, upon the weakest aspects of his work, because it has been determined by English critics who misunderstood him as I am convinced he misunderstood himself. I have a holy mission to reinstate the despised and rejected *Washington Square,* etc., to take James out of the hands of the Jacobites and to show that he spoke the sober truth in that phrase of his about the 'immense fantastication' of England (applied to himself, that is, and in consequence of certain weaknesses in his own nature)."[30]

To Brooks in the twenties, James's flight from America and from life slowly came to seem especially relevant to the contemporary literary situation. In 1920 he had found the "'strange experiments" in the *Dial* and *Little Review* merely eccentric and had patronizingly asked how Ezra Pound could be prevented "from becoming a bore." But a year later when Pound wrote in a *Little Review* essay that the great poets had had no moral preoccupations and had written solely to please themselves, Brooks answered angrily: "The fact is . . . that they have pleased themselves by formulating moral conceptions and that the history of literature in its main stream is inseparable from the history of morals." As Van Wyck was gradually forced to take Pound seriously, he was also forced to the conclusion that it was his own moral conception of art that was out of touch with the times. A "new literary era" had been entered, he announced in 1923, an era completely different from that of even six years before: "A strange, brittle, cerebral aristocratism has succeeded the robust democratism of the last age." The new mood sprang from "a fear of life, a disgust with life, from a cynicism so profound, a weakness so extreme that it can not but set aside the whole question of human destiny as a hopeless and irreducible tangle." To fellow spirits like John Gould Fletcher, Brooks was soon complaining that in America "A pedantic aestheticism has frozen everyone's blood, and we are getting farther and farther away from the underlying religious intention of great literature."[31]

Disappointed on the one hand by the purely esthetic orientation of the twenties literati, Brooks was disappointed on the other by the socialists' devaluation of culture. To Upton Sinclair's argument that his novels should be judged for their worth as revolutionary propaganda rather than as literature or art, Brooks replied that the failure of Sinclair's novels as literature made them worthless to the workers: "These false simplifications, these appeals to the martyr in human nature, these travesties of the psychologies of the powerful ones of the earth are so much dust thrown in the eyes of the proletariat." When Max Eastman ridiculed the concept of a revolutionary conflict of ideas and called for poets and artists to subject themselves to the discipline of the material forces of history, Brooks answered that Balzac and Christ, for instance, had created new cultural "moulds" for men to live in, be they businessmen or prophets. The authority of ideas, spirit, values, and culture was "unquestionable and incalculable," and to speak otherwise could only impede meaningful change. It was an evasion of reality to talk revolution "as if America had had its education and its art and literature." Eastman's estimation of literature as impotent was "unrealistic, feminine, and American, all too American."[32]

Brooks still wanted what he had always wanted, a middle ground, a "third ground," as he told Newton Arvin, "aside from the genteel tradition and the aesthetic tradition." In the logic of *America's Coming-of-Age,* Eastman was a Highbrow who professed an interest in literature but actually viewed it as powerless to affect reality. Pound, on the other hand, with his emphasis on technique over morality, was a Lowbrow in art, one more manifestation of the devaluation of ends in favor of means in a commercial and industrial society. What was needed was a man with the sensibility of an artist who would nevertheless recognize that because "a great literature presupposes an organized society, . . . the main task of criticism in America remains rather social than asthetic." America needed an artist of society, a Tolstoy, an Ibsen, "just one true-blue solitary rhinoceros" to deliberately reject American life, "not through any need to escape, but at the command of a profound personal vision. Such a man was Randolph Bourne."[33]

By now Brooks was coming to realize that Bourne had been right on the cultural consequences of the war. It had been a "victory" for the forces of industrialism and had "produced an art from which it no longer has anything to fear, an art which, driven by the very instinct of self-preservation, has withdrawn from the struggle by retreating from reality itself." Art, being social, must be more than the expression of one man's feeling, must be "in *rapport* with reality." Yet the enemy, the same old enemy — the insensate greed of the businessman and the industrialist — now appeared to have triumphed over the prophetic vision of art which had seemed to Brooks the prime mover in any betterment of the human condition.

The demoralization of art was therefore a double catastrophe; if the breach between the artist and reality was not healed it would mean "the death not only of the artist but of society itself as we now know it."[34] Such an opinion represented shattered hopes for Brooks. Instead of an American coming-of-age he seemed to be living through an American Armageddon, and evil was winning.

III

Having finally settled on James as his subject, Van Wyck soon found his arduous *Freeman* duties a distraction, so in May of 1922 he took an unpaid leave of absence from the magazine and departed with his family for California. Like *Mark Twain,* most of *Henry James* would be written in the house of his mother-in-law in Carmel. He worked hard on the book for two months and then, in mid-July, put it aside to earn some badly needed money by reading manuscripts for Harcourt, Brace and Company at a dollar and a half an hour. And he began to work on translations, though previously he had left this work largely to Eleanor, whose French was better than his. But as he grew increasingly baffled by problems in his treatment of James, he would turn to translation for the absorption in work which his temperament required.[35]

He had already expressed his fear that the James book would be beyond his power in letters to his mother, Gamaliel Bradford, Newton Arvin, and others, and now he lost confidence rapidly. In July, just before abandoning his writing in favor of translation, he wrote to Mumford: "I have been fairly drugged with work — I mean with the effort to understand my subject and seize the form of my book. I am not launched yet in spite of two months of the hardest work I have ever undertaken." He was losing weight, and photographs from this period show his clothes hanging on him loosely. In contrast, the skin was drawn tightly over his face, and his eyes stared intensely ahead, resisting distraction. He discussed James on long walks with Theodore Maynard, who was living in Carmel at the time and who later recalled Brooks's hair standing on end, "his wild eyes, his explosive chuckles, and his sudden lapses into dreaminess." Torn by doubts, Brooks vowed to Maynard that he would never take on a similar project again.[36]

The problem of form which he had mentioned to Mumford was created by his desire to tell the story of James's inner, spiritual life and yet at the same time, as he had written to Bradford, make the book "a narrative, as 'dramtic' as possible." He had been stung by what had become an almost universal criticism of *Mark Twain,* which Bradford expressed in a letter: "You did not take Mark quite first in his multiple, exquisite humanity, but used him as a mannequin to hang a rich and delightful garment of theory upon, and the tendency was to falsify, oh, only a trifle, but a trifle all the same." His treatment of James must be more artful yet at the same time permit him to make his point. By September he had hit on the solution which he later described to Sherwood Anderson: "The method is pretty much that of a novel — that is, I am attempting to tell the whole story through his eyes — with, of course, my own running interpretation."[37]

So he returned to the manuscript and worked hard through the fall until November, when he heard from B. W. Huebsch that he was needed on the *Freeman* in New York. Van Wyck answered that he was engaged in the most difficult task of his life and was now "on the brink of the 'big scene.'" Could he have three or four more weeks? If not, he would be glad to resign, so they could find someone more dependable and with whom Nock would be more willing to share responsibility. Huebsch responded that he could have a few weeks at most; Nock was on the verge of a nervous breakdown and had to have a vacation. (The emergency, however, could not be mentioned to the perverse Nock who would not take the needed vacation if he knew that it was being planned for him.) Once Nock was away in Germany, Van Wyck would have all the responsibility that he cared for.[38]

By Christmas Van Wyck was back in New York, leaving Eleanor and the children in California to return in the spring, and he was soon lonely and depressed. The Chelsea Hotel where he stayed on West Sixteenth Street was "full of low-caste college girls who are enough to destroy all the romance in the world." His numerous old friends in New York — Perkins, Sheldon, Wheelock, and Zinsser — gave him an active social life but could not cheer him up. His writing was affected, and he floundered for ideas for "A Reviewer's Notebook." Perkins wanted Scribner's to publish a collection of the essays, but when Van Wyck read through the back issues of the *Freeman* he decided that his labor "boils down to very little. . . . I really have been working all this time to no purpose." He urged Huebsch to let him give up his "vile" column which was a "disgrace to the paper," and despite Huebsch's refusal, the "Notebook" began appearing at increasingly infrequent intervals. To compensate for doing less writing he began reading manuscripts but felt guilty for threatening the job of Huebsch's regular reader.[39]

Evenings and weekends he worked on *Henry James*. When it had become apparent that he would not make his April deadline with Dutton, he had decided that he had to repay his $600 advance and that he would get the money by publishing a few of the finished chapters in magazines. Eleanor, who usually typed his manuscripts, was in California, and he could not risk mailing his one copy to her. Unable to afford a typist, he spent his spare time at the typewriter for the entire month of February, and in a state of exhaustion near the end wrote to Eleanor: "The whole matter has become a virulent disease, and I am beginning to think that the only thing to do is to burn the whole thing up, every note and scrap of it. What I want is another subject to switch to — and I shall never be sane again until I find it." On the last day of the month he submitted the typescript to the *Dial* and had to wait only two days for their answer — an enthusiastic yes. They would pay $400 for three chapters, so for the moment the money problem was nearly solved.[40]

But publication in the *Dial* brought new worries of "the howling storm that is going to arise when it begins to come out." The problem was that his interpretation "flies right in the face of the whole *Dial* school." The *Dial* had gradually become an organ of the pure estheticism Brooks detested, and the magazine was committed, he believed, to the idea that James "successfully mastered Europe and worked out his own life to the most triumphant conclusion. In short, I shall have to prove my thesis in the teeth of the very cleverest and most acute critics in the country. . . ." He attributed the *Dial*'s acceptance of his chapters to the absence of Scofield Thayer and Gilbert Seldes in Europe, which left the decision to subordinates. Actually, he was underestimating the respect with which he was still viewed by the *Dial* despite its disagreement with his basic position. Thayer and others on the magazine considered him one of the finest prose stylists in America and admired his writing for esthetic if not philosophical reasons.[41]

Still, his concern about the public reception of the chapters to appear in the *Dial* did show a realistic perception of what the "new literary era" signified for his own position and reputation. Not yet forty, he was coming to be regarded, he told Eleanor, "as belonging to a period of two or three generations back." Being *passé* had nothing to do with age; Ezra Pound, himself a year older than Van Wyck, casually dismissed "old gentlemen like Van Wyck Brooks."[42]

Feeling more and more alone, he increased his isolation by increasing the strain in his friendships with Waldo Frank and Sherwood Anderson. Frank had written him in California, accusing him of abandoning the ground which they had shared on the *Seven Arts*. Van Wyck had answered that he still felt as one with the Waldo Frank of *Our America* but not with the esthete author of *Rahab* and *Dark Mother* who "veils himself in impenetrable darkness." But then he seemed to admit the justice of Frank's charge that he was responsible for the rift between them: "Wait, Waldo, don't be impatient with me. . . . in time I shall swim again into your universe." Back in New York for the winter of 1923, Brooks met with Frank and "levelled" with him, apparently telling him that his work "lacks everything that means most to me in a novel."[43]

Similarly, he saw Anderson in New York and reported to Eleanor, "Fortunately, he didn't talk about 'sex,' of which I am sick, but there is an element of the fakir in him that makes him seem often not quite sincere." Anderson was also questioning Van Wyck's sincerity as a friend, having heard that Brooks had called him the "phallic Chekhov," which sounds uncharacteristic but possible, since the phrase did accurately represent his estimate of Anderson's talent. Anderson, who had also been disappointed by *Mark Twain* and felt that Brooks was feeding himself "on other men's failures," wrote in a letter, "Do you know I had, Van Wyck, a feeling that it was just the artist in Mark Twain you in some way resented." Still, Anderson spoke of "my immense debt to the man Brooks" and tried to keep up the friendship, but to no avail. He later said, "I did not put Brooks aside. He put me aside."[44]

With spring and the return of Eleanor and the children from California, Van Wyck cheered up and worked ahead slowly on *Henry James*. While he was committed to the method of a novelist, telling the story through the eyes of his central character, he did not have a novelist's freedom. The difference, as he explained to Anderson, was that ". . . every sentence I write must square with known facts — or facts that *may* be known to others than myself. Consequently, I can't let myself go or plunge ahead for an instant and I dare say it will take me another year to finish the book." Still, he believed he was making progress and told Anderson a month later: "Henry James really began to dawn on me about two months ago — came alive, I mean, inside of me, and since then the infant monster has been kicking and struggling so hard at the walls of my psyche that I am all out of breath." He longed to put everything else aside and finish the book. But Nock was still away, and he had to spend four days a week at the *Freeman* office in New York. Unable to devote himself steadily to the manuscript, he found it difficult to work out ideas and was gradually losing confidence. He pressed on in the same slow, tedious, harassed way for the rest of the year.[45]

Meanwhile, attacks on him increased and even friendly gestures were qualified. He received the annual *Dial* prize of $2000 for an American writer at the beginning of 1924, but the magazine's announcement of the award was hardly unstinting in its praise: "One can recognize the supreme importance of such a figure even if one fails to accept the whole body of his doctrine." Writing in the *Dial* just a year after that magazine gave Brooks its award, Gorham Munson would justly criticize the vagueness with which Brooks so often invoked the "poetic life." Munson first voiced what later became a common opinion — that Brooks was not a literary critic at all. Unable to "enter into the workings of the imagination," Brooks neither sought nor understood poetic creation but was a conservative seeking to reproduce "certain emotional experiences which he has found satisfying and has cherished. Crudely, what he desires is an American Charles Dickens, an American Carlyle, an American Thomas Hardy. Certainly, he has revealed no friendship for novelty, and if the coming American literature he has announced should turn out to be a new consciousness in new forms, there is reasonable doubt that Mr. Brooks would recognize his long-awaited Messiah." Those who recognized Brooks's past services expressed their appreciation but also their fear that he was incapable of understanding modern literature, the conditions for which in America he had helped create. Edmund Wilson thought Brooks was losing interest in "literature as an art" and cited the chapters of the James book which had been published in the *Dial:* "What we look for is a study of a man of genius who happened to be an American; but what we seem to be getting is a 'case history' of an American who had the temerity to try to be a man of genius." Waldo Frank said that Brooks was far from mastery in "the domain of literary criticism and of aesthetics." And Paul Rosenfeld, another old *Seven Arts* friend as well as Westport neighbor, published the severest criticism that had yet come Van Wyck's way from a friendly source. In *Port of New York* (1924), Rosenfeld wrote that by his failure to be interested in and appreciative of contemporary literature Brooks "exhibits the very want of sympathy for art and the artistic life of which he accuses society." Rosenfeld spoke the mind of many when he added that the James book would reveal whether or not Brooks had a future as a literary critic.[46]

Knowing as he wrote *Henry James* that his reputation hung in the balance, Van Wyck lost confidence, became cautious, and progressed still more slowly. He had read the manuscript to Mollie Colum in the *Freeman* office and despite her finding it satisfactory had insisted that it was marred by a mysterious flaw which he would not explain. It mattered little that Lewis Mumford had liked the parts Brooks had read to him or that Thomas Sergeant Perry, after reading the *Dial* chapters, had written to him, "Yes, you have my imprimatur, and more than that my gratitude for your comprehension, your sympathetic comprehension of Henry James." Brooks's friends began to be cautious in speaking to him of the book, and Mumford had a glimpse of his role of the next few years, urging Brooks to publish his work against Brooks's own criticism of it: "I forebear to ask you about the Henry James book, except to plead, as ardently as ever, for its publication." But by May of 1924 Van Wyck had given up for the time being and told Mumford that the book was "to go on the shelf" for a year: "It is finished in one sense, finished as a tract; but I haven't the heart to write tracts any longer. I mean to do the real thing, and can, with time. The *analytical work* is done, and it was a bit of a job — so much so that it wore me down most fearfully and convinced me that analysis is for me no longer. Another year of it and I should have killed what I have only temporarily benumbed."[47]

He had been further distracted that spring by the abrupt end of the *Freeman*, just four years after it had begun. The Neilsons would not tolerate Nock any longer and had stopped their subsidy, effectively killing the magazine.[48] Fortunately, Van Wyck had the $2000 from the recent *Dial* award to cushion the shock. But he had to have a job. Deciding that he was done with journalism forever, he turned down the editorship of the *Independent* and, the next year, Scofield Thayer's surprising offer of the editorship of the *Dial*. He had become increasingly friendly with Joel Spingarn, despite the latter's position in the enemy camp of new criticism, and Spingarn, who was associated with Alfred Harcourt, offered Brooks a half-time position in Harcourt, Brace's editorial office. Van Wyck happily accepted this job, which offered peace, anonymity, and above all, no public responsibility. He would not have to write to friends pleading that he not be judged by a weekly column written in a state of agony.[49]

With *Henry James* on the shelf, he began searching for that healing subject which, as he had told Eleanor, would make him "sane" again. This new book would require "synthesis" rather than the wearing "analysis" of the Twain and James projects, because the new book would deal with a success rather than a failure. Van Wyck believed it would be achievement enough to show that the literary life had been lived in America, without analyzing the reasons for success. In his essay in Stearns's *Civilization,* he had spoken of the courage required by the life of letters and added that few could summon that courage "unless they have *seen the thing done*."[50] European writers had many examples, but in America who offered, as he had asked in *The Malady of the Ideal,* "in . . . complete self-realization . . . an earnest of the human faculty"?

Having been an admirer of Melville's since first reading him at Stanford ten years earlier, Brooks had briefly considered him as a subject and had begun reading him again in 1923. But he believed that the Melville revival of the twenties was blighted by faddishness: "Next year Melville will have been forgotten again." And Melville, though a whale, "dived only on two or three occasions." This would not do. Brooks wanted a subject who contradicted the prevailing pattern he had outlined in *Civilization in the United States:* "The blighted career, the arrested career, the diverted career are, with us, the rule. The chronic state of our literature is that of a youthful promise which is never redeemed."[51]

Whitman, whom he had so long admired, would have been an obvious choice except that his "spontaneous life" was "the negation of discipline, struggle, selection," of just those things required by the art of society. In addition, perhaps Whitman did not bear a strong enough resemblance to Brooks, or rather, did not provide a suitable screen on which to project his own personal concerns, as he had done in his work on Twain and James. In the *Freeman,* Brooks had written that Whitman had had his success "thanks to a unique endowment, thanks only to that." Unlike most writers, unlike Brooks, Whitman had never, in Chekhov's phrase, "squeezed the slave out of himself," because he contained so little of the slave in the first place.[52] The proper example for Americans would be someone in whose life the principle of self-opposition had played a larger part, someone who appreciated material things but triumphed over them as Mark Twain had not, someone who admired Europe but remained American as Henry James had not, someone who had tried like Brooks to live the life of a prophet despite the claims of a bourgeois family.

He read through Poe and Hawthorne, rejecting them, and then with spirits brightening in May of 1924, he considered Emerson.

Reading the ten volumes of *Journals*, "for the first time attentively," as he later told Gamaliel Bradford, "was a sort of religious experience." Then he turned to Emerson's books, and finishing them, "I knew I had found my man." During the next year, when he was not at Harcourt's office or devilling away at a translation with Eleanor, he read extensively on Emerson and his times.[53]

On the surface, then, it was a happy year, and underneath probably a manic one. In Harcourt's office he acted strangely, according to Mollie Colum, who was coming to know him well but who did not specify exactly what was unusual about his behavior. However, he did help edit Sandburg's *Lincoln* and by himself brought in Parrington's *Main Currents of American Thought,* whose elaborate analysis of American literary history and hostility to Puritanism built on Brooks's own earlier and less developed ideas. Despite this distinguished publishing achievement, his strange behavior got him fired (apparently gently, since he remained friendly with Spingarn) after just a year with Harcourt. Such an event would have once caused severe depression but now Van Wyck blithely informed Eleanor that he was glad he had lost his job. He wanted time to work on his *Emerson,* and he temporarily solved the money problem by accepting Dutton's $1500 advance on that book and by, at last, publishing the James.[54]

He would eventually feel much guilt over publishing *Henry James* in its unfinished state. The reason for putting it "on the shelf" had been so that he could return to it in a year and "give it the right tone of feeling and be at peace with it." Yet a comparison of the chapters published in the *Dial* in 1923 with their final versions in the book shows that he made few meaningful changes. He altered a few words to get the right rhythm, but he did not substantially change the tone or feeling from its state in 1923 when he had told Mollie Colum that the manuscript had a mysterious flaw. Now, just before publication in April of 1925, he explained the flaw to her; the book was about himself rather than James. And sometime during this period he consulted his brother Ames, a lawyer, and asked if he could be sued for libelling a dead man.[55]

IV

The Pilgrimage of Henry James was the book of a sick man, as Edmund Wilson came near to suggesting in a lengthy and insightful review. Wilson questioned the spirit in which Brooks has come to undertake criticism. That spirit is one of intense zeal at the service of intense resentment. What Mr. Brooks resents and desires to protest against is the spiritual poverty of America and the discouragement of the creative artist by American conditions. But in preaching this doctrine he has allowed his bitterness to overshoot its mark and to excoriate the victims of America along with the conditions from which they are supposed to suffer. In the latter part of his new book, we have the feeling that he has set out to hound down poor old James, just as in the earlier one he set out to hound down poor old Mark Twain.

Brooks was a "romantic and a preacher" who could not understand an "equanimous artist" like James who wrote not to protest but to understand moral situations where there was no black or white. James took a "classic" view of such situations and saw them as universal and inevitable rather than as social or national. This being especially true of James's later work explained Brooks's preference for the earlier novels, where the contrast of American innocence and European experience made for more explicit social criticism. Brooks, Wilson said, "admires James in direct proportion as he [James] performs a function like himself."[56]

Thus Wilson touched on what Brooks himself considered the fundamental problem of the book — a confusion of subject with author. The problem had been compounded by the many similarities between Brooks and James. Both were from New York, which, unlike ante-bellum New England, Brooks said, kept its thoughts on America only during business hours and looked to Europe when it dreamed of culture. James, like Brooks, had suffered from feminine, genteel culture and the "extraordinary absence," as James had put it, "of a single male interest." James also had a father who seemed happiest in Europe and an older brother who would "plunge" pragmatically into the "muddy stream" of American things. Both Brooks and James had been taken to Europe at the impressionable age of twelve for a "sensuous education" and neither had ever after been content with America.[57] Despite the unreasonable hostility which Edmund Wilson had noted, Brooks also had some understanding, if not sympathy, for the young Henry James and his social and cultural situation.

Writing the book as a novel was both a result and a cause of Brooks's confusion of his own identity with James's. It was from

James himself that he had gained this interest in dramatizing inner psychological states, as if to say to critics that despite his dislike of the later novels he understood their technical achievement. More importantly, through this method he could exploit his own too-familiar knowledge of the cultural dilemma that troubled young Henry and the rest of the James family. Thus, early in the book he pictured the elder Henry James with his sons in Europe feeling very much as Brooks had often felt:

> It was all impossible. . . . And yet, and yet. . . . He could not surrender the beloved vision. He would walk up and down in his room at the hotel, "talking," as William James describes him, "of the superiority of America to these countries after all, and how much better it is we should have done with them." But the moment he stepped off the ship the illusion seized him once more. The Old World, was it not a paradise, of which, in the end, by some miracle, the gates might open to receive him? . . . Thus he lived with his eye ever turned across the sea.[58]

The ellipses in the passage are Brooks's; he used them to indicate not missing words but rather the natural hesitancy of thought. Like a novelist, he hoped to lay his characters' minds bare on the page, and to help accomplish this end he came up with the device of incorporating phrases from James's writings directly into his own text, usually without quotation marks. Brooks attempted to justify this unusual practice in the book's prefatory note: "The author has resorted to this expedient because he knows of no other means of conveying with strict accuracy at moments what he conceives to have been James's thoughts and feelings." Brooks would be wed to this method of unmarked quotation for the rest of his life and through it would often achieve vivid effects, as in *The Flowering of New England.* But a side effect of the device, as many critics would point out, was a blurring of the line between author and subject so that the reader could not always tell who was saying what. And in this case Brooks himself was confused, for when he pictured the James family hoping to pry open the heavenly gates of Europe, he could not be certain that it was not really himself dreaming, as he had in childhood, of Europe as a silvery shore with "very high spires and domes that gleamed like the City in *Revelations.*"

Because Brooks's objective was to portray James's artistic decline, he praised the early James as intensely as he attacked the later.

There were strident overtones in his insistence that James's early novels were filled with a community of characters "more real and coherent than any that exists in the world." Furthermore, James's understanding of his American characters in *Washington Square* and *The Bostonians* was "that born only of race." Brooks insisted also that in discovering the international scene as the background against which to depict the problem of civilized people from an uncivilized country, James had performed his greatest service for American literature. "Tragedy, satire, comedy are inherent in the situation," and for a time it had seemed that James, unlike Mark Twain, would be equal to his subject. The young James had been a true artist of society, the first American novelist "to challenge the herd-instinct, to reveal the inadequacy of our social life, to present the plight of the highly personalized human being in the primitive community. And James succeeds, where so many later novelists have failed, succeeds in presenting the struggle for the rights of personality — the central theme of all modern American fiction, because he is able to conceive personalities of transcendent value."[59]

But the central thesis of the book was the destruction of James's talent because, having given his own country a "good trial" and failing to find a world to interpret there, he went to Europe to find a subject. Knowing that the great writer "is the voice of his own people," James understood the risk in such a step, and he acquired a compensatory theory from Flaubert and Zola, Frenchmen who had stayed in France, that the great writer could "get up" any subject provided that he was sufficiently precise an observer. Settling finally in London, James committed himself to the English subject but never mastered it. His "fantastication" of Europe prevented him from seeing the object "as in itself it really was." He had the attitude of a humble American cousin toward the "great life" which he observed in England; hence his "deranged sense of values." Here Brooks displayed the same stern intolerance for ambiguity of character that had marred his work on Twain: "It is intolerable to be asked to regard as 'great' the Lion who is so afraid of his hostess, or as honorable the young politician who changes his party to save his house, or as worthy of our serious attention the lover who prefers his furniture to his mistress." The "astonishing integument of the 'later manner'" was the logical corollary of James's failure to master the English subject; its elaborate wit and manner were a protective covering meant to conceal the fact that he had not achieved his vaunted "saturation" in England but was possessed by the self-consciousness of a guest in a house where he was not at home. Having drifted farther and farther away from reality, from life, James sustained himself in later years with his commitment to technical achievement in the novel: "The old magician . . . had retained a craftsman's, but never, never an artist's view of the world."[60]

No summary such as the above can do justice to the intricacy and artfulness with which Brooks made his case and which almost made the book, if not convincing, at least consistent and worthy of serious attention. Given the prevailing wind in 1925 it is unlikely that he could have changed many minds on James, but he could at least have prevented the book from ruining his reputation as a critic if he had found the strength to work on it a little longer. What was needed was a thorough and consistent treatment of the English novels and James's imaginative relation to them. Such a treatment would at least have received a hearing. Edmund Wilson, for instance, agreed with Brooks that the later novels suffered from a "lack of emotional experience which is . . . partly to be accounted for by James's isolation among the English."[61]

At this point, however, Brooks's own dramatic, novelistic method broke down, and instead of treating the novels in the context of James's life, he subjected James to the same tendentious analysis of exterior evidence as he had Mark Twain. He made his most egregious error in arguing that James's later novels were not "the fruit of an artistic impulse that is at once spontaneous and sustained" but rather were stories "blown out to the dimensions of novels." As Wilson pointed out, Brooks did "not even pretend to go to the novels themselves to justify his critical conclusion about them." Instead, he cited a letter to Howells where James had said that *The Sacred Fount* was originally planned as a short story. Worse still, Brooks omitted James's remark in the same letter that he had planned short stories at this time because they were more salable than novels. As Wilson said: "That, in spite of this intention, he should have found the short stories growing uncontrollably into novels would seem to prove, not, as Mr. Brooks says, that his 'artistic impulse' was not 'spontaneous and sustained,' but on the contrary, precisely that it was." This "readiness to found upon such meagre and dubious evidence so sweeping a case against half of a man's whole work" led Wilson to doubt the "spirit" in which Brooks was practicing criticism.[62]

Wilson had seen that Brooks admired James so far as James practiced like himself the art of society, but he could not have seen that Brooks hated himself as much as he hated James. In his memoirs Brooks would say that he had learned in connection with this book "of the division within myself," and Leon Edel, reviewing the memoirs, would say that Brooks's biographer must "fathom" the remark.[63] It is easily enough understood if we remember Carl Van Doren's perceptive comment in reviewing *Mark Twain* that Brooks was too "rigorously monistic," viewing any dualism in the artist's personality as not only tragic but sinful. While Brooks had put much self-hostility into the Twain book, he had not understood it as such, partly because in that book he had stood outside his subject's psyche, at least pretending to analyze with scientific detachment. And even if he had used the interior, novelistic method in the earlier book, he was not enough like Twain to have mirrored himself very precisely in the picture. But by employing the novelistic method on a subject like James, whose origins and highly conscious dedication so greatly resembled his own, Brooks could easily explore his own mind and then, given his "rigorously monistic" standard, be appalled when he saw himself in the picture. For though he did it more subtly than in *Mark Twain*, he explained James's failure also as due to a split personality, or rather, a "double existence." Brooks himself had doubted, exactly as he accused James of doubting, "whether an American could be an artist at all," and in his compensatory theory of the art of society, the only art possible for Americans, he no less than James had made "the very substance of this art out of his own failure to grasp the materials of it."[64]

Through James, Brooks learned how far removed he still remained from the reality of American life, how little he had mastered his subject, how far short he had fallen of being an artist of society. Brooks's stern condemnation of what seemed to him the separate peace of Twain and James had prevented him from seeing whatever tensions there had been in their accommodations with America. The true artist of society, while deploring their compromises, would have salvaged whatever gains they had made and thus through them, as Randolph Bourne had said, touched "a certain eternal human tradition of abounding vitality and moral freedom, and so build out the future." By denying himself the opportunity to have learned what he could about the texture of American life from his subjects, Brooks had denied himself any basis on which to build, any grasp of his materials as an artist of American society. The negativeness of the works on Twain and James had precluded any positive statement, any formulation of what the "right composition in human things" would portend for America. Through his criticism of James,

Brooks recognized his own failure and learned that he had not overcome in himself the conflict between his desire for abstraction from life and his belief that the artist was a worldly man, the conflict between his desire to flee to Europe and his belief that the duty of an American artist lay in America. A year and a half after *Henry James* was published, Brooks was aboard ship, bound for England.

7

A SEASON IN HELL

VAN WYCK had not made life easy for Eleanor. Although he had kept a romantic feeling that must have been gratifying to her, it had not led him to share the housework when she labored on translations in order to help him earn a living. He encouraged her to hire a cook or maid, but she did not always do so, either because it would have neutralized some of her earnings or else because help was not available. Later, she told his doctors that she had "slaved" for him and that he had taken it as a matter of fact.[1] Actually, he had not only failed to be grateful for all her help but had been irritated by it. The sight of Eleanor engaged in housework bothered him greatly because it suggested his inadequacy as a breadwinner. He would have preferred a home at least as genteel as the one in which he was raised. The absence of servants in the Westport house and the consequent hard work for Eleanor were a daily reminder that by the standards of Plainfield he was a failure.

Another quality he found disturbing in Eleanor was her inability to enjoy entertaining as much as he did, partly because of the housework involved but also because of the shyness stemming from her lonely childhood. Van Wyck preferred, when finances permitted, to write intensely all week and then relax with company on weekends. Social life was his main diversion, and Eleanor was ill-equipped to provide him with it.

She went through bad moods, one of them in the winter of 1923 when she was in California with the children and Van Wyck was in New York. Apparently she compared her life unfavorably to his in a letter, for he answered that while his life might look satisfactory to her it was a trial to him. He had his own moods and "more often than you!" Fortunately, it was obvious what must be done in her case — break up her daily routine and "let the air in." He proposed to do that by getting her a book to translate. Her depression must have lasted some time, for a few weeks later he wrote to her: "We must continue to straighten out our complexes — yours as well as mine, and learn how to live with some firm and clear serenity of mind. I feel as if we were still babes in the wood and that we have everything to learn about life — that perhaps we both ought to be psychoanalyzed — for your ups and downs are just as bad and miserable as mine."[2]

The effect of their many separations was to heighten his feeling for her, as during her absence in 1923 when he wrote to her: "O my dear, man is a carnal being and a sadly sentimental one and I was never made to be a monk. Do come quickly!" But in addition to sexual desire, separations also heightened Van Wyck's love because he suffered, as Eleanor later told one of his doctors, from "the malady of the ideal." What she meant in this context was not that he shared Amiel's longing for the ether, though he did, but that he tended to idealize her when they were separated. Then he decided, as he once wrote to her, that it was "jaundice" which prevented him from being happy with her "all day long." She had gained weight in recent years, and she hated to be separated from him for very long lest the shock be too great when his ideal vision was confronted with the real Eleanor.[3]

One of the basic tensions with which Van Wyck had lived was the conflict between his desire for abstraction from life and his commitment to the idea that the artist must be a worldly man. As his emotional longing for abstraction began to predominate during his illness, his relationship with Eleanor deteriorated, for she and the children, with their material needs, represented the demands of the world. In a sense they were "reality," with all its mundane requirements, forcing him to spend long hours of drudgery teaching at Stanford or working at the Century Company. No wonder that later when he felt he had been unfaithful to Eleanor because of an "affair" with Mollie Colum, he said, "I became hysterical and ran away from reality."[4]

Mollie Colum was Irish, and Van Wyck, proud of his eighth of Irish ancestry, always found the Irish attractive. Mollie, who had a slender figure and bright red hair, was not only attractive but also literary. She had studied at the National University, taken the same degree as Joyce, and been on the scene of the Irish literary revival that had interested Van Wyck while he was at Harvard and helped convince him that great art was nationalistic. She had worked in the *Freeman* office, and it was there that Van Wyck had come to know her well and in 1923 asked her to listen while he read the James manuscript aloud.[5]

Mollie later said that she had been surprised by his request; he was usually very shy. In fact, his reserved nature had bothered Mollie, and she had said so in her essay "An American Critic: Van Wyck Brooks," which had appeared in the *Dial* when Van Wyck received the magazine's award. Brooks belonged, she said, "to the highest order of critics," falling below that order in only one regard — "intensity of temperament and emotion." He lacked

> that intensity, that almost wildness of emotion, that thrills us in the work of the great European critics. In comparison with them he seems a little cool and self-possessed. We cannot imagine him capable of shining, reckless enthusiasms, or capable of allowing his mind to wander off into that yearning and almost foolish ecstasy that Taine wanders into over Alfred de Musset. . . . the secret of a rich and nervous and swiftly-moving style such as Taine's lies just in that capacity for sublime emotional folly. Van Wyck Brooks, measured with these great Europeans, has an American sedateness.[6]

Mollie soon provided an opportunity for the sedate American to indulge in some "emotional folly." In the mid-twenties she moved with her husband, Padraic Colum, to New Canaan, Connecticut, only twelve miles from Westport, and as Van Wyck grew increasingly ill, Mollie became deeply involved in his treatment.

Publication of *Henry James* in April 1925 had brought on Van Wyck's worst depression yet, and at dinner with the Colums shortly after the appearance of the book, he began to speak of suicide. Mollie suggested that he needed a change of scene, so he moved in with the Colums for a few days. There he gained weight, cheered up, and talked about Emerson. Mollie decided that his problem was not guilt over the *James* book, but loneliness, and that he needed more literary companionship than Eleanor could provide. Concluding that Van Wyck and Eleanor were a mismatch, she also decided that in describing the stifling qualities in Mark Twain's marriage, Van Wyck had unconsciously described his relationship with Eleanor. To Mollie's surprise, Eleanor was irritated by Van Wyck's visit with the Colums. Mollie was not surprised, however, when Van Wyck became morose upon returning to Westport. She consulted a doctor who suggested that Van Wyck spend May of 1925 with Austen Riggs in Stockbridge, and he and Eleanor both accepted the suggestion.[7]

It is difficult to assess the lasting effects of Riggs's treatment, but at Stockbridge in May, Brooks felt that he was cured. Actually, he had passed from depression into mania, and a few months later he joyfully wrote to Mumford:

> You may know I had a bad breakdown last spring — it really lasted about two years; and when it came to a head and burst — on May 20th, when I woke up — I felt as if I had expelled from my system the gathering poisons of years. . . . I feel ten years older and ten years younger at the same time, and so conscious, deep down, . . . about the "good life," and the "mission" — what other word is there? — of literature, and the necessity of reasserting the idealistic point of view. . . . Everything I have done so far has been a kind of exploration of the *dark* side of our moon, and this blessed Emerson has led me right out into the midst of the sunny side.[8]

Returning from Stockbridge, he began to write *The Life of Emerson,* and in his elated mood told Joel Spingarn that the book "*seems* to be flowing like a mountain-stream in the springtime." He was discovering how little was known about American history; a half dozen interesting figures in Emerson's circle were virtually untreated in the standard histories. In August the book was still "flowing," this time like "distilled honey," as he told Gamaliel Bradford. Emerson's world was "really the most enchanting society my imagination ever worked itself into and hitherto seen by me only in two dimensions." For once he was exuberant instead of tortured as he wrote, and he believed that the book would win a Pulitzer Prize.[9]

Bradford lived in Wellesley, so in September when Van Wyck and Eleanor, accompanied by Mollie Colum, set out to visit Concord and the Manse they stopped at Bradford's house. This was Brooks's first meeting with Bradford, a bed-ridden invalid who, with heroic effort, had written dozens of plays and novels as well as the biographical studies Brooks had reviewed in the *Freeman.* The meeting was an opportunity for Van Wyck "to explain some of the silly things

I used to write . . . about the relative wanting interest of American history, etc. One lives and learns — a little." Those "silly" things had been the fruit of his life's work and thought. The door was opening to the feeling of guilt and futility he later described in his memoirs: ". . . I was consumed with a sense of failure, a feeling that my work had all gone wrong and that I was mistaken in all I had said or thought."[10]

Meanwhile, he was gradually losing confidence that he could deal with Emerson. In August he had told Spingarn that he was "on the road to carrying out my long-cherished idea of writing the paradise of the American man of letters, to follow the *Inferno* of Mark Twain and the *Purgatorio* of Henry James. The monster I am trying to pull ashore is several diameters larger than any Emerson I have discovered in the history books, etc. — almost as big as Goethe. . . ." A few weeks later he wrote: "My book *seems* to be going well, though I sit down every day with the fear of God in me." The manuscript kept expanding because of the many interesting characters he was discovering around Emerson, and he feared that his subject would not be manageable in a single volume.[11]

His pace slowed gradually through the fall, and by the end of 1925 he had largely ceased writing, telling Newton Arvin a few months later: "I'm not sure it will come to anything. . . . the subject is so volatile that I have often felt I was trying to shape a mass of air." Thus he acknowledged defeat in his attempt to show that Emerson's was the complete literary life, sanely balanced between the requirements of this world and the demands of a prophetic vision. Van Wyck seemed to have found that he had been right after all in *America's Coming-of-Age*: "Emerson is persistently abstract. . . . if he takes two or three paces on the earth they only serve to warm him for a fresh aerial adventure." In June of 1926 he told Spingarn that the Emerson project "went up in the air several months ago."[12]

Actually, *The Life of Emerson* was virtually completed. After Brooks's recovery from his five-year depression in 1931 he did some work on it but probably nothing more than the "tinkering" he always did when finishing a book, changing an occasional word or phrase but leaving the sense substantially the same. Read as a personal document, *The Life of Emerson* indicates the state of Brooks's mind, not in 1932 when it was published, but in 1925 when it was written.[13]

The Life of Emerson indicates, then, that despite Brooks's manic state in 1925, he was deeply concerned with death. The book began with a detailed description of old Mary Moody Emerson who "lived in her shroud" and apostrophized the creatures of the grave as "dear worms! Most valuable companions!" Emerson's feeling of being "adjacent to the One" was later figured in the phrase, ". . . he had died out of the world of men and existence." Because death was a figure for the good, the book was not mournful but joyful, as in the final sentence when Emerson had died and ". . . the universe had become his house in which to live."[14]

For the first two-thirds of the book, history was conspicuous by its absence. Perhaps the omission was intentional. Early in the book Van Wyck wrote that Emerson, to his credit, invited men "drenched in Time to come out of Time and taste their native immortal air." As Van Wyck described it, there was a static quality to Emerson's Concord, almost as if Emerson had lived in a picture rather than a society. But the last third of the book dealt with Emerson's life from 1850 through the Civil War, and though Van Wyck tried to preserve the same joyous tempo in which the first part of the book was written, the effect was of a great bird forced to earth: "1850. The Fugitive Slave Law had passed both houses of Congress. Emerson awoke each morning with a painful sensation. He carried it about all day. It robbed the landscape of its beauty and took the sunshine out of every hour." Until now, Emerson had been above the battle, and Van Wyck had affirmed his feeling that ". . . his own quarrel was not with the state of affairs. No: with the state of man." So the next paragraph had to begin limply, "But his feelings had gradually changed." Brooks perceived the shift in the book's mood and told Max Perkins, who read the manuscript in 1926, that ". . . it trails off at the end."[15]

The trailing off signified not only the increasingly mundane quality of Emerson's life but also the decline of Van Wyck's mania while he was writing the book in 1925. By early 1926 he had entered a deep depression, which would have its relative highs and lows, but from which he would not completely emerge until 1931. And the depression was based in part on the recognition that he had not written the book for which he had hoped, the story of a successful literary life, that is to say, an artist triumphant in America.

The exact point in which the book was a failure was the absence in Emerson, as Brooks portrayed him, of the principle of self-opposition. Emerson, like Whitman, seemed to have never "squeezed the slave out of himself." It was the absence of this quality of self-opposition which had led Brooks to say in the *Freeman* that Whitman, wonderful as he was, was not the proper fountainhead for

American literature. By failing to show that Emerson had emerged successfully from trials that had been an ordeal for Mark Twain and forced Henry James to go on a pilgrimage, Brooks failed to affirm his belief in free will, failed to create a proper example for Americans of the fully realized literary life.

What the *Emerson* book needed was the same kind of analysis Brooks had used in dealing with the early lives of Mark Twain and Henry James, the kind of analysis he had foresworn when he wrote to Mumford in 1924 that he was "going in for synthesis now." He devoted forty pages to Emerson's happy childhood and Harvard career, but then, in three brief pages, passed over the twelve dark years of Emerson's life, from his eighteenth year to his thirtieth. In that period his first wife died of consumption, a brother was stricken by the same disease, another brother was driven mad, Emerson himself was ill, and then, at thirty, he recognized that he had chosen the wrong career and left the ministry. In all this poverty and illness and mistaken endeavor there was an opportunity to show that Emerson had grown as a man and "squeezed the slave out of himself." But to have shown such development would have required the intense analytical thought of which Brooks no longer felt capable. Instead, he passed lightly, impressionistically, over Emerson's years of trial and concluded, "He knew he was born for victory." Thus, the mature Emerson, who had known no strife, lived passively, not in the world of time but in Elysium: "He felt as if he had drunk the soma-juice with the morning-moving deities of the Rig-Veda, as if life were all an eternal resource and a long tomorrow, rich and strong as yesterday."[16]

This constant concern with death and afterlife showed that Brooks had lost the equilibrium with which he had previously maintained that the artist was a worldly as well as a spiritual man. *The Life of Emerson* had been meant to be the capstone of a trilogy, Brooks's second trilogy, and beneath the Freudianism and cultural nationalism this trilogy had the same basic structure as the first. Mark Twain, like John Addington Symonds, was trapped in the world. Henry James, abstracted from America, was as far removed from mundane reality as Amiel in his ideal visions. Van Wyck had hoped but failed to show that Emerson, like H. G. Wells, had lived the true literary life with his feet on the ground and his eyes on the sky. But by letting the Emerson go "up in the air," Van Wyck revealed that he had reverted to the symbolism of his adolescence, when art was a surrogate death, an escape from the materiality of American life into some heavenly abstraction.

Beyond the failure of his book, Van Wyck had other reasons to be depressed. As always, the problem was partly financial; he had been forced back to translating in order to make a living. Mollie Colum thought, probably correctly, that he was upset because Eleanor's mother, now in her seventies, was coming from California to spend her declining years with the Brookses in Westport. Mrs. Stimson had continued in her reservations about Van Wyck as a son-in-law and especially as a breadwinner, and she did not hesitate to express these feelings.[17] Ill and unable to move her belongings across country by herself, Mrs. Stimson waited in Carmel for Eleanor to come and get her. Eleanor took the children with her and was gone from about the middle of January to the middle of April 1926. Rather than keep house by himself, Van Wyck spent that period in a New Canaan inn, writing to Eleanor that he was "still fiddling with Emerson. Some day I am sure I shall master it, but I shall have to get out of this rut of exhaustion and conflict. . . ." Max Perkins, who also lived in New Canaan, saw much of Van Wyck that winter, but there was little fun in it, Perkins told Scott Fitzgerald, because Brooks was so depressed over his book.[18]

The greatest attraction in New Canaan was Mollie Colum. Van Wyck had his fortieth birthday dinner and many others that winter at the Colums' house. It was in this period that he had his "affair" with Mollie, though even calling it an "affair" betrayed unreasonable feelings of guilt. Physically, nothing more portentous than a kiss and an embrace occurred. He later told a doctor that "nothing much happened," and Mollie said that his distressed state had made him display his affection more warmly than usual.[19] But it was the spirit which counted for Brooks, and on that level he had been unfaithful, becoming extremely dependent on Mollie's sympathy and interest and telling her that if he lost her half his life was gone. He had always believed in monogamy and by betraying that belief he had opened a rich new source of guilt.

When Eleanor returned with her mother and the children in April, she found Van Wyck more depressed than ever before and unlike himself in a "cold, terrible way." She could not reach him emotionally or physically. He said he was impotent and probably was, impotence being a symptom of manic-depressive illness.[20] But Eleanor seems not to have believed him, which probably increased his sense of guilt. He was troubled also by the belief that he had behaved dishonorably toward his friend Padraic Colum. Mollie phoned or visited every day, but if Eleanor had suspicions she kept them to herself, accepting Mollie as an ally in the struggle against

Van Wyck's illness. Eleanor tried to relieve his gloom by brightening the Westport house. Although their income now consisted of fifty dollars every month from his mother, twenty from hers, and the rent of "Hedgerows," a house in New Canaan which Eleanor had inherited a few years earlier, she bought flowers and new dresses and entertained as much as possible. She believed that he cheered up somewhat, but she could not be sure. He would not discuss his feelings or hers. In the face of his own terror he required that she at least seem to feel secure.[21]

The advance which he had accepted on the *Emerson* book worried him greatly now that he had decided the book was a failure. Having no way to repay the debt, Van Wyck collected some of his *Freeman* essays and six chapters from the early, joyous part of the *Emerson* life into a volume of miscellany which Dutton published in 1927 under the title *Emerson and Others.* He had hoped that this would be accepted as the book against which his advance had been issued, but John Macrae at Dutton insisted that it was *The Life of Emerson* for which he had paid $1500.[22]

Needing money and convinced that his literary career was finished, Van Wyck began looking for a routine office job, despite Max Perkins' warning that in an office he would be throwing away his most valuable asset, his reputation as a writer. If he could no longer write books, Perkins said, then he should go on the lecture circuit or else write essays, which would be more profitable than books. To prove the point he had Van Wyck sell the first chapter of the *Emerson* book to *Scribner's Magazine* for $300. But Van Wyck said that he could not write essays; that spring he had attempted a short piece on Henry Adams but considered it a failure. Lacking a large topic, a book, on which to "focus" himself, he could not write effectively.[23]

He did little work of any kind during 1926 except for some reviewing and editing. He joined Alfred Kreymborg, Mumford, and Rosenfeld in requesting writers to submit work for the first *American Caravan,* but he contributed little to the project and the next year his name was dropped from the list of editors. A new book by Stuart Sherman, who had recently begun to move left, dropping his erstwhile role of hatchet man for Babbitt and More, prompted a friendly review from Van Wyck: "Mr. Sherman has emerged on the other side of the morass — emerged, in fact, with a stronger position than ever." The word "morass" occurred several times in the review and may have characterized Van Wyck's idea of the experience through which he himself was passing.[24]

The most interesting thing that he wrote in this period was a review of John Freeman's study of Melville, whose own career, until the posthumous publication of *Billy Budd* in 1924, had generally been believed to have ended in middle life. Van Wyck drew comfort from the fact that Melville had not, as he had previously imagined, fallen "into a kind of madness." Instead, Melville had "preserved his spiritual faculties unimpaired. There is a note of sweetness and serenity in 'Billy Budd' that speaks of an inward peace." When the review appeared in May of 1926, Van Wyck was doing a second stint with Austen Riggs in Stockbridge, and from there he drove to Pittsfield to view the empty, ramshackle house where Melville had written *Moby Dick*. The famous piazza was still there, albeit with rotting planks, and Van Wyck, peering through cracks in the boarded-up windows, saw some old folios and a ship's model mounted on the wall. Despite the mournful scene, he told Eleanor, "... it was thrilling to think that in these rooms was written the greatest of all American books."[25]

But Brooks's illness was to prevent him from ever genuinely appreciating Melville, whom he believed shared his alienation from life. That same spring of 1926 he had read a chapter from Henry A. Murray's book on Melville and advised Murray to make more of the trip to the Holy Land "as an attempt to get hold of his world which was slipping away from him." Writing the Melville entry for the *Dictionary of American Biography* (1927), Brooks said Melville's career had died of "excessive subjectivity," the same point he had made in a *Freeman* essay reprinted in *Emerson and Others*. After a brief "equilibrium" in *Moby Dick*, the subjective element of Melville's mind dominated the objective and his soul became, Brooks quoted Melville, "diffused through time and space." One so alienated from the world "ceases in the end even to desire the narrow house of art."[26]

This last sentence, with its *art-nouveau* flavor, would easily have fit into *The Malady of the Ideal,* the malady from which Brooks believed he suffered. His belief that his depression was a spiritual malady was rooted in his early admiration for writers like De Quincey and Amiel and their belief in the ineffability of spiritual experience. Out of that nineteenth-century tradition evolved much of modern esthetics, anti-art, and the cult of silence. Ezra Pound said, "A man hurls himself toward the infinite and the works of art are his vestiges, his traces in the manifest."[27] It was only a step from there to believing, as Brooks had believed in youth and in 1926 apparently did again, that art, mere "vestiges" and "traces," was of no consequence beside the spiritual act of hurling oneself into the infinite.

II

Ames Brooks, about to satisfy one of his periodic bursts of wander-lust, offered to take Van Wyck to England. Eleanor, perhaps secretly anxious to get him away from Mollie Colum, was enthusiastic. But Van Wyck was torn, sometimes liking the idea, sometimes loathing it. In *Emerson and Others* he had noted that going to sea was Melville's "substitute for pistol and ball." Van Wyck may unconsciously have understood the danger which Europe held for him and believed that he "must cling to America to preserve his personality from disinte-gration," as he said years later.[28]

Nevertheless, Van Wyck sailed in August of 1926, his irresolu-tion supposedly ended by his decision to undergo treatment by an English psychoanalyst. Eleanor later believed, however, that the question of medical treatment was a subterfuge to attain his real goal: ". . . what he really wanted, as I discovered later, was to get out of the country. . . ."[29] He planned a long stay in England and may secretly have hoped to settle there permanently. Eleanor expected to follow shortly with the children, after she had sold her house in New Canaan in order to pay their fare.

Van Wyck spent the autumn of 1926 in a sanitarium, Bowden House, in Middlesex, near Harrow School, where an analysis was undertaken which he later believed had done him harm. Otherwise, the treatment consisted of a relaxed routine and exercise. The day began at ten o'clock with "Swedish exercises," including the goose step, followed by work in the garden or in the carpentry shop. Afternoons there were swimming and tennis. Swimming and espe-cially diving were difficult, but tennis was easier, a hopeful sign: ". . . it's supposed to be very important for me to learn to play tennis," he wrote to Eleanor. Evenings alternated between bridge and dancing: "I am resigned to these damned games and I *hope* I shall learn to like playing them." The treatment was meant to lower stress and focus his attention outside himself. But in his spare time he worried about money and his family, worked at translating books which Eleanor mailed to him, and felt guilty because of his rela-tionship with Mollie Colum.[30]

He had told the doctors of his "affair," and they convinced him that he must choose between Mollie and Eleanor. He found the choice easy and broke with Mollie by letter. She said that she had had no romantic feeling for him, but Van Wyck later said that she had once threatened suicide if he abandoned her. Whether this was truth or delusion on his part, it did not deter him. Fearful that

Eleanor would divorce him, he now wrote to her, explaining his relationship with Mollie and begging forgiveness. Eleanor offered him a divorce which, of course, he did not want, and then to his relief, she agreed to continue the marriage.[31]

With the air cleared Van Wyck improved dramatically and felt well enough to leave Bowden House. For the early months of 1927 he stayed in London with his old *Freeman* friend Walter Fuller and his wife Crystal Eastman. Their house was "quite a centre," and one evening there he met Bertrand Russell. Telling Newton Arvin that he was "rather looking up English things," Van Wyck attended plays, visited museums, and seemed almost happy in London.[32]

His improvement, however, was only temporary, and he soon entered his deepest cycle of depression yet. Hoping to find a job in London, he tramped all over the city in the winter cold, and having no luck, returned to the Fullers' house to lie awake worrying all night. At his doctor's request he returned to Bowden House, only to attempt suicide by smashing his watch crystal and swallowing the pieces. It was a lame, half-hearted attempt from which he apparently suffered no harm and which he reported to the staff himself. Nevertheless, a worried doctor threatened to commit him, against his will, to a stricter institution where he could be watched more closely. Suffering from increasingly severe delusions, Van Wyck gave the threat his own interpretation — Parliament had passed a special act permitting him to be "buried alive." Sometimes he believed he would be walled into a small chamber. Other times, when the maids raised the Venetian blinds, he interpreted the clatter as the hammering together of his "box." Always, "they" were coming for him. On a sunny spring day he looked out an open window at the grass and daffodils and was suddenly possessed by a guilt-ridden, egomaniacal vision that linked his own fate to that of the world. All who were attached to him would have breakdowns and be buried alive, and all who were attached to them would suffer the same fate, and so on, until "all mankind was engulfed, all movement ceased." He saw "the steamships stopping in the middle of the ocean, while invisible waves of horror encircled the world."[33]

Such was the state in which Eleanor found him when she finally arrived in April, having been delayed in her crossing by the lack of a buyer for the New Canaan house. She had decided that the only way to sell the house was to renovate it, though she would have to do the cleaning and painting herself. "My soul sickens at the thought," she had written to Charles at school but proudly reported soon after that she could hang paper as fast and well as the man who charged six dollars a day. She had turned down a low offer of $22,000 and lost another of $25,000 because the buyer was refused a loan. Receiving despondent letters from Van Wyck in February, she had decided that whether the house was sold or not she would sail, but then she had delayed again so that Charles could be with her during his school vacation. He was fifteen now and her main confidant during Van Wyck's illness. Finally, she had sold the house. With eleven-year-old Kenyon in tow and promising to bring Charles over in the summer, she had embarked at the end of March.[34]

Contrary to her expectations, they were home again by early May. In England she had moved Van Wyck from Bowden House to a hotel and been terrified by his attempts to throw himself in front of trains, though they were faint attempts since she could draw him back. Clearly, he could not earn a living in England as they had planned, but he said that he could not return to America either. Even so, Eleanor booked passage for April 30, and when the time came he only feebly resisted boarding. The ship's doctor wanted him locked in his stateroom, but Eleanor took responsibility for keeping him away from the rail. In New York he had to be forced to disembark, but the flight to Europe was over. He had returned to earth, to America.[35]

III

The next year was a dreary round of emotional ups and downs, mostly downs. Van Wyck worried about money, turned down an invitation to write an article for *Scribner's Magazine*, looked feebly and unsuccessfully for an office job, and performed the exercises and activities — carpentry, skating, tennis, bridge — which various doctors prescribed. He suffered from vertigo and delusions of all sorts. The sun was off-color, and when he slept he dreamed that he was about to be hanged. Suicide became an obsession, and the commonest objects suggested it to him. Knives existed for the purpose of slitting his throat, tall buildings were meant to be jumped from, and his belts were potential garrotes. He had never been a skillful driver, and now he became reckless. Since he would not often relinquish the wheel, Eleanor had to curtail the use of their car. There were few visitors because he was reclusive and because Eleanor was trying to keep his breakdown a secret. Mumford visited and for much of 1928 Henry Longan Stuart, the Anglo-Irish author of the fine novel *Weeping Cross* (1908), lived in the house and helped Eleanor keep a careful watch over Van Wyck. A Sandhurst graduate who had been wounded in the war and now lived by translating Italian novels and reviewing for the *New York Times,* Stuart was something of an invalid himself and would die later that year. But he was also a cheerful companion, and Van Wyck admired him greatly.[36]

April of 1928 brought a significant upturn in Van Wyck's spirits, due partly to his finally obtaining a routine job — reviewing books for the *Independent,* a weekly based in Boston. His reviews were well-written but uncritical summaries of books on subjects as diverse as Leonardo da Vinci, William Jennings Bryan, Zola, and Houdini. Reviewing Norman Foerster's *American Criticism* (1928), which contained a direct attack on himself, Brooks refused to respond in kind and instead praised the book for its "illumination and general solidity." Having found in Emerson's New England an American past he admired, Van Wyck could only agree with Foerster's harsh judgment of his early ideas as a revolt against a past which he had "not in the least really care[d] to know."[37]

When he suffered a relapse in May of 1928, Eleanor decided on a course of physical therapy recommended by a doctor and given in the summer on Monhegan Island by, of all people, Gerald Stanley Lee, the same man Van Wyck had attacked in *America's Coming-of-Age.* Angered by Lee's toadying book, *Inspired Millionaires,* Brooks had ridiculed him as the typical American prophet, "totally uninformed" but armed with a "bland smile." Still smiling, Lee visited Van Wyck in Westport, convinced him to take the course, and finding it an "almost tragically happy experience" to help the man who had attacked him, said that he was willing to defer payment. All Van Wyck needed, Lee told Eleanor, "is to be released from his reverie with a hopeful action and it will point the way."[38]

Accompanied by Henry Longan Stuart, Van Wyck arrived on Monhegan Island in mid-summer and submitted to two hours of exercise every day. Lee's idea was to reduce tension and strain by teaching "the substitution of floating into motions instead of pushing into them." This was accomplished by exercises like balancing three balls, one on the head and one on the back of each hand, while stepping up and down off a chair. Accomplishment of this task would show Van Wyck that he was "master of his fate" and prove "his right to self respect." By the end of August, Lee could offer Eleanor the encouraging news that Van Wyck had managed the feat thirteen times in a row. It is hard to know, however, whether Lee meant to hearten or discourage Eleanor by telling her than Van Wyck "laughed at himself this morning — at something he had just

said about the whole universe — beginning with you and Westport
being buried alive with him, God himself getting into the grave last."
Convinced that the exercises had been effective, Lee told Eleanor on
Van Wyck's departure: "I wish he could be further along with the
job of keeping the ball on his head before he has to face too many
people but he can take a job of writing."[39]

Lee did manage one intelligent recommendation — that Van
Wyck be kept away from his mother. She had come to Monhegan
Island to keep company and watch Van Wyck after Stuart, ill, had
been forced to return to New York. Observing her behavior with
Van Wyck, Lee warned Eleanor that Sallie agreed "unconsciously
. . . more than she should" with Van Wyck's conviction that he was
unfit for life. Hans Zinsser noticed the same thing when, on the way
back from Monhegan Island, Sallie deposited Van Wyck at Zinsser's
house in Cambridge for a few days. Later that autumn a doctor
would find it necessary to caution Sallie and Ames against censuring
or dictating to Van Wyck.[40]

In Cambridge, Zinsser, hoping perhaps to recall their happy
walks together in Palo Alto, kept Brooks outdoors. But Van Wyck
remained dejected and acted as sick as he was, crawling in the grass,
pulling weeds, and talking incessantly of his guilt and unworthiness,
of how he must inevitably be "incarcerated" — that is, buried alive —
and starved to death. Wouldn't it be better, he asked, if he were
dead, and wouldn't Zinsser please kill him?[41]

Zinsser and Mumford both now began to recommend more
intensive medical care to Eleanor, but Van Wyck interpreted any
move in that direction as the first step toward being "buried alive" in
an asylum. Mumford and Spingarn suggested treatment by Jung in
Zurich, but A. A. Brill, whom Eleanor had consulted, said that
analysis might be dangerous during a depression. Van Wyck's experience with analysis in England seemed to have verified Brill's
opinion. All of the doctors said that the illness was cyclical, and
Eleanor expected the next "up-curve" in the coming winter. Then
would be the time to see Jung and try to prevent a recurrence.
Meanwhile, she was "terrified at the thought of taking any drastic
step that might precipitate a tragedy."[42]

Van Wyck, following Lee's recommendation, continued to work
and write, but so unsatisfactorily that he only lowered his self-
confidence further still. He summarized rather than reviewed the
books which Edmund Wilson sent from the *New Republic*, and he
translated literally rather than idiomatically, the result of his "exag-
gerated respect for anything done by others," as Eleanor explained

to an understanding but dissatisfied Jack Wheelock at Scribner's. Still another blow to Van Wyck's self-respect came in October of 1928 when the *Independent* merged with the *Outlook* and stopped buying the weekly, uncritical reviews from which he had drawn, Eleanor said, a "pathetic satisfaction." Meanwhile, convinced that he could never write another book, he refused an invitation from one publisher to write a life of Swift and from another firm that wanted a book on Boswell. Eleanor told Mumford: "Oh, Lewis, if I could just get him started on another book I know, from of old, he would be well in a week."[43]

The "up-curve" which Eleanor had expected in the winter came in the fall and was short-lived. Van Wyck dropped his reclusiveness and happily received visits from Wheelock and Arvin. After reading Arvin's *Hawthorne* in manuscript, he sent his congratulations: ". . . you have written by far the best book on the subject. . . . better than Henry James." But by winter he had fallen into his deepest cycle of depression yet, and Eleanor, exhausted by caring for Van Wyck while keeping house and translating, finally agreed with Mumford and Zinsser that more professional care was necessary. She wrote to Jung, describing Van Wyck's symptoms and asking if she could send him to Zurich for analysis. Jung answered that Van Wyck's case would be difficult, perhaps impossible to treat, and he warned that analysis might be dangerous. Thus Jung implicitly agreed with most of Van Wyck's other doctors that he suffered from a physiological illness rather than a psychosis, a view consistent with much contemporary opinion on manic-depressive illness.[44]

By the time Eleanor received Jung's answer in April, Van Wyck had begun a determined fast, intending to starve himself to death. Sallie and Ames had said that they would pay for institutional treatment if it was necessary, and Eleanor now felt that she had no choice. On the twentieth of April 1929, Van Wyck was admitted, voluntarily, to Bloomingdale Hospital in White Plains, New York.[45] There he was strapped in bed and tube-fed until he abandoned his fast. It was probably at Bloomingdale, the very place where Dr. Sloper of *Washington Square* had caught his fatal cold, that Van Wyck was visited by visions of Henry James, who turned "great menacing luminous eyes upon me." Considering himself "emotionally atrophied" and "fathomlessly depressed," he said that his case was hopeless, and he wept and sobbed when talking of Eleanor, her great love for him, and his absence of feeling for her and the children. Still fearful of being buried alive, he told his doctors: "The custom is legally practiced in England if it is psychologically impossible to live." He believed that Bloomingdale was making him worse: "I am in confinement like a wild, raging animal." He could have effected his own release with a written ten-day notice, and all of Eleanor's persuasiveness was required to make him continue his voluntary stay at Bloomingdale.[46]

He was still further depressed by the hospital environment and by the therapy, a sort of shock treatment consisting mostly of insult and irony. Van Wyck had one of many doorless rooms looking onto a long, locked corridor where he mingled with other patients and played pinochle or bridge. The other patients ranged from a harmless general who rubbed poached eggs in his hair to a religious maniac who once tried to strangle Brooks's partner at bridge. When, just before noon, a file of inmates exited from the violent ward and, flanked by orderlies, marched around the exercise yard, Van Wyck supplied invisible whips to make it "a Doré picture, in real life, from the Inferno." After a brief improvement in May, he became seclusive and passive, stopped speaking, played solitaire, knocked the croquet ball around the exercise yard by himself, and began to pick and eat grass. Evenings he wept, dwelling on Eleanor's love for him and his guilt and selfishness in his relations with her.[47]

Hans Zinsser, moved by the "pathetic letters" he had been receiving from Van Wyck at Bloomingdale, urged that he be moved to Four Winds, a small private institution in Katonah, New York. There would be more individual attention at Four Winds, but it was also more expensive than Bloomingdale. Zinsser, however, told Mumford that ". . . the matter is so serious that a few thousand dollars more or less should not be taken into consideration," and he added that if necessary he was willing to raise or contribute the money. Mumford had already made a similar statement to Eleanor. In mid-June Zinsser finally travelled to Bloomingdale and found Brooks suffering "in a manner that is pitiful to see," his condition aggravated by the restrictions imposed to prevent suicide. Both Van Wyck and Eleanor agreed with Zinsser that Four Winds would be better. The supervision would be less intense, and while that would increase the possibility of suicide, it might also cheer Van Wyck up. Whatever was decided, Zinsser told Mumford, it was necessary to "push a consistent policy. . . . There has been much loss of time and altogether too long a period of desultory medical attention without responsible and frequent supervision."[48]

The rate at Four Winds was seventy-five dollars per week, twenty-five dollars more than at Bloomingdale. Sallie and Ames had said that fifty was all they could afford, and in fact they had frightened Eleanor by speaking of putting Van Wyck in a state institution to save money. So Eleanor made a "private" arrangement to pay the twenty-five dollar difference to Four Winds while Sallie and Ames would be billed for fifty, the same as at Bloomingdale. On the Fourth of July, 1929, Van Wyck was transferred to Four Winds.[49]

Upon admittance, according to staff notes, he was "cooperative and pleasant, but tense, uneasy and preoccupied," quick in his movements, and impulsive with a number of mannerisms. For instance, he would walk around a tree with his hands on the trunk, stooping occasionally to pull grass to eat. Speaking with attendants outdoors, he squatted on his haunches, pulled weeds, and averted his face. He admitted to a feeling of "unreality," said that his situation was "hopeless," and described himself as a "memory." When told that he could recover if he made an effort he answered, "There is nothing to make an effort with — I have nothing left." He went for days at a time without sleep, and sometimes he heard voices and felt that someone was about to lay hands on him. Then he could not stand still for fear that he would be strapped to his bed or pushed into a cell. About eight or nine o'clock in the evening he would brighten up, but at night he barked and moaned. He admitted to suicidal thoughts but said that he had no intention of effecting them. The staff concluded that he was actively suicidal.[50]

A few days after his arrival he tried to escape. Somehow, probably from Ames or Sallie, he had conceived the idea that on the first of September he would be committed to a state hospital in order to save money. "God help me there," he wrote to Eleanor, pleading with her to take him back to Westport before the dreaded date. She should not listen to the doctors or his mother or Ames: "If I am *dead* to the family — let me at least be dead finally in some humane way, not kept alive, with *feeding tubes* and bed straps for *30 years.*" And he told her that Four Winds was like the English hospital, Bowden House, "only 2 years [later] & 10,000 times worse. 'They' are coming for me this time with handcuffs and all the rest of it — in the shape of the state *Insane* warden, etc. — *in time* — unless you will do as I implore you. 'Give me liberty or give me death.' "[51]

Yet there were signs of gradual improvement that summer. He entered into conversations and activities with other patients, learned to weave and play baseball though he was handicapped by retarded motor control, and he began to gain weight. The improvement continued through the fall, and in September he began to lose his urge to eat grass. By November he was well enough to work a little on a translation which Eleanor had undertaken for Scribner's. On Christmas Day of 1929 Eleanor and the two boys visited and found him better. Progress, however, was very slow and he was still suicidal.[52]

Beneath the physiological basis of his illness, Van Wyck's depression had been deepened and prolonged by the great neurotic capacity for guilt which he had developed in adolescence and which had been intensified by the accusations of his family that he was "morbid."[53] Now those accusations seemed to have proved correct. He conjured up Doré pictures of the Inferno and thought of his illness as a "Season in Hell," because he felt that he was suffering a just retribution for his sins. Accepting his guilt, he consciously, willfully punished himself with all the purposeful intensity which he had previously devoted to his writing. Years later he would observe: "It is not easy by sheer inertia to sink to the lower depths. In order to sink as well as to rise, a well-organized person has to work, for he has to violate all manner of instincts which it is easier to satisfy. The line of least resistance is to float on a dead level."[54] The depth of his depression had been in part his own doing, but he had finally exhausted himself and now he ebbed toward life.

IV

Meanwhile, Eleanor had tried to deal with the problem of *The Life of Emerson*. She maintained that Van Wyck would not recover until the book was in print, and his doctors agreed that the unpublished book might be prolonging the depression longer than they had expected. She had sent the typescript to Mumford, who had replied that the book was "complete as it stands" and suggested that Eleanor show it to Macrae. She had done so, and Macrae answered in the winter of 1929 that he wanted to publish the book. But Van Wyck, still ashamed of the manuscript, refused his permission. So Eleanor decided to "let the matter drop, apparently, and bring it out on my own authority," without Van Wyck's approval or even knowledge. Mumford opposed this step, pleading that Van Wyck's spirits might be improved by working on the manuscript. Eleanor answered, "Lewis, he will never be able to work on it until he is well and it is my firm belief that he will never be well until it is out." And she added a rare note of despair: "I am beginning to believe that he will never be well anyhow." Mumford had warned that it might be an "unbearable humiliation" to Van Wyck to have the manuscript published while he was dissatisfied with it, but Eleanor replied that he could improve the book in a later edition. Anyway, she said, it was too late to stop publication. Once in the winter she had asked Macrae to return the manuscript and he had refused, citing his $1500 advance as justification. Mumford now bypassed Eleanor and wrote directly to Macrae that Brooks's work could not be published without his consent unless he was judged, as he had not been, incompetent. Macrae gave in and informed Eleanor that Van Wyck's approval was required for publication.[55]

Mumford, with his practical bent, had also begun to insist that when the book was finally published, it should be a profitable undertaking; he sent his copy of the manuscript to Carl Van Doren, then editor of the Literary Guild. Van Doren liked the book, wanted to adopt it, and asked Max Perkins to urge Brooks to publish. The Guild terms were $7000 in a lump sum, and Van Wyck would still receive his royalties on the book's retail sale. Perkins was soon deeply involved in the effort to persuade Brooks that the book was publishable.[56]

Meanwhile, Eleanor was forced by the doctors to reduce the frequency of her visits to Four Winds. Her mere physical presence still depressed Van Wyck. She tried to accept the doctors' verdict with good grace but could not entirely conceal the hurt, and she warned that if she was ever to resume a normal life with Van Wyck, she must see him often enough to prevent him from idealizing her. However, if Eleanor's presence depressed Van Wyck because she represented the demands of worldly life, then a solution was about to be achieved. Eleanor's cousin, Henry Stimson, Hoover's Secretary of State, created a trust worth almost $100,000 to guarantee Eleanor's support.[57] With an independent income, Eleanor would represent freedom from mundane responsibilities rather than enslavement to them.

Van Wyck continued his gradual improvement but with occasional relapses, as in March of 1930 when he wrote to Eleanor, begging her "to take me away in a car so that I can go up alone to the deserted farmhouse on the ridge above the Waldrons and stay there until I starve to death. . . . I would rather have thirty days alone in that old house with the rats, snakes and spiders than anything else I can think of. . . . My existence here is torture unbelievable. . . . Save me from drowning by helping me to starve."[58] The next winter when he was taken outdoors for exercise he went in light clothing and laid down in the snow, hoping to catch a fatal case of pneumonia. But this was the last of his feeble attempts at suicide, and the general trend during 1930 was upward. He seemed to be recovering his sense of humor, and he was more alert and spontaneous, usually concentrating well at baseball, though he would sometimes face left field when playing third base. He began to read again, and he learned to make hooked rugs with outdoor scenes which from a distance resembled paintings.

By the spring of 1931 he was so much better that Eleanor insisted, against the best judgment of Doctor Lambert, the medical director at Four Winds, that he be sent home to see how he fared. On April 12, 1931, he was released from Four Winds, though it would be a year yet before his record was finally marked "Discharged — cured." Once home, he slept well, seemed happier, and lost his fear of meeting people. But Eleanor was somewhat disappointed. He had not entirely recovered, she said, because he refused to return to his writing and still considered everything he had done "no good." In June she finally persuaded him to look at his Emerson manuscript again. She had retyped it so it would look new and fresh, and when he read it he exclaimed, "Why this is good! This is damn good!" The opinion showed that he was well into the upswing of one of his cycles, for in sober moments he would always be dissatisfied with the book. More than twenty years later he still felt "that I must make amends to myself for my abortive handling of RWE." Still, his willingness to publish the book was a clear sign that he had emerged from his depression.[59]

On the Fourth of July 1931, he wrote to Max Perkins that he had "cleared up the obscure parts" of the manuscript and asked if the Literary Guild still wanted the book. Perkins reopened negotiations with Van Doren, while urging Van Wyck to let Scribner's publish the trade edition rather than Dutton. Brooks answered that he needed a publisher not only for the Emerson manuscript but also for the Twain and James, which he had decided were "fundamentally sound books." He wanted to revise and reissue them with *The Life of Emerson* in a one volume edition with a preface explaining his intention: "a sort of trilogy — tracing through these three typical figures, as I saw them — Mark Twain (adaptation to the environment), Henry James (escape from the environment), Emerson (domination of the environment, which thus tends to create a more nearly 'ideal' society) — the history of the American man of letters, touching all of his characteristic problems & indicating the proper nature of artistic 'success' & what it means both to the individual

and to society." He wanted Perkins to be his publisher but only if
". . . the thing can be managed without hurting the feelings of Mr.
Macrae who has been so decent to me." Perkins felt that Dutton
should have pushed Brooks's books harder, but in the face of Van
Wyck's feeling of obligation to Macrae there was little that Perkins
could do except to make sure that Dutton let the Literary Guild have
the book. Macrae opposed book clubs, believing them bad for the
publishing business. But Perkins thought that Guild adoption would
introduce Brooks to a larger public and promote sales of his other
books, so he persuaded Macrae that this once a Dutton book should
also be published by the Literary Guild. Thanks to the Depression,
however, the Guild terms were not what they had been, and Van
Wyck realized only $3000 rather than the $7000 which Van Doren
had earlier mentioned.[60]

Eleanor was disappointed that Van Wyck devoted his energy to
revising his old work, and she refused to consider him cured until he
had begun something new. In her impatience for complete recovery, she did not see that before he could deal with the future he had
to come to terms with the past. In April he had still believed that all
his work was "no good," but by October he felt that the Twain and
James books only needed revision to make them satisfactory. The
guilt which he had felt for his early work was dropping away, to be
replaced by a vague embarrassment that, as he later put it, "I
conducted my education in public."[61]

Meanwhile, Lewis Mumford was opening the door to a new
interest by sending Brooks a copy of his book *The Brown Decades: A
Study of the Arts in America, 1865–1895* (1931), which treated the
Gilded Age far more sympathetically than Van Wyck had done in
his work on either Twain or James. Stimulated by Mumford's book,
Van Wyck wrote him a long and important letter, proposing that he
write a "History of American Culture." Mumford never wrote this
particular great book, but Brooks himself was to attempt something
like it — *Makers and Finders: A History of the Writer in America* — the
title of the series of five books that began in 1936 with *The Flowering
of New England*. Brooks's goal was to be similar to the one he
suggested for Mumford, the creation of that center in American life
whose absence he had spent his youth lamenting:

> What bowled me over all the time I was reading was the thought
> that all these sketches and ideas are properly fragments of the
> great book that has to be written and that nobody in the world

but Lewis will ever be able to write. I mean, the History of American Culture, in six volumes, on the scale of Gibbon's *Rome,* also written in the grand style and from a point of view that is absolutely and everlastingly *central.* . . . And what makes *The Brown Decades* so vaguely unsatisfying, in a sense, is because in reading it I found myself instinctively relating every new fragment to this more comprehensive work that must be written to give all your intuitions their proper value and setting. This is a defect inherent, it seems to me, in your conception. You discuss (always admirably) "neglected" figures like George Fuller. But it is pertinent to ask By whom are they neglected? Not by half a dozen people in this neighborhood who have always known Fuller's work. No, but by some "central," hypothetical audience, which in your mind you assume *should* exist, but which really doesn't exist and will not exist (in the sense in which a central audience exists in France or England) until it has been created by some critical historian, by some such work, for instance, as the great, grand and immortal History of American Culture I have spoken of, a work that rehandles all the *centrally accepted* figures (Howells, Whitman, etc. in all lines) and so provides the right angle at every point from which to study the lesser and "neglected" figures, etc. . . .

Lewis, read, if you haven't read it, Gibbon's autobiography and see what a wonderful thing it is to have a life occupied for years with an immense work like this that possesses all your thoughts. . . .[62]

Brooks was half-consciously mapping out a course for himself, and he could not fail to be stirred by Mumford's reply that, working together, they would "have a concentrated effect, multiplied far beyond the mere addition of our powers." Van Wyck quickly answered: "I have taken your letter so much to heart, as a sort of vote of confidence, that it has recreated in my own mind an idea that I have cherished for years — twenty, I guess — and that Eleanor is always driving me to carry out — of a History of American Literature in two or three volumes which I can spend the rest of my life writing!"[63] Van Wyck had cautiously found his way back to full recovery, measured even by Eleanor's rigorous standard; he would resume his work. In proposing that Mumford undertake a history of American culture, Brooks had suggested for his friend an undertaking of dimensions larger than he quite dared demand of himself. The advantage of writing to a friend was that he could point out, for his own benefit also, what a wonderful thing it would be to have life occupied by an "immense work" that would "possess" all his thoughts. As he often said, a writer "out of focus" was a writer "in hell." The long sustained effort to accomplish his history of American literature would keep him "focused" for the next twenty years and help prevent a recurrence of his "Season in Hell."

8

TENONED AND MORTISED IN GRANITE

"...there remained in my stomach as it were a hard ball of panic." So Brooks described his feeling in the years after his recovery, the years when he was at work on his five volumes of *Makers and Finders: A History of the Writer in America.* That history was addressed to contemporary writers and to the panic he supposed inhabited their stomachs also. In 1934 he quoted Malcolm Cowley's remark that "...ours is a 'homeless generation,'" adding that it "needs to be repatriated. It needs to find a home. But where? In what?" He said also that his early work needed revision in its conception "of 'America' in relation to 'Europe.'"[1] Thus Brooks seemed tacitly to acknowledge the largest error of his early career; he had judged America's history by Europe's rather than by an appropriately indigenous standard. Now, with the experience of twenty years of chaos in Europe and the recent turmoil of his personal life, Brooks felt that his generation must be "repatriated." He would turn once more to the American past to see if it offered lines of development toward the order, security, and community he always desired.

Van Wyck was committed now to knowing America, to mastering the facts of American life in a way that had not seemed necessary in his earlier psychological studies of Twain and James. Beginning work on his first volume, which would deal with New England from 1815 to the Civil War, he travelled frequently to Boston to read in the Athenaeum and to edit the papers of Gamaliel Bradford. Brad-

ford had died in 1932, naming Brooks as his literary executor. It was
a formidable task; there were ninety volumes of unpublished manuscripts. But Van Wyck was interested in Bradford and believed his
Journal was the only American book "to compare with Amiel's."
Bradford, a successful biographer, had failed in his strongest aspiration, to be a novelist. Brooks probably believed that Bradford's lack
of what Amiel called "fatal facility" was the logical result of having
lived through the New England *fin de siècle*. He hoped that editing
Bradford's papers would bring him closer to the New England past,
and he accepted the chore. It would occupy much of his time in the
next two years.[2] His trips to Boston brought him into contact with
such other men of letters as Judge Robert Grant and M. A. DeWolfe
Howe, representatives of the older generation he had scornfully
dismissed in *America's Coming-of-Age*. Now he dealt gingerly with
them, consulting them in his study of New England, and also studying them as later types of the writers he was preparing to treat in his
history. For instance, Bradford's courage in writing in the face of
illness reminded him of Prescott and Parkman.[3]

Even as he began the study of New England which would
occupy him through the thirties, he prepared to deal with the rest of
America. Among the older generation he cultivated friendships with
Hamlin Garland, Owen Wister, and Ellen Glasgow. And he began to
spend his winters in other parts of the country, Virginia, South
Carolina, Florida, and California. He had learned to drive some
years before his breakdown, and now he and Eleanor made long
journeys by car, mastering the country's contours on the winding
roads of the time.

The American scene reminded him of Europe. During the
winter of 1934 he did research at the Library of Congress and lived
in Alexandria, in an old brick house; ". . . looking over a forest of
chimney-pots, and the yellow fog, the street-cries and the mild air
make it seem like a shabby end of London." Two years later he and
Eleanor spent the winter in South Carolina, where Van Wyck was
thrilled by the stillness and the sense of timeless continuity with the
past. There was a monumental quality to everything; a statesman
had died in every four-poster, and the big houses all had marble
bureaus, rag rugs, mildewed brass and silver, and old family portraits. He was amused but also impressed by Miss Josephine
Pinckney's "lovely old lavender house, with blinds and trimmings in
two shades of green, facing a marble statue of William Pitt, with both
arms broken off by British cannon-balls in the Revolution."[4]

Farther south, he found resemblances to the Italian coast he

had loved since childhood. In 1933, on the way to Florida, he and
Eleanor stopped at the Bonaventure Cemetery in Savannah. Van
Wyck was stunned, looking down the avenues of oak and cypress
leading to lichen-covered tombs and the breaking waves of the surf
beyond. It was an otherworldly scene, like the one he had experienced in the monastery on the cliff above Naples in 1905. "That
cemetery is like nothing in the world," he wrote to John Gould
Fletcher, adding that he understood Poe for the first time.[5] They
went on to St. Augustine, where Van Wyck began to write *The
Flowering of New England* in a rented house under a magnolia tree.
The writing went well for a time, and he was very happy. From his
balcony he could look across an unkempt garden of palm and olive
trees to the Spanish fort and the ocean. It was a "heavenly place." He
and Eleanor took their meals in a hotel that seemed "European in
every respect."[6]

Even before his breakdown Brooks had begun to believe that
America had once had something like a national culture, and now as
he began *The Flowering of New England* he was convinced. He announced this change of opinion in 1934 when some of his earlier
work, including *America's Coming-of-Age,* was reissued in *Three Essays
on America.* He prefaced the new volume by explaining that in his
youth, "We had had too much of the old New England poets."
Therefore, he had dealt rashly with them, "even to the point of
impudence." Since then he had had "a vague horror of having
appeared to disparage these older worthies," because ". . . one finds
in them today — in some of them at least — the large mental bones
and the hardy sinews that mark an important race."[7]

He refused to change his mind, however, about the Gilded Age,
and in 1933 he reissued *The Ordeal of Mark Twain.* Although he
made twenty-five hundred changes in the text,[8] the revision was
slight, a toning down, not a shifting of the argument. Where the first
edition read ". . . his was a splendid genius which had never found
itself," the new edition read "never *fully* found itself."[9] Thus he
acknowledged the criticism that he had not appreciated the good
things Mark Twain had done. But the main argument was unchanged; the artist in Mark Twain had been thwarted by American
society.

Brooks still had a great capacity for work. In addition to issuing
new editions of his old books, he edited two large volumes of
Gamaliel Bradford's papers and translated Amiel's *Private Journal*
with his son Charles. Yet any work other than writing was still a
torment for him. At the beginning of 1934 he had hoped to finish

The Flowering of New England by the end of the year, but he was interrupted by his work on Bradford's papers and Amiel's journal. Although he still admired Amiel, he had only undertaken the translation in order to give his son Charles a start as a writer. Perhaps because his son's name was to appear with his own, he worked beyond reason on the project. He set to work in August, hoping to be done by October, but that month found him "buried alive" by the translation. In November he hoped to be finished by mid-December, and at Christmas he planned to be done in a week. But in mid-January he still labored at the "infernal" task, slowed as he told Waldo Frank, by "the diplomatic problem of doing it with my own son."[10]

Van Wyck had become most active as a parent only as his sons approached manhood. Children had never interested him, and he had been ill during his sons' adolescence. Troubled still, as in his illness, with feelings that he had not been a good father, he found it difficult to let his sons be independent. Rather than see them dissipate their energies in the workaday world, he contributed to their support long after they finished college. He hoped Charles would become a writer and the younger son, Kenyon, a painter, and he exhorted them as he did other American artists: "You have talent, o my intelligent son," he wrote to Charles at Harvard, "and how I would love to see you developing it." Both sons spent their youth before deciding that they did not want to be artists, and Van Wyck expended time, energy, and money. In addition to the five months he labored on Amiel's journal, he had sent Charles to France to work on the translation in the winter and spring of 1934. The return on this investment was about a hundred dollars in royalties during the first year the journal was in print.[11]

Although the Stimson grant to Eleanor enabled Van Wyck to "vow . . . that I would never take another job,"[12] it did not solve all of his financial problems. Even though Charles Brooks worked for the Federal Writers Project in 1935, Eleanor and Van Wyck were intent on sheltering and supporting him. There were medical fees for Charles, who was driven to the verge of a nervous breakdown by various pressures, including his parents' urges that he live at or near home. And there was tuition for Kenyon, who was at Harvard in the mid-thirties. Eleanor's income of $400 a month was not enough; Henry Stimson had to supplement it several times with a personal check. And Eleanor's income was not even secure. Her money was invested in Commonwealth and Southern stock, which fluctuated wildly because of Wendell Willkie's battles with the Tennessee Valley

Authority. In summer the Brookses often had to rent their house for $900 — Westport was fashionable and expensive — and retreat to a Maine cottage that cost only $150.[13]

Van Wyck earned little from his writing in the early thirties because of his debts to Dutton. The first royalties on the trade edition of *The Life of Emerson* were held against the $1026 he owed Dutton when he emerged from his breakdown. He liked to have Dutton send copies of his books to his friends and correspondents, charging the books against his future royalties. The practice was proper conduct for a man of letters, but it showed little regard for practical affairs. Of the $500 advance on *Sketches in Criticism* (1932), a collection of his *Freeman* essays, he received only $266; the balance was applied to his account with Dutton. In view of his past history Dutton and Company were understandably reluctant to make advances to him. He did not receive his $500 advance on *The Flowering of New England* until June of 1935 when it was nearly done. In September when he was forced to ask for $300 more, Dutton gave him only $200 and charged it against his current royalties rather than the future earnings of the new book as he had desired.[14]

Neither Dutton nor Brooks expected *The Flowering of New England* to be a best seller, though Van Wyck may not have been surprised that it won a Pulitzer Prize. As he finished the book in January of 1936, he felt that it was "the best I've ever done." But he expected a small sale and for once did not even feel that he could send free copies to all his friends, apologizing to John Gould Fletcher that his finances were "at an 'all-time' low." In March he read proof and exceeded the budget for changes, paying the printer an extra $200 out of his own pocket.[15] Then he began reading for *New England: Indian Summer,* which would deal with the period 1865 to 1915. He tried to write a chapter on Henry Adams and got into a state of "bad temper and general desperation." In fact, it was a severe depression. He was driven frantic by the "highbrow Coney Island" quality of Westport in the summer, and by noise, especially the telephone. He and Eleanor rented their house and fled to Maine in August, the month when *The Flowering of New England* was published.[16]

Van Wyck's spirits lifted at the response to *The Flowering of New England.* Carl Van Doren predicted that if succeeding volumes were written "with the same knowledge, range, insight, precision and grace," the series would be "one of the best literary histories in any language." There were dozens of similar reviews. An inspiriting impact was evident in R. P. Blackmur's reaction: the book showed that "Where we are aware of a lack, we can feel . . . that the cure is within us." Americans in the mid 1930's were ready for an inspiring book. By December 1936, four months after publication, twelve thousand copies had been sold. By the next December the book had gone through forty-one printings. A Book-of-the-Month Club edition alone earned Brooks $15,000. All told, the book probably brought him about $40,000. Early in 1937, with humility, he thanked Henry Stimson for past aid and with pride told him, ". . . it appears now that my work can well provide for our family needs."[17]

But his financial problems were far from over. Although *The Flowering of New England* had taken four years to write, most of the profits came in the single year 1937, so he had to pay a high income tax. After taxes he paid his debts, first $500 which he owed to his mother-in-law and then the substantial medical bills from his breakdown. Typically, he paid more than was necessary, sending a thousand dollar gift to Bowden House, the English hospital, because it had not charged him the full rate. He even paid the $200 "tuition" for Gerald Stanley Lee's exercise course on Monhegan Island in the summer of 1928.[18] Then he paid older debts, the mortgage on his Westport house and the $2000 he had borrowed from Ned Sheldon in 1910 so he could marry Eleanor. Sheldon refused the money, saying it had been a wedding present. So Van Wyck gave $500 to each of his own sons and to Sheldon's two sons, telling all four of them that the gift came from Ned Sheldon. By 1938 he had paid more than $7000 in debts. His pride had been deeply wounded by years of inability to support himself and his family, and he had paid his debts too hastily. He had counted on royalties from *New England: Indian Summer* by late 1939, but severe depressions and extremely careful research delayed the book for a year.[19] By 1939 he was again, in desperate financial straits.

"You see, " Eleanor explained to Mumford in January, 1939, ". . . it is not in Van Wyck's nature to think or plan about money matters." He placed bills, unopened, on her desk, and he refused even to discuss finances lest anxiety prevent him from writing: "He just shuts his eyes and goes ahead, hoping for a miracle, until circumstances bring him to an abrupt halt. Then, if there is no way out he goes into break." Unless she found $2000 by the first of May she would have to sell some of her securities, thus reducing her income and increasing Van Wyck's anxiety. She had heard that the Carnegie Corporation supported writers. Was there any way to apply for aid without telling Van Wyck? Mumford arranged for the Carnegie Corporation to inquire if Brooks needed help, and in

April he received a grant of $3000. Mumford must have smiled when Van Wyck told him what had "fallen from the sky." Eleanor reported that ". . . for the first time in weeks Van Wyck came cheerfully down to breakfast and then set to work tranquilly at his desk while I filled the kitchen with silent te deums." Still, the unhappiness would not depart immediately: "It never does."[20]

Although Van Wyck's health was good enough to enable him to work hard during these years, it was never unthreatened. He suffered one or two depressions a year, and sometimes they lasted for months, alternating with mild elations. The depressions were triggered by various causes — financial problems, his fiftieth birthday in 1936, a period of bad relations with his son Charles, or having to write about Henry James once more in *New England: Indian Summer*.[21] His mental health probably suffered also from his carelessness about his physical health. Viewing the idea that the one might depend on the other as a "heresy," he slept only six or seven hours a night, rose before dawn to begin his day's work, and drank huge quantities of coffee. He ate heavily and despite recurrent depression his slight, formerly emaciated body grew stout. Eleanor could seldom persuade him to diet, and in a few years he would suffer from heart disease. But the worst problems were depressions which made him irritable and sometimes violent. Then he might kick or break things or else go to bed in midday.[22]

The worst thing about his fits of depression was that he could not write during them. Working on *Makers and Finders,* he said with only slight hyperbole, "has saved my life." He observed of himself that he "had felt for a long time that he must cling to America to preserve his personality from disintegration. . . ." His study of the American past was his commitment to the world, his way of defeating the desire for abstraction which he felt had nearly killed him. For him, the inability to work was a threat to life itself, and he once exclaimed to Llewelyn Powys that "*Not* writing is the same thing as illness. . . ."[23]

Yet the threat was not as great as it had once been, because Van Wyck had developed a strategy for depression. Now he accepted it as illness, rather than compounding the trouble, as in the past, by blaming himself. Instead of forcing his writing, he put it aside, trying not to hold himself at fault, and then endured the depression, waiting it out until he could work again. He had finally learned to be gentle with himself. Eleanor stayed with him, avoiding the long separations that had earlier caused trouble. She might insist on a trip together for a change of scene and remind him of all the other times he had despaired and yet come out all right. She refused to regard any lifting of the spirits as an improvement unless it led to his writing again. Finally the depression would pass, perhaps into ela-tion, and in a "fever of excitement" he would begin to write in the happy tone that marked his later books.[24]

He had suffered the severest test of his recovered health in December 1931, when his brother Ames threw himself in front of a commuter train. Van Wyck had rushed alone to Plainfield, where his mother gave him Ames's room, furnished with a bed, a chair, and a set of pipes. The room could scarcely have been more barren if it had been in a boardinghouse, and it eloquently testified to the emptiness of Ames's life. Van Wyck laid awake in bed and imagined Ames lying there, planning his final act.[25] But the terrible shock was mitigated by a measure of comfort for Van Wyck in Ames's death. Van Wyck was vindicated for his youthful refusal to enter the business life which he now felt had killed his brother as well as his father. Where Ames had once seemed savage and "repressed," Van Wyck could now reflect peacefully on his memory — "a dear good and faithful man and brother" — because it was Ames's life rather than his own that seemed futile and unfulfilled. Ames "was a poet, all the time, in his heart."[26] After telling Ames's story in his memoirs, Van Wyck would ponder the comforting question, "How had I escaped . . . ?" Yet Ames's death also left a lurking fear of inherited instability.[27] Van Wyck was never quite sure that he would not end a suicide. His old feelings of guilt lingered on, submerged, and sometimes rose to the surface, as in a letter to his step-sister three years after Ames's death. Van Wyck had "always lived under a burden of guilt, a dark and gloomy burden, in connection with these primary family things; for I was a traitor in my heart . . . to all the assumptions of that little world."[28]

II

"I haven't a very clear perspective of the general movements and shiftings of the last three or four years," Brooks wrote to Newton Arvin, not long after his discharge from Four Winds. He counted on Arvin, whom he had always regarded as an ally, "to light them up for me." But Brooks had emerged from the sanatorium into a strange new world. A national economic depression had begun while he was being treated for his personal spiritual one. Where in the twenties he had deplored what seemed to him the retreat of literature from life and society, writers in the thirties reacted to the

Depression with a social consciousness so acute that Brooks feared they would lose sight of the ideal. Arvin, for instance, doubted that they were still allies, for he had become a Marxist, dedicated primarily to "the onslaught upon capitalism." Brooks passed lightly over this rift, saying that on economic questions he adhered to Marx. However, "Love, grief, nonsense, humor, tragedy, poetry are subjects on which Marx and Lenin have nothing to say . . . and culture is concerned with these things." Arvin was not mollified. Brooks's list of cultural concerns was too "intangible." Culture was also concrete and involved "the use of [material] things" — pictures, phonographs, newspapers, and so on. Culture was related to the system of production, on which Marx and Lenin had much to say.[29]

Arvin was then writing for the *New Republic,* and he held Brooks to the Marxist standard in public. At first, perhaps in the hope of converting him, Arvin gently implied that there was, or should have been, a Marxist intention in Brooks's work. *The Life of Emerson* was a worthy successor to books on "the man [Twain] who stultified himself by accepting his class culture uncritically, and the man [James] who crippled himself by trying to escape from it." Unlike them, Emerson had "transcended" his class culture. But as Brooks proved intransigently anti-Marxist, Arvin spoke more strongly. The revised *Ordeal of Mark Twain* failed to deal with "the question of the writer and his class." The fault was due to Brooks's "idealistic individualism." Arvin, on the other hand, was a materialist and a scientific socialist.[30]

Behind these differences lay Brooks's continuing belief in literature as an act of spiritual or prophetic leadership. He told Arvin that there was a "spiritual sphere as well as a social sphere, the one concerned with values, the other with applications." Literature dealt with values while science was "instrumental purely and altogether irrelevant to the question of ends." Clearly, then, literature should lead. Marxism reversed the proper order by making "the literary mind subsidiary to the economic mind." That was the problem with Arvin's *Whitman* (1938). Arvin had treated Whitman as an incipient socialist but had dwelled on the contradictions in his thought, showing that he had also embraced middle-class business life. Van Wyck agreed that Whitman was hardly a first-rate political theorist. But Arvin had missed the point — Whitman was great in his feelings. ". . . you have not sufficiently thought out your conception of a poet," he told Arvin. "Communist thinking is closed to a very large area of human feeling."[31] Brooks remained unabashedly romantic and idealistic.

Idealism was "the Open Sesame of the American mind," and Marxist materialism, therefore, actually impeded the development of American socialism. Marxist categories like "bourgeois" were European; the American character eluded them. Van Wyck refused to endorse an attack on "the influence of bourgeois ideas on American literature" because what seemed bourgeois to others was "to me sacred and real." Essentially this meant Emerson. He did not enjoy Newton Arvin's compliment that his *Emerson* was the "only book on the subject which will survive the final collapse of Emersonianism." When Granville Hicks said that *The Flowering of New England* was weakened by a "soft Emersonian idealism," Brooks reacted angrily: "It is the American Communists who are tender-minded." Idealism was a fact of American life; to ignore it was unscientific.[32]

Socialism in America implied development toward the ideal. Brooks liked to quote Herbert Spencer that the ultimate form of the American nation "will be high." On the political level this meant uplift of the masses rather than a dictatorship of the proletariat, which seemed to Brooks antagonistic to high culture. He irritated Newton Arvin by quoting George Russell's phrase: "Democratic in economics, aristocratic in thought." Aristocracy had a subtle appeal for Brooks, stronger than he perhaps knew. But he knew that he did not hate the upper classes; he liked the results of education, breeding, and travel, "and I am a socialist because I want everybody to be, in this sense, upper class." Dictatorship of the proletariat was too austere for him. From socialism he hoped for a material life that was reasonably comfortable and esthetic, secure and free from the middle-class anxieties that had felled his father and brother and nearly subdued him also. In this newer, better society one could work at one's craft and pursue "spiritual success."[33]

Brooks had not shifted very far from his youthful politics. In his book on H. G. Wells, he had said that America could profit from a socialist ideal. Now he felt that socialism could profit from American idealism. The difference was not in his politics but in his growing reverence for the American past. Beside the militant Marxism of Newton Arvin, Granville Hicks, or Edmund Wilson, Brooks's socialism seemed tame and aloof from the actual social problems of the Depression. But there were easier paths than Communism in the thirties, and Brooks refused these also. Albert Jay Nock, for instance, abandoned the faith in common people that had been the basis of his anarchism in the *Freeman* years. Now he believed only in the humanity of an elite "Remnant."[34] Brooks, however, remained committed to the Whitmanian vision of a high democratic culture.

Despite the Depression and partly because of it, Brooks was optimistic and talked, he said, "like a Babbitt." He had mellowed a bit after his breakdown, and besides, there were aspects of the Depression he liked. The business collapse probably seemed to him, like his father's business failure, a "sign of grace," an indication that America's true destiny was idealistic rather than basely economic. He hoped to see the production of needless goods restricted and the standard of living reduced. It pleased him that the younger writers abandoned belletristic interests for social concern, and he was struck by the "fact that almost all the American writers are on the Left side."[35]

So Brooks maintained close relations with Marxist friends and encouraged Arvin to write on Whitman, even against Arvin's early belief that such a book would "not adequately contribute to the struggle of cultures." Then he helped Arvin to win a Guggenheim Fellowship and to track down new sources on Whitman. He refused to reply to Arvin's critical reviews of his books, emphasizing that politics was not his forte, and exclaiming once in bewilderment, "God knows, I have no grievance against you." Arvin, for his part, warned Brooks in advance of his hostile reviews and tried to be conciliatory. But Arvin was thin-skinned and easily provoked, and he sometimes had to send an apologetic note after a letter or a visit to Westport. He need not have worried; he had an understanding friend in Brooks who had warned him early that they must not "let our lives and souls be eaten away by resentments and impulsive actions."[36]

"I know very well what my nerves can stand," Van Wyck explained to John Gould Fletcher in 1935, and so, much as he sympathized with radical politics, "I absolutely refuse to mix myself in political agitations." Self-doubt made politics difficult, for whenever he had to take a stand he was tortured by second thoughts. However, he did participate somewhat in electoral politics. He usually voted and gave speeches for Norman Thomas, and he joined a socialist local in Westport as a "sop to my conscience." Since there was no danger of her winning, he agreed to Eleanor's campaigning on the socialist ticket for a seat in the Connecticut legislature in 1934. But usually he was restrained from politics by his bad nerves and by his belief that ". . . my responsibility as a writer is much more comprehensive and complex than my responsibility as a voter or as a propagandist."[37]

But his literary responsibility did lead him into the League of

American Writers, and his experience there documented his frequent assertion that he was "no great shakes" at politics. He gladly
contributed his name and energy to the league until it "slowly
dawned" on him that "political sitters-in" were "taking the League
over for the communist party." Thus, even in writing his memoirs,
he seemed ignorant of what many had known at the time — the
Communists did not take over the league but, rather, founded it,
partly in order to use just such liberal writers as Brooks who refused
to be drawn into regular Party affairs. As early as 1935 he had
refused to sign the "Call" to the writers' congress which founded the
league because it was tinged with Marxist rhetoric.[38] Still, he joined
the league. He could only be sympathetic to the first attempt in
American history to organize writers on a national scale.

At first the league seemed to be the centralizing force for which
Brooks had hoped all his life. On his fiftieth birthday in 1936,
Malcolm Cowley, Kenneth Burke, and Waldo Frank telegraphed
congratulations on behalf of the league, saying that his writings had
marked the "turning point in American culture." The rise of the
Popular Front, in response to the Fascist threat, made the Marxists
more sympathetic than they had earlier been to Brooks and his
nationalist position. Where Newton Arvin had applied hard stric-
tures to Brooks's work in the early thirties, Malcolm Cowley responded generously to *The Flowering of New England* in 1936. The
Fascist menace threatened "all inherited culture," and therefore
Brooks's book served a useful purpose by "turning back to the great
past in order to see the real nature of the traditions that we are
trying to save, and in order to gain new strength for the struggles
ahead."[39]

The league was soon involved in the Spanish Civil War, and it
pleased Brooks that ". . . the U. S. writing guild is immensely on the
Loyalist side." Writers who supported the Loyalists were more "in
harmony with American traditions." Brooks attended the 1937
American Writers' Congress, where Hemingway spoke just after
returning from Spain, and he served with Hemingway and Sinclair
Lewis as sponsors of a farewell banquet for an ambulance corps
going to Spain. When a manuscript auction was held to provide
medical relief to the Loyalists, he donated a draft of *The Flowering of
New England,* and it brought $800, the highest price of the sale.[40]
This book's success had made Brooks's name a useful asset to the
league, so he signed statements, protests, and other documents, like
the letter offering an honorary membership in the league to

Franklin Roosevelt. And after the 1937 Writers' Congress decided to concentrate on regional organization, he was asked to chair the league's Connecticut Conference.

The Connecticut Conference, which met at a high school in New Haven in December 1938, seemed an especially important forum since, as Brooks wrote, Connecticut more than any other state "is known as a place where writers live and work." He had decided to use the opportunity to speak out against the Communists' increasingly apparent domination of the league, and he felt confirmed in this decision by an incident that occurred during the meeting. Wilbur Cross, then governor of Connecticut, had accepted an invitation to the conference and was sitting on the platform when a note was passed to Brooks saying, "Announce that Governor Cross has consented to be honorary president." It was untrue, and Brooks ignored the note, realizing it was a Communist ploy to gain the governor's prestige for the league.[41] Such methods were exactly what he meant when he said in his speech that the Communists were as opportunistic as the Fascists.

He had begun by saying he approved the league's policy of admitting Communists but not Fascists. He opposed the opportunistic methods of both groups, but the Communists at least had a good end. Collectivism was in the American tradition, he said, but in the post-Civil War period American ideals had been reversed and economic individualism held sway. American ideals must be reversed again to achieve collectivism. But that task could not be accomplished by a dictatorship of the American proletariat, who were "only the first half-pint, let us say, in the gallon." It was necessary to win the important people, or "swells," by which he meant the native Yankee farmers, rather than the "gilded savages of the country clubs." The Yankee heart, Brooks admitted, was fat and sleepy, unable to sympathize with the oppressed. But the Yankees would not be dictated to; their minds must be changed, "a long, slow process," but necessary in a free country. He asked if the Communists present "do not also love their freedom? — and whether they think they would have it if we had a Stalin?"[42]

Although the *New Republic* praised Brooks's "candid statement," there were enough critical reactions to cause him to ask Newton Arvin's counsel on his speech, "in which I am said to have misrepresented the Communist position." As usual he was torn by second thoughts, and he decided to swear off politics, telling Lewis Mumford that he had "said my say for good and all." Wanting to get back to his writing, he seemed to hope that the rest of the world would forswear politics also. He believed that the Fascists and Nazis "are all going to crash within, and then we'll have some fun in this world again." For several years, in fact, he had thought the Fascists might serve a useful historical purpose; while proving their ideas unworkable, they would make their countries "into 'corporate' bundles that can be socialized over-night. But I'd like to go to sleep for twenty years. . . ."[43]

If the Fascists did not disappear so easily, at least Brooks could soon feel vindicated in his attacks on Communist opportunism because of Stalin's non-aggression pact with Germany. When Arvin expressed hope that the league would condemn the pact, Van Wyck suggested that they issue an independent statement and break with the league if necessary. But Cowley and Hicks convinced Arvin it was enough for the league to keep silent and not praise the pact. Brooks had to submit his resignation alone. The league had seemed to offer the community and direction he desired, and he was hurt by the necessity of breaking with it. In the next few months he spoke of the "poor old League" and hoped it would be reconstituted so he could rejoin. James Farrell, who had also broken with the league, urged him to make a public statement, but Brooks refused. The Dies Committee was active, and he did not want to "give politicians a chance to stick their noses into the affairs of writers!"[44]

In a private statement to Malcolm Cowley, Van Wyck condemned the "mere political sitters-in" who were not really writers. He condemned the league's habit of dwelling on the sins of France and England, a practice that favored Hitler by implication. He condemned the league's alliance with "the unprofessed but actual dictatorship of Stalin." The league "must oppose *Fascism and Dictatorship together*." The league was "suspect by American writers, for, while we are democratic, the League is not so." Borrowing a phrase from William Carlos Williams, he said that the league "simply is not *in the American grain*. For there is an American grain, and I wish to live with it, and I will not live against it knowingly. . . . this country can only be socialized *in the American grain*."[45]

Brooks still believed that ". . . nationality is a primary instinct with human beings." He told Lewis Mumford that he drew solace from the non-aggression pact because it would destroy the myth of Communist internationalism and "result in a rapid growth of socialism, along the line of the psychologies of the various nations." He had become convinced that America had a national psychology, a peculiarly democratic instinct. America was one of Mazzini's national "workshops," after all, with a unique cultural product to contribute to civilization.[46]

While such beliefs had made him critical of Marxist friends like Arvin, they also separated him from interventionist friends like Mumford. Early in 1939 Mumford published *Men Must Act,* a call for America to fight Fascism. He advocated non-intercourse with the Fascist countries and the dropping of immigration restrictions so that the American population could be swelled for the coming struggle. Brooks agreed on non-intercourse but disagreed on immigration, although he wanted to accept "an army of refugees." He tried to aid a Viennese Jew whose case was brought to his attention, and he personally guaranteed the support in America of Eva Wasserman, a German dancer and political refugee. But refugees were different from immigrants, and Brooks opposed opening the gates. He believed immigrants were an obstacle to the discovery and centralization of American culture. The allegiance of the American Communists to Russia, for instance, was attributable to "the last wave of immigrants, who have not yet discovered that we have a tradition too." He told Mumford that America needed "a chance to shake down."[47]

Mumford translated Brooks's nationalism into isolationism. By early 1940, with war underway in Europe, he wrestled with Brooks, "like Paul with the men of Corinth, over your heretical belief in isolation" which "denies all the things that make you what you are." He warned that "When England and France are beaten, it will be too late for us to wake up. . . ." It moved him almost to despair that ". . . at a moment when — as in a shipwreck — there should be only men, those who best embody our manhood should think of themselves and their countrymen as *Americans.* We are men: other men are dying, other men are being tortured. . . . and we should go to their aid . . . simply because they are men, and men have a call upon other men when they need succour or love."[48] Mumford's eloquence evinced the depth of the disappointment and anger which would smolder beneath the surface of his friendship with Brooks and erupt years later over the award of a medal to the isolationist Charles Beard.

Brooks's beliefs were not so isolationist as Mumford thought, but they were nationalist. He favored preparedness in case Germany seemed to be winning, ". . . but otherwise I welcome anything that reduces British prestige in our population." Then, too, he feared for his sons and hoped that war could be delayed until they were too old for it. It was too soon, he told Mumford early in 1940, to be certain that England and France were beaten. And he persisted in his wishful hope that Fascism would collapse from within: "I cannot yet believe that Hitler will survive a year."[49]

He was gradually forced toward interventionism during the next year. France fell in June, five months after he had told Mumford it was too early to say that Germany was winning. In August he publicly endorsed Archibald MacLeish's *The Irresponsibles,* which attacked American writers for failing to oppose the Fascists. In November he voted for Roosevelt rather than Norman Thomas because of the preparedness issue. By the end of 1940 Germany had swallowed up Hungary and Rumania. The next April Hilter invaded Yugoslavia and Greece, and then, in the summer, Russia. Though England held out, Europe's fate seemed Fascist. Brooks could not countenance such a fate. Europe had always been his model for an America come of age. On September 1, 1941, the *New Republic* printed his letter: "Sir: I am for an immediate declaration of war."[50]

The war cloud had a silver lining. Brooks hoped for a positive effect on the literary atmosphere in which he had been uncomfortable in the twenties and thirties. When he endorsed MacLeish's *Irresponsibles* in 1940, he felt that the bellicose pamphlet "may turn the tide in American literature. . . . It asserts the free will of the writer, too long forgotten in a world that has been drugged by fatalism." He continued this reasoning after the war began. The religion of art could not prosper with writers united in the war effort and "dipped again in the central stream of human and social feeling." The war, with its daily heroisms, should "raise our respect for humanity," and writers would again feel themselves prophets as they considered "the future that such a race must have." His hope that the Second World War would accomplish his purpose was similar to the one he had mistakenly cherished during the First World War. Perhaps Randolph Bourne's memory nipped at his conscience, for he added defensively that there would be no postwar reaction. This time ". . . we went into it without illusions."[51]

Because Brooks was "no great shakes" at politics, he could hope for the best from the worst, and his optimism sometimes verged on intellectual opportunism. Before the Fascists collapsed from within they were to have prepared their countries for socialism. The non-aggression pact was to have hastened socialization along the lines of national psychologies. The war that revealed the horrors of Auschwitz was to have raised respect for humanity. He had opposed the Communists consistently and reasonably on philosophical grounds, but on the level of practice, as he well knew, he was out of his depth in the dangerous political waters of the thirties and forties. When he ventured into politics it was because he believed that duty called him, but his jangled nerves drew little comfort from that fact. He was always glad to return to his writing, his greatest source of happiness in the thirties.

III

The Flowering of New England was a book of nearly two hundred thousand words, twice as long as anything Brooks had previously written, and its length was essential to its success. The length was the logical solution to the formal problem Brooks had encountered in writing *The Life of Emerson*. The purpose of the Emerson book had been to show that the thing had been done, that the literary life had been lived in America. But for Brooks the literary life could not be lived in isolation; it required a national community and culture which would offer both resistance and recognition so that the man of letters, the artist-prophet, could be a moral influence in society. Without that resistance and recognition, the artist-prophet could exercise no leverage; he would spend his life in futility and end in despair. What had made Emerson increasingly attractive to Brooks was not only Emerson's own life and work but the setting in which he had lived. In 1925 he had been delighted with the number of interesting figures he had discovered around Emerson, for they indicated a congenial literary community. But because Brooks wished to portray not only Emerson but Emerson in his community, a large number of "subsidiary biographies" had been required. Consequently, the book had "expanded alarmingly," as Brooks had explained to Joel Spingarn in 1925, until he had concluded that it was not a book, or at least not a single volume.[52] That discouragement had helped bring on his depression. But now, with his confidence and courage restored, he had undertaken the representation not only of a single literary life but of an entire cultural community. It was a large goal and it required a large book.

The sense of being in touch with a cultural community and of working in the tradition of that community buoyed him up and gave him energy. Despite all the other projects on which he had worked since 1931, the Bradford papers, the Amiel translation, and so on, he had managed by 1936 to read more than eight hundred books by New England authors of the pre-Civil War period and then to write the more than five hundred pages of *The Flowering*. The words flowed out of him in a joyous but steady and rhythmic prose despite a heavy freight of detail. Actually, his indulgence in detail accounted in part for his happiness, for it reaffirmed his idea of himself as an artist. He felt moved to his intensely detailed treatment by his artist's love of the concrete — the idea of the artist he had learned from J. B. Yeats. And in fact *The Flowering of New England* resembled a vast painting. As early as the opening pages of *The Wine of the Puritans* (1908), when Brooks set the scene on the hill above Naples, it was apparent that his real gift was not for analysis or even narrative, but for vivid descriptions of scenes. Painting had first awakened his imagination, and later in youth he defined literature as "word-painting." The subjection of his visual or artistic sense to the analytical purpose of his early books had been difficult and sometimes torturing. In *The Pilgrimage of Henry James,* for instance, he had tried to employ the novelist's method, but his factual material and analytical, critical purpose had restricted his freedom and imagination. Now at last he gave free reign to his temperament. In 1932 he described his projected series as a "joyous panorama" to be "told in a continuous narrative, the surface of which will be as picturesque as I can make it."[53]

The purpose of the picturesque treatment was to make vivid the significance of communal surroundings for individual lives. Even if, as with Thoreau, it was solitude that counted, Brooks could draw a happy picture of him communing with nature. When Thoreau crossed a stream alone, he was not really alone, for painted tortoises on willow stumps, yellow pebbles in the stream bed, and the songs of the rush-sparrow and vireo played on his senses. There were similar scenes in the chapter "Emerson: Woodnotes," but then in the next chapter, "Concord: 1840–1844," Emerson was pictured in transcendental society, receiving "recognition" from Hedge, Ripley, Dwight, Alcott, Margaret Fuller, Jones Very, and Orestes Brownson. For "resistance" Emerson had Andrews Norton and the Unitarian theologians, the American subservience to Europe, and later Daniel Webster and the Fugitive Slave Law. All of these figures were brilliantly depicted, along with numerous other literati, who made New England a vital community though they moved in orbits far from Emerson's — Gilbert Stuart, George Ticknor, Jared Sparks, Bancroft, Prescott, Motley, Longfellow, Hawthorne, Dana, Lowell, Harriet Beecher Stowe, and Oliver Wendell Holmes senior. The chapter on Holmes colorfully evoked Boston and was at the same time a masterpiece of biographical portraiture. It ended with Henry James senior telling Holmes that he was intellectually the most alive man James had ever known: "And the little doctor replied, and he almost danced as he spoke, 'I am, I am! From the crown of my head to the sole of my foot, I'm alive, I'm alive!' "[54]

The joyousness of *The Flowering of New England* was a celebration of life, of Brooks's delight in life and his joy at being able to work and write again. His confidence was reinforced by the conviction that through this particular kind of writing he had resolved the problem of alienation from life or, as he would have put it, his excessive "subjectivity." His pictorial and detailed treatment of the American past brought him into contact with every possible object there. He was forced to deal with not only the major figures but also the decidedly minor, like Nathaniel Bowditch and Frank Sanborn. They were the essential connective tissue, the communal fabric of the tapestry in which the major figures were portrayed. This necessary all-inclusiveness reinforced Brooks's feeling that he was finally mastering reality, getting in touch with America. Then, too, the painstaking labor required to master the detail and work it into his rhythmic prose assured him that his days would be full for years to come. At best he never wrote more than a few hundred words a day. With the six volumes he planned he could be certain there was nothing immediately ahead like the terrible periods which had followed completion of his books on Twain and James. Instead, he was assured of a peaceful and steady routine. He wrote in the mornings, read in the afternoons, and made weekly trips with a canvas bag to the Yale library for the biographies and memoirs he needed.

As Brooks read he grew confident that, in Whitman's words, he stood "tenoned and mortised in granite" as no previous writer on American literature had been. Edmund Wilson, who had not seen Brooks since the early twenties, met him at a party in Westport in the late thirties and was amazed at the metamorphosis. The "pale, neat and shy little figure" he remembered had become "florid and portly and apparently quite heartily self-confident." Wilson congratulated him on *The Flowering of New England,* saying he had surpassed all other historians of American literature, and Brooks jauntily replied, "They've none of 'em read the books."[55]

Brooks's reading had carried him far from the day when Barrett Wendell had been his light on American literature. Wendell had said that Emerson's idealism was unrelated to worldly life, and Brooks had repeated the charge in *America's Coming-of-Age*. But in *The Flowering of New England*, Emerson "watched with awe the life of his farmer-neighbours," hoping to see in the facts of their everyday lives the connection between ideal and real. In youth Van Wyck had thought of Hawthorne as a "phantom in a phantom world," but in *The Flowering* he showed how New England society had drawn Hawthorne "out" and how New England history had "pressed against and filled his consciousness." Van Wyck had begun his career by picturing the Puritans and their descendants clinging tenaciously to European ideals unsuited for life in America. But by 1942 he believed that ". . . our early culture diverged from Europe in accordance with our native experiences and needs."[56]

For Brooks, criticism remained a moral science. Strictly esthetic judgment was not his purpose, although *The Flowering of New England* contained many such judgments. He observed, for instance, that Whittier's mind was not "poetic in grain" and that he wrote "with almost no distinction of language." Nevertheless, Whittier "glowed with moral feeling. . . ." Brooks insisted that while Whittier's poetic weakness denied him major significance, it could not, in the face of his moral feeling, his abolitionism, and his relation to society, render him insignificant. Decades earlier Brooks had said that the important question in the study of men and books was "How far do they . . . add to the number of ways in which personality can achieve itself?"[57] How far do they offer new modes of being to the community, to the people? Now he asked that question of the history of American writers and concluded that they had been, in Whitman's phrase, "makers and finders."

Brooks's moral concerns had led him into sociology, though the transition was not immediately clear to him. In the preface to *The Flowering* he said that his subject was "the New England mind." But as some reviewers objected, there was no analysis of ideas in the book.[58] Only gradually did it dawn on him that his real subject was *A History of the Writer in America*, as he eventually subtitled the *Makers and Finders* series. What interested him was the relationship of American writers to each other and to American society. Where he had once believed that they were part of an irrelevant highbrow culture, he now believed American writers had created the central culture or middle ground which he had previously thought missing in American life. The New England writers had conceived of literature as "Promethean":

They were teachers, educators, and bringers of light, with a deep and affectionate feeling of obligation towards the young republic their fathers had brought into being. Sometimes they suggested Miss Ophelia reforming Dinah's kitchen; but . . . they came to be accepted as fathers and sages. . . .

What was the cause of this transfiguration? The breadth of their conscious horizon, the healthy objectivity of their minds, their absorption in large preoccupations, historical, political, religious, together with a literary feeling, a blend of the traditional and the local, that gave the local wider currency while it brought the traditional home to men's business and bosoms. They filled the New England scene with associations and set it, as it were, in three dimensions, creating the visible foreground it had never possessed. . . . In their scholarship, their social thought, their moral passion, their artistic feeling, they spoke for the universal republic of letters, giving their own province a form and body in the consciousness of the world.[59]

Such men had been prophets, and they offered a useful model. Brooks's purpose in this book was to show that the literary life had been lived and could be lived again in America. His own chosen area of prophecy was in American literature itself. He did not hope now so much to affect American society as to affect American writers, who would in turn become social prophets. The joyous tone of the book was due in part to his delight in the discovery of material suitable for the inspiriting role he wished to play. And some of the reviews must have convinced him that he had succeeded, that his book would help inspire a new golden age in American literature.

In the most perceptive review *The Flowering of New England* received, R. P. Blackmur called the book "prophecy." By celebrating "the highest period of American culture . . . he [Brooks] brings us to the brink, the very possibility, of another such period." Brooks's narrative of appreciation was a useful inspiration for artists suffering from "lack of theme and the rootless malaise," the disorders, Blackmur pointed out, that Brooks had seen in Mark Twain and Henry James. In those books he had pointed out the failings but not "the actual achievement — the greatness of imagination" of his subjects. But in *The Flowering of New England* he had declared "not only what greatness was there but also the greatness of the possibility that was never enacted." Blackmur believed that the possibility of greatness had not been "taken up" in New England, but the possibility "persisted and persists now. . . . How shall it be taken up?" The answer lay in Brooks's depiction of greatness, albeit unenacted, which made it possible for artists to "feel the direction of magnitude and the stretch of scope," to feel, in short, what greatness feels like. ". . . we can feel . . . that the cure is within us."[60] *The Flowering of New England* was an inspiriting, prophetic book.

The Flowering of New England must be judged, then, as prophecy. And prophecy must be judged by its accuracy, not of prediction but of spirit. In Brooks's case that means its Americanness — an outmoded standard but the one by which he would have most wished to be judged. In short, the question is to what degree he had overcome his tendency of earlier years to believe that an America come of age would resemble a European nation. The answer is that his success was qualified, that though he had imposed a heavy burden of American fact on his imagination, it labored in its old course and dreamed of Europe.

In 1915 in *America's Coming-of-Age,* Brooks had predicted the development of an American nation similar to a European, where culture would be relevant to life and not sliced off into "Highbrow" idealism. The fulfillment of this prophecy had been frustrated, he felt, by the estheticism and spiritual disillusionment of the World War generation. Now, as he turned from the future to the past, he saw in the New England of 1815 a proper example for his own time — "the coming-of-age of the Boston mind." In its "appointed hour," New England had sloughed off the colonial mentality that prevented a "centre of its own."[61] *The Flowering of New England* depicted in 1815 the Europeanization of America which Brooks had mistakenly hoped for in 1915.

Thus, Brooks described New England in dozens of European metaphors: Massachusetts was a smaller England, Boston another Edinburgh, Cambridge a second Heidelberg, and Harvard a "provincial Oxford." Webster resembled Burke, Everett seemed another Abelard, and Holmes was an American Pope.[62] New England conformed to the model that Spengler had developed for older societies in *The Decline of the West*; New England had passed through a "culture-cycle," and *The Flowering of New England* dealt with the climax, the high point of the cycle: "Here we have a homogeneous people, living close to the soil, intensely religious, unconscious, unexpressed in art and letters, with a strong sense of home and fatherland." New England was, in the words of D. H. Lawrence, "a living, organic, believing community." And the New England authors were not highbrow but rather an integrated part of the community: "They were as completely of their people as any authors of the oldest nations. . . ."[63]

The New England writers had been related not only to their community but also to each other in a fashion typical of Europe. Brooks had always wished, as he told John Cournos in 1933, "that we could have in America the guild-life that writers have in England." The loneliness of the artist in America, his isolation from his fellow artists as well as from his community, had been a recurrent theme of Brooks's. One of the things that most pleased him about New England was the number of contacts between writers, and his narrative was intricately interwoven to reveal those contacts. American writers had formed a "guild" after all, Brooks concluded when he finished the *Makers and Finders* series.[64] Living American writers, working in the tradition of this guild, need never feel alone; they had the exemplary past which Brooks had once believed the exclusive heritage of the European artist.

Brooks had remained a romantic and an organicist, and he was profoundly impressed when he read Spengler's *Decline of the West* a few months before he finished *The Flowering of New England*. The idea of a "culture-cycle," with societies passing through the life stages of an organism, seemed a perfect explanation of New England's history. In *The Flowering of New England* he had pictured New England at the highest point of the cycle, and his next book on New England from the Civil War to 1915 had inevitably to be a tale of declension. At the conclusion of *The Flowering of New England*, Brooks indicated his expectations for the sequel:

> . . . gradually the mind, detached from the soil, grows more and more self-conscious. Contradictions arise within it, and worldlier arts supplant the large, free, ingenuous forms through which the poetic mind has taken shape. What formerly grew from the soil begins to be planned. The Hawthornes yield to the Henry Jameses. Over-intelligent, fragile, cautious and doubtful, the soul of the culture-city loses the self-confidence and joy that have marked its early development, — it is filled with a presentiment of the end; and the culture-city itself surrenders to the world-city, — Boston surrenders to New York, — which stands for cosmopolitan deracination. What has once been vital becomes provincial; and the sense that one belongs to a dying race dominates and poisons the creative mind.[65]

Spengler provided not only a model but also a working title — "The Decline of New England" — for the second book. In the end, however, Brooks found that though the latter period lacked the strong color of New England in its flowering, it had some autumnal brilliance, and he called the book *New England: Indian Summer* (1940).

Henry James, predictably, was the symbol of New England's decline. Deracinated and driven to Europe, James could not take root in English soil — hence the later manner "in which he seemed to abandon the objective role" and "drifted further and further from life itself." In the twenties Brooks had called James's later manner arachnoid, and now he wrote that the later novels were "grey webs of speculation, peopled with phantoms in a fog." But he insisted on ending his treatment of James on a happy note, so he saved for last his admiration for the shorter tales, "flawless and full in their tone and structure," where one saw James "in his clearest autumnal beauty."[66]

Brooks's treatment of Howells was happier still. As he researched *Indian Summer* his opinion of Howells underwent a drastic reversal, and before long he was writing to Stephen Vincent Benét: "Do read *Their Wedding Journey* and see if you don't think it is a *real American poem*."[67] Howells' career was threaded through *New England: Indian Summer* and drew the book together. Raised in the province of Ohio, Howells looked to Boston as his culture-city. Settling there, he cultivated older worthies like Holmes and Longfellow, and he befriended younger writers as disparate as Mark Twain and Henry James. Brooks still thought Howells' squeamishness had crippled Twain's genius, but he added now that Twain had profited from Howells' esthetic sensibility.[68] With James, Howells had created the realistic novel, and as a critic he had recognized talents who received little recognition elsewhere, such as John W. De Forest. Howells was the linchpin of the book, and even Brooks's subtitle, *Indian Summer,* paid tribute to Howells, who had written a novel under that title.

Still, Brooks found problems in Howells' career, and told Benét that Howells was "always worst in his big attempts, for reasons I am trying to uncover." He had not far to look; the answer lay with the "feminization" of literature in Howells' time. The post-Civil War audience seemed mainly composed of women, and Howells wrote for them. That was why Howells' realism was tempered by prudishness and a "tendency to the namby-pamby." Despite his literary friendships he was "never thrown closely with men," and he saw the world through the eyes of women; hence his preoccupation with domestic affairs and his "tendency to fuss."[69] Though Brooks no longer saw the problem as resulting from the heritage of the Puritans, he still believed that American culture in the Gilded Age had been effeminate and highbrow.

Despite Howells' weaknesses, he was the most accurate observer of the American scene in his time. If he was weakened by his associations with women, he evened the score, for his portraits of them realistically captured "their foibles and their instinct for manoeuvre."[70] According to Brooks, Howells remained an honest and simple man, with none of the crippling complexities of Henry James, Henry Adams, and other latter-day New Englanders. Once settled in New York, Howells' fine moral concerns came to the fore. In his rediscovery of Tolstoyan socialism and his defense of the Chicago anarchists, he revealed himself as a prophet. Less able than James as a technician, Howells was greater as a man. Howells alone of Brooks's subjects in *Indian Summer* had the point of view of a great writer. Regrettably, his point of view developed too slowly, stunted perhaps in the early years in the West, and therefore it never developed enough: ". . . he never sounded the depths of the minds that are oceans. He was rather like some great fresh-water lake. If these lakes have their shallows, they are transparent, and, if they have their narrows, they are also large; and all manner of living things foregather in them, as they foregathered in Howells."[71]

The New England books, *The Flowering* and *Indian Summer*, were unquestionably the best that Brooks ever wrote; in them he had achieved his perfect subject and form. Of all the regions and periods in American history, New England in its flowering was undoubtedly closest to the Europeanized ideal of a literary community that gripped Brooks's imagination. New England's literary culture was more densely interconnected and more truly a part of the larger community than were those of the other regions. The intricately interwoven detail of the New England books was appropriate for creating the impression of density that was an essential part of Brooks's picture.

The question that remained for Brooks when *New England: Indian Summer* was finished was whether or not he would find subjects other than New England which were appropriate for the same treatment and form, and if not, would he be able to adjust his treatment and form accordingly? Gradually the subjects of his books would lead him out of New England to New York, to the South, and to the West, away from the nineteenth century and toward the twentieth. As he progressed in that direction, away from old Europe and toward modern America, there would be the danger that the "method," as he called it, which he had developed in *The Flowering of New England* would be inadequate for these new subjects. His method was appropriate for painting a richly detailed picture of a unified society and culture, but if society and culture were harsh, crude, and fractured, then his method might lead to an inaccurate picture and stand in the way of his desire to fathom American reality.

9

CERTAIN ROOT IDEAS

BY arguing in the New England books that literature had after all been a meaningful part of nineteenth-century American life, Brooks had reversed himself at just the time when his earlier position was becoming the conventional wisdom. "I miss some of the accents of the sterner son-in-law of the Voice of God that you once were," Lee Simonson said as he congratulated Brooks on *The Flowering of New England.* Simonson was hardly unique in this feeling. In 1930 when Sinclair Lewis had received the first Nobel Prize for Literature ever awarded to an American, his acceptance speech, "The American Fear of Literature," seemed almost to have been written by the young Brooks, with its attack on Howells and its criticism of the "divorce in America of intellectual life from . . . reality." Those like F. O. Matthiessen who continued to admire *America's Coming-of-Age* inevitably found *The Flowering of New England* "too like a piece of glowing brocade . . . from the drawer of a highboy." Malcolm Cowley, calling Brooks worthy of the Nobel Prize, dedicated his anthology *After the Genteel Tradition* (1937) to Brooks but included in it an essay characterizing *The Flowering of New England* as a "withdrawal from the battle." F. W. Dupee wrote in the *Partisan Review* that Brooks was incapable of meeting the problems of his own epoch and therefore had permitted "the spiritual New Englander in him to absorb the modern critic, the visionary to consume the sceptic."[1]

Brooks, who was under attack from another quarter in the thirties, must have felt trapped in a cross fire. While some attacked his later writings, others, notably Bernard DeVoto, took aim at his earlier work. DeVoto conducted a frenzied, decade-long pursuit of Brooks, beginning with *Mark Twain's America* (1933). By describing Mark Twain as a humorist in the tradition of the Southwest, DeVoto scored heavily on Brooks's assertion that there was no folk tradition in America and also on Brooks's faulty Freudianism. Later, from his post as editor of the *Saturday Review of Literature,* DeVoto sniped at Brooks, and then declared war in *The Literary Fallacy* (1944), almost half of which was about Brooks. Like many books in the early forties (including Brooks's *Opinions of Oliver Allston*), *The Literary Fallacy* blamed the dreary world prospect on the spiritual defeatism of its author's literary enemies and their belief that ". . . life is subordinate to literature."[2]

Although Brooks thought his critics were unjust, he did not often reply. His nerves could not stand such exchanges, and he usually preferred to be above battle with "literary pugilists." Still, his resentments were strong. When Sinclair Lewis defended Brooks by savagely denouncing DeVoto as a "tedious and egotistical fool, . . . a pompous and boresome liar" with a "frog-like face," Brooks congratulated him on putting "that poor devil through such a wringer. . . ." For a time, Brooks's resentment of his Marxist critics had been focused on Edmund Wilson, and he once burst out to Arvin that he doubted the "intellectual integrity" of those who had defended Joyce and Gertrude Stein but who "*now* throw over all literary considerations and plump for communism. . . ." Academic critics like Matthiessen held to the religion of art, sailing in the wake of T. S. Eliot, as it seemed to Brooks. While serving on the Visiting Committee of Harvard's English Department in the thirties, he had been ill at ease during his visits and sick with the conviction that Harvard, the school for writers, had been captured by "Elioteers." They were "almost as bad as the Germans," and he was glad only that ". . . they choose to live in a concentration camp, so nobody will have to put them there."[3]

During the thirties he had seldom expressed these thoughts on contemporary literature and his reticence added weight to charges that he had withdrawn from the battle into nostalgia and scholarly story-telling. He had inevitably translated such criticisms into the worst charge he could imagine — that he had indulged in mere art and forsaken his prophetic responsibility. It was harder still to withstand the blandishments of supporters and friends. When Lewis

Mumford asked him in 1940 what he was writing for the present moment, it gave him a "very guilty feeling." He said that he was "not enough of a Pharisee" to ask "Am I not [already] writing for the present?" Actually such an answer would have been justified, since all of his writing on the American past was motivated by his perception of present needs. But he told Mumford that what was needed was "immediate thought for immediate action." Handicapped by "habits of long-range thinking," he nevertheless promised to do what he could.[4] He had sporadically kept a journal of his opinions on contemporary literature and politics during the thirties, and now he began to prepare it for publication.

The 1940 Conference on Science, Philosophy and Religion gave him a more immediate opportunity to speak out. These annual conferences at Columbia University in the early forties were the creation of Rabbi Louis Finkelstein, president of the Jewish Theological Seminary. Ostensibly, the purpose of the conferences was "the protection of the intellectual life of the United States against a growing infiltration of totalitarian thought," but in fact Rabbi Finkelstein proposed restriction of intellectual activity so that democracy would have "free unity and yet have the strength that totalitarianism has obtained by imposing uniformity." He wished "to clarify the limits within which the sciences, the philosophies and the theologies must operate." Those limits were traditional, fundamentally anti-modern and anti-science. The first conference was hardly underway in 1940 before Finkelstein chastised Albert Einstein, a participant, for engaging in "speculation." Einstein had said that modern science rendered untenable the traditional anthropomorphic concept of God, an idea hardly suited to Finkelstein's goal of demonstrating "the close relation of modern science and history with traditional ethics and religion. . . ." What appealed to Brooks in all this was Finkelstein's indictment of "writers and teachers whose self-defeating skepticism has played directly into the hands of the totalitarians."[5] Ever since the rise of the Popular Front in the mid-thirties, Brooks had felt that intellectual currents were moving his way. Now finally he was ready to put his history aside, as Lewis Mumford and others had been urging him to do, in order to attack totalitarianism and, not incidentally, the "Elioteers."

Excited by his first contact with Finkelstein and by the fact that hundreds of leaders in the fields of philosophy, religion, and science had agreed to participate, Brooks agreed to cull a paper out of his journal for the conference in September 1940. The paper would serve him as a "focus," and he promised Finkelstein that he would work on nothing else.[6] This was one of the most important summers of his life. He and Eleanor retreated to a Maine cottage where he developed the ideas that would dominate his mind for the next fifteen years and mar the last three volumes of the *Makers and Finders* series. From Maine he wrote to Mumford of his intention of working out what he *"really thought,* not about American literature but about life."[7]

He could not work out his thoughts on anything in the abstract, however, and he turned to American history and literature for the flesh of his ideas. Beginning to read Jefferson, Franklin, and Paine that summer in preparation for *The World of Washington Irving* (1944), he hit on the paradox that revolution was the American tradition. The Irving book, he told Mumford, would attempt to show "that America has a *monopoly of Revolution,* that we really started the whole thing and have our chance *for the last word also.* . . ."[8]

That summer of 1940 he also read Mumford's *Faith for Living* and predicted that the book would be misunderstood by "liberal intellectuals." Mumford's recurrence to tradition made Brooks certain that ". . . the intelligentsia will not know how to take it. What, talking of love, family, sacrifice, talking of first and last things, when everybody knew there wasn't such an animal. . . ." Mumford was "striking down into the *folk* mind, and you have the reputation of a highbrow writer." Brooks added, "The same thing is happening to me . . . ," meaning not only that he also was striking into the folk mind but that he too expected to confuse and disenchant the intelligentsia.[9] And he did.

Despite his promise to Finkelstein, Brooks did not have a paper ready for the Conference on Science, Philosophy and Religion in September 1940, but he chaired one of its sessions. In his "Opening Remarks" he made clear his belief that the American tradition was based on the traditional values of the conference leaders but was at the same time democratic and revolutionary. Contemporary literature, he said, was "sick" and "off-centre." In the previous quarter century writers had "ceased to be voices of the people." Yet the fault was not entirely that of writers; the people themselves had ceased to possess "centrality" — that is, "certain postulates that were held in common, postulates regarding the aim and meaning of life. . . . [and] that afforded their values to science and to literature also."[10]

Brooks never identified just what those "certain postulates" were, though he was to refer to them often in the next few years, sometimes as "certain root ideas" or "unchanging truths." His vagueness on the point was to cost him the respect of many former admirers and encourage derision rather than argument from his opponents. His imprecision was due, as he said, to his lack of training in philosophic thought.[11] As a romantic, however, he believed it was as valid to feel an idea as to think it. He knew what he felt if not what he thought, and he expressed his feelings to Finkelstein in April of 1941:

> I do not believe that the sensitive modern mind is as far astray as it thinks it is, as it has been *sophisticated into being,* — by its willing acceptance of sophistry, — and I think people would find themselves on much firmer ground if they really followed their noses, their consciences and their hearts. All the sages of all the races and all the ages have agreed on certain root ideas, and it is the business of grown men to identify their minds with these ideas. We still have Moses and the prophets and we have no excuse if we do not listen to them. (To the prophets I add the classics.) Regarding man himself and his values, I think that most modern talk about relativity, etc., is merely sophistical chatter.[12]

He had found Finkelstein's first conference a "thrilling affair." It was hardly over before he was badgering Mumford to participate in the next year's conference: "This is not *just another damned thing;* and Dr. Finkelstein is one of the most remarkable men whom I have ever known." Mumford refused the invitation, but Brooks, undeterred, delivered a paper at the second annual meeting in September 1941. His paper, "Primary Literature and Coterie Literature," was a vehement denunciation of those who had abandoned "root ideas" — Eliot, Pound, Stein, Joyce, Hemingway, and all other spokesmen for the modern sensibility. These were the "coterie-writers," deniers of progress — Eliot especially — who disparaged the "myth of human goodness" in order to justify following their "personal bent." Primary literature, however, favored progress and the "life-drive" by treating the great themes "by virtue of which the race has risen, courage, justice, mercy, honour, love." The paper was taken from the book Brooks published that fall — *The Opinions of Oliver Allston* (1941).[13]

During the previous year, stimulated by his involvement in Finkelstein's conferences and his consequent meetings with many like-minded men, Brooks had prepared his journal for publication. As in youth he preferred to write of himself as if he were dead, so he attributed the journal to the fictional Oliver Allston and saved for himself, Brooks, the role of literary executor who introduced and commented upon the fragments of the deceased man's journal. It was the life-and-letters format in which the literary remains of nineteenth-century men of letters were customarily buried. Thus, even in the form of his book, Brooks expressed his preference for traditional manners. So too with the title — "Oliver" was an old family name, and "Allston" suggested Brooks's sense of identity with the painter Washington Allston, whom he had portrayed in *The Flowering of New England* as tied to an American "roost" that did not quite suit him, laboring for twenty years on his painting of "Belshazzar's Feast."[14] Similarly, Brooks labored long on his vast canvas, his projected six volumes of American literary history.

To Brooks's long-time readers *The Opinions of Oliver Allston* must have seemed familiar. His old thoughts were in the new book — the horror of the business life, the necessity of socialism, the freedom of the will, the prophetic calling of the artist, and the importance of writers being rooted in a national tradition. The Ruskinian influence was as strong as ever, and he objected to advertising, mass production, industrialism, bigness, and modern urban life in general. He hoped "to see all the skyscrapers filled with bats" and the Empire State Building dropped "in the Atlantic near the spot where the Titanic lies." Horrified by the development of sporting events into giant spectacles, he no longer merely detested football but saw it as one with the power philosophy of Fascism, and he warned that ". . . the war-scuffle . . . has begun already in every mind that likes competitive football on the mass-production scale."[15]

But what gave the book notoriety was its attack on the religion of art and its *devotées*. He had said similar things in the *Freeman,* but now, with his New England books behind him, he spoke to a larger audience in harsher words. His large sales had made him confident, overconfident in fact,[16] even as they had increased his resentment of esthetes and their belief, as he saw it, that *popular* was a synonym for *superficial.* Years earlier he had complained to George Russell of the "cults of *elegant privacy* in our literature, the T. S. Eliot cult, the E. E. Cummings cult, etc. — types of intellectual snobbishness created by reaction from the other cult of 'a million readers.'"[17] With the large audience he could now command in a country on the brink of war, he hoped to force a reaction against such privacy. If writers were to be "voices of the people," they could not hide in a closet. If literature was to be prophetic, it must also be public, and therefore Brooks attacked the "coterie-writers."

Alfred Stieglitz

Clockwise from upper left: Randolph Bourne, Mollie Colum, Sherwood Anderson, Waldo Frank

Eric Schaal

Morton Dauwen Zabel

Clockwise from upper left: Maxwell Perkins, Lewis Mumford, Malcolm Cowley, Newton Arvin

Upper left, the Westport house; lower left,
Brooks about the time of *The Flowering of New
England*; right, Van Wyck and Gladys Brooks

Above, the Weston house; below, the Bridgewater house

Van Wyck Brooks

Brooks's study in Bridgewater just after his death

In *Oliver Allston* he made his case against privacy in modern literature, attacking especially T. S. Eliot for making up a tradition "to suit himself." Based on personal impression and sectarian orthodoxy, Eliot's tradition was not traditional. Brooks defined tradition as "all that humankind has kept alive for its advancement and perfection." This definition implied a faith in progress. The "coterie-writers" denied the idea of progress, but they were cut off from country, family, and "the life that is natural to mankind." Thinking they possessed the sense of the age, they actually possessed only the sense of "a decade of defeat and disappointment." Their cold intellectual sense of poetry as "superior amusement" or a problem in construction did not square with Brooks's romantic idea of the inspired artist. They treated poetry as if it were engineering and thus "made literature a training ground for science." In sum, they made literature into one more technology in an industrialized society and thus inadvertently strengthened the chaotic and ugly forces which caused their despair. Direction for such a society could only be provided by a literature concerned with values and ends rather than techniques.[18]

Criticism especially "exists to determine values, to cherish them, define them and maintain them." There were universal standards and objective truths, and Brooks's purpose as a critic was "to establish the principles by which writers should write, or, rather, by which they should live. . . ." Hence the biographical, sociological emphasis of his criticism, and though he did not say so in *Oliver Allston*, he must especially have resented Eliot's statement that "Poetry . . . is not the expression of personality, but an escape from personality." By dissociating art from the artist, Eliot had dissociated it from life. But Brooks insisted that art, however properly critical of life and reality, had nevertheless to be related to them. The very nature of the artist's role as prophet, as exemplary spirit, as "maker and finder," required that he express his personality. And it had to be a great personality, not a mere "catalyst" of which no trace appeared in the finished work of art. Brooks's basic difference with Eliot was theological, though again he did not state it very clearly. Eliot, like Brooks, used "personality" interchangeably with "soul," and Eliot's opposition to the idea of poetry as expression of personality led him to question, as Brooks would never have done, "the metaphysical theory of the substantial unity of the soul."[19]

Unfortunately, instead of clearly stating these, at bottom, reasonable objections to avant-garde writers in general and Eliot in particular, Brooks resorted to jeers, violent rhetoric, and, as Lionel

Trilling said, "savagery." Brooks called Joyce "the ash of a burnt-out cigar." Was not a poet like Eliot "a clever artificer merely," a craftsman rather than an artist? Such writers were the logical heirs of "the naughty brat Laforgue" and "the spoiled child Proust." Hemingway and half of all American novelists were "boys, determined to remain boys." To follow the theories of Gertrude Stein was "to utter gibberish by definition." The new criticism had "no visible relation to the world of men." All of these were "merely bats . . . who had flown in the twilight between the wars."[20]

Yet Brooks had actually restrained himself in the book. In private he was capable of still more violent expressions of hatred for those who had made contemporary literature meaningless for him. Poetry, even Whitman's, palled on him when he was in this mood, and he told John Hall Wheelock in 1950 that "The Elioteers have killed it [poetry] for me." He could never discuss Eliot calmly, and he told Wheelock that he hoped Eliot would contract cancer and die in agony.[21]

Brooks's violence indicated the intensity of his feelings, heightened in part by self-hatred and continuing fear of insanity. By attacking the "coterie-writers" and their *fin-de-siècle* progenitors, he was attacking his old self; in his youth and at Harvard he had mixed in the same literary circles as Eliot and had shared the world-weary mood of the *fin-de-siècle*. Eliot was the perfect symbol for the aspect of his own past which Brooks most disliked. Similar considerations accounted for his accusation that the "coterie-writers" favored the "death-drive" over the progressive tradition of great literature and its moral values for survival. He had been plagued by recurrent depression all through the thirties and by a continuing sense of unreality and alienation from life. At such times he had not been able to work and had turned to his journal to slay the dragon of his youth that seemingly still beset him — the temperamental preference for unworldliness, for death. The "coterie-writers" seemed to share the preferences of his youth, and he attacked them for inflicting the death-wish on the contemporary mind. For the same reasons he concluded, ". . . the literary mind of our time is sick." He was not certain that he did not share some of the responsibility for that sickness, and his sense of guilt had led him to consider "Ashworth" or "Ashwell" for his alter ego's name before settling on the milder "Allston."[22]

Brooks had changed a number of other youthful opinions, and his new views, while not always explicitly stated in *The Opinions of Oliver Allston,* nevertheless helped account for some of the book's vehemence. His cruel jab at Joyce as a "sick Irish Jesuit" was rooted in the fact that the Spanish Civil War had led him to view Roman Catholicism, as he told Newton Arvin, "much more darkly than in my more aesthetic youth." He worried about the church's political strength in America, telling Mumford that it opposed "every measure for decent living." Neither did the high rites of the Anglican Church or for that matter England itself appeal to him as they had once done. Eliot's English citizenship and Anglican faith constituted the kind of rebellion against American life which would have once been attractive to Van Wyck. But now, with his belief in a native radical tradition, he found Eliot's oppositon to "revolution" treasonous. On a vacation in Canada in 1938, Brooks had seen an altar cloth from the coronation of William the Fourth treated "as if it was a piece of the Cross." He had never been so glad of the American Revolution: "One feels as if no one ever had an idea in Canada." A year later he noted that two London periodicals had ceased and that he knew of four good English writers who wished to emigrate to America — "a remarkable sign of the times." In a speech at Hunter College in 1940 he said: "Europe is reaping whirlwinds far worse than ours. . . . It has thrown us back upon ourselves, and America has risen immensely in its power to charm us. Thousands of novels, biographies and histories, published in recent years, have shown us what multifarious strivings and failures and what multifarious victories lie behind us. . . ."[23]

Now Van Wyck looked back scornfully on his early years when he had lost faith in art and had depreciated American literature in particular. He felt some guilt for the harsh things he had said of Howells, whose novels he had not then read, and he said that Allston was "forty-five before he knew how good they [Howells's novels] were." He also repeated in *Oliver Allston* a regret he had first expressed in 1934: he should not have attacked Puritanism, which had "ceased to menace any sentient being." As a youth he had considered rhetoric a form of poetic untruth and longed like Amiel for pure form or, short of that, pure spirit. Now he considered rhetoric the "social element" of style, which explained the opposition of the "coterie-writers" to it. Defending the relative pronoun against the cult of Hemingway, Brooks said, "All the great literary ages have exalted the study of rhetoric."[24]

Despite what appeared to be a great many changes of opinion, Brooks insisted that he had been fundamentally consistent throughout his career — he had always sought a meaningful idealism. In his youth, businessmen had "professed to march under Emerson's banner," and he had therefore attacked Emerson. In middle age he had discovered the true Emerson, an idealist properly, meaningfully critical of American reality. Whatever his basic consistency as an idealist, Brooks now believed he had read American history wrongly, and his changed viewpoint had cost him his early following. He said in *Oliver Allston* that this loss did not trouble him and explained that he did not believe in "worshipping his own dead self."[25]

Despite the claim on the jacket that it contained "material for a literary revolution," *The Opinions of Oliver Allston* had slight effect on opinion except to reduce Brooks's reputation to a new low. Although there were numerous favorable reviews, they were due mainly to the book's pro-war, anti-Fascist politics. Thus Clifton Fadiman praised the attack on the "death-lovers (now headed by the Fascist stooge Ezra Pound)." Only the unfavorable reviews dealt with Brooks's literary position. Joseph Wood Krutch pointed out that many of the nineteenth-century writers in Brooks's canon had been accused of decadence in their time, and he characterized *Oliver Allston* as "stuffed-shirt literature." Malcolm Cowley accused Brooks of the "heresy" that a good book "expresses the proper opinions." If that were true, "Critics could be replaced by policemen. . . ." Even Alfred Kazin, who of all the younger writers had the greatest understanding and appreciation for Brooks, concluded that ". . . the pressure of the times was too great for him." There was nothing in the book, Kazin said, from which writers could learn, and Brooks showed as little sympathy for artists as did the Fascists he ostensibly opposed.[26]

Dwight Macdonald labelled Brooks "our leading mouthpiece for totalitarian cultural values," and recalled how at the end of 1938 Brooks had asked in a letter to the editor of *Time*, "Why should not committees be formed in towns to make house-to-house collections of objects made in Germany, which might be destroyed in public bonfires?" Actually Brooks had meant to suggest only a voluntary anti-Hitler gesture rather than the adoption of terroristic methods, but he was learning now that anti-Fascist criticism was a two-edged sword. Just before *Oliver Allston* was published, Carl Sandburg had warned Brooks that Eliot was supporting the English war effort and that it would be best to "reserve attacks on him as a fascist, royalist, anti-democrat, anti-Jefferson, anti-Lincoln, anti-Brooks-and-Sandburg, till after the war." Events quickly proved Sandburg correct. The *Partisan Review* held a symposium on the "Brooks-MacLeish Thesis" (MacLeish was included because of his *Irresponsibles),* and a number of contributors found latent Fascist or totalitarian tendencies in Brooks. Allen Tate pointed out that Hitler also had attacked modern art. Louise Bogan called Brooks an "official critic," and James T. Farrell accused him of "setting the basis for staging a kind of Moscow Trials of American culture." In the next issue Eliot himself said that Brooks's use of figures like "life-drive" and "race-survival" was "depressingly reminiscent of a certain political version of biology."[27]

Yet if Brooks had argued his case with more reason and in a better temper he might have won sympathy in surprising quarters. For instance, although he had included John Crowe Ransom among the "coterie-writers," Ransom agreed with him on some issues, calling modern poetry "brilliantly unsuccessful" and a "tinkle without resonance." But Brooks had pitched the controversy in a tone that united his opponents and encouraged scornful rebuke rather than intelligent discussion. William Carlos Williams called him an "ignorant sap," and Henry Miller wrote, "My impression was that Brooks was dead — years ago. I see now he's deader than dead."[28]

The Opinions of Oliver Allston, Brooks's worst book, should never have been published. It is one thing to write personal grievances in a journal and another to print them in a book as if they offer "faith for living."[29] The device of "Allston," Brooks's dead alter ego, served little formal purpose, except to let him string his unfinished and hardly crystalline ideas together with little attention to exposition. Many of his ideas were relevant at the time of the Fascist menace, but *Oliver Allston* was so inadequate as a book that it had little value in the face of the menace. Brooks's later years would have small claim for attention if *The Opinions of Oliver Allston* had been the only book he wrote.

II

Brooks thought of *Oliver Allston,* however, as a mere interlude in his continuing search for the American past. Two decades of life still remained to him, and he would spend them with his customary intensity, writing three more volumes of *Makers and Finders* and then a dozen more books, many of them dealing with hitherto untouched subjects and all of them related in some way to the question of the writer in America.

But none of these later books was to be the equal of *The Flowering of New England* or of *New England: Indian Summer,* the books in which he had "let himself go," as he once said Mark Twain had in

Huckleberry Finn. In the New England books, he had abandoned analysis and gone in for synthesis, had given free rein to his visual sense and scenic imagination, and had indulged his artist's temperament. That indulgence was a focus in this period for the feelings of guilt and inadequacy from which he was never free, and he suffered qualms of conscience for having "let himself go" at the expense of his prophetic responsibility. Brooks did not wish to be merely an artist but an artist of society, and he could not conceive of an art worthy of the name that was not socially uplifting or morally didactic. In 1932 he told George Russell that American literature was "off-centre" because the critics had not "stated the unchanging truths . . . in relation to the concrete life our men of genius know."[30] If this had been his hope for the New England books, he had partly failed. Though his work was full of concrete life, it had contained few clearly stated "truths." The old angry stance of the prophet was gone, and he had failed to convince his critics and ultimately himself that he had held his ground in the thick of the battle. Therefore, in the last three volumes of *Makers and Finders* he would rein himself in and not indulge his visual and artistic sense as freely as in the New England books. Instead, he would impose on these later books the burden of the thesis which he had begun to argue in *The Opinions of Oliver Allston.* As Carl Van Doren had said in his review of *The Ordeal of Mark Twain,* Brooks was too "conscious" to tolerate ambiguity and so must ever walk a "fraying path" between his instincts and his conscience.

Van Wyck later felt that *The World of Washington Irving* (1944) was the best of all his books. The feeling was understandable; it was the best written of *Makers and Finders,* and it was a remarkable record of discovery. He had grown tired of the introspective and self-conscious New Englanders while he was writing *Indian Summer* and complained of "the wily old cuttlefish Henry James and Henry Adams" and their "cold old hearts." With relief he turned to what seemed simpler times and places — New York, the South, and the West in the time of Irving and Jefferson, Cooper and Poe. Irving and Cooper suggested the New York of his maternal ancestors, and as he turned from New England to these subjects, he had the sense of "coming home."[31] But he had never hoped for as much from home as he had from New England, and he mistakenly expected the material for the book to be thin. In the complete *Makers and Finders* series, he thought of *The World of Washington Irving* as preceding and setting the stage for *The Flowering of New England.* But as he began to read for the book he discovered that while literary culture in Irving's time may not have been high, neither was it thin. He discovered dozens of characters who fascinated him and seemed indicative of a primitive literary community at the nation's beginnings — Matthew Carey, Parson Weems, Charles Brockden Brown, Thomas Paine, Joseph Priestley, Barlow, Trumbull, Dwight, Freneau, Hamilton, Aaron Burr, Fisher Ames, Joseph Dennie, William Byrd, John Randolph, William Wirt, John Taylor, Charles Wilson Peale, Alexander Wilson, Brackenridge, Paulding, Audubon, Bryant, Simms, J. P. Kennedy, N. P. Willis, and many more. They travelled, both in America and Europe, met each other, or at least some of the others, exchanged letters, and were perfect warp and woof for one of Brooks's densely interwoven tapestries. Each of the major figures was portrayed as part of a circle or community of other writers. Jefferson had Paine, Fulton, Barlow, and countless others. Irving was drawn out of himself by Paulding and the circle of the theater manager William Dunlap. Cooper had his Bread and Cheese Club, and even Poe had Kennedy and Wirt.

Despite the myriad facts and details of the scenes Brooks drew, there was also an intentional blurring and lack of clarity. The book was written as if it looked back hundreds and thousands of years, rather than a century and a half, to a dimly perceptible folk history saturated with a mythic lore difficult to separate from reality. Jefferson had grown up in the country and at sixteen had not seen a village of twenty houses. He had "read Homer as a boy on canoe trips down the Rivanna, while he had pored over Virgil stretched under an oak tree. . . ." Educated among his countrypeople, Jefferson possessed manners and morals "homogeneous with the country itself." Irving as a boy hunted along the banks of the Pocantico River, a cheerful region in the day but haunted at night by Hulda the Witch, wizard chieftans, and the headless horseman. The Revolution had faded almost into pre-history though there were still strange cries round the great tree where André was taken. What could be better for a writer than to be brought up like Irving "in the midst of history and romance?" And even Poe had primitive beginnings that included "weird tales in the slave-quarters, whither his mammy took him, about graveyards, apparitions, corpses and spooks."[32]

It was little wonder that Brooks felt *The World of Washington Irving* was his finest book; in it he seemed to have discovered a primitive folk history like that of the Angles, Celts, Saxons, and Franks. America was not after all founded by "full-grown, modern, self-conscious men," as he had written in *The Wine of the Puritans*, but by men who had origins resembling those out of which European folk cultures had grown. It was to the intangible power of those folk cultures that Brooks had in part attributed the admirable centralization of modern European cultures. Now he could reasonably hope for such a culture on this side of the water. America too had a primitive, mysterious, somewhat shrouded, and therefore useful past.

But in *The World of Washington Irving* Brooks also began to attempt to mark out the line of native radicalism which he called "the American prophetic tradition." This tradition was expresssed in Jefferson's eighteenth-century faith in human perfectibility. For Van Wyck, though, the Jeffersonian faith took only its language from the Enlightenment; the essence of the faith was American. There was a common, humanistic strain running through Jefferson's rationalistic faith in man, Emerson's romantic self-reliance, and "Lincoln's mystical faith in the wisdom of the people." Brooks believed the nation's literature expressed that central humanistic tradition, that contribution of the American folk to the civilizations of the world. In *The World of Washington Irving* Brooks had created a primitive setting appropriate for the dawn of an epic folk tradition, and in Jefferson the tradition had its first voice: "Like Emerson and Whitman later, he saw man in the morning of time, with his best future all before him, and he regarded the earth as belonging to the living, and the living in the widest commonalty spread. He expressed an American way of thinking that had never been put into words before, as the writers and artists of his time recognized at once. . . . In surprising numbers they knew by intuition that he was one of them, he was their man, and within a generation virtually every writer of eminence had found and followed the Jeffersonian line."[33] This thesis was much like Parrington's though, as Brooks would have marked the distinction, it was more "literary" than Parrington's purely economic standard of judgment. In the vocabulary of *Oliver Allston,* the Jeffersonian tradition represented "primary literature," not merely because it stood for economic and social justice but because it supported the spiritual progress of the "living" and had ideal hopes for the "future."

Nevertheless, Brooks encountered problems much like Parrington's in arguing the primacy of the Jeffersonian tradition, and he resorted to Parrington's solution of defining the disagreeable out of American history. The major problems in *The World of Washington Irving* were Cooper, Irving, and Poe, none of whom followed Jefferson in politics or philosophy, though with Cooper and Irving it was possible to salvage something while dismissing their disagreeable qualities. Just as Parrington had done, Brooks discounted Irving's politics as due to "atomsphere and habit" rather than conviction. His "antiquarian tastes" made him a "natural Tory" but a benign one, "singularly untroubled by thoughts of his own." As for Cooper, Brooks explained his distrust of democracy by saying that he was "at war with himself" (the exact words Parrington had used) and that ". . . his heart and his tastes were not always the friends of his conscience." Yet Brooks insisted that Cooper's essential loyalties were proved by the fact that "his heart went out" to "men of the humbler sort who were essentially noble in their low disguises." These were his "vividest characters" and "the men that Cooper's genius loved."[34]

But Poe? What saving qualities were there in him? He had never paid the least lip service to Jeffersonian ideas but had mocked the notions of human progress and perfectibility. Worse still, he had been as private, undemocratic, and difficult as the modern "coterie-writers." The conclusion was as inescapable to Brooks as it had been to Parrington that, in the latter's words, Poe was "outside the main current of American thought." For Brooks that fact explained the smallness of Poe's impact on American literature: "Poe himself had never shared the developing mood of the American tradition, which his fellow-Virginian at Monticello had done so much to shape, and as he never shared it he could not guide it. So American literature flowed past Poe, without dislodging him indeed, but without ever being diverted or seriously affected by his presence. Nothing could have proved more clearly the toughness and reality of the American tradition than the patent fact that Poe *was* outside it."[35] If the "American tradition" had not been diverted by Poe, neither had he been moved by it, and that raised a question. Of what use was an American tradition that left Poe unaffected? He was a "consummate artist," the possessor of a "literary genius that had had no parallel as yet on the American scene." *Makers and Finders* was meant to prove that the literary life could be and had been lived in America, because there was a community of spirit between artists and the people. "The silent spirit of collective masses is the source of all great things," Renan had said, and Brooks had echoed the sentiment all his life with his insistence that writers were "voices of the people." But Poe had not been a voice of the people, not if Brooks had correctly defined the American tradition. The only possible conclusion for Brooks was that it was Poe rather than the American tradition which had proven inadequate. Poe was not only not

American but not suited to worldly life; he could not have been the voice of any people because he was "sick." His "nervous and mental organization would have made havoc of his life in any society, at any moment of time."[36]

Many other American lives had had a dark side, and Brooks treated several of them — Lincoln, Twain, and Melville — in *The Times of Melville and Whitman* (1947). The vehemence with which he had begun to argue a single American tradition forced a difficult choice on Brooks. Either the darkness of these later lives made them "sick" like Poe and placed them outside the American tradition, or else the lives were divided between darkness and light and the light was all that mattered. Van Wyck chose the latter course, conscientiously depicting the blackness, then ruling it un-American. Lincoln, for instance, was ridden with melancholy and fears of madness and suicide, but what counted was that he was also a "man of letters," a prophet of great moral force who believed in the "religion of humanity that Jefferson had shared. . . ." The same was true of Mark Twain, whom Brooks had read again, telling S. K. Ratcliffe that he was "astonished to find that my old book on Mark, *The Ordeal*, is just inescapably true. . . ."[37] But if Mark Twain had often despaired, he had also been a "natural democrat" who raged against injustice. He was "the serio-comic Homer of this old primitive Western world," and a civilizing force who made the Mississippi "a dwelling-place of light . . . where the mind had never been at home and where henceforth it was always happy to rest." Even Melville, for all his blackness, had praised the "kingly commons," and though he had lost much of his faith, it "super-abounded in him in the great productive years that reached their highest point in *Moby Dick*, when he shared the general Mazzinian belief that nations have their missions and Whitman's special belief in the mission of his own." Melville was thus a spokesman of the Jeffersonian tradition, one of those like Emerson and Whitman in whom "America as a whole had found its voices."[38]

Whitman, however, was infinitely more the hero of the book than Melville. Brooks's initial working title had been "Whitman and His Contemporaries" because, as he had explained to Mumford, "Whitman seems to me bigger and bigger, but I find that Melville doesn't wear so well. So much of him seems just rhetoric, and I find I dread going through him again." Distressed by this comment, Mumford had replied that in his own *Melville* (1929) he had missed his "real opportunity; and that was to treat Whitman and Melville together, as complementary aspects of the spirit, contrasting, antagonistic, yet united." Brooks had been impressed by this idea and, finding Melville more readable than he had expected, in fact "more wonderful than ever," had decided to make the book "a sort of interweaving of darkness and light, using Melville and Whitman as my two colours. . . ."[39] In *The Times of Melville and Whitman,* Brooks wrote that both *Moby Dick* and *Leaves of Grass* were "planetary" books: "One gave the dark side of the planet, the other the bright." Van Wyck's preference was for the bright. Though he praised Melville, his heart was not in it, and he expressed his true feeling in *The Confident Years* (1952) when he condemned the postwar reaction of the 1920's: "Then the great myth of Moby Dick rose in the American imagination and Melville's overpowering sense of the omnipotence of evil blacked out the sunniness and whiteness of Emerson and Whitman."[40]

Against Melville's blackness Brooks painted a bright portrait of Whitman, a prophet in touch with the common people, a great stylist moved by a religious rather than an esthetic impulse. Where Brooks had once thought Whitman's great spirit was a sort of historical accident which, taken as a model, would endanger those less fortunately constituted, he now felt that Whitman was a useful example for American writers. Whitman was a student of perfection whose great personality was the result of a struggle and who had after all, though Brooks once thought he had not, squeezed the slave out of himself. Whitman offered evidence of the power of the will, an example much needed in America.

Whitman's sexuality could have been the flaw in the picture. Brooks still believed that a great writer was a great man writing, and he could not believe that a homosexual could be a great man. On an ideal level he still believed, as he had in youth, that the artist's (and the critic's) nature combined both masculine and feminine qualities. He later criticized Mencken's intellect as devoid of "feminine traits," and he called Hemingway's cult of toughness anti-art: "For what does 'sissyness' comprise if not the traits of the sensitive man that art has hitherto cherished and nourished?" Admitting to being "soft-boiled" himself, he protested near the end of his career that "Be gentle!" was as manly an injunction as "Be hard."[41] But masculine and feminine qualities had to be balanced in a great writer, and then only in an ideal sense. So Brooks abstracted Whitman's homosexuality to the level of the ideal. When he said that ". . . there was much of the woman in Whitman's composition," he meant it only in an ideal sense, on the level of poetry, where it balanced his masculinity and produced a whole-souled vision. On the level of the real or physical, Whitman was "mildly bisexual and mostly unconscious of the homosexual implications in *Calamus*. . . ." Too drawn to "all that was bracing, hardy and sane" to be interested in the perverse, Whitman's supposed expressions of homosexual longing were the result of his great "manly affection" for the "comrade-apostles" of democracy whom he figured in "the sweet-flag called the calamus."[42]

Brooks argued the Jeffersonian thesis even more strongly in *The Confident Years: 1885–1915* (1952), especially in the last five chapters, beginning with the chapter that treated his own early career, "The Younger Generation of 1915." That generation had announced that America "was somehow coming of age" and had been a "united army," hopeful like Jefferson for humanity, and consciously preparing the way, as Randolph Bourne had done, for a "socialized world-culture." It was questionable, however, whether or not Brooks's generation actually had been united behind this particular vision, and he hardly proved the point by mentioning Ezra Pound's 1913 essay *Patria Mia* in the same breath as his own *America's Coming-of-Age*. Pound's book (unpublished until 1950 because the manuscript had been misplaced) was startlingly similar in many respects to *America's Coming-of-Age*; Pound hated the implicitly materialistic values of the business life, disliked Howells, deplored American genteel culture and the practice of leaving art "to the care of ladies' societies," and nevertheless predicted an "American Risorgimento." But the differences between the two books were just as striking, and they suggested Brooks's later disagreements with the "coterie-writers." As early as 1913 Pound had admired Whistler and Henry James, declared that the test of art was in technique, and opposed the idea of art as social prophecy to which Brooks had already committed himself.[43]

If Brooks's picture of his own "Younger Generation of 1915" was not quite accurate, it nevertheless would have been an appropriate end for *The Confident Years: 1885–1915*. Unfortunately, he further marred the book by adding four more chapters which raced through American literature from 1915 to 1950. In these four he made his most careful attempt to define the American Jeffersonian tradition, and then harshly judged the contemporary religion of art against that standard. He defined the American tradition as a faith in the goodness of man and a "vision of a good life and world that had sprung from the Enlightenment and the age of revolutions." The tradition included figures as intellectually diverse as Thomas Paine, Emerson, Whitman, Lincoln, Ellen Glasgow, and Sinclair Lewis. But the tradition Brooks was outlining was attitudinal and emotional rather than intellectual. What mattered was that both

Emerson and Jefferson had owned visions of a better life and world. They had been prophets of hope and "on the side of life," as Brooks said of Ellen Glasgow.[44]

In a two-page summary, Brooks related the American Jeffersonian tradition to humanistic faiths from classical times to the present, and then criticized modern literature against this standard of the ages. The modern literary mind had thrown over Jefferson's "religion of humanity" in favor of the religion of art. Writers fled their homelands and the humanity the homelands symbolized, preferring to live as exiles in Paris, gathered about the goddess of art. Rather than being voices of the people, they thought of the people as rabble. Their preference for difficulty was the consequence of their desire for a style immune from defilement by the rabble. This and the dehumanized "instinct of workmanship" that alone survived in a technological society accounted for an esoteric literature divorced from life.[45]

This line of argument was of course familiar to readers of *The Opinions of Oliver Allston*, and though Brooks tried to make his points with more restraint than in the earlier book, he could not entirely subdue his strong feelings. Though he did not now call the avant-garde writers lovers of death as he had in *Oliver Allston*, he wrote that life had ceased to be "real" to them because their ideas and esthetics devalued humanity. Again, as in *Oliver Allston*, Brooks's prose became lame and halting, and he resorted to rhetorical questions where only detailed and careful argument could have sufficed: ". . . craftsmanship in any form justified for Hemingway a life in which 'nowadays' everything was 'murder.' Was not this what the colonel was to say in *Across the River and into the Trees*, adding that to have 'shot well' was enough to have lived for, though this would have justified an ordinary gangster's life?" Eliot, however, remained the primary villain because of his rejection of the "myth" of the innate goodness of man. Repudiating that basic premise, he had to repudiate also the democratic liberalism which was based on it and which was "the only American tradition that ever affected the outer world. . . ." Eliot had not only ignored the American tradition, he had reversed it. Hence, "the intellectual dictator of the literary West" distrusted humanity and sought solace through religious sectarianism. Pound also, with his "commands to the militia," had broken faith with democracy. Nevertheless, Brooks put in a good word for Pound, who was then imprisoned for his support of Fascist Italy: "In the venal sense Pound was scarcely a traitor"; he was only, in the phrase of Jefferson, "a traitor to human hope."[46]

What then could Brooks make of American literature in the first half of the twentieth century? Was it totally dissociated from the Jeffersonian tradition, alienated not only from America but from life itself? This was a difficult conclusion for a series of books meant to show that the literary life had been and could be lived in America. He rejected such a conclusion and argued instead that American writers continued to be men of faith "behind the masks they were generally apt to wear, underneath the cynicism that covered them like a film of steel. . . ." If Dreiser had been a fatalist and an admirer of power, he had "acted as if he believed in free will" with his youthful plans for reform and his "genuine compassion for the woes of the weak." Hemingway, for whom a true story must end in death, had "acquired in Spain a respect for human nature" and thus "reaffirmed the position of Jefferson." Even Ezra Pound, in his attack on "usurers," was "defending the America of Jefferson's ideal." American writers were disillusioned "because of the failure of a promise that Europe had never felt." Brooks asked, ". . . was it not, in fact, because they cared for the fate of men on earth that they seemed so chagrined and disenchanted? Were they not denunciatory in proportion as they cared for this, in proportion as America had fallen short of its promise, as the gap had widened between reality and the idea of the country that Americans had always had in mind?" Dreiser, Hemingway, and Pound were in the American tradition after all. And while he would not say such a thing about Eliot, Brooks nevertheless felt he too was defined by America, or rather, as he told S. K. Ratcliffe, by his "comprehensive rejection of everything American. Turn it [Eliot's point of view] inside out and you have America."[47]

Brooks was having it both ways, calling the avant-garde writers to account for their denial of the American tradition and then using the vehemence of their denial as evidence of the continued vitality of the tradition. Thus in *The Confident Years* he could sweepingly declare it an "obvious fact that the American imagination had been on the side of the 'Left' since Jefferson's days," that is, on the side of the people.[48]

These ideas suggest why Brooks never wrote the projected sixth volume of *Makers and Finders,* attempting to deal with American literature from 1915 to 1950. He could not have sustained for an entire volume the tenuous argument that the avant-garde writers were both denyers and, by the strength of their denial, affirmers of the American tradition. He would have had difficulty forcing American literature in the twentieth century into the idealized picture of a community that the form of *Makers and Finders* was best suited to convey. He had glimpses of this problem, and in his memoirs recalled how Sinclair Lewis once asked him what kind of man Steinbeck was, ". . . and it struck me then that we had no community of literature, such as we had had in the nineteenth century and even later. . . . now they [writers] were as solitary as the rhinoceros roaming the veldt. . . ." Still, as late as 1947 when *Melville and Whitman,* the fourth volume of the series, was published, he had expected to do not only the fifth book but also the sixth and had told Mumford, "The next two volumes are the crucial ones, the two generations of our own lifetime, 1885–1915, 1915–1950." Mumford had warned him that in *Melville and Whitman* he had left out "the bitter tragic element." If he failed to recognize the dark side of American life he would not, when the time came, "have a key to our present generation."[49] Brooks did indeed lack that key, and in the end he quietly dropped the idea of writing a sixth volume.

In these later years Brooks hoped for too much from the American past, just as in his earlier phase he had undervalued it. Then his criticism had been based on a mistaken but commonly agreed upon hostility to American history. Only his insistence that America could and would have a central culture had been new. Now he had so completely reversed his opinion of the American past that he seemed unable to criticize it at all. He was willing to maintain his idea that America after all had a central cultural tradition even at the expense of narrowing American history. Rather than criticizing, he cut out whatever seemed unhealthy. Whatever was not part of the Jeffersonian tradition was not part of the American past but simply sickness and aberration.

In his later no less than in his earlier career, Brooks's failures as a prophet were due to his failures as a historian. *Makers and Finders* was a "synthetic" achievement, quite different from the analytic tasks which he had suggested for American critics in his 1918 essay "On Creating a Usable Past." Yet that essay had betrayed a lack of respect for the reality of the past that had continued into and weakened his later career. He had tended to idealize history ever since his childhood, when he had been taught that the only mean-ingful past was across the water in the heavenly sphere of Europe. Committed now to mastering the reality of America, he nevertheless let his hopes for what would be shape his vision of what had been. The subjects of his books had led him westward, out of nineteenth-century New England toward the modern America in which he actually lived, and he had been unable to come to grips with a present that was not continuous with his idealized vision of the past. Therefore he could not write the sixth volume that would have dealt with his own bitter era. What then of his prophetic hopes for the future? America has had a different and fiercer destiny than he could have envisioned.

III

Brooks was an artist rather than a philosopher, and he was most convincing where he did not have an explicit thesis, as in the New England books. In *The Flowering of New England* he had said that his subjects were "friends of the human spirit. They stood for good faith and fair play and all that was generous and hopeful in the life of their time."[50] But this was only in the conclusion, and he had not made the book depend upon the idea. The later books would have been better if there too he had not explicitly argued his thesis, but relied solely on his artistry to create his vast picture of an American literary community. *The Times of Melville and Whitman* and *The Confident Years* were as scenic and colorful as the earlier books and taken alone, without the blemish of a thesis, the scenery and color were powerfully convincing.

Brooks's scenes were regional scenes. This limited focus was appropriate, for he still remained, as in his youth, a moral scientist interested in charting the interaction between people and their environment. He was still following the "natural method" of Sainte-Beuve. Yet Brooks was a physician as well as a scientist, a prophet as well as a scribe, and he meant to improve as well as observe the moral condition of life in America. He believed he could prescribe or prophesy the conditions necessary for the fulfillment of the American spirit. That fulfillment would come "when the life of all the regions, taken together, formed a final synthesis." This idea was Brooks's American counterpart for Mazzini's interpretation of European nationhood — that the nations were "workshops" of the peoples, in which they forged individual cultures for the benefit of the ultimate community into which they would merge. The regions of America were analogous to the nations of Europe. That was why *Makers and Finders* was organized along geographical lines, first with the New England books and then with the chapter headings in the later books — "The South," "The Middle West," "The West," and so on. Each of these regions, "to establish its independence," had "turned against New England," just as ". . . the East had turned against the mother-country." Regional feeling, Brooks said in 1941, would unite "the artists and the people as they had been united in New England." And when each region possessed its own tradition, ". . . what a synthesis would follow that."[51]

Despite his commitment to a regional interpretation, the last three books of the series were national in scope. After the New England books one would have expected whole volumes devoted to New York, to the South, and to the West. Instead, the later books were about the entire country in specific periods; only the chapters were organized around regional themes. This method of organization committed Brooks to pictures of several regional communities between the covers of each book. He had to paint the entire nation, section by section, in each volume, and the result was that in addition to the communal spirit for which he always strove, there was also a sense of division in these later books. He could not hope to achieve anything like the unified effect of the New England books with this method of organization, and yet he probably felt driven to it. The only other choice would have been separate books on New York, the South, and the West, but this was not feasible because Brooks still could not imagine that the literary life could be lived outside the Northeast. A volume on the South would have had Poe, whom Brooks regarded as sick, as its main figure, and that would not have suited his goal of showing that the literary life had been lived in America. And he had not changed his mind on Mark Twain, who would inevitably have dominated a book on the West. By organizing the books chronologically he could use Irving and Cooper in one volume and Melville and Whitman in another, rather than expending them all in one book on New York.

Because the regions of America were for Brooks analogous to the nations of Europe, he admired them to the degree that they reminded him of Europe. Thus, he was better disposed to the South than to the West. As the oldest region the South most resembled Europe in age, an important fact to Brooks, who believed that ". . . writers flourish best in the oldest part of any country." But unlike New England, the South had produced few "prophets" in the nineteenth century. Much of its history was sordid, Brooks believed, and it had been a difficult place for men of conscience to live. The South maintained a colonial attitude toward England, and T. S. Eliot's main strength came from the Vanderbilt neo-classicists who were "really taking out their grudge against the North for winning 'the war.' . . . Eliot makes common cause with them in a common sympathy for the eighteenth century Tory England from which America broke away."[52] Still, the South was the home of Jefferson, and unlike the West, it was venerable for its age.

The West, a place of raw newness, least resembled Europe, and for Brooks it remained least lovely of the sections. It would have depressed him terribly to write an entire book on the West and its towns with their "litter of curled up boots and shoes, pieces of bottles and rags and played out tin-ware, the hog-wallows and broken-down fences and the gates with hinges of old leather or none that Mark Twain later deplored in the American scene. The town drunkard slept with the pigs in the tanyard and only returned to life at the sound of a dog-fight. Old worm-eaten boards staggered over the graves on the hill-side, and the gardens were full of jimson-weeds. . . ." To Brooks the inadequacies of contemporary literature seemed related to the West's achievement of "supremacy in American letters" in the twentieth century. He thought of Eliot and Pound as Westerners, along with others whose work seemed morally inadequate — Dreiser, Anderson, Hemingway, Farrell, and Fitzgerald.[53]

His treatment of the West showed the problem with Brooks's detailed and pictorial method; it was appropriate for describing an integrated and settled community but was inadequate to a history of struggle in a harsh environment. After *The Times of Melville and Whitman* was finished, Brooks admitted to Newton Arvin that his chapters on the West were "thin and perfunctory." His "method" had failed in treating the West because ". . . there were so few writers (Lew Wallace, Riley, etc.) that they couldn't be brought into relation with the wealth of the background." For Brooks there was still no meaningful community in the West, but his commitment to his "method" had led him to a mistaken effort at depicting what never existed. He would have come closer to the inspiriting effect he hoped for by drawing the harsh West of his imagination and then showing whatever heroism he could have found there. Instead, he created a picture no one believed in. Even as friendly a reviewer as Lewis Mumford objected that if Brooks would let his readers down occasionally, he would lift them up more often. Instead, Brooks followed the method of *The Flowering of New England,* a method wonderfully fresh and appropriate for that book but which, Mumford said, "has now become pat."[54]

The West was where Brooks's method met its most glaring defeat, but there were problems with it even in the East. His attempt to sustain the joyous mood of *The Flowering of New England* led to a lack of discrimination. In *The Confident Years,* for instance, he argued the very questionable point that Weir Mitchell, H. H. Furness, and Henry Charles Lea gave Philadelphia "the sort of distinction that Lowell and Dr. Holmes conferred on Boston. . . ." Then, also, his search for community often led to too great an emphasis on the contacts between writers. Melville's loneliness in New York, for instance, was difficult to countenance, and Van Wyck mitigated it in every way he could. He said that Melville had "seen and read" the travel writer John Lloyd Stephens. In fact, it was only once, as a boy, that Melville saw the man Stephens, and at a distance, in church. To Brooks "nothing seemed stranger" than that Melville and Whitman had hardly known of each other and probably never met. After he had finished *Melville and Whitman,* he learned that as an old man Melville had belonged to the New York Writers' Club, and he passed the information along to Newton Arvin, who was working on his own *Herman Melville* (1950): "It shows at least that Melville was not ignored by the New York writers and might be worth at least a little mention."[55]

Just as he had not changed his mind on the West, Brooks maintained many of the other opinions of his youth in *Makers and Finders.* He still deplored the latter half of the nineteenth century when young men like his father had been drawn into a "frenzy of speculation," and when literature "by default" had fallen into the hands of women. And he was still appalled at the "hard and loveless" life on the frontier. His psychological theory was unchanged; to be "whole-souled" was best. To wish unconsciously to be an artist and at the same time be uncritically representative of the objective facts of American life, especially commercialism, was to be, like Mark Twain, a "dual personality." But to fly from the fact of America was to drift "further and further from life itself," as Henry James had done in England with his late manner which "seemed to abandon the objective role."[56]

But there was little social content in the psychology of *Makers and Finders,* even though Brooks treated many of his new subjects along the lines of his old. When George W. Cable became, like Henry James, "an expert professional novelist," he lost his Creole traits and ". . . the flavour vanished from his work." Jack London, like Mark Twain, had possessed the "sensitive spirit" of the artist, but he "repressed this spirit too effectively, too long." In this way, Brooks maintained his early belief in a balanced personality; the artist should be a worldly man with a heavenly vision. As he had applied this psychology to Twain and James, "America" had meant "world," and "Europe" had meant "heaven." This social content was what had made his interpretation significant, but now he failed to analyze his subjects in terms of their place in American society. He showed Melville, for instance, passing from a too worldly or objective state in his early books to a moment of equipoise that produced *Moby Dick.* Then he slid into an "excess of the subjective" that "all but extinguished the creative power in him." Melville had passed through an ordeal, but Brooks's analysis of it was abstracted from Melville's anguished experiences in American society. It was no wonder that he told Mumford, ". . . the Melville problem strikes me as a bore now." One would have expected, as Edmund Wilson remarked, a different feeling and treatment from the author of *The Ordeal of Mark Twain.*[57]

When he had begun the *Makers and Finders* series, Brooks had intended for it to be "critical and psychological," but he found this goal difficult to achieve. In his early career his artistic sense had suffered for the sake of psychological analysis, and analysis suffered now for the sake of art. By the time he wrote *The Opinions of Oliver Allston,* he claimed to have lost interest in psychology because it was useful only to the scientist interested in "causes." Brooks was interested in the "moral and aesthetic spheres," in "significance." History, he insisted, could not be a science, which meant it was an art. His work, as he had said of Prescott's in *The Flowering of New England,* possessed "colour" rather than depth, and ". . . its pageantry of picturesque detail was calculated to feed as never before the starved imagination of the country."[58]

Still, there was a psychological interpretation, however removed from society, in *Makers and Finders.* Brooks saw a cyclical pattern in American history that resembled the cycles of manic-depressive illness. In *The Flowering of New England* he had shown the inchoate Boston of 1815 rising till it was, in Oswald Spengler's term, a "culture-city." Then, in *New England: Indian Summer,* he had portrayed New England's decline and passage "through the valley of the shadow," a necessary passage before there could be "another springtime." He drew hope from this cyclical pattern resembling his illness, for if he had sounded the depths and risen, so should American literature recover from its contemporary morbidity. In *The Confident Years* he pictured the flowering, as it might be called, through which he had lived before the First World War, when he and Bourne and the *Seven Arts* had expected the growth of a public literature. Then had come the postwar decline dominated by Eliot and the "coterie-writers." It was a "time of life-denial," as his own worst depression had been, but the prognosis was as good for the literary mind as for the manic-depressive. Time would bring an upswing. In the final paragraph of *The Confident Years* he declared again his belief in progress and his agreement with Thomas Wolfe that ". . . the true fulfillment of our spirit . . . is yet to come."[59]

There were many problems with *Makers and Finders*. Minor figures often received as much space as major ones and seemed to be of the same stature. Books themselves were not often discussed, only the lives of their writers. Quotations were unmarked, creating a blurred effect in which the reader could not distinguish Brooks from his subject. Reviewers and critics harped on these problems over the years and little purpose would be served by discussing them in detail here. It is important to note, however, that the problems with the series were not egregious errors but the logical consequence of Brooks's old-fashioned idea of literary criticism as a study of morals. To him the work of art was ultimately a document of the moral relationship between the artist and the world. Hence he turned more quickly from the art to the artist than the new critics could abide. But he in turn could not tolerate the separation between the man and the work that was a basic principle of the new criticism.

What finally needs to be emphasized is the heroism and the significance of Brooks's reading through all of American literature from its national beginnings. It is true that he drew a measure of needed comfort from his work, but the comfort was purchased dearly. Writing his series had given him a "wonderful existence," he once told Mumford, "but I have bought it at the price of many things human." He was referring to the single-mindedness that often made him deny the demands of others, in this case Mumford's request that he write a memorial essay on their old friend Paul Rosenfeld. But Brooks denied himself also. There were days when his spirit flagged and his torpor was almost physical.[60] Yet he scourged himself into his study to work virtually every day for twenty years, reading four thousand books and writing the twenty-six hundred pages of his five volumes. Such sustained effort accounted, no doubt, for many of the weaknesses of the series, including the absence in the later books of the tautness that had characterized his early prose. He had energy enough, but he refused himself the respite in which his concentration could have peaked. He had lost whatever little capacity he had once had to refresh himself, to loaf like Whitman and invite the soul. Perhaps he feared the introspection and "subjective" knowledge that such refreshment might have brought. Fearing for his sanity with more reason than most, he must to some degree consciously have seen his absorption in work as a strategy for keeping himself sane. The more important point, however, is that he chose meaningful work, and his sustained effort accounted also for the massive completeness of his series, a quality essential to its numerous discoveries.

In *Makers and Finders* Brooks helped set the pace for the astonishingly rapid growth of scholarship devoted to American cultural history. In later years he was deluged with queries on sources from younger writers and scholars provoked to book-length studies by his treatment of neglected subjects. And he provided all the aid he could. Thus, Victor von Hagen's book on *John Lloyd Stephens,* the explorer and travel writer, was not only inspired by Brooks and dedicated to him, but was written in Brooks's house in the winter of 1946 while Brooks was in California. Another discovery was the Civil War novelist John W. De Forest. When Brooks checked De Forest's books out of the Yale library in the late 1930's, he found that some of them had last been taken out in the 1890's. Edmund Wilson treated De Forest in his *Patriotic Gore,* and in a letter acknowledged so great a debt to Brooks that he was not sure how much he had contributed himself. Wilson doubted that he could have written his book without Brooks's exploratory efforts, and later Wilson would pay tribute to Brooks for "his importance to American culture, his heroism in pulling himself together and carrying out his great achievement. . . ."[61]

In the end, however, heroic striving had not been enough to achieve the oneness with America, with life, for which Van Wyck longed. He could not escape the dream of the old world that played on his imagination, however much more subtly in these later years. He offered America the best past that he could imagine, a past which resembled the community of culture and national purpose that to him seemed the essence of nineteenth-century Europe. So too, was his own life lived out along European lines. Believing in "the approach . . . of the great old fellows of the nineteenth century," he wrote in the tradition of European critics and literary historians — Taine, Sainte-Beuve, Brandes, Symonds, Pater, and Ruskin. They had all been admired for the substance as well as the art, the content as well as the form of their writing, and some of them had been powerful, prophetic voices. Brooks was a prophet, and he labored forward in America, hoping his work would strike such a spark as had, say, Standish O'Grady's *History of Ireland: Heroic Period* (1878) when it ignited the Irish literary revival. He received no such reward, but only, as it seemed to him, the carping of small and "life-denying" critics. It was not easy to be a man of letters in the modern world, and harder still in America. The great Europeans had been threatened by industrialism but never by the question of what was their native land or the community to which they spoke. Brooks faced that question daily, with heroic resolve, trying always, as he said in *Oliver Allston,* for a "philosophy of American life," and never quite succeeding.[62]

MAN OF LETTERS

BOTH critically and financially, *New England: Indian Summer* (1940) had been as great a success as *The Flowering of New England* (1936). Van Wyck had seemed well established as a best seller, and he had believed that his future was financially secure. Once again he had been wrong. *The Opinions of Oliver Allston* (1941) had disappointed him with its low sales, and the last three volumes of *Makers and Finders,* beginning with *The World of Washington Irving* (1944), were not nearly as popular as the earlier New England books had been. By 1943 he was again living on advances.[1] This new financial crisis was in part due to his desire for, and his belief in 1940 that he could finally afford, the well-upholstered life of a man of letters. To begin, he had built a new house.

The Westport house in which he had lived for twenty years was old and rickety, and when the maid walked heavily upstairs the entire structure rattled. It was difficult to have the quiet he required in his study, and even though his children were grown he believed that he needed more space than his "cottage," worn out "at the knees and elbows," could provide. He wanted something more stately, and he built it with $40,000 provided by a new mortgage.[2]

The site was a clearing of four acres on a wooded hill in Weston, Connecticut, four miles from Westport. The new house stood at the top of the hill, facing south, and the ground dropped steeply in front. On a clear day Van Wyck could look out across the Sound and see Long Island twenty miles away. The large, imposing, two-story, white brick house was well proportioned, with graceful lines, large windows, and a long stone terrace in front. There was a verandah at each end, and the roofs of these were railed sundecks, approached through French doors upstairs. On the ground floor in front, three more pairs of French doors opened on the terrace, which led in turn to the garden. So much glass would have been more functional in a Mediterranean climate. And in fact, from the rear, where one of the windows was round, the house suggested the sort of Italian villa in which Van Wyck and Eleanor had dreamed of living when they were young.

In his memoirs Brooks said that the advantage of the Weston house, with its isolated site, was that he and Eleanor were "disentangled from village affairs" and "could live more serenely with our work and with the friends who came to see us."[3] However, he had never allowed Westport affairs to entangle him, and his life in this period was not serene but, rather, troubled and hectic, so that he actually lived in the Weston house for barely half of the six years he owned it. What appealed to him in both the prospect and the memory of the new house was the image of himself living out his later years at remove from the world but not in isolation. The world would seek him out as it had always sought out men of letters; where Voltaire had been, *there* was Paris. Van Wyck had always liked to entertain rather than visit because when he was host he had only to deal with the company he chose, and as a man of letters he wanted to play the role of host on a large scale. As soon as he had moved into the new house in May 1941, he was inviting all his old friends to visit for long weekends or for large dinner parties, up to thirty guests on the terrace.[4]

There were problems with the new house, however. Because of its situation on the top of the hill it was buffeted by storms, and the living room was once flooded by rain when wind burst the French doors open. Another time a hurricane left Brooks on his hill without electricity or water for five days. The Second World War, with its gasoline and tire rationing, soon cramped his hospitable ways. Guests could not often drive to his house, and even if they came by train, he could not always spare the gasoline for the fourteen-mile round trip to the station. Without company life was "grim . . . on top of this hill." Van Wyck was soon tired of his isolation, and he thought of selling the house. But property values were down during the war, and he could not afford a loss. Another problem created by the war was the shortage of servants to maintain the large house and help Eleanor, who was often sick during these years. Still worse, their ration of fuel oil would not heat the house in winter, and they had to move into New York for the winters of 1943 and 1944.[5]

They spent both winters in two-room apartments just above Times Square. During the first winter, even with rent payments, it was cheaper to live in New York than to maintain and staff their house. But during the second winter in New York they paid $225 a month for an apartment with no kitchen, only a refrigerator and an electric hot plate. Both winters they were cramped, and for a time Van Wyck had to write at a card table. Despite such inconveniences, he was delighted with the stimulus of the city and his escape from the isolation of Weston. He had dozens of meetings, dinners, and parties with old friends like Robert Frost, Paul Rosenfeld, Lee Simonson, and Jo Davidson. When he needed books he walked to the Public Library on Forty-second Street. Winter in New York was "delicious," he told M. A. DeWolfe Howe. Yet to Eleanor he soon complained that the city was too hectic. Although his writing seemed to be going well, he wanted peace for concentration, and he looked forward to returning to the country in the spring. But they were hardly back in the big house before he was lonely again and longing for the city.[6]

To add to his troubles, his health began to deteriorate. At the beginning of the first winter in New York he suffered a spasm of a blood vessel in his brain. His left arm and leg were temporarily paralyzed, but in a few days he was better. A year later, spring 1944, he experienced severe chest pains. His physician diagnosed these as angina pectoris, but at Eleanor's urging told Van Wyck that the problem was hardening of the arteries. Van Wyck's father had died of angina, and she said he had a "horror" of it. For a time he had to stay in bed till ten in the morning and avoid excitement and exercise. He was hardly on his feet again before Eleanor had one of her frequent cases of pneumonia. Van Wyck had to go for the groceries, do other chores that were usually hers, and climb the stairs a dozen times a day to see her. He strained his heart, suffered a mild thrombosis, and was soon in bed again himself. For the next few weeks he was on his back, but reading from six in the morning till ten at night for *The Times of Melville and Whitman*. His illness and other problems in the next few years no doubt contributed to making it one of the weakest books in the *Makers and Finders* series.[7]

Meanwhile, his daughter-in-law had a nervous breakdown. Charles had married suddenly in 1936, and Van Wyck, who had never met the girl, had hardly been able to sleep for the "misery" of what he had been certain was a mismatch. He had been quickly reconciled, however, when, meeting the girl, he learned that she was a fine painter. Now in 1944 her breakdown led Van Wyck to think back on his own nervous crisis. He advised Charles not to place too much confidence in doctors, who could not understand "what goes on in an 'artist's' mind, but such cases virtually always come right of themselves." Eleanor concurred; the "pure artist type" had special needs, and Charles should understand that his wife loved him "as Papa loves me." And she offered the consolation that Van Wyck's crisis had "enriched . . . the relation between us." Charles had taken his wife to California several years earlier and there they had a son, Peter, who was to be Brooks's only grandchild. Eleanor had always worried, probably too much, about Charles and had wanted to visit him in California. But she had been unable to go alone because Van Wyck was "wretched," she said, when she was gone for even a single night. Now Eleanor and Van Wyck decided to go together for the winter of 1945. The climate, they hoped, would be good for Eleanor with her dangerous tendency to pneumonia.[8]

Van Wyck and Eleanor had a reunion with Charles in San Francisco and then returned to Carmel after an absence of more than twenty years. They rented a house on the ocean, looking out toward Point Lobos, and as in times past, the blue water and winter verdure reminded Van Wyck of Italy: "Carmel is unique, like Capri and a few other places." He met John Steinbeck and Robinson Jeffers, and he was greatly impressed by the latter's intensity, if not by the darkness of his vision. Eleanor had taken charge of their five-year-old grandson for a month, and the boy irritated his grandfather by interrupting dinner conversation. Brooks was trying to begin the writing of *Melville and Whitman,* and he suffered the depression that came with each new book. Then an artery burst in his right eye, causing a large clot, and he could not use his eyes for six weeks while it dissolved. For a time it was not certain that he would recover his sight and his depression worsened. Eleanor lifted his spirits somewhat by reading and typing for him for six hours a day, showing him that he would be able to continue his work, even if permanently blind. Then Eleanor's mother, who had remained in her small house in Westport, suddenly died. Henry Stimson, Eleanor's cousin and now secretary of war, arranged train reservations, and they returned East for the funeral and, as Van Wyck said, a "general overhauling."[9]

But there was to be no respite. They had hardly returned from California before Van Wyck was hospitalized for ten days by a hydrocelectomy — surgery to drain his scrotum of an accumulation of serous fluid. It was a minor operation but a depressing prospect nonetheless, and he feared "the knife." He had not written a line in two months, and he worried about money as medical bills mounted for his own illnesses, the breakdown of his daughter-in-law, and Eleanor's recurrent pneumonia. They returned to the big house for the spring and summer, but the only servant available was a German woman, pro-Nazi, prone to violence, and probably insane. They put up with her for two months but finally had to let her go. Eleanor, weakened by constant colds, had to do the cooking, marketing, gardening, housework, and laundry as well as "be always on tap to listen to Papa." He invited six for Sunday dinner when Eleanor had no cook, and she found this "hard." Later they hired a Japanese-American who was loyal but who did not know how to cook. Van Wyck had trouble with his writing during the summer and suffered a severe depression. The end of the war did not lift his spirits. The peace was a "horrid mess," and had it not been for his belief in "the constancy of certain human facts," the atomic bomb and the population explosion would have made him "feel that life had passed utterly out of control."[10]

For the fall and winter of 1945–46 he and Eleanor returned to California, by automobile now that gasoline and tires were available. Soon afterward their son and grandson suffered minor injuries in a car accident. In February, Van Wyck suffered his sixtieth birthday. Eleanor tried to ease his pain by soliciting messages from his old friends. Mumford responded with an encomium: ". . . no one since Emerson himself, has worked to better purpose than you have." Van Wyck took heart from this. He felt his best work had just begun, and he hoped for twenty more years. He drew cheer also from the discharge in San Francisco of his younger son, Kenyon, who had served in the Navy and was on a destroyer in the Pacific at the end of the war. For the first time in eight years Van Wyck, Eleanor, Charles, and Kenyon had a family reunion — a fortunate event since Eleanor would be dead in six months.[11]

First, however, there were to be several other deaths. In April 1946, Van Wyck's old college friend Ned Sheldon finally succumbed to the arthritis which had crippled and blinded him years earlier. Van Wyck had been a frequent visitor to his bedside and had drawn strength from Sheldon's unfailing courage and cheer. Still, his life had been painful and death hardly seemed to have come too soon. Perhaps more troubling was Paul Rosenfeld's death of a heart attack in July. Rosenfeld's sudden death was a sobering reminder of the difficulty of the life of the spirit in straitened material circumstances. He had lost most of his money in the Depression and thus been deprived of his role of patron of the arts. His health had begun to fail, too, and though he had continued to write critical essays, they had seldom had the old zest. Van Wyck, who knew too well the danger of reclusiveness in times of trial, had tried to keep in touch with Rosenfeld. But usually he "seemed to take flight," and they had had few meetings in recent years.[12]

Van Wyck's mother also died in 1946. Sallie Brooks had lived out her life in Plainfield with her second husband, Henry Hibbard, a successful engineer. Van Wyck thought their life, centered on bridge and golf, was "pathetic," but their marriage was happy. Hibbard, a stronger figure than Charles Brooks, had resisted Sallie's imperious manner, but at the same time had provided the travel and stylish living she loved. But Sallie had been broken by Ames's suicide in 1931. Soon afterward her mind had begun to wander, and she would forget what she had started to say. She was an invalid by the time her second husband died in the summer of 1942. Van Wyck had visited her once a week that summer, traveling almost four hours each way by public transportation since he could not get gasoline. Sallie's memory was gone by this time, and she could hardly finish a sentence. But as her presence faded Van Wyck could love her more: ". . . much that is large and serene in the depths of her nature has . . . come to the surface." The other side of Sallie's nature continued also; she was prone to childish rages when she would throw and smash whatever was at hand. But Van Wyck took pleasure in believing she had outgrown the meretricious ways of the New York suburb. He still could not forgive Plainfield, which had "poisoned the well of my family life," but at least he had displaced his resentment of his mother onto history: "What a terrible phase of America we all grew up in!" he wrote to his stepsister. He visited his mother often in her final years and usually found her happy, easily pleased, and "unbelievably gentle." She was all "sweetness and kindness" to Van Wyck, whom she ceased to recognize several years before she died in her sleep at the age of eighty-seven.[13]

II

Van Wyck, Eleanor, and Kenyon had returned East ten days before Sallie Brooks's death in March 1946. They had driven through the South, and Eleanor had caught a cold in a Texas norther. Van Wyck had insisted on a brief rest in Florida, and she was all right, sitting quietly in the car, till they reached home. Then she had to unpack, open the house, and do other errands. She was soon in bed with her twelfth case of pneumonia. It was an almost standard pattern; the effort required to maintain the large house would wear her down, and she would catch a cold which might develop into pneumonia. She was ill, for instance, just after they moved into the new house, and it was no wonder. Much of the work of moving fell on her, so that Van Wyck would miss as little of his writing as possible. She had even done much of the landscaping herself, clearing away rocks, preparing garden beds, and moving many plants from the old house to the new. Living in the big house in the grand style Van Wyck enjoyed was hardly less trying for Eleanor. Whenever they had enough supplies, he insisted — despite rationing — upon entertaining, and often for the entire weekend. In May 1944, they had company three weekends out of four, and Eleanor, fatigued, caught a cold each following week. She spent the summer in bed with pneumonia. "Papa cannot understand," she complained to Charles, "why a house cannot be run as in . . . his childhood, when they had three maids and a gardiner [sic]."[14]

Eleanor had spent her married life maintaining appearances, not only to the outside world but also to Van Wyck. While he did not like to think about practical affairs, he also did not like to be reminded that his refusal to do so forced still more work on Eleanor. The proper companion for a man of letters was a wife who was pretty and serene rather than one worn down by cares and hard work. Early in their marriage he had been irritated to see her tired and drab after housework, and as Eleanor later explained to Charles, her first reaction had been to resent his unreasonableness: "If what he disliked happened because it was the only way to give him a chance to do his work, which he always put first, then I felt he should stop disliking it." But Eleanor had early decided that ". . . he couldn't help it, that it was just the way he was made," and she decided "to be philosophical about it." So she continued to do the best she could to shield him from worldly cares and to protect him also from the knowledge of how hard she worked in doing so. And she kept many of her personal problems to herself, rather than upset him to the point where he could not write. She had not told him when she went through menopause in 1939 because he had always dreaded the experience for her. Still, she sometimes backslid; on an excursion together one rainy day in 1943, she wore an old hat instead of her bright new one, and this unromantic prudence made him unhappy with her for hours.[15]

In the summer of 1943 in a series of long letters to her son Charles, Eleanor had reviewed her life with Van Wyck and how she had sacrificed her own hopes of writing in order to care for him and the children. Her writing had been "the thing by which I was to vindicate and fulfill myself, . . . earn my own respect and that of the community. I needed this respect and reassurance very badly." She had consoled herself about the writing by promising herself that she would do it later, after the children were grown. Meanwhile, as a compromise, she had tried translating, but had eventually found that it required more concentration than she could muster while maintaining the protective shell that Van Wyck needed for his work. Someone had to answer the doorbell and the telephone and "meet the thousand interruptions." But she still wanted creative work of her own, so she next tried the "social question," which had interested her since childhood. In Westport in the thirties she had thrown herself into politics, running for the state legislature on the socialist ticket and "fighting the water trust, the graft on the roads, the politicians in the schools. . . ." But this "displeased Papa, and he burned with embarrassment if I got up and spoke at a town meeting." So she had given up politics and put her creative energies into her garden: ". . . when Papa complained of the hours I spent in it (almost all of them before breakfast) I turned a deaf ear. I knew by now that for some reason he felt an uneasy resentment when I was really absorbed in some private work of my own, and I decided that this was too unreasonable and I would not humor him."[16]

Yet Eleanor had humored him more often than not, giving up even her friends for him. Van Wyck was "truly noble" in "big things," she told Charles, but in small matters ". . . he always was and still is a 'snob.' "

> He will forgive a great deal to well bred, well mannered people. He will forgive nearly anything to genius. Yet he can be mercilessly snobbish to innocent, well-meaning everyday people, if he is thrown into close contact with them, and he has really caused me a good deal of unhappiness by disliking most of my old friends. . . .
>
> I have never condoned this and never will. As you will remember, I insist on seeing my friends now and then and on his being nice to them. But I have come to recognize that this, too,

is part of his nature. . . . So though I know he has no right to demand it, it is usually his friends who come to the house. And this is my own choice. After all, Papa means more to me than those old friends.[17]

Eleanor was ambivalent on the question of whether or not her marriage had been worth her sacrifices. Usually she said so, as in the passage above, but at other times she wondered if she had done right to stand so steadfastly beside Van Wyck. Her own mother had been happier in divorce than in marriage, and her great aunt, Eliza Kenyon of the Plainfield Seminary, had lived alone but usefully. Eleanor would never have deserted Van Wyck when he was down, but when he was prosperous and confident, ". . . he could have had his freedom at a word." But then he did not want it: "When his work went well he loved me and all the world." And Eleanor had been held fast by her belief that children needed two parents and a secure home. She had loved her children, she told Charles, but she wondered if he knew "that I had never liked doing the things that took my time and strength for 18 hours out of the 24?" If she had been able to afford help in raising them, things would have been better, but instead she had been their "constant companion" at the expense of her intellectual and creative powers: ". . . if one must keep one's mind constantly bent to their tiny level one acquires a sort of crick in one's mind, which is just as distressing as a crick in one's back." She had felt stooped and cramped, "trapped by my best instincts [and] forced into the sort of life I had always abhorred, become a sort of pack horse for those who were very often indifferent to me, ground down into a monotony that either supified [sic] me or drove me to fury."[18]

Eleanor had been a feminist in youth but that had not protected her against Van Wyck's "nature." He was of "the pure artist type," and such exotics "concentrate on ends and demand them insistently and continuously, often absolutely ignoring whether or not there are human means of achieving those ends." This was the case with Van Wyck: ". . . when a difficult, ugly fact arose, he simply ignored it until it knocked him down." Eleanor had spent her life paying attention to facts, so that they did not knock Van Wyck down too often. She had known from her childhood experiences with her father that life was not easy with an artist, and that had been one of the reasons why she had hesitated to marry Van Wyck. This ideology of the artist's idealistic and imperial nature, which both she and Van Wyck accepted, gave him the upper hand despite her feminist beliefs. When he was unreasonable they both attributed it to the artist in him, and the burden of understanding inevitably fell on her. "And after all," she wrote to Charles, "these 'unreasonable' characteristics of his which have been rocks in my path and thorns in my side . . . during the thirty odd years we have travelled together are all part of the things that make him the beautiful artist he is. If he did not have his sense of perfection, his love of beauty and form, his insistence on avoiding trivialities he could not do what he does, and probably he could not change one without the other."[19]

Related to Van Wyck's artistic nature was his manic-depressive illness, which Eleanor had interpreted as a "malady of the ideal." Before his illness she had not always repressed her own feelings, and there had been times when she stormed and raged. But with his illness she had given up her right to protest the main source of her problems — the strain placed on her by his needs. His doctors had cautioned her that she should not discuss his depressions with him but rather let him talk all he chose and only make suggestions when he asked for them. Against the combined weight of the theory of the artist and the demands of Van Wyck's illness, Eleanor could not raise a hand: "I cannot change him. He cannot change himself. So far as [I] can I will not do things to make him unhappy." From the time of his illness she gave even less thought to herself than she had before.[20]

Eleanor's belief in the psychology of the "pure artist type" also led her to the belief that she had never been meant to write. The self-sacrifice which she had displayed in her marriage was not characteristic of artists who "concentrate on ends and demand them insistently." It followed, then, that Eleanor was not an artist, not "a born writer as Papa was." She had let herself be turned away from writing, "and he let *nothing* deflect him." She realized now that her wish to write had been only a "personal instinct, a will to power, and not the artistic instinct which is the only true basis of an art." Concluding now that she had never been meant to write, she decided she might have made a good labor leader, and she wished she could have had a try at that.[21]

But no matter what occupation she was best suited for, if she had had her life to live again, she would have given up hope of mixing marriage and a career. She would either have married without reservations and hopes for creative work of her own, or else she would have not married and "gone into the struggle for social reform." During much of her marriage she had felt that she was "waiting all day at a station" for the train on which "my own life would begin." Now she realized that her train "passed long ago and I did not even hear its whistle."[22]

Eleanor insisted that her bitterness and resentment against her married life, "and with poor Papa, for somehow being the cause of it, has steadily decreased with the years." She had found compensations, and except "in the matter of vanity" she did not now believe that it was any better to be an artist than an ordinary person: "If one does necessary work and does it well why has one not led an honorable and useful life? . . . I have always been a great believer in life and in happiness, too. I have always put it first, and I deliberately and for quite selfish reasons, chose to find my happiness in trying to help those I loved." Van Wyck was depressed at the time, and as she watched him struggling at his desk, "I feel the most enormous admiration for him." She still hoped, however, "to have a fling all by myself."[23]

Not all of Eleanor's problems stemmed from her marriage to Van Wyck. She had been insecure and worried since childhood, and it was part of her own nature to throw herself into material cares and sacrifice her desires to those of others. Mrs. Stimson, after her divorce, had relied too heavily on Eleanor and trained her too well in concern for others and in eking out a living on a small income. Sacrifice was the work which Eleanor came to know best, and she performed it too readily. The letters to Charles in which she recorded the numerous details of Van Wyck's dependence upon her reveal also a measure of gratification in that dependence. Van Wyck and the children could have managed without all of her sacrifices, and to some degree she caused some of Van Wyck's needs with her worry and insecurity. When he was in one of his high, fine moods they were a good match, but when he was depressed Eleanor's own usually high level of anxiety made things worse.

No doubt there were other women to whom Van Wyck might have been more happily married. No doubt there were other lives that Eleanor could have lived and in many of them been happier than with Van Wyck. But hers was also a complex personality, and it is impossible to know the circumstances that would have served her better. If there were other choices, Eleanor had refused them. Like Van Wyck, she stood by her commitments with uncommon faith and intensity. They both believed in the family, and they maintained theirs with love, courage, and sacrifice — most of the last on Eleanor's part, admittedly, but to her it also served a need.

Eleanor had hardly recovered from her pneumonia in the spring of 1946 before her right leg began to ache. In mid-May a doctor diagnosed her problem as water on the knee and sent her to bed for three weeks. Her condition worsened and was finally diagnosed as cancer, a sarcoma above the knee, and she underwent surgery for removal of the tumor. The operation seemed successful, and early in June she was discharged on crutches from the hospital. She had not been home an hour when she fell and broke her leg, just below the incision. After a day and a half of great pain she was taken back to the hospital, where the leg was amputated. In lucid moments between alternating extremes of wearing pain and drugged stupor, she worried about Van Wyck and her children and their finances. From bed she wrote letters of advice to her son Charles in California and letters on money matters to her cousin, Henry Stimson, who had helped her so generously in the past.[24]

Van Wyck stayed in Weston, writing for part of each morning and then driving to the hospital in New York. Eleanor, who had learned to predict his phases, had expected him to be depressed that summer anyway, and she had unsuccessfully tried to persuade her doctors not to tell Van Wyck that she had cancer. The news left him "dreadfully unstrung," she wrote to Charles. He still hoped, however, for Eleanor's recovery, and he planned on selling the Weston house and moving to a condominium apartment on East Fifty-seventh Street, across the hall from his college friend, John Hall Wheelock. The apartment was on one floor with no stairs, and he hoped Eleanor would be able to live there. Despite a minor heart attack she gained strength in July and was taken home. But her lungs and heart, weakened by strain, became involved in the illness. On August twenty-sixth Van Wyck wrote to Mumford that she could not live another month, and she died three days later.[25]

Van Wyck, "infantile as I am in so many ways emotionally," told Mumford he was not sure that he could go on without her and the home she had provided. His life was "cast adrift without a rudder." But Charles had come briefly from California, so both his sons were present to help him. And his writing, to which he soon returned, served him as a "life-line." *The Times of Melville and Whitman* was four-fifths written, and he counted on its momentum to carry both itself and himself through the time of grief. He drew strength also from his memory of Eleanor's courage. "It was really beautiful, dear S. K.," he wrote to Ratcliffe, "and I realized for the first time that if you are made in a certain way there is nothing really to fear in death." He was comforted also by the universality of death. It was the common lot, and his sense of alienation was subdued for once in a "community of grief." In October, he and Kenyon moved into the apartment on East Fifty-seventh Street, and Margaret Cobb, a Westport neighbor and the widow of newspaperman Frank Cobb, came to keep house for them. So Van Wyck still had a home and the woman's touch his life required.[26]

In New York his old friends took charge of him. He sat for a bust by Jo Davidson, and they went about the city together as they had in youth in London. Davidson even took Van Wyck to the 21 Club, a place where it is difficult to imagine Van Wyck being comfortable. But Van Wyck admired Davidson's extroversion, which reminded him of Whitman's "orbic" personality, at home with all kinds of people. Van Wyck was still most comfortable as host in a closed set of literary and artistic friends. On Sunday afternoons he invited such people — the Davidsons, the Walter Pachs, the John Sloans, and the Wheelocks — to dinner and conducted the conversation on a high plane. Jack Wheelock sought invitations for Van Wyck and in November obtained one for dinner at the home of Gladys Rice Billings. Van Wyck had met her once before at the Wheelocks' home in 1944, and even before that she had once written to him, inquiring about a speech in which he had given his opinion of the "coterie-writers." Despite her knowledge of Van Wyck's ideas she also invited her friend Allen Tate to dinner and introduced the two men as if the meeting were long overdue. Van Wyck had always thought of Tate as a "coterie-writer" and "highbrow snob," but he tried to parry the awkward moment with a smile, even as he greeted Tate, "You're a literary enemy." A pleasant friendship, however uneasy at first, began with this meeting.[27]

Gladys, whom Van Wyck would marry the next June, admired people more than ideas and possessed a social quality that appealed to him. She was about Van Wyck's age, married twice and divorced twice, most recently from the painter Josh Billings. Her first husband had been John Saltonstall of Boston, and from that marriage she had an independent income. The daughter of a society doctor in New York, she had memories that intrigued Van Wyck. Mark Twain had been one of her father's patients when she was a girl, and as a young woman in Paris she had been one of Henry Adams' adopted nieces. An accomplished violinist, she was a friend of writers and artists, and she understood, as Van Wyck later explained to one of his sons, "our kind." Cheerful and energetic, she was intensely interested in all around her and was adept at keeping a conversation in motion. She was, as Kenyon Brooks explained to Charles, attractive and fashionable, a "man's woman" who would give Van Wyck the social life he desired.[28]

Van Wyck had first asked Gladys to marry him during the winter, after they had known each other only a few months. She had agreed but then he changed his mind. Eleanor had died too recently, and he felt guilty. Gladys accepted this calmly, and a few days later he changed his mind again. They were married on June 2, 1947, in New York at City Hall, with two each of their children serving as witnesses. After the ceremony the small party took a train uptown to the Ninety-fourth Street home of the Carl Bingers, who gave the reception. Twenty or thirty friends were present, among them Max Perkins, to whom Van Wyck had dedicated *New England: Indian Summer*. Van Wyck had seldom seen Max in recent years, and he saw him for the last time that day. Perkins, soon to die of pneumonia, took Gladys aside and counseled her to keep Van Wyck away from Mollie Colum. After the reception they returned to Van Wyck's apartment, and a few days later he came down with mononucleosis, brought on perhaps by the strain of working at his old pace while courting Gladys. His recovery required a few weeks and then they spent the summer together in a house she owned on Martha's Vineyard.[29]

So began the happiest years of Van Wyck's life. None of his friends or Eleanor's felt that he had found a new life too soon. They understood how difficult it was, with his temperament, to live alone, and Gladys was ideally suited for him. She sensed his need for protection from the ordinary trials of living and his simultaneous need for a social life that would overcome his feeling of alienation from the world. She both protected him from life and exposed him to it. How wonderful, he would say gratefully in his memoirs, that she "could be so much of the world yet not be worldly in any sense at all." In return, she felt, he gave her a love greater than she had known. The financial problems which had always been so threatening were finally solved. At his mother's death he had inherited the capital of his Grandfather Ames, probably not a large amount. But his sons' security was at least partially guaranteed by the Stimson trust which passed from Eleanor to them, and Gladys had her own income. On a base that secure, the literary life could continue.[30]

III

Brooks's conception of himself as a man of letters was reinforced by the almost continuous stream of honors bestowed on him in the last third of his life. These included a Pulitzer Prize and the Gold Medal for Literature of the National Institute of Arts and Letters, which was awarded only once every ten years. He also received honorary doctorates from Harvard, Columbia, Pennsylvania, and half a dozen other universities. He was elected to the Century Association, the Players, the American Academy of Arts and Letters, the American Philosophical Society, and the American Academy of Arts and Sciences, which awarded him its Emerson-Thoreau Award. Especially pleasing, no doubt, were his invitations from the Saturday Club in Boston and his election as a fellow of the Royal Society of Literature in Great Britain.

Noblesse oblige. As a man of letters, Brooks felt he should administer to the needs of fellow writers less successful than himself. He disliked correspondence, for instance, but out of duty and kindness he devoted many hours to it. After reading an incoming letter he usually dropped it on the floor of his study where an unsorted pile accumulated. Two or three times a month he made his way through the pile, answering every letter, usually perfunctorily and in his cramped handwriting, but occasionally doing far more than necessary. He read all unsolicited manuscripts, made criticisms, and in cases where he saw promise, offered extraordinary amounts of aid. He wrote to publishers on behalf of writers he had never met, secured advances and grants for them, loaned or gave them hundreds of dollars (even when he was himself in financial trouble), and occasionally sheltered them in his own home so they could write.[31]

Attempting to use his large reputation to encourage the study of American culture, he was always glad to lend his name or write a letter for a young scholar engaged in literary history or biography. And he tried to persuade such friends as his Westport neighbor Hamilton Basso to undertake important studies, in Basso's case a biography of William Gilmore Simms. To older allies, Brooks's generosity continued as of old. He had helped Constance Rourke in the *Freeman* days, and her *American Humor* (1931) had built on and surpassed his understanding of Mark Twain and Henry James. He had aided her in the thirties in her search for fellowships and other means of support, and she in turn produced several important books. After her death he edited her unfinished *Roots of American Culture* (1942). Newton Arvin had begun the 1940's with a nervous breakdown and was hospitalized at White Plains. Van Wyck visited him there, despite his terrible memories of the place from his own illness. He still did not believe that doctors could understand artists and their maladies, but he assured Arvin that he would recover: ". . . the misunderstanding of doctors in no way alters the process of cure." When Arvin did recover, Van Wyck encouraged and aided him in the writing of *Herman Melville*.[32]

All of this was secondary, however, to the real service he had hoped to render. When he received the Gold Medal of the National Institute in 1946, he said that he had "written mainly for other writers. . . ." He hoped the cultural tradition he had discovered would be as meaningful to others as it had been to him: "It means much to feel that one is connected with a living stream of imaginative life, . . . that one is not working in the dark and working alone." Those who spoke of "tradition and the individual talent," he said, took it for granted that no American tradition existed, but he believed that he had proved them wrong.[33]

But his conception of himself as a man of letters was in some ways a barrier to the inspiriting and prophetic role he wished to play. The almost stuffy rectitude with which he had scolded the "coterie-writers" alienated many whom he wished to convert. He talked down to American writers and called them "boys." They had produced a contemporary literature that was "infantile," and he sternly reproved them as if he were more advanced than they, not only in years but in morals. Their resentment of his avuncular rebukes baffled and frustrated him. In his 1940 Hunter College speech, for instance, he had said that though James T. Farrell was a writer of great power, his writing was negated by its moral emptiness. Farrell and others seemed "to delight in kicking their world to pieces." Farrell, who had admired Brooks's actions in the League of American Writers, protested in a personal letter and in a meeting, and Van Wyck decided that perhaps he was wrong on Farrell. Except for compliments he had omitted Farrell's name from *The Opinions of Oliver Allston*, but Farrell had still been angered by the tone of the book and in a *New Republic* article in 1944 called Brooks a "frightened Philistine." Van Wyck angrily resigned from the *New Republic*, where for years his name had been carried on the masthead as a contributing editor. Farrell's attack troubled him because he admired *Studs Lonigan* and because Farrell was the sort of younger man whom he would have liked to influence. But his patronizing manner merely turned younger men away. And in turn their anger seemed childish and recalcitrant to him. He could not see that Farrell had as much right to criticize Brooks as Brooks did Farrell. It was Van Wyck, after all, who was the man of letters.[34]

Brooks failed not only in his didactic and hortatory efforts but also in his continuing attempt to find or create a central organization of American writers. He had failed to achieve this goal with the League of American Writers in the thirties, so in the forties he turned to the American Academy of Arts and Letters. Several years before his election to membership in 1937 he had expressed a dim view of the academy. The country was "too large and too chaotic" for it to accomplish anything. The men of genius in America were anarchistic in temperament "and prefer to live in their own unlighted caves." But after the collapse of the league, Brooks decided to do what he could with the academy. It was "hollow at present, a mere list of names, when it might be solid, alive, and active," he wrote to Stephen Vincent Benét in 1940.[35]

In vain he conceived a number of projects to make the academy a useful force in American life. First of these was his idea in 1941 for a study of all the academies in history to see what they had accomplished or hoped to accomplish. The project "should present us with many suggestions," he said, and he urged the academy to finance such a study by a competent scholar. But after Pearl Harbor he opposed the idea, feeling that the academy's money would be better spent on grants-in-aid to keep writers and artists at their work during the war. Later he suggested that the academy pay for a standard plaque which local communities could use to mark houses associated with the history of art and literature. He had always envied Europe its monuments to artists and writers, and this idea, which was never realized, would have been an inexpensive beginning along such lines in America. Although these ideas and others did not bear fruit, he had become so active in the academy that in 1943 he was elected secretary, a post he held for five years though it placed on him a large burden of correspondence in addition to his own writings. Later he served on many academy committees and from 1956 till his death in 1963 he was chancellor.[36]

As a member of the academy's inner circle, he worked energetically to influence nominations and elections, not only to the academy but also to the National Institute of Arts and Letters, from which the academy drew its smaller, more elite membership. He believed that "If we once get a majority of first-rate members, the future of the Academy is assured." He wished, therefore, to elect "really eminent writers" instead of the usual "scholars, college presidents, and constitutional historians." He suggested Faulkner, Dos Passos, Steinbeck, Robinson Jeffers, and Archibald MacLeish as worthy candidates, and in time they were all elected. He later nominated Carl Sandburg and Frank Lloyd Wright. As secretary he kept the slates small, so that some of his candidates, if not all, were certain to be elected, and he campaigned actively for his nominees. Sometimes, however, the obstacles were insuperable, as when he nominated John O'Hara for the institute, only to have him blackballed.[37]

There was opposition also from American writers themselves, many of whom, like Henry Miller, thought of the institute and the academy as stuffily genteel and were surprised to be elected. Some writers, Brooks found, took election "for a kind of insult." Hemingway, for instance, refused membership, and his absence in turn angered Steinbeck, who did not know that membership had been offered to Hemingway.[38] And most of Brooks's candidates who were elected would nevertheless not join him in his effort to make the academy count for something. Their maximum participation was attendance at dinner meetings if they happened to be in New York. Although his effort to improve the quality of the membership was generally successful, he seemed also to have proved his earlier foreboding that the academy could accomplish little among America's anarchic men of genius.

Still, Van Wyck drew a great deal of comfort from the academy in his later years. It was something, at least, that the academy offered a community of writers and artists with whom he could mingle in friendship and good works. The academy awarded a considerable number of grants to younger writers and artists, and Van Wyck drew satisfaction from serving on committees that made such awards to the needy and worthy. He sat on prize committees also and tried to see that the prizes were awarded to the right persons — a medal for achievement in the novel, for instance, to Hemingway despite his refusal of membership in the academy. In 1957 Brooks nominated Robinson Jeffers for a poetry medal, though his oldest friend, John Hall Wheelock, had also been nominated. This act troubled him, but he refused to allow "friendship to sway my judgment."[39]

The severest test of Brooks's friendship and judgment had come in 1947, when he voted with other members of the National Institute of Arts and Letters to award a Gold Medal for History to Charles Beard. Consequently, Lewis Mumford resigned from the institute. Mumford and Beard had once been friends but had split over American involvement in European affairs. Beard's isolationism during the Second World War accounted for the break. Mumford's belief in the necessity and justice of the war had been intensified by the loss of his son, killed in action in Italy in September 1944. Later that year Beard had published his *Basic History*, with its account of Roosevelt leading a reluctant and unwary nation into war. Mumford, believing it was Roosevelt who had been too reluctant, had said in print that Beard was "a passive — no, active — abetter of tyranny, sadism, and human defilement." In a letter to Brooks, Mumford had added that he believed Beard had betrayed his trust as a scholar and warped the facts of history to justify his politics.[40]

Van Wyck was hardly surprised, then, in 1947 when Mumford said that he would resign from the institute if it awarded Beard the Gold Medal. But Van Wyck could not believe that Beard had knowingly falsified facts, and, valuing Beard's early work, he asked Mumford, "What other historian . . . would you prefer to the Beard of *forty years?*" Mumford answered immediately, stating again his belief that Beard's books had "suppressed the case for the democracies" and thus strengthened the case for the Fascists. "Can you be so wilfully blind . . . ?" Mumford asked. Van Wyck replied that he had been too immersed in his own work to read Beard's recent books: "If I have been mistaken, I am sorry." He begged Mumford not to resign from the institute, and he hoped they could clear up the "misunderstanding."[41]

The difference between them was "more than a misunderstanding," Mumford answered in a l.. ⁄er-like brief. Instead, ". . . it goes to the very bottom of each of our lives." Van Wyck was not absolved by the simple statement that he was too busy to read Beard: ". . . by voting for Beard you voted against me. You were not above battle at that moment. You were in the thick of it *on the wrong side.*" Then Mumford thrust home by relating the dispute to Van Wyck's work. The recently published *Times of Melville and Whitman* had seemed a failure to Mumford, who identified strongly with Melville, of whom he had written an early biography. Mumford had expressed only mild criticisms in a published review, but now he spoke his mind. Brooks, by closing his eyes to what had been going on around him, had placed himself on the side of proper "gentlemanly men" who had thought Thoreau, Melville, and Whitman uncivilized for raising unpleasant issues: ". . . the tragic choices and the tragic decisions in the lives of our great writers, all those elements that caused them to be despised and rejected by their own countrymen, not only in their own lifetimes but long after, have somehow escaped you; and the reason for that is that you have not let yourself see them when they were under your nose. It would be better to leave your series unfinished and to produce at least one book which, out of your sympathy and understanding for your own period, would run the full gamut of our experience." Then finally: "In the eyes of God,

Charles Beard and I are both sinners: perhaps indistinguishably so. But you have long been a friend, dear Van Wyck; and in the eyes of a friend I expect a friend's loyalty and a friend's understanding. If I have failed you here as you have failed me, I am sorry."[42]

For many gentlemanly men the receipt of such a letter would have ended a friendship. But as Van Wyck explained to another friend, he was disturbed at least partly on Mumford's account, for he believed that Mumford's vehemence was attributable to the loss of his son in the war.[43] Wishing to respect Mumford's troubled feelings and at the same time maintain his own self-respect, Van Wyck was gentle but firm in his reply. Acknowledging the truth of some of Mumford's charges, he also insisted that his convictions were "not very much involved in this matter of elections and medals." He agreed that ". . . my treatment of Melville was very inadequate . . . " but still hoped someday to write the book which Mumford said he should, and he counted on Mumford to aid him. Bewildered, he said, by the results of a "more or less empty gesture towards a man whom I never associate with you," he continued to believe in the strength of his "bond" with Mumford and sent "real love." Mumford responded with "love" also in order to "heal the wounds we've both, alas! inflicted," and the danger of a permanent breach was thus avoided.[44]

The "affair Beard," as Brooks and Mumford called it, had a shabby ending. After Mumford resigned and made a statement to the newspapers, several other members of the institute threatened to resign also. Henry Seidel Canby, who was to have presented the medal to Beard, now refused, and Van Wyck, as secretary, was left with the task. He resented these latter protestations and felt they showed simply that ". . . the band-wagon has turned around." He resigned as secretary though he was determined to make the presentation. He now felt, however, that he could not praise Beard's later work, and he would speak only of "the Beard I used to know." In his speech he said that though Beard had sometimes "grieved his friends," the medal was for his "main life-work," and he stressed Beard's early battles for academic freedom and civil liberty.[45]

Meanwhile, a movement had begun to get Mumford back into the institute, but he had concluded that ". . . the honor of staying out . . . is as great, almost, as the honor of being in." Six years later, after Beard's death, Mumford decided that his action had been "ill-timed and ill-directed." He should have acted before rather than after the medal was voted. Van Wyck felt all who understood how his son's death was involved would "forgive" him. Mumford withdrew his resignation, returned to the institute, and was elected to the academy.[46]

Although Van Wyck's friendship with Mumford survived it, the Beard incident revealed some problems in the friendship. As early as 1933 Mumford had told another friend that he and Brooks were so eager to be on good terms that ". . . we tend to understress our differences." Mumford doubted that Brooks accepted "half the things I believe in," and he rejected many of Brooks's ideas, especially his "notion of progress." Mumford shared Melville's sense of tragedy in life and thus also shared the modern sensibility to a degree that Brooks could not. In his *Herman Melville* (1929), Mumford had depicted a reserved Hawthorne rejecting the younger Melville's proffered intimacy, and like Melville, Mumford felt that he too had been disappointed by an older friend who had been an early inspiration. After Brooks's death, Mumford would write that ". . . our friendship, however loving, never became deeply intimate."[47] Much as Brooks admired Mumford, perhaps because of that admiration, there was always something of the official in their friendship, almost as if they were heads of neighboring states whose friendship was only incidental to diplomacy. Perhaps this was because Mumford was last in the line of male culture heroes — Ryder, Marshall, Yeats, Zinsser, and Bourne — whom Van Wyck had admired almost as if they were more than human. Hence his inability to be entirely human with them and hence, too, the lack of intimacy which Mumford regretted.

Then, too, the stiffness and reserve in Van Wyck that Sherwood Anderson, Paul Rosenfeld, and others had commented on when he was a young man had continued into his old age. He was wary, guarded, and correct with strangers, and the consequent difficulty in approaching him reinforced the image of him as a genteel prude that became popular after *The Opinions of Oliver Allston*. His sense of humor was usually indicated by a mild, slightly mischievous smile and a few wrinkles around the eyes. He could open himself only to old friends and not all of them. It was only loud, strong, humorous natures like that of his Westport neighbor Hendrik Van Loon that could make Van Wyck unbend in laughter, and he cultivated such friends for just that reason. Although Van Wyck called Van Loon a "modern Erasmus" because of his human-centered histories, he was also a vulgarian who would sometimes enter Van Wyck's garden with his hulking three-hundred-pound body bent as if in pain, raising his arms warningly, pretending to be a leper, and crying

"Unclean! Unclean!" Van Wyck, to the astonishment of visitors, would roar with appreciative laughter.[48]

The lack of intimacy that Mumford regretted was based only in part, however, on Brooks's innate shyness and reserve; it resulted also from his hopes that Mumford would develop into a man of letters in the nineteenth-century tradition. Mumford did not quite fit this mold, yet Brooks thought of him as another Taine, Carlyle, or Ruskin — in short, as a prophet, a "chosen man," a "giver of laws." He was fourth in "the American line of Emerson, Whitman and William James."[49]

Mumford was as adequately equipped as anyone in this century for the role of prophet, yet he sometimes disappointed Brooks because of his style. Van Wyck admired a style based on mastery of language as it already existed: "The wish to explore and use existing resources is the mark of a sound economy." The American tendency to create new words was "a pioneer habit, like the rest." In this respect Mumford was too American; steeped as he was in scientific texts, he occasionally resorted to neologisms. His reading, Van Wyck told Mumford in 1952, "has for years been too exclusively scientific." Van Wyck believed that "a year's discipline in the style and thinking of the literary moralists might work wonders for you," and he suggested in particular Edmund Gosse and his own beloved Amiel. A year so spent would not only improve Mumford's style but might also enable him to achieve a "new ethical synthesis . . . the 'one thing necessary' for our time." Thus Mumford would fulfill his destiny as a man of letters, as a prophet.[50]

Mumford reacted with astonishment to this casual suggestion for a year of his life. In a twenty-five-hundred-word letter he defended his style as a "new kind of writing . . . in which the imaginative and subjective part is counter-balanced by an equal interest in the objective, the external, the scientifically apprehended." His style was not an attempt to shore up his statements with scientific jargon but to square the subjective element of his thought "with what William James called 'hard, irreducible facts.' " This combination of the thinker's individuality with collective research "characterizes the best thought of our time." Mumford concluded that in looking for connections between his work and "past work of the same order," Van Wyck had "overlooked what is fresh and original in my own statement." Thus he had also failed to see the "esthetic fact" that Mumford's work required "a different formal presentation."[51]

Although Van Wyck was "rather hurt" by this explicit statement, he missed the point. He told Mumford he had not meant to say that he should write "in 'imitation' of classical writers — but because this vein is natural to you." But Mumford had meant exactly that the vein of the classical writers was not natural or appropriate for him. Van Wyck, for whom a classic writer wrote in a classic style, could only feel that Mumford, like many others in the twentieth century, had gone astray in the bypaths of science. Mumford replied one more time, and the debate on style ended.[52]

After the poignantly brief encounter with Randolph Bourne, the friendship with Mumford was the most important of Van Wyck's life, and it continued until his death in 1963. The younger Mumford, who enjoyed the rough and tumble of debate, either in person or correspondence, had to restrain himself to gentle tributes as Brooks grew older. But he probably felt that Brooks did not understand him, and he occasionally lashed out in irritation, as in 1951 when Van Wyck gave Harcourt a statement for Mumford's *Conduct of Life* — "the wisest book we will see this year." Mumford resented this "comically restricted superlative" and felt that Van Wyck should have called it simply a "wise book" rather than speaking like a "cagey reviewer." Nevertheless, Van Wyck continued to feel as he had on his sixtieth birthday: ". . . if I am remembered at all it will be as a friend and contemporary of Lewis Mumford." But he insisted also that Mumford was as lonely in the twentieth century as himself. Mumford was one of the "great classic literary types," Van Wyck wrote in 1952, to explain his statement that "Mumford is an anachronism." By thus casting his friend "in bronze," as Mumford once said, Van Wyck underscored not only the lack of intimacy in his friendship but also his loneliness as a man of letters in the modern world.[53]

DISSOLUTION

GLADYS BROOKS, Van Wyck once said, was what his mother ought to have been. Like Sallie Brooks, Gladys was a New Yorker, a musician, and a woman of charm who enjoyed society. In 1947 Kenyon Brooks described her to his brother Charles in California as possessing a "wispy manner" and a fashionable "Hepburn" accent. Gladys had a slim figure, and the physical resemblance to Sallie, except for Gladys's blond hair, was strong. The important difference to Van Wyck was that Gladys had dealt more boldly and critically with life. She had ended her first marriage, despite its monied security, and had married an artist. But thanks to a favorable divorce settlement, she had never known the economic insecurity that had led Sallie, contrary to fact, to call herself "poor." This, too, was one of Gladys's attractions. Yet, like Sallie, she was a "man's woman," as Kenyon explained to his brother, who would find her own satisfaction in making Van Wyck's life go smoothly.[1]

The resemblance between Sallie Brooks and Gladys may have accounted for Van Wyck's fears that Gladys would distract him from his writing. Early in their marriage he was unable to conceal his fear that she would make too many social engagements, and she later recorded her hurt "at his doubt of my motives."[2] He spent the summer of 1947, when they honeymooned on Martha's Vineyard, compiling a book of selections from his previous writings — *A Chilmark Miscellany* (1948). It was a cut-and-paste effort requiring no

concentration, but he worked daily on it that summer. In the un-
familiar circumstances of his new marriage, he enjoyed the familiar
routine of work, and he hoped also to establish at the beginning with
Gladys the pattern that he desired for their life together. Above all,
he wanted her to understand that he must have time for his work.

Where Eleanor's somewhat anti-social nature had failed to provide enough relief from the tedium of work, he worried now that
Gladys would provide too many distractions. Often in the next few
years he would issue the mock lament: "I have far *too popular* a
wife."[3] Certainly his concentration weakened in these later years; he
did not, for instance, write the projected sixth volume of *Makers and
Finders*. But that was due in part to his advancing years and also to
problems in his conception of his own period, with which the book
would have dealt. If Gladys gave him a busier social life than he had
known, it was at least partly because he wanted it. She restrained her
own social impulses, and she made astonishing sacrifices to his
needs, playing her violin less frequently, for instance, lest the noise
disturb him at his work. He had little to fear. Her devotion was
complete.

Again like Sallie Brooks, Gladys was an energetic woman, always in motion. Van Wyck was more contemplative and not as
physically active, partly because of his heart condition. His slower
ways sometimes taxed Gladys's patience. It required a very sharp
curve to make her violate her policy of driving at fifty miles an hour
on narrow, winding country roads. Van Wyck was more cautious,
and when he drove she grew restless in the car and protested their
slow speed. "Very well, I shall give up the wheel," he angrily replied
on one such occasion, getting out of the car and beginning to walk.[4]
Gladys was soon reconciled to his slow driving. As she knew him
better, she related his slow physical pace to qualities that she admired in him, especially his appreciation of scenery, buildings, paintings, and books which spoke of the past and which most Americans
rushed by without a backward glance. He turned her interests not
only toward writing but toward history, as was evident from her
book *Three Wise Virgins* (1957), a study of Dorothea Dix, Elizabeth
Peabody, and Catherine Sedgwick.

Van Wyck, in turn, was not always happy with Gladys's busy
manner, but he too found offsetting advantages. Thanks to her
energetic and capable ways, she could manage a large house and
active social life with the occasional aid of a cook and part-time maid.
Thus the servant problem which had troubled his first marriage was
solved, and he recorded happily in his memoirs that Gladys, who

once had nine servants, had discovered "the pleasure of doing for oneself."[5] In short, he was fortunate to have found her. Gladys was the person he needed as he entered his last decade and completed the circuit of his life by peacefully revisiting, even as in a sense he had done in his second marriage, the scenes of his troubled youth — Europe, California, Harvard, and Plainfield.

Before undertaking such travels, however, he and Gladys had to settle in a permanent home. Van Wyck was tired of New York, of too many telephone calls and invitations, and of "the eternal cocktail glasses and half-smoked cigarettes."[6] Gladys's talents as a hostess would give him all the society he wanted in the countryside, so they began to search for a house in Connecticut. Van Wyck disliked such work and was easily depressed by it. "These people had a gift for the commonplace," he would say wearily to her after looking at an ordinary house. So the task fell to her, and in June of 1948 she spent days driving through the country, trying to narrow the choices for his final consideration. In Bridgewater, a village north of Danbury, she found a large, "monstrously ugly," gray house by the edge of the common. It was shrouded by trees and had a large piazza and fumed oak panelling. The house was too wide to be graceful, and the high deck-like verandah gave it the appearance, as their friend William McFee later said, of an old Fall River steamboat. But with some of the trees cut down and part of the piazza removed, she could envision it as sunny and comfortable. It had a large garden which pleased Van Wyck when he saw it, but he objected to the piazza: "Too much like the houses of my youth in Plainfield. . . ." They put off the decision till the next spring, and for the winter they rented a house in Cornwall, Connecticut. They were happy there, and Van Wyck, certain now that he wanted to live in the country, was willing to buy the Bridgewater house, even if it did remind him of his youth. After the purchase they renovated the exterior according to Gladys's plan, cutting down trees and removing part of the piazza. Indoors, they had a brick fireplace and Edwardian furnishings installed, and some of the dark panelling was painted white. They moved in during the summer of 1949, with Van Wyck hoping that they would spend the rest of their life together there. And they did.[7]

They made friends in the village, and Gladys began to attend the church across the common. On Sundays, Van Wyck always put on his special suit, but he could seldom force himself to attend services. Sermons bored him, so he usually spent Sunday mornings in his study. There were numerous friends within a half hour's drive of Bridgewater — the Mumfords, Malcolm Cowley, Peter Blume,

Francis Hackett, Louis Untermeyer, Matthew Josephson, William McFee, Alexander Calder, Hamilton Basso, and others. And Van Wyck made the acquaintance of younger writers in the area — Norman Mailer, Arthur Miller, and William Styron. With Gladys as hostess, Van Wyck could entertain in the large manner appropriate for a man of letters. Their large annual party, on either Christmas or New Year's eve, was a glittering literary event. World-renowned figures stopped to visit Brooks in Bridgewater — Robert Frost, Carl Sandburg, Peyton Rous, Alan Paton, Sir Alfred Zimmern, and even Van Wyck's brother-in-law, Frank Stimson, who was beginning to receive recognition for his work in Polynesian ethnology.

Although Gladys found that he required "a great deal of cheering up," these were the happiest years of Van Wyck's life. He breakfasted every morning by a sunny window in the dining room, under portraits of his ancestors, and then began the day's work. If some mornings it was still an act of courage to carry his gloomy spirit into his study to write, such mornings at least occurred less often now. On the mantel in his study were the mementos of a lifetime — a portrait of Sainte-Beuve, a photograph of Lincoln, the death mask of Randolph Bourne, and souvenirs of his first trip to Europe in 1898. The study was in the front of the house, and he could look out across the village green, with its white houses and churches, to the store and post office that supplied his worldly needs. The garden of his own house, with its rhododendrons and white birches, its magnolias in bloom, and chairs set about under the trees, reminded him of a Sargent watercolor. Where the Bridgewater house had first suggested the horrors of Plainfield, it now brought back "the peace of fifty years ago."[8]

A similar development occurred in his attitude toward Plainfield itself. In 1947 he had buried Eleanor's ashes there with misgivings; she should rest where she had been happy, and she had not been happy in Plainfield. Later he moved her ashes to Westport and eased his conscience. Gladys found it difficult to draw him out either on his mother or on Plainfield, but she persuaded him to stop there during a holiday trip shortly after their marriage. They parked their car in front of the house on East Ninth Street where he was born, but they did not get out. Van Wyck sat rigidly, frowned, and spoke only of his Grandmother Ames. And he refused to visit the large yellow house on West Eighth Street where he had spent his adolescence.[9] But within a few years he dealt more sympathetically with Plainfield. In 1951 when he spoke at the seventieth anniversary celebration of the Plainfield Public Library, he recalled the narrow world of his mother's generation against which "the young people rebelled." Thus had begun an attack on family life which still continued and which he now felt was "getting rather tiresome." Looking back, he discerned some good things in Plainfield at the turn of the century, not least the security of its world view: ". . . one felt that there was a very stable world behind and beneath everything." Having lived out his life in great insecurity, he valued that earlier feeling even if it was, as he said in his memoirs, an illusion.[10]

In 1951 he also visited Europe for the first time in twenty-five years, sailing for Ireland in April. When he had crossed to England to begin his literary career in 1907, he had glimpsed Ireland from shipboard and felt his eighth of Irish blood stir. Now, forty-four years later, he was too excited to sleep the night before he and Gladys landed at Cobh. He had come armed with letters from Padraic Colum that introduced him to the Irish literati — Francis MacManus, Monk Gibbon, Mary Lavin, Maud Gonne, and numerous others. He and Gladys called on the painter John Yeats, son of J. B. Yeats, who had befriended Van Wyck in New York forty years before.[11]

With the exception of an easier entrée into literary circles, Van Wyck's visit resembled the European tours of his youth; he and Gladys visited the Dublin galleries and literary landmarks like the Pearl Lounge and Abbey Theatre. Later, in Galway, they climbed Yeats's tower and visited the grounds of Lady Gregory's house. The Irish countryside with its paucity of modern buildings, its dolmens and empty castles and bronze age tombs, gave Van Wyck the eerie sense of a timeless other world that was for him the essence of Europe: "It was . . . as if pre-history and the Dark Ages still continued there and the people of these times had simply withdrawn for a day."[12]

"Europe remains Europe, with few changes, and Baedeker knew it better than anyone else," Van Wyck would say to Gladys to explain his preference for the half-century old guidebooks that he had saved from his earliest trips to Europe. By 1951, however, Europe had been through some momentous changes. In England, the next stop after Ireland, he and Gladys had planned to stay in a small hotel where his father had lived eighty years before, and though they had not reserved a room, Van Wyck gave the taxi driver that address when they arrived in London. Instead of a hotel, the taxi pulled up in front of a fenced-in bomb crater.[13]

Still, the English past was more vivid than the American. In Dorchester, the native town of Thomas Hardy, Van Wyck studied the writer's statue and reflected sadly, "England remembers her great literary men. In America they're forgotten by the next generation." He repeated the observation in France, provoked this time by Parisian houses that bore the names of famous writers who had lived in them. They visited the French countryside and at Bêcheron saw Jo Davidson, who would shortly die, as had many in Van Wyck's life, of pneumonia. Then, at the end of July, they sailed for home so that Van Wyck could continue to labor at giving America a memory.[14]

Beyond New England, however, America remained an enigma to Van Wyck. He and Gladys drove across the United States in 1955, the sixth time he had crossed the continent. On his first trip, by train in 1911, he had felt that he was passing through a desolate wilderness, a vast limbo of sand and silence into which only Eleanor had been able to draw him. By 1955, however, the West had ceased its silence. Now its desolation consisted of garish billboards, ugly motels, drive-in restaurants, and automobiles that were "mobile caves." On the road Van Wyck observed the "common run" of his countrymen and concluded they were the "strangest" and "most uncivilized people on earth," who ate their hamburgers and french fries "to the accompaniment of the raucous strains of a radio singing about LUV." He preferred the older, less travelled roads to the modern highways. The by-passes that moved the traffic around the towns denied access to what patches of civilization there were and made America seem, he later said, like "Danbury three thousand miles long," referring to a Connecticut town blighted by too many gasoline stations and garages. Yet, in the midst of all this ugliness he found Americans who were solicitous and kind. However barbarous their manner, their greeting sometimes came from the heart. And at the end of the journey into the western limbo there remained, as in 1911, the miracle of California.[15]

The literary life in California, where Van Wyck and Gladys spent a few months at the Huntington Hartford Foundation, astonished Van Wyck yet again. The painter George Biddle, an old friend, was there, along with several young composers and novelists. Van Wyck worked on a small book on Helen Keller, a friend of many years, and Gladys wrote her *Three Wise Virgins*. On excursions from the foundation he met Upton Sinclair, Aldous Huxley, Will Durant, and numerous other writers. Later the Brookses visited Carmel, where Van Wyck renewed his admiration for Robinson Jeffers, "that great man," as he told Gladys. There too they met Henry Miller, who was delighted to find that Van Wyck was not a "stuffy old man" as he had supposed. In Berkeley they unsuccessfully searched for the boardinghouse where Van Wyck had first stayed forty-four years before while seeing *The Soul* into print. There is no indication that California seemed otherworldly now to Van Wyck, or suggestive of Europe as it once had. Instead, he was amazed at the "vitality" of California and its growth since the war.[16] He had no reason to long for a surrogate Old World in the New, since he permitted himself three visits to Europe itself during his marriage to Gladys.

He visited Italy in 1956, spending the winter in residence at the American Academy in Rome and working on a volume of memoirs, *Days of the Phoenix: The Nineteen-Twenties I Remember* (1957). It was a cold winter in Rome, and he and Gladys both caught bronchial pneumonia. But the attacks lasted for only a week, and he managed to write in his unheated apartment by sitting with an electric heater under his knees. Despite the cold he reported to Mumford that the academy was "a kind of paradise." Actually, it was Italy that seemed paradisaical, and he and Gladys used the academy as a base from which to explore it. In Rome they visited Keats's grave and then Raphael's sarcophagus, where Van Wyck became morose and muttered "Dust and bones, dust and bones . . ." until Gladys drew him away. They went to Amalfi and stayed in the Hotel Luna, the converted monastery where Van Wyck had stayed with his mother, brother, and grandmother in 1899. And they met many Italian writers, among them Ignazio Silone, Mario Praz, Alberto Moravia, and Benedetto Croce.[17]

But it was the American writers in Italy who interested Van Wyck. Most distinguished of these was Bernard Berenson, ninety years old and an expatriate who lived in remove from the world in his villa atop a hill in Settignano. The great art critic was, in short, a figure reminiscent of Henry James, a symbol of things Van Wyck had feared, both in himself and in American culture. The greater equanimity of Van Wyck's later years is documented by the fact that he nevertheless enjoyed his visit with Berenson. He and Gladys found Berenson living in his villa "like another Voltaire," like a man of letters, with guests and scholars from all over the world. Van Wyck was no doubt glad to hear Berenson say that T. S. Eliot was his "mortal enemy," that Santayana "had no heart," and that Irving Babbitt was a "dull heavy sulker." But Berenson's opinions on contemporary politics were conservative, and Van Wyck thought there was much in him that was "ambiguous." His manner, however, was large, his interests "universal," and ". . . there was great sweetness and liberality in all he said."[18]

Van Wyck celebrated his seventieth birthday that winter in Rome, and his advancing years no doubt accounted in part for his greater equanimity and the absence of his old vehemence. Still, his ideas continued along the old line of literary nationalism. He met many younger Americans in Rome and at the academy, including several writers — Ralph Ellison, Theodore Roethke, and John Aldridge — whose work he admired. But what pleased him most about the Americans in Rome was their homesickness and how they "nowadays really feel that our part of the U.S. is the most attaching and desirable corner of the world."[19]

Although New England remained his favorite region, even it contained places of danger. Van Wyck and Gladys spent the early months of 1958 at Harvard, where he researched his book on Howells, and they were overwhelmed with hospitality. In the Widener Library he was assigned to the Norton Study, and he spent his days there working happily. Evenings and weekends he and Gladys were in Boston and Cambridge society. He visited his old friend, Mark DeWolfe Howe, now aged ninety-two, and he had dinner with Edward Forbes, Emerson's grandson. At an afternoon tea he found himself defending Henry James against a harsh remark from the novelist's nephew. He was delighted by these encounters with the previous century, but he was no more pleased by the university than he had been as an undergraduate. From the cocktail hour onward the social life was fatiguing, and there was no time for reflection. He was predisposed to find literary life there uninteresting since "English departments everywhere are entirely governed by fashion." He could hardly be comfortable in academia, where, as he had once told Mumford, "I am invariably treated as the scum of the earth." Even though this remark turned out not always to be true, he was still ill at ease. He enjoyed himself and was pleased by the friendly attention he received at Harvard, but he was not sorry to leave.[20]

He traveled once more to Europe, to England and the Low Countries, in 1959. It was his third European voyage with Gladys and the eighth of his life if one counts, as he did not, the tragic journey of 1926. The three voyages with Gladys were no doubt a kind of reward, a visit to the promised land sweetened by the self-denial and dedication of his work in the American wilderness. "How could there not be more travelers," he asked, "from a land where everything changed to the timeless world of the Pantheon. . . ?"[21] He made these latter voyages peacefully, with none of the old fear and guilt that he had fled his duty in America. With his twenty years of labor on *Makers and Finders*, he had justified himself, even in his own eyes.

II

In the books of his later years, as well as in his travels, Brooks peacefully revisited the scenes of his youth. He published three volumes of reminiscence — *Scenes and Portraits: Memories of Childhood and Youth* (1954); *Days of the Phoenix: The Nineteen-Twenties I Remember* (1957); and *From the Shadow of the Mountain: My Post-Meridian Years* (1961). At his own request, the three books were collected into a single large volume after his death, but it is doubtful that he would have approved the title, *An Autobiography* (1965). In fact, he had disclaimed any intention of writing an autobiography.[22] He had forsworn introspection and subjectivity forever, and despite the first person narrative, he told the story of his life objectively with few references to his inner feelings. He analyzed somewhat his ambivalence on the subjects of Europe and money, wondering if he had been influenced by his parents. But this was the only intense bit of self-examination in his memoirs. The rest of his life — his childhood, his marriages, his friendships, his writing, his breakdown — he described dispassionately and from the outside of the experiences.

Though his lack of introspection made his memoirs a disappointment to some,[23] the deeper emotions of Van Wyck's life were only incidental to what the three books were about, which was "scenes and portraits" from American literary life as he had personally observed it. He recalled all of the literary people he had known, from Plainfield luminaries like Eliza Elvira Kenyon to world figures like Lewis Mumford. In one way or another he had brushed against the greats of his time — Frost, Pound, Robinson, Anderson, Hemingway, Wolfe, Fitzgerald, and so on. He had known the smaller fry also, and the index of *An Autobiography* was as complete as one would have expected in a reference book on twentieth-century American literature. *An Autobiography* was meant to contribute to the same objective as *Makers and Finders*, a vivid description of the density and interconnectedness of American literary culture. In a sense *An Autobiography* was the sixth volume of *Makers and Finders*, the book that dealt with Brooks's own time and that he had been unable to write in the manner of his earlier books. By using his own life as a principle of selection and organization, he was able to ignore the complex and tangled politics of the period, to ignore the question of the contemporary significance of the Jeffersonian tradition, and to salvage something of his original intention to carry his history of the writer in America up to his own present day. Yet how important was it that he had once dined with Robinson, met Wolfe socially, or heard Hemingway make a speech? Just as with *Makers and Finders,* one must question whether literary culture was as densely interconnected as Brooks pictured it in *An Autobiography.*

When Brooks had finished *The Confident Years,* he had vowed that he would write no more history, and he had hoped to "go through two or three more phases."[24] But he could not relinquish his grip on the American past. In the twelve years left to him after *Makers and Finders* was finished he wrote, in addition to *An Autobiography,* six more books that carried on the work of recovering the American literary past. Of these later books, the last one, *Fenollosa and His Circle* (1962), was probably least satisfactory, and yet it was an original effort, like most of his books. No one had written a life of the New Englander who had studied and preserved much of the art and culture of Japan and whose life was, as Ezra Pound said, "the romance par excellence of modern scholarship." Van Wyck set out to write a book but instead wrote a seventy-page essay. It was a crowded picture that included not only Fenollosa but also Henry Adams, John LaFarge, Lafcadio Hearn, Sturgis Bigelow, Ezra Pound, W. B. Yeats, Edward S. Morse, and numerous others, with much Japanese detail in the background. The book was filled out with similar sketches of other adventurers and scholars — Fanny Wright, John Lloyd Stephens, George Catlin, Charles Wilkes, Charles Godfrey Leland, and Randolph Bourne. The purpose and method, in short, was the same as in all his other later books — to describe an American literary community and culture.

There was a difference, however, in these later books. He had largely ceased to argue the Jeffersonian thesis that had marred the last three volumes of *Makers and Finders* and had returned to the strictly pictorial narrative that had made the New England books the best of the series. This was still one more indication of the greater equanimity of his later years — that he could cease his preaching and rest content with the hope that mere artistry would give his pictures significance. Without the massiveness of the *Makers and Finders* series, however, these smaller pieces lacked a significant context. It was as if an old weaver of huge but minutely detailed tapestries had begun to produce mere patches of what should have been larger work. The problem was most glaringly evident in *The*

Dream of Arcadia: American Writers and Artists in Italy, 1760–1915
(1958), a disconnected series of short sketches which lovingly recreated the Italian scene but suggested little about the significance of
that scene for the writers who were the book's ostensible subjects.

The three biographies which he wrote in these later years were
done in the same detailed and pictorial manner as his other books.
Helen Keller: Sketch for a Portrait (1956) was just that, a sketch, though
he was able to indulge himself with some literary history because
Helen Keller's teacher, Ann Sullivan, married the critic John Macy.
John Sloan: A Painter's Life (1955) was an excellent book, probably the
best of Van Wyck's later years, vividly drawn and moving, thanks to
his intimate acquaintance with the subject. *Howells: His Life and
World* (1959) was not equal to Brooks's interesting treatment of
Howells in *New England: Indian Summer.* Van Wyck continued, however, to identify strongly with Howells, and he probably thought of
himself when he said that Howells was ignored in the twentieth
century because he was "too sane to seem exciting" and hence "could
not command the homage of a time that was wholly submissive to
the 'power of blackness.' "[25]

Van Wyck was moved at least in part to write his books on
Howells and Sloan and Keller because he unfashionably wished to
assert the power of goodness. Sloan was a "good man, fearless,
truthful, innocent and wise, who had always lived in a world that
knew no time." *Helen Keller* was an attempt at "hagiography," a
picture of a modern saint to counter the contemporary obsession
with evil, and for the same reason Brooks considered a life of
Channing. He never wrote that book, but some of the intention got
into *Howells,* which concluded with Kipling's remark that Howells
"had the natural kindness of the good and the utter simplicity of a
great man." In his book *The Writer in America,* Brooks asserted that
"goodness abounds."[26]

He wrote *The Writer in America* (1953) to defend *Makers and
Finders* against the attacks of the "avant-garde critics and professors"
and their assertations that his work was old-fashioned and, above all,
not literary. His resentments remained intense, and he sometimes
erupted in anger, as when in 1952 he broke off what had been ten
years of friendly relations with Alfred Kazin because of Kazin's
"dishonesty" in reviewing *The Confident Years.* Kazin's *On Native
Grounds* (1942) had contained what was probably the most accurate
and sympathetic treatment of Brooks's career published during his
lifetime and had earned Brooks's gratitude and respect. But Van
Wyck believed that Kazin, in his review of *The Confident Years,* had

quoted as his "total opinion" of Pound and Eliot a paragraph that concerned Hemingway's bull fighting only: "That sort of foul play," he wrote to Kazin, "disqualifies a critical mind for me." Actually, Kazin had done no such thing, but his review had been harshly negative in its treatment of Brooks's attack on the modern sensibility. Furious, Brooks told Kazin, ". . . you repeat all the canards that all the yes-men of the avant-garde have been throwing at me for fifteen years. . . . I am taking care of all these canards in a book I am now writing."[27]

Specifically, he intended in *The Writer in America* to defend himself against the charge that since he had not dealt with literary forms there was nothing literary about his history. He turned the argument easily by insisting that there was no standard form for literary history: ". . . it has varied in all times like other kinds of writing." There were few inventors of form in any age, and in America there had been only Poe and Whitman. Therefore, Brooks had written not a history of forms but, as he had said in his subtitle, a *History of the Writer in America*. He insisted that ". . . the main interest of American literature resides in other aspects than the purely aesthetic." That this was particularly true of American literature was a virtue rather than a defect; to insist that the main interest of literature should be esthetic was to imply "that literature is nothing but an art."[28]

For forty years Brooks had believed in a broad humanistic justification for literature. He had long ago rejected, at least consciously, the abstract spiritualism that had been one of his predilections in youth. There was a common ground for his rejection of artistic formalism or, as he would have said, "mere art" and his insistence that the "content" of literature was what mattered. He was in revolt against the modern devaluation of humane knowledge, or the "object" of consciousness, in favor of knowledge of consciousness itself. Consciousness turned inward upon itself must inevitably result in a sort of implosion. No wonder that ". . . the integrity of the individual consciousness has broken down. . . ." He was fond of E. M. Forster's remark that modern psychology and psychoanalysis had "split and shattered the idea of a 'person.' " Character and personality were reduced, as Aldous Huxley had said, to "collections of psychological atoms." Thus, the twentieth century was a "comparatively dehumanized time."[29]

Human character and personality were what interested him now that he had given free rein to his imagination in *Makers and*

Finders. Character and personality were the appropriate interests for a pictorial prose style such as his, and they were also the subjects of interest in such great ages as the Victorian era, he said. Nothing better demonstrated the enervation of the modern mind than the lack of interest in character. But he felt certain that society would recover from "this epoch of confusion," and when it did, writers would return to character and portraiture. In the great ages artists had relished the humanity of the characters they created. Carlyle and Taine, Hugo and Thackeray, Velasquez and Rembrandt had laughed and wept with their characters. Modern writers, incapable of this sort of attachment, could only examine their characters psychologically. They could only analyze rather than synthesize, and this incapacity had serious consequences for art: "I suppose no writer in our time can see life steadily and see it whole." Perception and feeling were required for the appreciation of character, but psychology stood in their way. Psychology required too large a use of the intelligence and thus blocked the intuition on which feeling and perception depended. No one in this age of psychology could achieve an integrated vision of life similar, say, to that of the nineteenth-century Russian novel, which still seemed to Brooks, "the most deeply human of all types of modern writing."[30]

He was never very successful in articulating the reasons for his rejection of the modern sensibility, but he came closest to successfully speaking his mind in *The Writer in America.* He believed that thinking about the form of art was bad strategy. It would lead to self-consciousness, which, as he knew from his youth, would inhibit "the flow of the unconscious from which all art springs." That there was no spontaneity and no free will expressed in modern literature was due much less to industrialism and the machine than to "Freudian analysis and Marxian determinism [which] destroyed man's belief in himself." That was why Brooks now opposed the psychological analysis that had marked his own early books and had gone in for "synthesis" in *Makers and Finders.* It was not merely wars and concentration camps and "human failure," but also "human thought" itself which had led to the modern failure of nerve.[31]

"Modern" probably struck Brooks as a poor appellation for the bleakness of contemporary thought, which he continued to feel was the logical result of the *fin-de-siècle* mood. Fifteen years earlier he had written in a notebook: "All the 20th century so far a dying of the 19th. The real 20th still to begin." The question was how it would begin, and as always his faith was in the poet as prophet. A new great

poet, he had told Rabbi Louis Finkelstein in 1941, would simply cut
the Gordian knots in which the modern mind was snared. Brooks
spent his later years reading new books, visiting conferences and
artists' colonies, scanning the crowd of young writers, searching for
the "promised man . . . in whom the 20th century will turn the
corner."[32]

Sometimes he grew impatient for the "great original writer of
genius who will dominate the coming time," and in *The Writer in
America* he asked, "Are we obliged merely to wait . . . ?" He suggested a number of measures to prepare for the dawn of the new
age. To begin, it was necessary to "rehumanize literature" and
"think better of man." The only possible escape from modern self-
consciousness was through an intentional lapse of memory. It was
necessary "to break the habits of the recent past," especially reading
habits; St. Francis, Plutarch, and Rabelais should be read instead of
Augustine, Donne, and Pascal. And he suggested "an hour of silence
regarding Melville and Henry James before they have been killed
for all time with kindness." Instead of critics who "analyze," he
recommended those who "synthesize" and "reveal the fruitful interaction of literature and life." These last included Sainte-Beuve
and De Quincey and though he did not name him, the author of
Makers and Finders.[33]

Yet Van Wyck grew ever gentler in his attitude toward the
avant-garde critics. *The Writer in America* (1953) was far more restrained than *The Opinions of Oliver Allston* (1941), and by 1956, when
he published his essay "Reflections on the Avant-Garde," he felt that
the avant-garde served a useful purpose. In 1952 he had been a
guest lecturer at the "Rocky Mountain Roundup of the Arts" at the
University of Montana, and he had been impressed by the number
of young talents who had stayed at home, albeit at the university,
rather than being driven to Greenwich Village or Paris as they would
have been thirty years before. In *Oliver Allston* he had said that while
the sensitive spirits of America had "not chosen their dwellingplace,
everything depends on their staying there."[34] By the mid-fifties he
saw a new trend toward writers staying at home and the reason was
precisely the strength of the avant-garde, who provided young
writers with literary contacts. University colloquia, writers' workshops, teaching posts, little magazines, and even the exclusive snobbishness and "party-line" of the avant-garde gave writers a sense of
community and security that let them live in and face down their
hostile towns and regions. In this respect the avant-garde movement

was good. It was a "life-line for the sensitive young, a sort of national 'hook-up' that brings them into relation with a powerful circle." The avant-garde resembled, more than anything he had observed in his lifetime, an American literary community.[35]

Still, avant-garde culture was unsatisfactory, led as it was, not by prophets but by monks. They were the " 'Initiated' of our time," who "occupy a sort of magic island that has no connection with the mainland of American thinking." The avant-garde's sense of security was purchased at the expense of a self-imposed exile from America. This was tragic: "Never has society needed more the aid and direction of the literary minds which the avant-garde encourage to stand aloof. . . ." Yet not to remain aloof would be to violate the isolation which was the basis of their security. Thus Brooks understood "this literary quietism" which was guilty of "teaching literature in terms of itself rather than in terms of humanity and emptying it more and more of its vital content." No wonder that much contemporary literature, however well accomplished, was "peripheral rather than central."[36]

But "historically speaking," the avant-garde was only a "phase," and the question was "What is to succeed it?" Van Wyck hoped that the next phase would combine "the great subject matter of the 'middle-brow' writers with the technical expertness bequeathed by the formalist critics, restoring in turn the notion of literature as a mirror and guide of society. . . ." He wanted to preserve what was good in the avant-garde, and he especially did not want to "jeopardize the avant-garde machinery that has been a blessing (with its magazines and summer conferences) for the sensitive young." Therefore he did not want to launch an offensive but preferred to hope for a "coup d'etat within the avant garde restoring its lost tie with the main intellectual body."[37]

That such an event might transpire within the avant-garde seemed likely in view of the special situation of America after the Second World War. As so often in the past Brooks supplied a reading of the historical present that made his hopes seem like certainties. The modern temper, his argument went, was based on the disorders of Europe in the twentieth century and the consequent disappointment of such turn-of-the-century prophets as his own H. G. Wells. But Americans could not share this "European mood of the moment." America "is too vigorous for this and it has lost too little." Thus, American writers should be the first to reject avant-garde attitudes and lead the way toward the twentieth century which

Brooks believed had not yet begun. The time had finally come for America to fulfill its destiny and accept Melville's injunction to "set, not follow precedents."[38]

Brooks was an artist, not a philosopher, and he could not argue history convincingly. When he made such attempts, his prose lost its sure rhythm, and he thrashed about with the idea nearest at hand. For instance, he defended the idea of human progress by saying that in the Middle Ages torture and inhumanity were "taken for granted, unlike Dachau and Buchenwald, which every human being knows were wrong."[39] The answer was sadly obvious that at least the thousands who operated the death camps seemed not to have known.

Yet many of Brooks's beliefs did cohere, however unsystematic his expression of them. His opposition to the avant-garde and the modern sensibility, its abstractness, its self-consciousness, and its tendency to analysis, was related to the role that he believed criticism should play in a world threatened by disorder, war, and nuclear destruction. It was possible, he admitted in *The Writer in America,* that civilization might end in atomic fire and human life would have proved an illusion that passed "like a dream in the night." But if so, history would have ended "at 12:01 in the morning," for civilization was only five thousand years old and ". . . the life-expectancy of man is several million years."[40] Perhaps mankind had only an even chance, but that left as much reason for belief as for despair. And belief was a positive act that might stave off war. Brooks was struck by Leo Stein's idea, when he read *Journey into the Self* in 1950, that society had two alternatives, more war or more "appreciation." The avant-garde was engaged in depreciation when what was needed was "the appreciation of life and man that would lead people to give up the resistances and repressions that must otherwise lead them to fight." Appreciation required that the contemporary mind be done with its "over-conscious" introspection and its "tiresome ideal of sophistication." Instead, it was necessary to recover a sense of innocence and the "lost capacity for wonder."[41]

Stein's idea provided a significant defense of *Makers and Finders,* for the series was an act of faith at a time when faith was a positive act. Brooks's later career, from *The Life of Emerson* on, had been one long bout of American appreciation. Now he declared explicitly his belief in "the old American messianic belief that this country was divinely appointed to deliver the world from European inequality, intolerance and corruption, as well as from the squalor and darkness of Africa and Asia." The old faith had new significance in a nuclear age, and he quoted Wyndham Lewis that America was the "ante-chamber of a world state," the place "where Cosmopolis is being tried out." This was hardly a new idea to Brooks or anyone else, but it justified his old-fashioned cultural nationalism, which was, "in American terms, really a defense of Whitman's 'orbic' mind. . . ." As one of Mazzini's "workships" of humanity, America's contribution to civilization was precisely the idea of one government for a culturally pluralistic world. America remained the hope of the world, the place where the necessary "planetary mind" should first emerge.[42]

This continuing faith in America required courage in the face of a lifetime of disappointments. America had not come of age as he had predicted in 1915, nor even by 1941 when he had written that "America as a whole has had its adolescence in our time." In 1958, when he was seventy-two, he admitted that America was still divided between the "esprit précieux" and the "esprit Gaulois," equivalents of Highbrow and Lowbrow, and that ". . . the great thing is the central thing we lack which reconciles the two." Americans in the flesh still struck him as "childish" in the extremity of their interest in competitive sports and their susceptibility to the "foolish cult of advertising, which exists for the breeding of desires. . . ." American literature was now a world literature but only through the default of Europe: ". . . is it [American literature] not still, on the whole, con-fused and as far from equal to this world role as the foreign policy of the nation has proved to be?" American writers were still "boys," he said on a national television program in 1958, adding, "Our Presi-dent is a boy." America was, in fact, so "brazen" that there was nothing in it to defend except "the idea that lies behind it."[43]

Tempered by the experiences of a lifetime, Brooks still affirmed the ideal in the face of a harsh reality. In fact, he comforted himself, affirmation of the ideal was an American trait. Thus, by engaging in it, he established still one more connection between himself and American reality. To be yea-sayers was natural for Americans, who were too young as a people to "sincerely think of the world as dead." Yet he still longed also for the comforts of the Old World, and there remained a large confusion about what the American ideal was. When he said that America "is far from having the homogeneity a country should have," he looked backward to nineteenth-century Europe rather than forward to the pluralistic world state of which America was supposed to be the model. Yet what was significant in Brooks's later years was not his continuing ambivalence between the urge to embrace and the urge to flee. In that respect his life might almost be taken as representative of American literature. What indicated a new level of spiritual maturity and courage was his willingness to live with this tension. His sanity no longer depended on an absolute identification with the course of American history. He had hopes for America, but if they were not fulfilled that would not indicate that the ideal was wrong or insanely divorced from reality. He had been disappointed too often in the past for any overbearing confidence in the future. He drew as much comfort now from the act of belief as from the expectation of fulfillment. Though faith alone would not raise life to the ideal, it might heighten or at least preserve it. So he continued to believe in and hope for America, "not for the country that is but for the country that promises to be, even if it always breaks its word."[44]

III

Brooks was seventy-five years old on February 16, 1961. A special birthday celebration was held in the library of the American Academy of Arts and Letters, and more than sixty writers, artists, and musicians came to hear Brooks saluted as "our chief living man of letters." Old friends like Lewis Mumford, John Hall Wheelock, and Louis Untermeyer were there to pay homage, and congratulatory messages were read from those who could not be present — Newton Arvin, Malcolm Cowley, Edmund Wilson, and many others. Mumford recalled that he and Van Wyck had had their differences but "to have quarreled with someone as magnanimous, as generous as Van Wyck Brooks, is one of the high privileges of friendship." Mumford turned to Van Wyck and said, "We love you and we're grateful for the fact that you have lived."[45]

Yet those present did not agree on what it was in Van Wyck's life that they should be most grateful for. He may have been most pleased with the remark of Isabel Bishop that he had enhanced for her and other painters "the sense of belonging to a place, to this place — I mean, to this country — and for giving us a deeper sense of its characteristics." Such a tribute was appropriate for the picturesque qualities of his later books, in which he had tried to give America a vivid memory of its cultural past. He believed *Makers and Finders* was his major work, on which his chances for a lasting reputation would rest. Yet Mark Van Doren saluted him for *America's Coming-of-Age*, of which the kindest word that Brooks would have said was "immature." Van Doren, however, felt that the early book was "heartbreakingly wise" and said "things about American society that are true now, that I fear may perhaps always be true."[46]

Thus Brooks received notice, even on this evening of homage, that his career would continue to be viewed as broken into two halves, early and late, and that many would view his early work as best. He believed in progress, however, both his own and the country's, and he believed that the superiority of his later work would be recognized when the country reached its own maturity, which he continued to hope was not far distant.

The politics of the early 1960's were balm for Brooks's spirit and helped renew his old faith that America would yet come of age. In 1948 he had voted Socialist, abandoning the Democrats after his wartime support. But in the fifties, with the advent of Adlai Stevenson on the national political scene, he had begun to vote Democratic again. He thought Stevenson was the most interesting political mind to appear in America in his lifetime, but Stevenson's defeats depressed him and reinforced his conviction that Americans suffered from "a general distrust and suspicion of superior people."[47] All this changed in 1960 with Kennedy's election. Kennedy was a writer, interested in American history, and from Boston. He was not of old New England stock, but Van Wyck's Irish blood warmed to him. Kennedy wooed Brooks in the summer of 1960 by sending, at Allan Nevins' suggestion, a collection of his speeches and a personal letter saying he would be glad to have comments. By the end of August, Van Wyck had decided to support Kennedy, and he let his name be used by the National Committee of Arts, Letters and Sciences for the Democratic candidate. But his enthusiasm was motivated as much by antipathy to "Dirty-Dick" Nixon and the "tiresome grinner" Eisenhower as it was by admiration for Kennedy.[48] Only after Kennedy took office and began a policy of government support for the arts unprecedented since the time of John Quincy Adams did he win Brooks's heart.

Kennedy invited Brooks to the White House dinner for Nobel Prize winners in April 1962. Van Wyck wanted to decline and keep on with his writing, but he relented when Gladys said such an invitation was a command. At the dinner they saw many old acquaintances — Fredric March, Pearl Buck, William Styron, Samuel Eliot Morison, John Dos Passos, and Robert Frost. The White House, glittering with formal dress and the uniforms of Marine escorts, had something of the quality of a European court. In the receiving line Van Wyck quickly shook Kennedy's hand and modestly passed on, but the President called after him that he had read *New England: Indian Summer* when he was in the hospital recovering from war wounds. After dinner Kennedy remarked that it was the most extraordinary collection of talent ever assembled at the White House "with the possible exception of when Thomas Jefferson dined alone." So much interest in American history and culture at the head of the government seemed a portent to Brooks. Exhilarated, he told a reporter to expect to witness soon "the flowering of America."[49]

Since America was the prototype for the world state of the future, not only the American but the world prospect seemed to have improved in the Kennedy years. One of the last things Van Wyck wrote was an introduction to a collection of interviews of American and European writers. He could see little difference between the Americans and Europeans but felt they all spoke for "the one world toward which the modern mind is aiming." It no longer mattered where a writer lived, for ". . . everybody lives everywhere at present." Literature had become "denationalized," Brooks said, as if he could casually dismiss the major concern of his life. Actually, he believed that the rest of the world, represented by Kennedy's somewhat old-fashioned patriotism, had come round to nationalism, and he cited, for instance, the fact that Ezra Pound said he felt "more American all the time."[50]

Brooks's Americanism was still an expression, in a continental symbol, of his concern for the proper relationship between the ethereal spirit of the artist and earthbound reality. Therefore, he was as fascinated as ever by the lives of other American writers, including that of Randolph Bourne, about whom Van Wyck wrote one of his last essays. To research the piece he had interviewed Bourne's surviving relatives and corresponded with his old friends. He was happy to find, as he told Alyse Gregory, that Bourne was well remembered forty years after his death, "a rather remarkable record in our much forgetting country." In his essay on Bourne, published in *Fenollosa and His Circle,* Brooks recalled Bourne's brave and lonely life: "It is no fun being a free man in a slave world," Bourne had once said. Bourne's courage had been nourished on his belief that the liberal idealism of the nineteenth century would produce a new age of social justice in the twentieth. He had seen at once that the door was slammed on this vision when the "monster" of war burst on the world and had cried out in vain protest. Still, Brooks believed that the Elioteers and de-humanizers "would have had a more difficult victory if Bourne had lived long enough to counterattack them."[51]

Van Wyck, however, was still ambivalent on the correctness of Bourne's politics in the *Seven Arts* crisis: "I could not see why a magazine of art should destroy itself by opposing the war."[52] There were depths of conservatism in Brooks from which he had never escaped and which made it difficult for him to carry his idea of the artist as a social prophet over into politics. In this respect he shared some of the genteel qualities he and Bourne had early condemned, for by divorcing art from politics he was also divorcing it, in part, from life. He said in later years that he admired Berenson's justification of art as "life-enhancement," but this was not too far distant from Eliot's idea of poetry as "superior amusement." Brooks would have admitted that his own vision was not totally integrated and his conception of culture still somewhat unreal, but to him that seemed as much a fault of the age as of himself. He had long since given up hope that the fractured modern mind could see life "whole."

Still, some came closer than others, and one of the closest was Edmund Wilson, who lived, Van Wyck said, "the uncloistered life of a many-sided free-ranging man of letters and the world." Wilson's immense talents and varied interests fascinated Brooks and reminded him of Sainte-Beuve. In later years Brooks had taken to justifying his portly figure by saying that all good critics were overweight: "Look at Sainte-Beuve. Look at Edmund Wilson." At other times Wilson reminded him of Samuel Johnson and other men of letters in times when the psyche was healthier and could better comprehend life. Wilson was a *"character,"* he told Mumford, "and quite eighteenth century."[53]

Brooks and Wilson met several times in the late fifties, once at Harvard and occasionally on Cape Cod, where both Wilson and Gladys Brooks owned property. Their last meeting was in August 1958, at Talcottville, New York, in the ancestral home Wilson described in *Upstate* (1971). Wilson spent summers alone in the old stone house; his wife, Elena, preferred Cape Cod, and rather than living at Talcottville, she only visited. Van Wyck and Gladys found Wilson standing in front of his house in the summer afternoon, waiting impatiently, apparently eager to see them. He had planned their entertainment carefully, and he showed them about the region and gave them a picnic beside the Independence River. For Van Wyck, who had often journeyed upstate in the summers of his youth, the visit must have brought poignant memories. He was distantly related to the Noyes family, and he was delighted with the visit Wilson arranged to Oneida. He met the son of John Humphrey Noyes, Pierrepont Noyes, who was in his late eighties, and they discussed their mutual relatives. Van Wyck and Wilson explored the old Mansion House and examined the transoms to see if it was possibly true that young men had escaped through them when they did not want to sleep with the girls to whom they had been assigned.[54]

Brooks and Wilson disagreed on many subjects, but they talked easily and enjoyed each other's company. Wilson was ten years younger, but he said he had given up trying to follow new writers and books. Van Wyck, still watching for the great young poet-prophet of the future, did read new books, but could "scarcely understand" many of them. He was glad to hear that Wilson, whom he regarded as the most intelligent writer in the country, had simply given up. He thought of Sainte-Beuve's saying that in old age the river "flows past us," and he told Wilson that the two of them were "the only men of letters left."[55]

They discussed old books instead of new, and Brooks, who was at work on *Howells*, spoke of his growing admiration for *The Rise of Silas Lapham*. Wilson could not bear the book or Howells either, and he found Brooks's interest depressing. To Wilson it was just one more instance of the "lack of discrimination" in Brooks's later phase. Never having known Brooks well enough to appreciate that his later synthesizing phase was underway before his breakdown, Wilson felt that this "cult of mediocrities . . . was something itself of a sedative to the deep agitation, the near despair of his breakdown." Yet Wilson also admired Brooks's work and thought it "of great importance to American culture." Brooks had displayed "heroism" in recovering from despair and writing his massive books. Later Wilson wrote that America owed a huge debt to Brooks for opening up the whole field of American literary history.[56]

Wilson was also troubled by Brooks's continuing hatred of T. S. Eliot, and he linked it to the difference in their attitude toward Europe: "Eliot represents the growth of an American internationalism; Brooks, . . . the beginning of the sometimes all too conscious American self-glorification which is a part of our American imperialism." Wilson kept off modern literature at Talcottville, having unsuccessfully protested in previous meetings Brooks's theory that Eliot had misled the young toward a greater interest in form than in content. But to other guests at Talcottville, Brooks spoke his mind on modern literature, saying that Proust and Joyce were "haters of life." To Wilson this seemed childish and indicative of a very narrow idea of literature; Brooks could regard as great only a writer who resembled Tolstoy or H. G. Wells or some other exhortatory figure. Wilson was repeating his 1925 criticism of *Henry James* that Brooks was incapable of dealing with the equanimous artist who was not a "voice of the people." Now Wilson attributed this failing to an imperfect education in the classics and in French. Wilson did not know that in youth Van Wyck had had a quasi-religious faith in art for art's sake, had lost faith, and then replaced it with his belief in the art of society. Therefore, Wilson could not understand how "a man who writes so well, who is very much himself an artist, should not understand style and form in other writers."[57]

Brooks also wrote critically about the visit to Talcottville. He found Wilson a "highly unreasonable rationalist, abounding in violent prejudices." Wilson's remark that Aldous Huxley was not an artist signified to Van Wyck as narrow an idea of literature as his own seemed to Wilson. Despite Brooks's nationalism, he had always admired the English personally, while Wilson was repelled by "British impudence." When Brooks questioned him on this point, Wilson answered that during the Revolution one of his ancestors had been shut in a British prison ship. Wilson's distaste for Howells seemed equally unreasonable, a mere echo, Brooks felt, of the sneers of Mencken and Sinclair Lewis. Wilson was inadequately educated in things American, a result perhaps of having, like Saint-Beuve, "no-centre." Brooks felt that Wilson had shifted allegiances rather easily during his career, and in exactly the metaphor he had inscribed in his notebook during Irving Babbitt's lecture on Sainte-Beuve more than half a century before, Brooks now wrote of Wilson, "He was afloat, his ship had no anchor." Like Sainte-Beuve, Wilson suffered from a lack of commitment, so that his great intelligence "seemed to look down on his heart."[58]

For all their disagreements, however, the two men felt they were kindred spirits in that they took a larger view than most. Wilson thought Brooks heroic, and Brooks saw that Wilson, like Sainte-Beuve, "possessed supremely the gift of wonder." Brooks and Wilson were not great friends but they had an affinity. That they had met so infrequently during the forty years of their acquaintance was only one more example of the loneliness in American life against which Brooks had fought. The end of the two-day visit at Talcottville, as the Brookses drove away early on a rainy morning, depressed both men. Perhaps they sensed it was their final meeting. Wilson felt "let down" after the Brookses left, and Van Wyck was troubled by his memory of Wilson seeing them off, standing sleepily alone in his robe in front of the stone house with the rain beating down.[59]

One of the loneliest American lives of which Brooks had personal knowledge was Newton Arvin's. He felt that Arvin had too fine a critical talent to be spending his time and energy at Smith College, and he had often urged him to attempt to make a living solely by writing. Still believing in talents that were death to hide, Brooks feared that Arvin was betraying his gifts just as Mark Twain had done. In 1941 when Arvin was recovering from a nervous break-down, Brooks had urged him not to return to Smith. If he would announce that he was available as a reader and reviewer he would have a decent income, Brooks had said. But Arvin, nervous and insecure, had believed that he needed the stability and certain income which Smith gave him. Brooks had cautioned that to go back to Smith might bring on a recurrence of the breakdown, and feeling prosperous after the success of the New England books, he had hinted that he would loan Arvin money if asked: ". . . you probably don't know how deeply your friends care about you, and how glad they would be to take steps that would serve you best in the end."[60]

Arvin had not taken Brooks's advice but had gone back to Smith, and during the last twenty years of his life he was tortured by emotional problems. His brief marriage to a Smith student had ended unhappily, and so too had his Marxist theories of the thirties. In 1948 when Brooks voted for Norman Thomas, Arvin urged him to vote for Truman and explained that he now thought of socialism in a more "pluralistic" sense than he once had. In the thirties Arvin had prided himself on his scientific materialism and chastised Brooks for his idealism. But by 1954 Arvin had been through several emotional crises and, needing comfort, he began to attend church. These experiences made Arvin sympathetic to Brooks's campaigns against the avant-garde and against "coterie literature," and he began again to consider himself a follower of Brooks, "the only man we have who can tell off the pedants as they need to be told off." Borrowing Emerson's phrase for Channing, he often spoke of Brooks as "our bishop."[61]

Although Arvin and Brooks did not meet often in the fifties, they corresponded regularly, and Van Wyck continued in his old role of mentor, exhorting Arvin to focus his efforts on a book. That they met so seldom was probably due to Van Wyck's increasingly active social life with Gladys and perhaps also to the fact that Gladys found Arvin a "subdued and sad man." She did not understand, as Van Wyck did, that Arvin was a "quiet man with a violent mind," who "would gladly have stood against a wall and faced a fusillade for his convictions."[62]

Brooks had always believed it was the lack of "resistance" in American life, the lack of sharp issues and causes and traditions, that made life difficult for men like Arvin. In Europe such men would have found careers as critics, but in the confused cross-currents and swirling eddies of American culture they could not grasp a point of view and only swam wildly about. In his *Makers and Finders* Brooks had attempted to provide a central tradition of native radicalism for American writers, and for his friend Arvin, a specific case of the need for direction, he had personally supplied all the help he could. It is doubtful that without Brooks's assistance and prodding Arvin could have written his four fine studies of Hawthorne, Whitman, Melville, and Longfellow.

Despite all his torments and insecurities Arvin had lived humanely and usefully, and it was exceedingly unjust that his last years were spent in humiliation, following his arrest by the Northampton police in 1960 for possession of homosexual pornography. He was charged also as a "lewd person." The arrest resulted in another breakdown, a sojourn in a mental institution, and a forced early retirement from Smith. As soon as Brooks heard of the incident he wrote to Arvin, offering his support. The letter does not survive, but Arvin's answer does: "I would never have doubted for a moment your being beside me — with whatever very reasonable reservations. . . ."[63]

The reservations probably expressed Brooks's continuing fear of seeming to countenance homosexuality. Because his early life and career had been, in one sense, a revolt against sexual roles, he had always been somewhat on the defensive regarding his sexuality. His strenuous, lifelong insistence that literature had practical consequences was in some part a defense of his masculinity. Homosexuality had always been a difficult problem for him to deal with in writers, especially in writers whom he admired like Symonds and Whitman. Arvin, unlike Brooks, could directly face Whitman's homosexuality, and this difference in their attitudes had been made clear by Brooks's reaction to Arvin's *Whitman* (1938): ". . . how fine," he had praised Arvin, "the way you treat the fact of his homosexuality and generalize it as I have always felt it." This was the way Brooks would treat it in his *Times of Melville and Whitman* (1947), by "generalizing" or idealizing it away from the physical level. But there had been a depth of affection in Arvin's treatment of Whitman that Brooks had not understood, and, puzzled, he had added in parentheses, "I must say that Whitman has never been *personally lovable* to me." Arvin, in turn, would respond critically to Brooks's idealization of Whitman's homosexuality in *The Times of Melville and Whitman:* "I think Whitman was really pretty far off the middle line in these matters, farther off than he 'knew,' and certainly than he wanted anyone else to know."[64]

Brooks refused to let his reservations on homosexuality stand in the way of friendship. He visited Arvin in the hospital after his arrest, and when Arvin had recovered and begun to consider editing a four-volume guide to American literature, Brooks agreed to contribute a chapter, a rare exception to his policy of refusing to write piecemeal.[65] Arvin also started another book on Hawthorne and planned an unspecified project to occupy himself "for six or eight *years* — if I last so long." Perhaps he was finally taking Brooks's advice, now that he was retired from Smith, and mapping out ambitious projects that would "focus" him over a long period of time. If so, it was too late. He was soon to weaken and die of cancer of the pancreas. Arvin did, however, find strength to finish his *Longfellow*. He could not overcome the feeling in his final years that he was a pariah, and when he decided to dedicate the *Longfellow* to Brooks, he cautiously asked permission and added that he would "understand it perfectly well if you preferred that I didn't."[66] Van Wyck of course accepted the dedication.

Lewis Mumford had managed the most social existence of all of Brooks's literary friends. With his large books and vast correspondence, his astutely managed finances which gave him independence for the life of the mind, and his diverse interests, he still seemed to Brooks an ideal case of the many-sided man of letters. Their friendship had continued unabated, and as Brooks grew older, Mumford was less demanding, though he still occasionally urged Brooks toward politics. After the U-2, a United States spy plane, was shot down over Russia in 1960, he asked Van Wyck to drop his work and join in demanding "a complete overhauling of all our aggressively psychotic plans. . . ." Such a demand from Brooks would be very effective because he occupied "a unique place in the minds of our countrymen." Such compliments were a staple of Mumford's later letters to Brooks. He understood better than most what Brooks's career had been about, and he offered all the assurance he could in Brooks's final years that his life had been well spent. On Van Wyck's seventy-first birthday Mumford had written:

> I have no hope of being able to say adequately how much I owe to you: how your integrity has kept before me . . . the image of the true man of letters, following his mission, to stir up the creative forces in our life in defiance of all that deadens the spirit. . . . this land would now be a drearier and emptier place,

were it not for all the good things, the books, the places, the people, that your imagination and insight have brought to light. . . . You have enlarged both our past and our potentialities: and I anticipate the verdict of generations to come when I record my gratitude. . . .[67]

To Brooks, who had spent his later career attempting to show that the thing had been done, that the literary life could be lived in America, Mumford was an exemplary figure, and he had wanted for years to write about Mumford. In 1940 he had said that treating Mumford was "to be one of the joys of my old age." Mumford would be a central figure in "my sixth volume." But he had never written the sixth volume of *Makers and Finders,* and he had decided to make amends by writing a life of Mumford. The idea did not appeal to Mumford, who had not liked an essay on himself which Brooks had included in *The Writer in America.* He felt that at bottom his was a deeper and more tragic view of life than Brooks's, and he may have doubted that at seventy-six Brooks had the capacity to deal even with the surface of his work. But Mumford could hardly say no to so old a friend, and in the spring of 1962 Brooks began to read and collect information for the book. Mumford said that he did not want to overburden Brooks with information, so while he would supply information, he would not volunteer it. If the book was too much trouble, Van Wyck should not let any fear of disappointing Mumford prevent him from dropping it. The mere fact that he had wanted to do it would be satisfaction enough and would "remain an invisible and untarnishable gold medal." Brooks replied that he would not give up the book, and he hoped that Mumford would volunteer information: "I *count* on writing about you. . . ."[68] But Brooks's work was interrupted by a slight stroke that summer and by other illnesses and decreasing strength thereafter. In the end all that was written was one chapter.

A tumor in Brooks's colon has been discovered and removed in the winter of 1960, and his health had gradually declined from that point on. After his stroke in August 1962, he underwent surgery again at Grace Hospital in New Haven, this time on a carotid artery in order to prevent another stroke. The operation was performed under a local anesthetic, and as soon as it was completed Van Wyck asked the surgeon, "Will you be good enough to have me wheeled back to my room so that my wife can read to me?" Shortly after his return to Bridgewater he began to have difficulty digesting his food. The tumor in his colon had recurred, and at the end of November it was removed in a small hospital in New Milford, only a few miles from Bridgewater. He was weak, but he survived the operation and on New Year's Day 1963 he returned to Bridgewater.[69]

Gladys had had his bed moved to the dining room. It received more light than any other room in the house, and he enjoyed looking at the portraits of his ancestors on the dining room walls. She helped him walk at first and later wheeled him down the short hall to his study to read. Newton Arvin, dying himself, sent an advance copy of his *Longfellow,* which Van Wyck read in his study chair. On February sixteenth Van Wyck was seventy-seven, and Lewis Mumford saluted him as America's best critic. In March, Edmund Wilson took space in a review of Arvin's *Longfellow* to call Brooks one of the top American writers of his time. Of those who had devoted their lives to the study of American literature, Wilson said, only Brooks and Arvin were themselves fine writers.[70] Arvin died the same week that Wilson's review appeared.

Van Wyck, who had believed it right to love life, struggled on. However troubled he may have been about his relationship to the world, he had always addressed himself to the problem intensely, and that had been the true measure of his vitality. The long test was nearly over, and he was ready to live, in Emerson's words, "out of time." With Whitman, he would have said, "I laugh at what you call dissolution. . . ." Van Wyck told the village rector that what he had written was a "reflection of something beyond me in the universe; I have to believe in God. . . ." The length of the visits to the study shortened gradually until they were only ten minutes long. He grew too weak to hold a book and then he would say to Gladys, "Read to me." The last book she read aloud was his own *Scenes and Portraits: Memories of Childhood and Youth.* Early in the afternoon of May 2, 1963, he whispered to Gladys, "You must have rest."[71] Then time stood still.

NOTE ON SOURCES

In addition to the printed works cited in the Notes, this book was largely written from manuscript sources housed in the following collections.

ANDERSON, SHERWOOD. Papers. The Newberry Library, Chicago, Illinois.

ARVIN, NEWTON. Papers. The W. A. Neilson Library, Smith College, Northampton, Massachusetts.

AUSTIN, MARY. Papers. The Huntington Library, San Marino, California.

BENÉT, STEPHEN VINCENT. Collection of American Literature, Beinecke Rare Book and Manuscript Library, Yale University, New Haven, Connecticut.

BLAKE, WARREN. Papers. The Houghton Library, Harvard University, Cambridge, Massachusetts.

BOURNE, RANDOLPH. Papers. The Butler Library, Columbia University, New York City, New York.

BRADFORD, GAMALIEL. Papers. The Houghton Library, Harvard University, Cambridge, Massachusetts.

BROOKS, VAN WYCK. Papers. The University of Pennsylvania Library, Philadelphia, Pennsylvania.

CANBY, HENRY S. Papers. Collection of American Literature, Beinecke Rare Book and Manuscript Library, Yale University, New Haven, Connecticut.

CANE, MELVILLE. Papers. The Butler Library, Columbia University, New York City, New York.

COWLEY, MALCOLM. Papers. The Newberry Library, Chicago, Illinois.

FARRELL, JAMES. Papers. The University of Pennsylvania Library, Philadelphia, Pennsylvania.

FLETCHER, JOHN GOULD. Papers. Special Collections, University Library, University of Arkansas, Fayetteville, Arkansas.

FRANK, WALDO. Papers. The University of Pennsylvania Library, Philadelphia, Pennsylvania.

GREGORY, ALYSE. Papers. Collection of American Literature, Beinecke Rare Book and Manuscript Library, Yale University, New Haven, Connecticut.

HOWE, M. A. DEWOLFE. Papers. The Houghton Library, Harvard University, Cambridge, Massachusetts.

HUEBSCH, BENJAMIN W. Papers. Manuscript Division, The Library of Congress, Washington, D.C.

JORDAN, DAVID STARR. Papers. Stanford University Archives, Stanford, California.

LEE, GERALD STANLEY. Papers. The Forbes Library, Northampton, Massachusetts.

MCFEE, WILLIAM. Papers. Beinecke Rare Book and Manuscript Library, Yale University, New Haven, Connecticut.

NEVINS, ALLAN. Papers. The Butler Library, Columbia University, New York City, New York.

PERRY, BLISS. Papers. The Houghton Library, Harvard University, Cambridge, Massachusetts.

POWEL, HARFORD, JR. Papers. The John Hay Library, Brown University, Providence, Rhode Island.

POWYS, LLEWELYN. Papers. Collection of American Literature, Beinecke Rare Book and Manuscript Library, Yale University, New Haven, Connecticut.

SCRIBNER'S ARCHIVES. Papers. Princeton University Library, Princeton, New Jersey.

SPINGARN, JOEL. Papers. Manuscripts and Archives Division, The New York Public Library, Astor, Lenox and Tilden Foundations, New York City, New York.

STIMSON, HENRY L. Papers. Yale University Library, New Haven, Connecticut.

STIMSON, JOHN F. Papers. The Peabody Museum, Salem, Massachusetts.

VILLARD, OSWALD GARRISON. Papers. The Houghton Library, Harvard University, Cambridge, Massachusetts.

NOTES

In the notes Van Wyck Brooks's name has been abbreviated to VWB and that of his first wife, Eleanor Stimson Brooks, to ESB.

PREFACE

1. James P. Spradley, *The Cultural Experience: Ethnography in a Complex Society* (Chicago: Science Research Associates, 1972), p. 8.
2. Christopher Lasch, *The New Radicalism in America, 1889-1963: The Intellectual as a Social Type* (New York: Vintage, 1965), p. 65.

PLAINFIELD, 1886-1904

1. VWB, "The New Temple of Taste," Brooks MSS.
2. VWB, "Memorial of Charles Graeling," Brooks MSS.
3. Anne Van Wyck, *Descendants of Cornelius Barente Van Wyck and Anna Polhemus* (New York: T. A. Wright, 1912), pp. 23, 39, 60; VWB, *Autobiography* (New York: Dutton, 1965), pp. 76-83; "Gatherings," Brooks MSS.
4. VWB, *Autobiography*, pp. 20, 65; "Gatherings," Brooks MSS.
5. VWB, *Autobiography*, p. 84; "Gatherings," Brooks MSS.
6. Dorothy Whyte to VWB, Mar. 12, 1935, courtesy of Mrs. Whyte; Brooks file, Four Winds, Katonah, New York.
7. "Gatherings" and "Scrap Book," Brooks MSS.
8. "Gatherings" and "Scrap Book," Brooks MSS.
9. "Gatherings" and "Scrap Book," Brooks MSS.
10. VWB, *Autobiography*, pp. 14-15.

11. Ibid., pp. 10–11.
12. VWB, *The Wine of the Puritans* (London: Sisley, 1908), pp. 54–55.
13. VWB, *Autobiography*, pp. 67–68; "Family History," Brooks file, Four Winds.
14. VWB, *Autobiography*, pp. 70–71; Interview with Oliver Kenyon Brooks, Jan. 1972.
15. VWB, *Autobiography*, p. 69; "Family History," Brooks file, Four Winds.
16. "Gatherings," Brooks MSS.; Charles E. Brooks to VWB, Jan. 23, 1899, courtesy of Charles V. W. Brooks.
17. VWB, *Autobiography*, p. 11.
18. VWB, *The Opinions of Oliver Allston* (New York: Dutton, 1941), p. 120.
19. VWB's baby book, Brooks MSS.
20. Ames's and VWB's baby books, Brooks MSS.; *Burlington, Vermont, Free Press*, Apr. 23, 1932.
21. VWB, *Autobiography*, pp. 7–9.
22. Ibid., pp. 12, 15.
23. Ibid., pp. 36–40; ESB to Charles V. W. Brooks, Aug. 3, 1943, Brooks MSS.
24. VWB, *Autobiography*, p. 33; "Gatherings," Brooks MSS.
25. VWB, *Autobiography*, pp. 72–73; VWB, "Memorial of Charles Graeling," Brooks MSS.
26. ESB to John F. Stimson, Nov. 23, 1898, John F. Stimson MSS.; VWB, "Diaries," Brooks MSS. These diaries and VWB's account in his *Autobiography*, pp. 85–94, are the source, except where otherwise noted, for the following account of the Brookses' year in Europe.
27. Charles E. Brooks to VWB, Dec. 13, 1898, courtesy of Charles V. W. Brooks.
28. VWB, "Memorial of Charles Graeling," Brooks MSS.
29. Sallie Brooks quoted by Ames in his letter to Charles E. Brooks, Mar. 22, 1899, Brooks MSS.
30. VWB's baby book and "Books Read," Brooks MSS.
31. George Winokur, *Manic Depressive Illness* (St. Louis: Mosby, 1969), p. 23; VWB, "Verse and Prose Miscellanies, I," Brooks MSS.
32. VWB, "Diary and Commonplace Book," Brooks MSS.
33. A complete file of the *Oracle* is in the library of the public high school, Plainfield, New Jersey; VWB, "Memorial of Charles Graeling" and "Diary," Brooks MSS.
34. VWB, *Autobiography*, p. 6; "Homage to Van Wyck Brooks," *Proceedings* of the American Academy of Arts and Letters, Second Series, No. 12 (1962), p. 161; VWB, *Oliver Allston*, p. 89; VWB, *The Wine of the Puritans*, p. 26.
35. *Oracle* (June 1904)—this issue in the Brooks MSS.; VWB, *Autobiography*, p. 29; Gladys Brooks, *If Strangers Meet: A Memory* (New York: Harcourt, 1967), p. 98.
36. Elting E. Morison, *Turmoil and Tradition: A Study of the Life and Times of Henry L. Stimson* (Boston: Houghton Mifflin, 1960), p. 15; VWB, *Autobiog-*

raphy, pp. 295–97, 333–35; "John Francis Stimson," *New York Times,* Nov. 1, 1958, p. 19.

37. ESB to Charles V. W. Brooks, Aug. 3, 1943, Brooks MSS.; VWB, *Autobiography,* pp. 289–90.

38. ESB to Charles V. W. Brooks, Aug. 3, 1943, Brooks MSS.

39. Ibid.

40. VWB, "Diary," Brooks MSS.

41. VWB, "Verse and Prose Miscellanies, I," Brooks MSS.

42. VWB, *Autobiography,* p. 90; VWB, "Verse and Prose Miscellanies, I," Brooks MSS.

43. VWB, "Diary," Brooks MSS. VWB was apparently still under the influence of the "theory of curves" during his sophomore year at Harvard when he published a story entitled "The Rest of the Circle" in the *Harvard Advocate,* Nov. 10, 1905, p. 57.

44. VWB, "Diary," Brooks MSS.

45. Charles Ames Brooks to Sallie Brooks, Aug. 10, 1901, Brooks MSS.; VWB, "Diary," Brooks MSS.

46. Dorothy Whyte to VWB, Sept. 5, 1934, courtesy of Mrs. Whyte.

47. VWB, *Autobiography,* p. 7.

48. Ibid., p. 14; VWB, "Diary," Brooks MSS.; VWB, *The Times of Melville and Whitman* (New York: Dutton, 1947), p. 183.

49. VWB, *Autobiography,* p. 70.

50. Ibid., p. 439.

51. Ibid., pp. 243–44; VWB, "Diary," Brooks MSS.

52. VWB to Sallie Brooks, Aug. 12, 1901, Brooks MSS.; VWB to ESB, Oct. 21, 1903, Brooks MSS.; VWB, *Oliver Allston,* p. 237.

53. VWB, "Diary," Brooks MSS.; *Oracle* (June 1904) — this issue in the Brooks MSS.

54. Ryder to Charles Ames Brooks, Apr. 11, 1899, Brooks MSS.; VWB, *Autobiography,* p. 93.

55. VWB, "Brooks, Charles Ames," *National Cyclopedia of American Biography* (New York: James T. White, 1933), XXIII, 133; "Charles Ames Brooks, '05," *Princeton Alumni Weekly,* January 8, 1932, p. 310; VWB, *Wine of the Puritans,* p. 30.

56. VWB, *Autobiography,* pp. 242–43; Gladys Brooks, *If Strangers Meet,* pp. 97–98.

57. Gladys Brooks, *If Strangers Meet,* pp. 97–98.

HARVARD, 1904–1907

1. VWB, *Autobiography,* p. 120; VWB, *Oliver Allston,* p. 97.

2. VWB, *Autobiography,* pp. 26–28.

3. Wheelock, "Foreword" to VWB, *Autobiography,* p. ix.

4. VWB, *Autobiography,* pp. 104–06; Francis Biddle, *A Casual Past* (Garden City, New York: Doubleday, 1961), p. 226.

5. Biddle, *A Casual Past,* p. 105; Wheelock, *Poems Old and New* (New York:

Scribner's, 1956), p. 40; VWB, "Verse and Prose Miscellanies, II," Brooks MSS.

6. VWB, *Autobiography,* p. 113; "Homage to Van Wyck Brooks," p. 159; Interview with John Hall Wheelock, Jan. 1972.

7. VWB, *Autobiography,* pp. 102–06; Interview with Joan Terrall, Feb. 1972.

8. Granville Hicks, *John Reed: The Making of a Revolutionary* (New York: Macmillan, 1936), p. 25; Hugh Hawkins, *Between Harvard and America: The Educational Leadership of Charles W. Eliot* (New York: Oxford, 1972), p. 170; VWB, *Autobiography,* pp. 102, 231; Cleveland Amory, *The Proper Bostonians* (New York: Dutton, 1947), p. 300; VWB to Harford Powel, Jr., Aug. 22, 1953, Powel MSS.

9. VWB, *Autobiography,* pp. 101–02.

10. VWB, *Verses by Two Undergraduates* (Boston, 1905).

11. ESB to Charles V. W. Brooks, Aug. 3, 1943, Brooks MSS.

12. ESB to VWB, Feb. 28, 1907, Brooks MSS.

13. VWB, "Diary" and "Verse and Prose Miscellanies, II," Brooks MSS.

14. VWB to ESB, Jan. 4, 1906, Brooks MSS.; Biddle, *A Casual Past,* p. 226; Henry James, *The American Scene* (Bloomington, Ind.: Univ. of Indiana Press, 1968), p. 69.

15. Brooks's transcript, Office of the Registrar, Harvard University.

16. VWB, "The New Advocate," Brooks MSS.

17. VWB, "Harvard and American Life," *Contemporary Review,* Dec. 12, 1908, pp. 613, 617; VWB, "The New Advocate," Brooks MSS.

18. Hawkins, *Between Harvard and America,* p. 220; VWB, "Verse and Prose Miscellanies, I," Brooks MSS.; VWB, *Oliver Allston,* p. 120.

19. Hawkins, *Between Harvard and America,* p. 220; VWB, "Verse and Prose Miscellanies, I," Brooks MSS.; VWB, "Harvard and American Life," p. 613; VWB, "Varied Outlooks," *Harvard Advocate,* 83 (Apr. 12, 1907), 35–37.

20. VWB, "Harvard and American Life," p. 618.

21. Brooks's transcript, Office of the Registrar, Harvard University; Interview with Gladys Brooks, Feb. 1972.

22. Samuel Eliot Morison, *Three Centuries of Harvard, 1636–1936* (Cambridge, Mass.: Harvard Univ. Press, 1936), pp. 370–71.

23. VWB, "Verse and Prose Miscellanies, II," Brooks MSS.; J. Donald Adams, *Copey of Harvard* (Boston: Houghton Mifflin, 1960), p. 89; VWB, *Autobiography,* p. 122.

24. VWB, *Oliver Allston,* p. 96; VWB, *Autobiography,* pp. 109, 121.

25. VWB, *Autobiography,* p. 123.

26. Harold Nicolson, *Sainte-Beuve* (Garden City, New York: Doubleday, 1956), pp. 4–6, 64.

27. VWB, "Class Notes," Brooks MSS.; VWB, "The Quality of Romance," *Harvard Monthly,* 43 (Christmas 1906), 212.

28. VWB, "Italian Journals," Brooks MSS.; VWB, *Autobiography,* p. 99; VWB to ESB, Sept. 10, 1905, Brooks MSS.

29. VWB, "Italian Journals," Brooks MSS.; VWB, *Autobiography,* pp. 97–98.

30. VWB, *Autobiography*, p. 99
31. VWB, "Italian Journals," Brooks MSS.
32. Ibid.
33. VWB to ESB, Sept. 10, 1905, Brooks MSS.
34. Wendell, *A Literary History of America* (New York: Scribner's, 1900), p. 10.
35. Rollo W. Brown, *Dean Briggs* (New York: Harper, 1926), p. 60; Leon Edel, *Henry James: The Treacherous Years* (Philadelphia: Lippincott, 1969), p. 143; *Barrett Wendell and His Letters*, ed. M. A. DeWolfe Howe (Boston: Atlantic Monthly Press, 1924), pp. 138, 162, 128.
36. VWB, "Verse and Prose Miscellanies, I," Brooks MSS.; Wendell, *The Privileged Classes* (New York: Scribner's, 1908), pp. 87–88; *Barrett Wendell*, ed. Howe, p. 131; VWB, *The Wine of the Puritans*, pp. 53–54, 15.
37. VWB, "Preface," in Lewellyn Powys, *Thirteen Worthies* (New York: American Library Service, 1923), p. 7; VWB, "Class Notes," Brooks MSS.; VWB, "Verse and Prose Miscellanies, I," Brooks MSS.; VWB, "Juvenile, College, and Early Essays," Brooks MSS.
38. VWB, "Dante and the Literary Temperament," Brooks MSS.
39. VWB, "Verse and Prose Miscellanies, I," Brooks MSS.
40. Ibid.
41. VWB, *Oliver Allston*, p. 162; VWB, "Imaginary Letters," Brooks MSS.
42. VWB, "Imaginary Letters," Brooks MSS.
43. VWB, "Memorial of Charles Graeling," Brooks MSS.

THE LIMITATIONS OF LIFE

1. VWB to ESB, Jan. 3, 1907, Brooks MSS.; More to Colby, Dec. 26, 1906, Brooks MSS.; James Vitelli, *Van Wyck Brooks* (New York: Twayne, 1969), p. 30.
2. Mildred Howells to VWB, June 20, 1958, Brooks MSS.; VWB, *Oliver Allston*, p. 22; VWB to ESB, Jan. 3, 1907, Brooks MSS.
3. VWB to ESB, Jan. 3, 1907, Brooks MSS.
4. VWB, *Autobiography*, pp. 130, 150.
5. VWB, *Oliver Allston*, p. 23; VWB to ESB, Aug. 1, 1907, Brooks MSS.
6. Charles S. Graves to VWB, Aug. 30, 1907, Brooks MSS.; VWB to ESB, Aug. 8, 1907, and "Wed. eve." [Aug. 1907], Brooks MSS.; VWB, *Autobiography*, p. 136.
7. VWB to ESB, "Wed. eve." [Aug. 1907], Brooks MSS.; VWB, *Autobiography*, p. 137.
8. VWB, *Autobiography*, p. 139; ESB to "Alice," July 19, 1911, courtesy of Charles V. W. Brooks.
9. VWB, *Autobiography*, p. 139.
10. Ibid., pp. 134–35.
11. VWB, *The Wine of the Puritans*, pp. 131–32.
12. VWB, "Harvard and American Life," pp. 610–11; VWB, "A Book of Limitations," Brooks MSS.

13. VWB, *Autobiography*, pp. 148–51; VWB to ESB, Mar. 31, 1908, Brooks MSS.

14. VWB to ESB, Mar. 31 and May 20, 1908, Brooks MSS.; VWB, *Autobiography*, p. 151; VWB, "The New Temple of Taste," Brooks MSS.

15. VWB, "The New Temple of Taste," Brooks MSS.

16. VWB, *Oliver Allston*, p. 23; Interview with Gladys Brooks, Jan. 1972; VWB, "The New Temple of Taste," Brooks MSS.

17. VWB, "The New Temple of Taste," Brooks MSS.

18. Ibid.

19. Ibid.

20. Eliot, rev. of *The Wine of the Puritans, Harvard Advocate*, May 7, 1909, p. 80; John Hall Wheelock and Charles Seeger also reported strong reactions to the book in interviews, Feb. 1972.

21. VWB, *The Wine of the Puritans*, pp. 11, 12, 93, 22, 13.

22. Ibid., pp. 14, 17, 15, 18.

23. Spiller, *Literary History of the United States* (New York: Macmillan, 1948), p. 1138; VWB, *The Wine of the Puritans*, p. 16.

24. Wendell, *Literary History of America*, pp. 319–20.

25. Santayana, *The Genteel Tradition: Nine Essays*, ed. Douglas L. Wilson (Cambridge, Mass.: Harvard Univ. Press, 1967), pp. 30, 52.

26. VWB, *The Wine of the Puritans*, p. 51; Wells, *The Future in America: A Search after Realities* (New York: Harper, 1906), pp. 100, 152–54, 235; Dickinson, *A Modern Symposium* (New York: Frederick Ungar, 1962), pp. 98–101; Arnold, *Civilization in the United States* (Boston: Cupples, 1888), pp. 90, 177.

27. VWB, *The Wine of the Puritans*, pp. 64, 78.

28. Ibid., pp. 86–88, 93, 95–98, 105–09.

29. Ibid., pp. 55, 116, 119, 118.

30. Ibid., p. 98.

31. Ibid., pp. 48–49, 78–79, 21, 83.

32. Ibid., pp. 37–40.

33. VWB, *Autobiography*, pp. 132–33; VWB, *The Wine of the Puritans*, pp. 9–10.

34. VWB, *The Wine of the Puritans*, pp. 120–21, 123, 125–26.

35. *The Portable Matthew Arnold*, ed. Lionel Trilling (New York: Viking, 1949), p. 237; VWB, *The Wine of the Puritans*, pp. 133–36, 142. This interpretation of the dialogue rests on the correction of a typographical error on page 134. There is no quotation mark following the word CAPITAL at the end of the first paragraph, but clearly Brooks meant to shift speakers at that point. If a quotation mark is not supplied, then it is Brooks who speaks of "sacrifice" on page 133 and Graeling who says ". . . that is what I mean by sacrifice" on page 134.

36. Wells, *The Future in America*, p. 17; Dickinson, *Modern Symposium*, p. 94; VWB, *The Wine of the Puritans*, pp. 89–90.

37. ESB to "Alice," July 19, 1911, courtesy of Charles V. W. Brooks; Perkins to VWB, Aug. 21, 1908, Brooks MSS.; VWB to ESB, Aug. 4 and 7, 1909, Brooks MSS.

38. VWB, "Mr. Howells at Work at Seventy-two," *World's Work* (May 1909), p. 11548; VWB, *Autobiography*, p. 157.

39. Kennerley to VWB, June 4, 1909, Brooks MSS.; VWB to ESB, Aug. 4, 1909, Brooks MSS.

40. VWB to ESB, Aug. 4, Sept. 23, and Oct. 7, 1909, Brooks MSS.; VWB, *Autobiography*, p. 158.

41. VWB to ESB, Nov. 6, 1909, Brooks MSS.

42. VWB to ESB, Nov. 18, Dec. 3, and Dec. 29, 1909, Brooks MSS.

43. VWB to ESB, Nov. 18, Dec. 3, Dec. 29, 1909, and Jan. 3, 1910, Brooks MSS.

44. VWB to ESB, Jan. 3, 1910, Brooks MSS.

45. VWB, *Autbiography*, pp. 153–55; VWB, *Oliver Allston*, p. 25; Conrad Aiken, *Ushant* (New York: Duell, Sloan and Pearce, 1952), p. 71.

46. VWB, *Autobiography*, pp. 173–80; VWB, "John Butler Yeats," Box 37, Brooks MSS.; VWB, "A Reviewer's Notebook," *Freeman*, 4 (Mar. 1, 1922), 598; *John Sloan's New York Scene*, ed. Bruce St. John (New York: Harper, 1965), p. 446; William I. Homer, *Robert Henri and His Circle* (Ithaca, N.Y.: Cornell Univ. Press, 1969), pp. 205–06.

47. Aiken, *Bring! Bring!* (New York: Boni, 1925), p. 168; VWB to ESB, Sept. 23, 1909, Brooks MSS.; VWB, *Autbiography*, p. 176.

48. VWB, *Autobiography*, pp. 122, 184, 191; VWB, *America's Coming-of-Age* (New York: Heubsch, 1915), p. 161.

49. *John Sloan's New York Scene*, p. 372; VWB, *Joan Sloan: A Painter's Life* (New York: Dutton, 1955), pp. 71–76; See also Bennard Perlman, *The Immortal Eight* (New York: Exposition, 1962).

50. VWB to ESB, Jan. 31, 1910, Brooks MSS.; Homer, *Robert Henri*, pp. 158–64; VWB, *John Sloan*, pp. 10, 74.

51. VWB, "Notes on Vernon Lee," *Forum* (Apr. 1911), pp. 448–49.

52. Ibid., pp. 453–55.

53. Hackett to Harry Steger, Jan. 17, 1910, Brooks MSS.; VWB to ESB, June 5 and 12, 1910, Brooks MSS.

54. ESB to Charles V. W. Brooks, Aug. 3, 1943, Brooks MSS.; *John Sloan's New York Scene*, p. 449; ESB to VWB, Sept. 6, 1910, Brooks MSS.; VWB to ESB, Aug. 4, 1909, Brooks MSS.

55. VWB, "The New Temple of Taste," Brooks MSS.; VWB, "Notes on Vernon Lee," p. 454.

56. VWB, "Notes on Vernon Lee," p. 454; VWB, *The Soul: An Essay Towards a Point of View* (San Francisco: privately printed, 1910), p. 6.

57. VWB, *The Soul*, pp. 10, 5, 6, 9, 7.

58. Ibid., pp. 5–8, 10.

59. Ibid., pp. 19, 29.

60. Ibid., pp. 12, 15, 16, 31, 32.

61. Ibid., pp. 22–27.

62. Ibid., pp. 35–39.

63. Ibid., p. 40.

THE ART OF SOCIETY

1. VWB to ESB, Jan. 6, 1911, Brooks MSS.
2. VWB to ESB, Aug. 7, 1909, Brooks MSS.
3. VWB to ESB, Jan. 3, 1911, Brooks MSS.
4. VWB, *Autobiography,* p. 71.
5. VWB to ESB, Mar. 13, 1911, Brooks MSS.
6. Ryder to VWB, Jan. 13, 1911, Brooks MSS.; ESB to "Alice," July 19, 1911, courtesy of Charles V. W. Brooks; ESB to Charles V. W. Brooks, Aug. 3, 1943, Brooks MSS.
7. ESB to "Alice," July 19, 1911, courtesy of Charles V. W. Brooks.
8. Ibid.
9. ESB to VWB, Apr. 27, 1907, Jan. 22, 1911, and Feb. 28, 1907, Brooks MSS.; VWB to ESB, "Sunday" [Mar. 1911] and July 6, 1907, Brooks MSS.
10. VWB, *Autobiography,* pp. 114–15; ESB to Sallie Brooks, Feb. 26 [1912], Brooks MSS.
11. VWB, "The Twilight of the Arts," *Poet Lore* (Autumn 1913), pp. 322, 331; VWB, Stanford lecture notes, Box 47, Brooks MSS.
12. VWB, *Autobiography,* pp. 207–08.
13. Dayal to VWB, Aug. 1, 1912, Brooks MSS.; VWB to Warren Blake, Oct. 10, 1912, Blake MSS.
14. VWB, *Autobiography,* pp. 201–03.
15. VWB, "Hans Zinsser," Box 37, Brooks MSS.; VWB, *Autobiography,* p. 202.
16. VWB, *The Malady of the Ideal* (Philadelphia: Univ. of Pennsylvania Press, 1947), pp. 22–24.
17. Ibid., pp. 85–86.
18. Ibid., p. 28; VWB, *Johnson Addington Symonds: A Biographical Study* (New York: Mitchell Kennerley, 1914), pp. 44, 46, 50, 234, 136.
19. Horatio F. Brown, *John Addington Symonds: A Biography Compiled from His Papers and Correspondence* (New York: Scribner's, 1895); Phyllis Grosskurth, *John Addington Symonds: A Biography* (London: Longman's, 1964), p. 270; VWB, *John Addington Symonds,* pp. 211, 19–20.
20. VWB, *The World of H. G. Wells* (New York: Mitchell Kennerley, 1915), pp. 25, 38, 42–43.
21. Ibid., pp. 14–15.
22. VWB, *The Malady of the Ideal,* pp. 47, 52; VWB, *John Addington Symonds,* p. 232.
23. VWB, *H. G. Wells,* pp. 153, 155, 178–79, 168.
24. Ibid., pp. 183–84; VWB, *The Wine of the Puritans,* p. 136.
25. VWB, *Autobiography,* p. 214.
26. VWB to ESB, July 30 and Nov. 11, 1913, Brooks MSS.
27. VWB to ESB, July 24, 1913, Brooks MSS.; VWB, *Autobiography,* pp. 221–28; Lippmann, *A Preface to Politics* (Ann Arbor: Univ. of Michigan Press, 1962), pp. 11, 229, 59–60; VWB to ESB [July 1913], Brooks MSS.

28. VWB to ESB, July 24 and 30, 1913, Brooks MSS.

29. VWB to ESB, July 24 and 28, 1913, Brooks MSS.

30. VWB, *Autobiography*, pp. 216–19; VWB to ESB, Aug. 8, 1913, Brooks MSS.

31. VWB, "Toward a National Culture," *Seven Arts*, 1 (Mar. 1917), 535; VWB to ESB, Aug. 8, 1913, Brooks MSS.

32. VWB, *Autobiography*, p. 215.

33. *Editor to Author: The Letters of Maxwell E. Perkins*, ed. John Hall Wheelock (New York: Scribner's, 1950), p. 10.

34. *Cambridge Review* (May 6, 1914) and *Mercure de France* (Nov. 6, 1913), clippings in Brooks MSS.

35. VWB, *Autobiography*, p. 236.

36. Ibid., p. 210; ESB to Lewis Mumford, Jan. 31, 1929, Brooks MSS.

37. VWB to Jordan, July 21, 1914, Jordan MSS.

38. ESB to Sallie Brooks Hibbard, Aug. 9, 1914, Brooks MSS.

39. Ibid.

40. Ibid.

41. ESB to Charles V. W. Brooks, Aug. 29, 1934, Brooks MSS.; VWB, *Autobiography*, p. 504.

42. VWB to ESB, Aug. 31, 1914, Brooks MSS.

43. Ibid.

44. VWB, *America's Coming-of-Age*, pp. 6–7.

45. Ibid., pp. 8–10.

46. Ibid., pp. 45–46, 70.

47. Ibid., pp. 78–79, 91–92.

48. Wendell, *A Literary History of America*, p. 439.

49. VWB, *America's Coming-of-Age*, pp. 112–13, 118.

50. Lippmann to VWB, Sept. 2, 1913, Brooks MSS.; VWB, *America's Coming-of-Age*, pp. 141–42.

51. VWB, *America's Coming-of-Age*, pp. 148, 153–54, 160.

52. Ibid., pp. 164–65, 33.

53. Ibid., pp. 33–34.

54. Ibid., pp. 176, 168, 180.

55. Ibid., pp. 34, 128, 176.

56. Ibid., pp. 177–80.

57. Ibid., pp. 179, 183.

58. Ibid., p. 183.

59. Ibid., p. 120.

60. Ibid., p. 181.

61. Ibid., p. 29. Cf. Lippmann, *A Preface to Politics*, pp. 19, 38. Another clear example of the influence of Lippmann's book on *America's Coming-of-Age* is offered by a comparison of Brooks's opening discussion of the "tree-top dream of the economic man" taught in American universities (p. 4) with Lippmann's account of his Harvard economics course (pp. 60–61).

BEGINNING LOW

1. VWB, *Autobiography,* pp. 269–71; VWB to ESB, Aug. 3 and 4, 1915, Brooks MSS.; Shevchenko Scientific Society, *Ukraine: A Concise Encyclopedia* (Toronto: Univ. of Toronto, 1963), p. 705.

2. VWB, *Autobiography,* pp. 241–42.

3. ESB to Charles V. W. Brooks, Mar. 31, 1942, Brooks MSS.; Lippmann to VWB, Sept. 20, 1916, Brooks MSS.; VWB to ESB, July 2 and Aug. 11, 1914, Brooks MSS.

4. VWB to ESB, July 27, 1915, Brooks MSS.

5. Huebsch to VWB, May 1916, Brooks MSS.

6. Sherman, "The Battle of the Brows," *Nation* (Feb. 17, 1916), p. 196; Traubel, rev. of *America's Coming-of-Age, Conservator* (Jan. 1916), p. 169.

7. Van Doren to VWB, Mar. 13, 1934, Brooks MSS.; Frank to VWB, n.d., Brooks MSS.

8. *The Memoirs of Waldo Frank,* ed. Alan Trachtenberg (Amherst: Univ. of Massachusetts Press, 1973), p. 87.

9. "Editorials," *Seven Arts,* 1 (Nov. 1916), 52–53, and in the same issue, "A Preface to the December Number," p. 95.

10. VWB, "The Splinter of Ice," *Seven Arts,* 1 (Jan. 1917), 270.

11. VWB, "Enterprise," *Seven Arts,* 1 (Nov. 1916), 57, 60.

12. VWB, "Young America," *Seven Arts,* 1 (Dec. 1916), 146–47, 150–51.

13. VWB, "The Splinter of Ice," pp. 270, 273, 276, 279–80.

14. VWB, "An American Oblomov," *Dial,* 62 (Mar. 22, 1917), 244–45.

15. VWB, "Introductory Note," in *The Shock of Recognition,* ed. Edmund Wilson (Garden City, New York: Doubleday, 1943), pp. 1256–57; *Letters of Sherwood Anderson,* ed. H. M. Jones (Boston: Little, Brown, 1953), pp. 10, 35–36.

16. VWB, "Toward a National Culture," pp. 541, 544, 537–38, 546–47.

17. VWB, "The Culture of Industrialism," *Seven Arts,* 1 (Apr. 1917), 662, 664, 665.

18. Ibid., pp. 665–66.

19. VWB, "Our Critics," *Seven Arts,* 2 (May 1917), 104, 108, 113.

20. VWB, "Our Awakeners," *Seven Arts,* 2 (June 1917), 236, 242.

21. VWB, "The Splinter of Ice," p. 278; VWB, "Our Awakeners," p. 242.

22. VWB, "Our Awakeners," pp. 240, 245, 243.

23. VWB, "Toward a National Culture," pp. 539, 547.

24. VWB, "The Splinter of Ice," p. 271.

25. VWB, "Randolph Bourne," in *Fenollosa and His Circle* (New York: Dutton, 1962), p. 260; Bourne, *History of a Literary Radical and Other Essays,* ed. VWB (New York: Huebsch, 1920), pp. 17–18.

26. VWB, *Fenollosa,* p. 265; Bourne, "Youth," *Atlantic Monthly,* 109 (Apr. 1912), 441.

27. Louis Filler, *Randolph Bourne* (Washington: American Council on Public

Affairs, 1943), p. 61; Bourne, "John Dewey's Philosophy," *New Republic* (Mar. 13, 1915), p. 154.

28. VWB, "Our Awakeners," pp. 244–45; VWB, *Letters and Leadership* (New York: Huebsch, 1918), pp. 111–12.

29. Bourne, "Trans-National America," *Atlantic Monthly*, 118 (July 1916), 86–97.

30. "Who Willed American Participation?" *New Republic*, 10 (Apr. 14, 1917), 308–09.

31. Bourne, "The War and the Intellectuals," *Seven Arts*, 2 (June 1917), 133; Bourne, "A War Diary," *Seven Arts*, 2 (Sept. 1917), 547.

32. ESB to VWB, July 29, 1917, Brooks MSS.; VWB, "War's Heritage to Youth," *Dial*, 64 (Jan. 17, 1918), 47–50.

33. VWB, *Autobiography*, p. 286; *Memoirs of Waldo Frank*, pp. 90–91, 94.

34. VWB, "Our Awakeners," p. 242.

35. Bourne, "The War and the Intellectuals," pp. 140–41; Dewey, "The Future of Pacifism," *New Republic* (July 28, 1917), p. 358; Bourne, "Twilight of Idols," *Seven Arts* (Oct. 1917), pp. 690, 695; VWB, "Our Awakeners," p. 238.

36. VWB to ESB, July 27, 1917, Brooks MSS.; ESB to VWB, July 29, 1917, Brooks MSS.

37. VWB, *Autobiography*, pp. 285–86; John Moreau, *Randolph Bourne: Legend and Reality* (Washington: Public Affairs Press, 1966), p. 191; VWB to ESB, July 27 and Aug. 8, 1917, Brooks MSS.

38. VWB to ESB, Aug. 8, 1917, Brooks MSS.; Bourne's letter to Gregory quoted in Moreau, *Randolph Bourne*, p. 191.

39. "Personal History," Brooks file, Four Winds, Katonah, New York: VWB to ESB, Sept. 6 and 12, 1917, Brooks MSS.

40. VWB to ESB, Sept. 12, 1917, Brooks MSS. For the various and occasionally contradictory accounts of the end of the *Seven Arts* see also William J. Wasserstrom, *The Time of The Dial* (Syracuse, New York: Syracuse Univ. Press, 1963), p. 74; Nicholas Joost, *Years of Transition: The Dial, 1912–1920* (Barre, Mass.: Barre, 1967), p. 141; Oppenheim, "The Story of the Seven Arts," *American Mercury*, 20 (June 1930), 164; *Memoirs of Waldo Frank*, p. 93.

41. VWB, "War's Heritage to Youth," p. 50.

42. VWB to ESB, Sept. 6 and Oct. 1, 1917, Brooks MSS.

43. VWB to ESB, Oct. 1, 1917, Brooks MSS.

44. VWB, "On Creating a Usable Past," *Dial*, 64 (Apr. 11, 1918), 339.

45. Ibid., p. 341.

46. *The World of Randolph Bourne*, ed. Lillian Schlissel (New York: Dutton, 1965), p. 325; Bourne to VWB, Mar. 27, 1918, Brooks MSS.

47. Bourne, "Traps for the Unwary," *Dial*, 64 (Mar. 28, 1918), 277–78; Monroe, "Mr. Bourne on Traps," *Poetry*, 12 (May 1918), 91–94; Bourne and VWB, "The Retort Courteous," *Poetry*, 12 (Sept. 1918), 341–44.

48. *World of Randolph Bourne*, p. 325; VWB, *Fenollosa*, p. 259; Bourne to VWB, Aug. 5, 1918, Brooks MSS.; VWB to ESB, Sept. 6, 1917, Brooks MSS.

49. VWB to Frank, Nov. 6, 1918, Frank MSS.

50. VWB to Frank, Feb. 15, 1919, Frank MSS.; VWB to Sallie Brooks Hibbard, Mar. 15, 1919, Brooks MSS.

51. VWB to Sallie Brooks Hibbard, Mar. 15, 1915, Brooks MSS.; VWB, *Autobiography,* pp. 195–96; VWB to Frank, Feb. 1 and May 22, 1919, Frank MSS.

52. Frank, *Our America* (New York: Boni, 1919), pp. 196–97; VWB to Frank, Nov. 27, 1919, Frank MSS.; Frank, *Salvos* (New York: Boni, 1924), p. 173; Hackett, "Creative America," *New Republic,* 16 (Sept. 28, 1918), 262.

53. Anderson to Crane, in *Letters of Sherwood Anderson,* p. 52; Anderson to VWB, June 7, 1918, Brooks MSS.; Bourne to VWB, March 1918, Brooks MSS.; Bourne, *History of a Literary Radical,* p. 29.

54. VWB to Frank, May 22, 1919, Frank MSS.

55. VWB, "Introduction," in Bourne, *History of a Literary Radical,* pp. xii, xiv, xxxi.

56. Ibid., pp. xvi, xxxiii.

57. Ibid., pp. xxxv, xiv, xxxiv.

58. VWB to Huebsch, June 5, 1919, Huebsch MSS.; VWB to Frank, Sept. 23, 1919, Frank MSS.

59. VWB, *The Ordeal of Mark Twain* (New York: Dutton, 1920), pp. 15–16; Sherman, *On Contemporary Literature* (New York: Holt, 1917), p. 45.

60. VWB, *Mark Twain,* pp. 10, 29–30, 61.

61. Ibid., pp. 21–22, 73, 97, 111.

62. Ibid., pp. 207, 211.

63. Ibid., p. 225.

64. Brooks told Robert Spiller, years later, that Hart was his source. See William Wasserstrom, *Van Wyck Brooks* (Minneapolis: Univ. of Minnesota Press, 1968), p. 10.

65. Hart, *The Psychology of Insanity* (Cambridge, Cambridge Univ. Press, 1912), pp. 29, 48.

66. Paine, *Mark Twain: A Biography* (New York: Harper, 1912), I, 74–75.

67. VWB, *Mark Twain,* p. 42.

68. Ibid., p. 95.

69. Ibid., pp. 68, 106.

70. Ibid., pp. 107–08.

71. VWB, *America's Coming-of-Age,* p. 34.

72. VWB, *Mark Twain,* p. 267.

73. VWB, *Autobiography,* p. 426; Van Doren, *The Roving Critic* (New York: Knopf, 1923), p. 54.

FAILURE

1. VWB to ESB, Feb. 24, 1920, Brooks MSS.; Oppenheim to VWB, Sept. 18, 1919, Brooks MSS.; VWB to Huebsch, Dec. 18, 1919, Huebsch MSS.

2. VWB to Sallie Brooks Hibbard, Dec. 30, 1919, Brooks MSS.; VWB to ESB, Feb. 24, 1920, Brooks MSS.

3. VWB to ESB, Mar. 1, 1920, Brooks MSS.

4. VWB to ESB, Mar. 6, 1920, Brooks MSS.

5. VWB to ESB, Apr. 10, 17, 23 and "Thursday," 1920, Brooks MSS.

6. VWB to ESB, Apr. 25, 1920, Brooks MSS.; VWB to Sallie Brooks Hibbard, Dec. 30, 1919, Brooks MSS.

7. VWB, *Autobiography*, pp. 253–68, 362–79; Interview with Oliver K. Brooks, Mar. 1972.

8. VWB, *Autobiography*, p. 254; Interview with Oliver K. Brooks, Mar. 1972.

9. Burton Rascoe, "A Bookman's Notes," *Bookman*, 66 (Oct. 1927), 188–89.

10. VWB, "The Literary Life," in *Civilization in the United States*, ed. Harold Stearns (New York: Harcourt, 1922), pp. 180, 182, 191, 197.

11. Susan Turner, *A History of* The Freeman: *Literary Landmark of the Early Twenties* (New York: Columbia Univ. Press, 1963), pp. 20–28: VWB to ESB, Apr. 17, 1920, Brooks MSS.; Frank Luther Mott, *A History of American Magazines* (Cambridge, Mass.: Harvard Univ. Press, Belknap, 1968), v, 88–91; Francis Neilson, *The Story of "The Freeman,"* supp. to *American Journal of Economics and Sociology*, 6 (Oct. 1946), 6, 30–31.

12. VWB, *Autobiography*, p. 306; Nock to VWB, Apr. 16, 1922, Brooks MSS.

13. Albert Jay Nock, *Memoirs of a Superfluous Man* (New York: Harper, 1943), pp. 167–74; Huebsch to VWB, Nov. 30, 1922, Brooks MSS.; VWB to Huebsch, Nov. 23, 1922, Huebsch MSS.

14. Llewelyn Powys, *The Verdict of Bridlegoose* (New York: Harcourt, 1926), pp. 103–04.

15. VWB to Fletcher, Feb. 25, 1924, Fletcher MSS.; VWB, *Autobiography*, p. 312.

16. "Lewis Mumford," in *Twentieth Century Authors*, ed. Stanley J. Kunitz and Howard Haycraft (New York: H. W. Wilson, 1942), pp. 995–96; Mumford, "The Beginnings of a Friendship," *The Van Wyck Brooks — Lewis Mumford Letters*, ed. Robert Spiller (New York: Dutton, 1970), p. 1; Mumford, "The Image of Randolph Bourne," *New Republic*, 64 (Sept. 24, 1930), 151–52.

17. Mumford, "The Beginnings of a Friendship," pp. 1–2.

18. Mumford, *The Story of Utopias* (New York: Boni, 1922), p. v; Mumford, *The Golden Day* (New York: Boni, 1926), pp. 10–11.

19. Neilson, *The Story of "The Freeman,"* p. 25; *Brooks-Mumford Letters*, pp. 14, 16–17.

20. VWB to Arvin, Nov. 5, 1920, Arvin MSS.

21. Arvin, "The Everlasting No," *Freeman*, 3 (June 1, 1921), 283; VWB to Arvin, May 3, 1921, Arvin MSS.; Arvin, "The Foundering Grandsons," *Freeman*, 4 (Jan. 18, 1922), 451; Arvin, "Tilting at Windmills," *Freeman*, 7 (July 11, 1923), 430.

22. VWB to Arvin, June 8, 1921, and Feb. 13, 1922, Arvin MSS.

23. VWB, *Autobiography*, p. 223; Turner, *History of* The Freeman, p. 77.

24. VWB, "A Reviewer's Notebook," *Freeman*, 1 (June 9, 1920), 311; Mary

Austin to the Freeman, June 8, 1920, Brooks MSS.; VWB to Eleanor Manson Stimson, Feb. 12, 1921, Brooks MSS.; VWB to Austin, July 1, 1920, Austin MSS.; Austin to VWB, Aug. 12, 1920, Brooks MSS.

25. *Freeman,* 2 (Oct. 13, 1920), 119; i (Aug. 18, 1920), 550; 2 (Nov. 17, 1920), 239; 5 (Mar. 22, 1922), 47.

26. *Freeman,* 4 (Nov. 2, 1921), 191; Stuart Sherman, "Is There Anything to Be Said for Literary Tradition?" *Bookman,* 52 (Oct. 1920), 111; VWB, "Professor Sherman's Tradition," *Freeman,* 2 (Oct. 27, 1920), 154; *Freeman,* 7 (June 20, 1923), 358–59; 5 (Apr. 5, 1922), 94–95.

27. *Freeman,* 3 (Mar. 23, 1921), 47; 1 (June 16, 1920), 334; 5 (Apr. 5, 1922), 95.

28. VWB to Arvin, Aug. 8, 1921, Arvin MSS.

29. VWB to ESB, Apr. 17, 1920, Brooks MSS.

30. *Freeman,* 1 (Apr. 28, 1920), 164; 4 (Feb. 1, 1922), 502; VWB to Bradford, Apr. 17, 1922, Bradford MSS.

31. *Freeman,* 2 (Sept. 15, 1920), 23; 1 (June 16, 1920), 16; 4 (Nov. 30, 1921), 186; 7 (Aug. 8, 1923), 527; VWB to Fletcher, Feb. 25, 1924, Fletcher MSS.

32. *Freeman,* 4 (Sept. 21, 1921), 47; 1 (May 12, 1920), 215; 3 (June 29, 1921), 383; 3 (Aug. 31, 1921), 599.

33. VWB to Arvin, Oct. 15, 1921, Arvin MSS.; *Freeman,* 6 (Jan. 24, 1923), 479; 3 (Aug. 10, 1921), 511.

34. *Freeman,* 7 (July 25, 1923), 479.

35. ESB to Wheelock, Aug. 27, 1929, Scribner MSS.

36. VWB to Sallie Brooks Hibbard, May 19, 1922, Brooks MSS.; VWB to Bradford, May 4, 1922, Bradford MSS.; VWB to Arvin, Feb. 13, 1922, Arvin MSS.; *Brooks-Mumford Letters,* pp. 16–17; Maynard, "Van Wyck Brooks," *Catholic World,* 140 (Jan. 1935), 416–17.

37. Bradford to VWB, June 19, 1923, Brooks MSS.; VWB to Anderson, June 18, 1923, Anderson MSS.

38. VWB to Huebsch, Nov. 23, 1922, Huebsch MSS.; Huebsch to VWB, Nov. 30, 1922, Brooks MSS.

39. VWB to ESB, Jan. 12, Jan. 25, and Feb. 12, 1923, Brooks MSS.

40. VWB to ESB, Jan. 29, Feb. 28, and Mar. 2, 1923, Brooks MSS.

41. VWB to ESB, Mar. 2, 1923, Brooks MSS.; Nicholas Joost, *Scofield Thayer and the Dial* (Carbondale: Southern Illinois Univ. Press, 1964), p. 85.

42. VWB to ESB, Jan. 25, 1923, Brooks MSS.; Ezra Pound, "Historical Survey," *Little Review,* 8 (Autumn 1921), 40.

43. VWB to Frank, Dec. 3, 1922, Frank MSS.; VWB to ESB, Jan. 12, 1923, Brooks MSS.

44. VWB to ESB, Jan. 12, 1923, Brooks MSS.; *Letters of Sherwood Anderson,* pp. 78, 84, 130; Anderson, *A Story-Teller's Story,* ed. Ray Lewis White (Cleveland: Case-Western Reserve Univ. Press, 1968), p. 300.

45. VWB to Anderson, June 18, July 23, and "Sunday evening" [Sept.], 1923, Anderson MSS.

46. "Comment," *Dial,* 76 (Jan. 1924), 96; Munson, "Van Wyck Brooks: His Sphere and His Encroachments," *Dial,* 78 (Jan. 1925), 36, 42; Wilson,

"Imaginary Conversation: Mr. Van Wyck Brooks and Mr. Scott Fitzgerald," *New Republic* (Apr. 30, 1924), pp. 249, 251–52; Frank, *Salvos,* p. 174; Rosenfeld, *Port of New York* (New York: Harcourt, 1924), pp. 57, 63.

47. Mary Colum, "Statement," Brooks file, Four Winds; Perry to vwb, Sept. 21, 1923, Brooks mss.; *Brooks-Mumford Letters,* pp. 25, 27.

48. Turner, *History of* The Freeman, p. 172.

49. vwb to F. E. Kenyon, Mar. 26, 1924, Brooks mss.

50. *Brooks-Mumford Letters,* p. 27; vwb, "The Literary Life," p. 190.

51. *Freeman,* 4 (Oct. 26, 1921), 166; 6 (Feb. 14, 1923), 551; vwb, "The Literary Life," p. 180.

52. *Freeman,* 3 (May 18, 1921), 239. I have not found a single source to support William Wasserstrom's statement that Brooks substituted Emerson for Whitman as his subject on learning of Whitman's homosexuality from Malcolm Cowley (Wasserstrom, *Van Wyck Brooks,* p. 19). Lewis Mumford informed me by letter that he had no memory of Brooks's having considered Whitman as a subject in 1924. Cowley said in an interview that he had only a vague memory of Brooks considering Whitman as his subject and no recollection of the incident Wasserstrom recounts. Wasserstrom offers no documentation except for ". . . so the story goes."

53. *Brooks-Mumford Letters,* p. 27; vwb to Bradford, Aug. 23, 1925, Bradford mss.

54. Mary Colum, "Statement," Brooks file, Four Winds; "Personal History," Brooks file, Four Winds.

55. *Brooks-Mumford Letters,* p. 27; Mary Colum, "Statement," Brooks file, Four Winds; "Personal History," Brooks file, Four Winds.

56. Wilson, rev. of *The Pilgrimage of Henry James, New Republic* (May 6, 1925), pp. 283–85.

57. vwb, *The Pilgrimage of Henry James* (New York: Dutton, 1925), pp. 12, 18, 1.

58. Ibid., pp. 7–8.

59. Ibid., pp. 103–04.

60. Ibid., pp. 49, 51, 67, 133–34, 86–87, 139.

61. Wilson, rev. of *Henry James,* p. 284.

62. vwb, *Henry James,* p. 122; Wilson, rev. of *Henry James,* p. 285.

63. vwb, *Autobiography,* p. 439: Edel, "Under Skies Always Shining," *New York Herald Tribune Book Week* (Feb. 21, 1965), p. 10.

64. vwb, *Henry James,* pp. 88, 138.

A SEASON IN HELL

1. "Personal History," Brooks file, Four Winds.

2. vwb to esb, Feb. 12 and 28, 1923, Brooks mss.

3. vwb to esb, Mar. 29, 1923, July 27, 1917, and Feb. 24, 1920, Brooks mss.; esb to Charles Lambert, n.d., Four Winds.

4. "Personal History," Brooks file, Four Winds.

5. VWB, *Autobiography*, pp. 324-25; Mary Colum, "Statement," Brooks file, Four Winds.

6. Mary Colum, "Statement," Brooks file, Four Winds; Mary Colum, "An American Critic: Van Wyck Brooks," *Dial*, 76 (Jan. 1924), 41.

7. Mary Colum, "Statement," Brooks file, Four Winds.

8. *Brooks-Mumford Letters*, p. 33.

9. VWB to Spingarn, June 17 and Aug. 28, 1925, Spingarn MSS.; VWB to Bradford, Aug. 23, 1925, Bradford MSS.; "Personal History," Brooks file, Four Winds.

10. VWB to Bradford, Aug. 23 and Sept. 29, 1925, Bradford MSS.; VWB, *Autobiography*, p. 439.

11. VWB to Spingarn, Aug. 28 and Sept. 15, 1925, Spingarn MSS.

12. VWB to Arvin, Apr. 30, 1926, Arvin MSS.; VWB, *America's Coming-of-Age*, p. 77; VWB to Spingarn, June 20, 1926, Spingarn MSS.

13. Brooks told Spingarn (June 20, 1926, Spingarn MSS.) that he had written eighty thousand words before he gave up, and that was approximately the length of the published volume. Six of the book's twenty-three chapters appeared almost intact in a collection of miscellany, *Emerson and Others,* which Brooks published with Dutton in 1927. And the first chapter, on Mary Moody Emerson, appeared as "The Cassandra of New England" in the February 1927 issue of *Scribner's Magazine.*

14. VWB, *The Life of Emerson* (New York: Dutton, 1931), pp. 7, 9, 126, 315.

15. Ibid., pp. 30, 243, 245-46; VWB to Perkins, n.d., Scribner MSS.

16. VWB, *Emerson*, pp. 43, 124.

17. Interview with Oliver K. Brooks, Mar. 1972.

18. VWB to ESB, Feb. 19, 1926, Brooks MSS.; *Dear Scott/Dear Max: The Fitzgerald-Perkins Correspondence,* ed. John Kuehl and Jackson Bryer (New York: Scribner's, 1971), p. 140.

19. "Personal History," and Mary Colum, "Statement," Brooks file, Four Winds.

20. Winokur, *Manic Depressive Illness,* p. 17.

21. ESB to Charles V. W. Brooks, July 18, 1943, Brooks MSS.

22. ESB to Mumford, June 8, 1929, Brooks MSS.

23. *Dear Scott/Dear Max,* pp. 119, 140.

24. *American Caravan,* ed. VWB *et al.* (New York: Macaulay, 1927), p. x; VWB, "The Evolution of a Critic," *New York Herald Tribune Books,* Apr. 18, 1926, p. 5.

25. VWB, "Herman Melville," *New York Herald Tribune Books,* May 16, 1926, pp. 1-2; VWB, *Autobiography,* pp. 441-42; VWB to ESB, May 15, 1926, Brooks MSS.

26. VWB to Henry A. Murray, Apr. 2, 1926, courtesy of Professor Murray; VWB, "Herman Melville," *Dictionary of American Biography* (New York: Scribner's, 1927), VI, 524; VWB, *Emerson and Others,* pp. 174, 192-93;

Lewis Mumford, who wrote his *Melville* (1929) during Brooks's illness, said years later that Brooks had passed "through a period of blackness not altogether unlike that which Herman Melville encountered at a similar moment of his life." Mumford, "Van Wyck Brooks," *Proceedings* of the American Academy of Arts and Letters, Second Series, No. 14 (1964), p. 399.

27. Pound, "Brancusi," *Little Review*, 8 (Autumn 1921), 3.

28. ESB to Charles V. W. Brooks, July 18, 1943, Brooks MSS.; Mary Colum, "Statement," Brooks file, Four Winds; VWB, *Emerson and Others*, p. 188; VWB, *Oliver Allston*, p. 259.

29. ESB to Mumford, Aug. 8 [1928], Brooks MSS.

30. VWB to ESB, Oct. 19, 1926, and "Friday morning," Brooks MSS.

31. Mary Colum, "Statement," Brooks file, Four Winds; ESB to Charles V. W. Brooks, July 18, 1943, Brooks MSS.

32. VWB to Arvin, Feb. 15, 1927, Arvin MSS.; "Personal History," Brooks file, Four Winds.

33. ESB to Charles V. W. Brooks, July 28, 1943, Brooks MSS.; "Personal History," Brooks file, Four Winds; VWB, *Autobiography*, pp. 442–43.

34. ESB to Charles V. W. Brooks, Feb. 21, Mar. 2, and Mar. 12, 1927, Brooks MSS.

35. ESB to Charles V. W. Brooks, May 11, 1927, Brooks MSS.; VWB to Charles V. W. Brooks, Apr. 20, 1927, Brooks MSS.; "Personal History," Brooks file, Four Winds; ESB to Mumford, Aug. 8, 1928, Brooks MSS.

36. Brooks file, Four Winds; VWB, *Autobiography*, pp. 440, 364–66.

37. VWB, "Four Aces in Criticism," *Independent*, 120 (June 16, 1928), 580; Foerster, *American Criticism* (Boston: Houghton Mifflin, 1928), pp. 224–25.

38. Lee to VWB, Apr. 6, 1937, Brooks MSS.; Lee to ESB, July 25, 1928, Brooks MSS.

39. Lee, *Rest Working* (Northampton, Mass.: Coordination Guild, 1925), pp. 281–82; Lee to ESB, July 25 and Aug. 26, 1928, Brooks MSS.

40. Lee to ESB, Aug. 26, 1928, Brooks MSS.; Zinsser to Henry A. Murray, Sept. 26, 1928, Brooks MSS.; ESB to Zinsser, Oct. 9, 1928, Brooks MSS.

41. Zinsser to Murray, Sept. 26, 1928, Brooks MSS.

42. *Brooks-Mumford Letters*, pp. 54–55; ESB to Mumford, Oct. 31 and Aug. 8, 1928, Brooks MSS.

43. Wheelock to ESB, Feb. 18, 1929, Brooks MSS.; ESB to Wheelock, Feb. 23, 1929. Scribner MSS.; ESB to Mumford, Oct. 31, 1928, Brooks MSS.; Wilson, *Upstate* (New York: Farrar, Straus and Giroux, 1971), p. 186.

44. ESB to Lee, Nov. 29, 1928, Lee MSS.; Wheelock to VWB, Oct. 30, 1928, Brooks MSS.; VWB to Arvin, Nov. 16 and Dec. 9, 1928, Arvin MSS.; Jung to ESB, Mar. 24, 1929, Brooks MSS.; Winokur, *Manic Depressive Illness*, pp. 2–3.

45. ESB to Spingarn, Apr. 16 and 29, 1929, Spingarn MSS.; ESB to Mumford, Apr. 21, 1929, Brooks MSS.

46. Brooks file, Four Winds.
47. VWB, *Autobiography,* pp. 439, 443–44; Brooks file, Four Winds; ESB to Charles V. W. Brooks, Aug. 27, 1943, Brooks MSS.
48. Zinsser to Mumford, May 5, May 14, and June 21, 1929, Brooks MSS.; *Brooks-Mumford Letters,* p. 56.
49. ESB to Henry Stimson, Oct. 4, 1930, Stimson MSS.; ESB to Charles V. W. Brooks, July 28, 1943, Brooks MSS.
50. Brooks file, Four Winds.
51. VWB to ESB, n.d., Brooks file, Four Winds.
52. Brooks file, Four Winds: ESB to Wheelock, Nov. 10 and Dec. 27, 1929, Scribner MSS.
53. "Although psychologic factors are rarely etiologic, they play a major role in the character of the symptoms and in prolonging the illness beyond its normal course" (Samuel H. Kraines, *Mental Depressions and Their Treatment* [New York: Macmillan, 1957], pp. 76–77). There are studies which indicate that the illness is most prevalent among "socially established families with traditions of intellectuality," who, by pressuring their children to conform and achieve, breed in them "a need for social approbation and success" (Winokur, *Manic Depressive Illness,* p. 24). These, certainly, were the conditions of Brooks's childhood and may explain his ambivalence toward money and success, which, in order to be consistent with his radical position, he ought to have scorned unequivocally. There seems to be no reason to question the diagnosis of Brooks's illness as manic-depressive; he had most of the symptoms Winokur describes — feelings of having committed the unpardonable sin and being an abomination on the face of the earth, along with delusions of persecution, phobias, hallucinations, decreased sexual interest, apathy, anorexia, weight loss, listlessness, sleep disturbance, and psychomotor retardation (p. 17).
54. VWB, *From a Writer's Notebook* (New York: Dutton, 1959), pp. 1–2.
55. *Brooks-Mumford Letters,* pp. 55–56, 60–61; ESB to Mumford, Aug. 29, 1928, and Feb. 26, Mar. 18, and June 8, 1929, Brooks MSS.; Macrae to Mumford, July 12 and 16, 1929, Brooks MSS.
56. *Brooks-Mumford Letters,* p. 59; Van Doren to Perkins, Feb. 10, 1930, Scribner MSS.
57. ESB to Charles Lambert, n.d., Brooks file, Four Winds; ESB to Henry Stimson, Oct. 4, 1930, Stimson MSS.; ESB to Charles V. W. Brooks, July 28, 1943, Brooks MSS.
58. VWB to ESB, Mar. 5, 1930, Brooks file, Four Winds.
59. ESB to Spingarn, Apr. 22, 1931, Spingarn MSS.; ESB to Lambert, Apr. 28, 1931, Brooks file, Four Winds; ESB to Charles V. W. Brooks, July 28, 1943, Brooks MSS.; VWB to Arvin, July 23, 1955, Arvin MSS.
60. VWB to Perkins, July 4, 1931, and "Wed. eve." [Oct. 1931], Scribner MSS.; Perkins to VWB, July 6, Oct. 17, and Oct. 27, 1931, Brooks MSS.; Macrae to Perkins, Nov. 30, 1931, Scribner MSS.

61. ESB to Lambert, Aug. 17, 1931, Brooks file, Four Winds; VWB, *Oliver Allston*, p. 27.
62. *Brooks-Mumford Letters*, pp. 68–72.
63. Ibid., pp. 74, 76.

TENONED AND MORTISED IN GRANITE

1. VWB, *Autobiography*, p. 451; VWB, *Three Essays on America* (New York: Dutton, 1934), p. 12.
2. VWB to Frank, Jan. 14, 1932, Frank MSS.; *Brooks-Mumford Letters*, p. 79.
3. VWB, "Preface," in *The Journal of Gamaliel Bradford* (Boston: Houghton Mifflin, 1933), pp. xi–xii.
4. VWB to M. A. DeWolfe Howe, Feb. 3, 1934, Howe MSS.; VWB to Llewelyn Powys, Feb. 20, 1936, Powys MSS.
5. VWB, *From a Writer's Notebook*, p. 23; VWB to Fletcher, May 18, 1935, Fletcher MSS.
6. VWB to M. A. DeWolfe Howe, Feb. 17, 1933, Howe MSS.; VWB to Charles V. W. Brooks, Jan. 19, 1933, Brooks MSS.
7. VWB, *Three Essays*, p. 11.
8. *Brooks-Mumford Letters*, p. 86.
9. VWB, *Mark Twain* (New York: Dutton, 1920), p. 17; (New York: Dutton, 1933), p. 30.
10. *Brooks-Mumford Letters*, pp. 98, 105, 109–11; VWB to Perkins, "Tues. eve.," Scribner MSS.; VWB to Frank, Jan. 12, 1935, Frank MSS.
11. ESB to Henry Stimson, Oct. 9, 1934, Stimson MSS.; VWB to Charles V. W. Brooks, Oct. 8, 1931, Brooks MSS.; Macmillan Co. to VWB, Dec. 29, 1936, Brooks MSS.
12. VWB to H. S. Canby, Feb. 24, 1944, Canby MSS.
13. VWB to Charles V. W. Brooks, July 3, 1938, Brooks MSS.; ESB to Henry Stimson, Oct. 9, 1934, and Nov. 11, 1935, Stimson MSS.; Henry Stimson to ESB, Oct. 16, 1933, Brooks MSS.; ESB to Lewis Mumford, Jan. 31, 1939, Brooks MSS.; VWB to Fletcher, Apr. 22, 1936, Fletcher MSS.
14. John Macrae to VWB, Oct. 28, 1932, Brooks MSS.; Elliot Macrae to VWB, Sept. 5 and 9, 1935, Dutton file, Brooks MSS.
15. *Brooks-Mumford Letters*, p. 122; VWB to Fletcher, Aug. 17, 1936, Fletcher MSS.; Dutton and Co. to VWB, Apr. 17, 1936, Brooks MSS.
16. *Brooks-Mumford Letters*, pp. 136, 139.
17. ESB to Oliver K. Brooks, n.d., Brooks MSS.; Carl Van Doren, *Books* (Aug. 16, 1936), p. 1; R. P. Blackmur, "A Prophecy of Possibilities," *Nation*, 143 (Aug. 22, 1936), 218–19; Dutton to VWB, Dec. 7, 1936, and Nov. 25, 1940, Brooks MSS.; VWB to Henry Stimson, Feb. 28, 1937, Stimson MSS.
18. ESB to Mumford, Jan. 31, 1939, Brooks MSS.; ESB to Charles V. W. Brooks, "Sunday," [Nov. 1936], Brooks MSS.; Crichton Miller to VWB, May 28, 1937, Brooks MSS.; Lee to VWB, Apr. 6, 1937, Brooks MSS.
19. VWB to Charles V. W. Brooks, Nov. 13, 1937, Brooks MSS.; ESB to

Charles V. W. Brooks, Apr. 27, 1938, Brooks MSS.; ESB to Mumford, Jan. 31, 1939, Brooks MSS.

20. ESB to Mumford, Jan. 31 and Apr. 6, 1939, Brooks MSS.; Carnegie Corporation to VWB, Apr. 3 and Apr. 11, 1939, Brooks MSS.; *Brooks-Mumford Letters,* p. 161.

21. ESB to Charles V. W. Brooks, Feb. 16, 1936, and Apr. 17, 1933, Brooks MSS.; ESB to Mumford, Jan. 31, 1939, Brooks MSS.

22. ESB to Dorothy Hibbard Whyte, Dec. 15, 1935, courtesy of Mrs. Whyte; ESB to Lambert, Aug. 17, 1931, and June 26, 1938, Brooks file, Four Winds.

23. ESB to Henry Stimson, Nov. 11, 1935, Stimson MSS.; VWB to Alyse Gregory, Nov. 13, 1944, Gregory MSS.; VWB, *Oliver Allston,* p. 259; VWB to Powys, Jan. 17, 1937, Powys MSS.

24. ESB to Charles V. W. Brooks, "Sunday night" [May 1933], Sept. 19, 1937, and Aug. 11, and Oct. 16, 1939, Brooks MSS.; ESB to Lambert, July 19 [1938?], Brooks file, Four Winds.

25. Interview with Oliver K. Brooks, Dec. 1973; ESB to Lambert, n.d., Brooks file, Four Winds.

26. VWB to Dorothy Hibbard Whyte, Dec. 15, 1934, courtesy of Mrs. Whyte; VWB to Melville Cane, Dec. 28, 1931, Cane MSS.

27. VWB, *Autobiography,* p. 243; Lewis Mumford to the author, Apr. 30, 1972.

28. VWB to Dorothy Hibbard Whyte, Dec. 15, 1934, courtesy of Mrs. Whyte.

29. VWB to Arvin, Jan. 9 and 20, 1932, Arvin MSS.; Arvin to VWB, Jan. 13 and 24, 1932, Brooks MSS.

30. Arvin, "Brooks's Life of Emerson," *New Republic,* 70 (May 11, 1932), 358; Arvin sent a copy of the review in his letter to VWB, Feb. 20, 1933, Brooks MSS.

31. VWB to Arvin, Apr. 1, 1932, and Dec. 28, 1938, Arvin MSS.; VWB to Harcourt, Brace and Co., Jan. 2, 1938, Brooks MSS.

32. VWB, *Oliver Allston,* p. 140; VWB to Arvin, Dec. 28, 1928, Arvin MSS.; VWB to Frank, Jan. 12, 1935, Frank MSS.; Arvin, "Brooks's Life of Emerson," p. 358; VWB, "Journal," p. 15, Box 48, Brooks MSS.

33. VWB, *Oliver Allston,* p. 77; Arvin to VWB, Jan. 24, 1939, Brooks MSS.; VWB, "Journal," Box 48, Brooks MSS.; VWB to Arvin, Jan. 2, 1932, Arvin MSS.

34. Michael Wreszin, *The Superfluous Anarchist: Albert Jay Nock* (Providence: Brown Univ. Press, 1972), pp. 106–09.

35. *Brooks-Mumford Letters,* p. 132; VWB to G. S. Lee, Apr. 17, 1934, Lee MSS.; VWB, *Autobiography,* p. 534; VWB to Arvin, May 6, 1937, Arvin MSS.

36. Arvin to VWB, Feb. 4, 1932, Brooks MSS.; VWB to Arvin, Oct. 8 and Nov. 11, 1934, and Apr. 1, 1932, Arvin MSS.

37. VWB to Fletcher, May 18, 1935, Fletcher MSS.; *Brooks-Mumford Letters,* pp. 113, 141; VWB to Arvin, Nov. 11, 1934, Arvin MSS.

38. VWB to Arvin, Nov. 11, 1934, Arvin MSS.; VWB, *Autobiography,* p. 535; Daniel Aaron, *Writers on the Left* (New York: Avon, 1965), pp. 300–03; VWB to Frank, Jan. 12, 1935, Frank MSS.

39. Cowley, Burke, and Frank quoted in ESB to Charles V. W. Brooks, Feb. 16, 1936, Brooks MSS.; Cowley, "The Puritan Legacy," *New Republic* (Aug. 26, 1936), p. 80.

40. VWB to Arvin, Mar. 22, 1937, Arvin MSS.; VWB quoted in "An Attack on Democracy," *Commonweal*, 25 (Mar. 12, 1937), 537-38; League of American Writers *Bulletin*, 4 (May 1938), 3.

41. League of American Writers *Bulletin*, 5 (Fall 1938), 3; VWB, *Autobiography*, p. 535.

42. VWB, "The League of American Writers: A Personal Statement," *New Republic*, 98 (Feb. 22, 1939), 66.

43. "Connecticut Get-Together," *New Republic*, 97 (Dec. 14, 1938), 159; VWB to Arvin, Dec. 28, 1938, Arvin MSS.; *Brooks-Mumford Letters*, pp. 140, 158-59.

44. Arvin to VWB, Sept. 24 and Oct. 2, 1939, Brooks MSS.; VWB to Arvin, Sept. 26, 1939, Arvin MSS.; *Brooks-Mumford Letters*, pp. 168, 171; VWB to Farrell, Nov. 1, 1939, Farrell MSS.

45. VWB to Cowley, Oct. 31, 1939, Cowley MSS.

46. VWB, "Journal," p. 39, Box 48, Brooks MSS.; *Brooks-Mumford Letters*, p. 167.

47. VWB to O. G. Villard, June 4, 1938, Villard MSS. On Eva Wasserman, see the file for the American Guild for German Cultural Freedom, Brooks MSS.; VWB, *Oliver Allston*, p. 136; *Brooks-Mumford Letters*, p. 160.

48. *Brooks-Mumford Letters*, pp. 177-79.

49. *Brooks-Mumford Letters*, p. 180; VWB to Arvin, May 6, 1937, Arvin MSS.

50. VWB to O. G. Villard, Sept. 29, 1940, Villard MSS.; *New Republic*, 105 (Sept. 1, 1941), 280.

51. VWB to O. G. Villard, Aug. 6, 1940, Villard MSS. An anonymous contributor paid for five hundred copies of MacLeish's pamphlet to be sent, with Brooks's statement, to influential persons. VWB, "Writers and the War," Box 38, Brooks MSS.

52. VWB to Spingarn, Sept. 15, 1925, Spingarn MSS.

53. VWB, *Autobiography*, p. 291; VWB, "Imaginary Letter from a Purist to a Journalist," Box 46, Brooks MSS.; VWB to Clarkson Crane, May 7, 1932, Brooks MSS.

54. VWB, *The Flowering of New England* (New York: Dutton, 1936), pp. 30, 358.

55. Wilson, *Upstate*, p. 186.

56. VWB, *The Flowering of New England*, pp. 202, 386; VWB, *America's Coming-of-Age*, pp. 66, 76-79; VWB, "Preface," in Constance Rourke, *The Roots of American Culture* (New York: Harcourt, 1942), p. xi.

57. VWB, *The Flowering of New England*, pp. 398-401; VWB, *The Malady of the Ideal*, p. 85.

58. For instance, F. O. Matthiessen, rev. of *The Flowering of New England*, *The New England Quarterly* (Dec. 1936), p. 703.

59. VWB, *The Flowering of New England*, pp. 528-29.

60. Blackmur, "A Prophecy of Possibilities," pp. 218-19.

61. vwb, *The Flowering of New England,* pp. 17, 5, 19.
62. Ibid., pp. 82, 7, 166, 41, 94, 100, 355.
63. Ibid., pp. 526–28.
64. vwb to Cournos, Nov. 3, 1933, Brooks mss.; vwb, *The Writer in America* (New York: Dutton, 1953), p. 46.
65. vwb, *The Flowering of New England,* p. 527.
66. vwb, *New England: Indian Summer* (New York: Dutton, 1940), pp. 397–98, 408.
67. vwb to Benét, Jan. 19, 1938, Benét mss.
68. vwb, *New England: Indian Summer,* p. 212.
69. vwb to Benét, Jan. 9, 1938, Benét mss.; vwb, *New England: Indian Summer,* pp. 212, 215.
70. vwb, *New England: Indian Summer,* p. 222.
71. Ibid., p. 494.

CERTAIN ROOT IDEAS

1. Simonson to vwb, Aug. 11, 1936, Brooks mss.; Matthiessen, rev. of *The Flowering of New England, New England Quarterly,* 9 (Dec. 1936), 709; Bernard Smith, "Van Wyck Brooks," in *After the Genteel Tradition,* ed. Malcolm Cowley (1937; rpt. Carbondale, Ill.: Southern Illinois Univ. Press, 1964), p. 66; F. W. Dupee, "The Americanism of Van Wyck Brooks," *Partisan Review,* 6 (Summer 1939), p. 85.
2. DeVoto, *Mark Twain's America* (Chataqua, N.Y.: Chataqua Institution, 1933), p. 101; DeVoto, *The Literary Fallacy* (Boston: Little, Brown, 1944), p. 43.
3. vwb to Frank, July 23, 1943, Frank mss.: vwb to Vera McWilliams, Aug. 20, 1942, Brooks mss.; Sinclair Lewis, "Fools, Liars and Mr. DeVoto," *Saturday Review,* 27 (Apr. 15, 1944), 9; vwb to Lewis, Apr. 23, 1944, quoted in Mark Schorer, *Sinclair Lewis: An American Life* (New York: McGraw-Hill, 1961), p. 712; vwb to Arvin, Apr. 1, 1932, Arvin mss.; vwb to Bliss Perry, Oct. 18, 1933, Perry mss.
4. *Brooks-Mumford Letters,* p. 187.
5. Finkelstein quoted in the *New York Times,* Sept. 10, 1940, p. 24; Sept. 11, p. 30; Sept. 12, p. 27.
6. vwb to Finkelstein, June 20, 1940, Brooks mss.
7. *Brooks-Mumford Letters,* p. 187.
8. Ibid., p. 187.
9. Ibid., p. 191.
10. vwb, "Opening Remarks," Finkelstein file, Brooks mss.
11. vwb, *Oliver Allston,* p. 158.
12. vwb to Finkelstein, Apr. 17, 1941, Brooks mss.
13. *Brooks-Mumford Letters,* p. 193; vwb, *Oliver Allston,* pp. 229–30, 211.
14. vwb, *The Flowering of New England,* p. 161.
15. vwb, *Oliver Allston,* p. 16.
16. Brooks thought so himself (interview with Gladys Brooks, Mar. 1972).

17. vwb to George Russell, Jan. 8, 1932, Brooks mss.

18. vwb, *Oliver Allston*, pp. 223, 229, 232, 233, 236.

19. vwb, *Oliver Allston*, pp. 187, 179; Eliot, *The Sacred Wood* (London: Methuen, 1920), pp. 53, 50.

20. Trilling, "On the 'Brooks-MacLeish Thesis,'" *Partisan Review*, 9 (Jan.-Feb. 1942), 46; vwb, *Oliver Allston*, pp. 225, 231, 235, 236, 300, 239, 246.

21. vwb to S. K. Ratcliffe, Feb. 22, 1947, Brooks mss.; vwb to Wheelock, May 8, 1950, Brooks mss.; Interview with Wheelock, Feb. 1972.

22. vwb, *Oliver Allston*, pp. 231, 213; *Brooks-Mumford Letters*, p. 131.

23. vwb, *Oliver Allston*, p. 225; vwb to Arvin, May 6, 1937, Arvin mss.; *Brooks-Mumford Letters*, p. 154; vwb to M. A. DeWolfe Howe, Aug. 6, 1938, and May 22, 1939, Howe mss.; vwb, *On Literature Today* (New York: Dutton, 1941), pp. 28–29.

24. vwb, *Oliver Allston*, p. 22, 63, 291; vwb, *Three Essays*, p. 11.

25. vwb, *Oliver Allston*, pp. 168, 193.

26. Fadiman, rev. of *Oliver Allston*, *New Yorker*, 17 (Nov. 8, 1941), 92; Krutch, "An Invitation to Minerva," *Nation*, 153 (Dec. 13, 1941), 615; Cowley, rev. of *Oliver Allston*, *New Republic*, 105 (Dec. 1, 1941), 738; Alfred Kazin, *On Native Grounds* (New York: Reynal, 1942), p. 517.

27. Macdonald, "Kulturebolschewismus Is Here," *Partisan Review*, 8 (Nov.-Dec. 1941), 446; *Time* (Dec. 5, 1938), p. 4; Sandburg to vwb, Sept. 24, 1941, Brooks mss.; "On the 'Brooks-MacLeish Thesis,'" pp. 38, 42, 46; Eliot, "Letter to the Editors," *Partisan Review*, 9 (Mar.-Apr. 1942), 115–16.

28. "On the 'Brooks-MacLeish Thesis,'" pp. 40, 39, 41.

29. *Brooks-Mumford Letters*, p. 147.

30. vwb to Russell, Jan. 8, 1932, Brooks mss.

31. vwb to Arvin, Aug. 14, 1938, Arvin mss.; vwb, *Autobiography*, p. 29.

32. vwb, *The World of Washington Irving* (New York: Dutton, 1944), pp. 147, 165, 166, 339.

33. Ibid., pp. 150–51.

34. Ibid., pp. 164, 420, 419, 423, 425; cf. Parrington, *Main Currents in American Thought, Vol. II, The Romantic Revolution in America* (New York: Harcourt, 1927), pp. 208, 223.

35. vwb, *Washington Irving*, pp. 453–54.

36. Ibid., p. 350; Parrington had a similar opinion (*Main Currents*, II, 58).

37. vwb to Ratcliffe, Feb. 22, 1947, Brooks mss.

38. vwb, *Melville and Whitman*, pp. 229–33, 300, 297, 160–61, 476.

39. *Brooks-Mumford Letters*, pp. 250, 254–55.

40. vwb, *Melville and Whitman*, p. 175; vwb, *The Confident Years* (New York: Dutton, 1951), p. 587.

41. vwb, *The Confident Years*, p. 465; vwb, *Autobiography*, p. 544; vwb, *The Writer in America*, p. 190.

42. vwb, *Melville and Whitman*, pp. 183, 187.

43. vwb, *The Confident Years*, pp. 492, 494; Pound, *Patria Mia* (Chicago: Ralph Fletcher Seymour, 1950), pp. 24, 33, 36, 42, 45, 50–51, 56.

44. VWB, *The Confident Years,* pp. 577, 350.

45. Ibid., pp. 557, 561–63.

46. Ibid., pp. 569, 573, 576–77, 596, 595, 579.

47. Ibid., pp. 607, 312, 608, 602, 591, 608–09; VWB to Ratcliffe, July 30, 1950, Brooks MSS.; Brooks made similar arguments about the "inverted idealism" of modern American literature in *On Literature Today* (1941), p. 47, and in his speech before the National Institute of Arts and Letters, May 17, 1946, Box 41, Brooks MSS.

48. VWB, *The Confident Years,* p. 608.

49. VWB, *Autobiography,* p. 488; *Brooks-Mumford Letters,* pp. 313, 326–27.

50. VWB, *The Flowering of New England,* p. 529.

51. Ibid., p. 530; VWB, *Oliver Allston,* p. 263.

52. VWB, *Oliver Allston,* p. 265; VWB to Ratcliffe, Feb. 25, 1951, Brooks MSS.

53. VWB, *Melville and Whitman,* pp. 299–300; VWB, *The Confident Years,* p. 325.

54. VWB to Arvin, Nov. 2, 1947, Arvin MSS.; Mumford, "Our Rich Vein of Literary Ore," *Saturday Review,* Nov. 8, 1947, pp. 11–13.

55. VWB, *The Confident Years,* pp. 26–28; VWB, *Melville and Whitman,* pp. 152, 20 n.; VWB to Arvin, Jan. 25, 1948, Arvin MSS.

56. VWB, *New England: Indian Summer,* pp. 100, 397–98; VWB, *Melville and Whitman,* pp. 400, 461–62.

57. VWB, *Melville and Whitman,* pp. 394, 166; VWB, *The Confident Years,* p. 237; *Brooks-Mumford Letters,* p. 250; Edmund Wilson, *Classics and Commercials* (New York: Farrar, Strauss, 1950), pp. 423–30.

58. VWB to Clarkson Crane, May 7, 1932, Brooks MSS.; VWB, *Oliver Allston,* p. 64; VWB, *The Flowering of New England,* p. 135.

59. VWB, *The Flowering of New England,* pp. 526, 528; VWB, *New England: Indian Summer,* p. 433; VWB, *The Confident Years,* pp. 605, 610.

60. *Brooks-Mumford Letters,* p. 313.

61. Victor von Hagen, *Maya Explorer* (Norman, Oklahoma: Univ. of Oklahoma Press, 1947); Wilson, *Patriotic Gore* (New York: Oxford, 1962), p. 669; Wilson to VWB, Jan. 2, 1962, Brooks MSS.; Wilson, *Upstate,* p. 186.

62. VWB, *Oliver Allston,* p. 77.

MAN OF LETTERS

1. ESB to Charles V. W. Brooks, Dec. 9, 1941, and Feb. 26, 1944, Brooks MSS.

2. VWB to M. A. DeWolfe Howe, Dec. 31, 1940, Howe MSS.; VWB, *Autobiography,* p. 257; Interview with Oliver K. Brooks, Dec. 1973.

3. VWB, *Autobiography,* p. 547.

4. ESB to Charles V. W. Brooks, Aug. 4, 1941, Brooks MSS.

5. VWB to William McFee, Sept. 22, 1944, McFee MSS.; VWB to Howe, Oct. 4, 1943, Howe MSS.; VWB to Dorothy Whyte, Oct. 4, 1943, courtesy of

Mrs. Whyte; ESB to Charles V. W. Brooks, Sept. 28, 1943, and Aug. 4, 1941, Brooks MSS.

6. ESB to Charles V. W. Brooks, Feb. 1, Mar. 15, May 7, and June 13, 1943, Brooks MSS.; *Brooks-Mumford Letters,* pp. 229–30; VWB to Howe, Mar. 25, 1943, Howe MSS.

7. *Brooks-Mumford Letters,* p. 206; ESB to Charles V. W. Brooks, Mar. 25 and June 25, 1944, Brooks MSS.; VWB to H. S. Canby, May 7, 1944, Canby MSS.; VWB to Arvin, July 4, 1944, Arvin MSS.

8. VWB to Dorothy Whyte, Dec. 3, 1936, courtesy of Mrs. Whyte; VWB to Charles V. W. Brooks, Aug. 26, 1943, Brooks MSS.; ESB to Charles V. W. Brooks, May 7, July 2, July 18, and Oct. 15, 1943, Brooks MSS.

9. VWB to Hamilton Basso, Feb. 19, 1945, courtesy of Mrs. Basso; ESB to Charles V. W. Brooks, Jan. 6, Jan 27, and Feb. 5, 1945, Brooks MSS.; VWB to Elliot Macrae, Feb. 22, 1945, Brooks MSS.; Henry Stimson to ESB, Feb. 27, 1945, Stimson MSS.

10. ESB to Charles V. W. Brooks, Mar. 19, June 12, June 24, and Aug. 1, 1945, Brooks MSS.; VWB to William McFee, Mar. 29, 1945, McFee MSS.; VWB, *Autobiography,* p. 549; *Brooks-Mumford Letters,* pp. 202, 283.

11. VWB to Hamilton Basso, Jan. 27, 1946, courtesy of Mrs. Basso; *Brooks-Mumford Letters,* pp. 293–94.

12. *Brooks-Mumford Letters,* p. 278.

13. ESB to Charles V. W. Brooks, Jan. 21, 1932, Aug. 4, 1942, and Oct. 31, 1944, Brooks MSS.; VWB to Dorothy Whyte, Apr. 29, 1937, Dec. 5, 1939, Mar. 26, 1943, and Sept. 21, 1946, courtesy of Mrs. Whyte.

14. ESB to Charles V. W. Brooks, Mar. 12 and 20, 1946, May 12 and 15, 1941, and June 1, 1944, Brooks MSS.; VWB to Arvin, May 8, 1946, Arvin MSS.

15. ESB to Charles V. W. Brooks, July 2, Aug. 6, and Sept. 9, 1943, Brooks MSS.

16. ESB to Charles V. W. Brooks, Aug. 24, 1943, Brooks MSS.

17. ESB to Charles V. W. Brooks, July 2, 1943, Brooks MSS.

18. ESB to Charles V. W. Brooks, Aug. 24, 1943, Brooks MSS.

19. ESB to Charles V. W. Brooks, July 2 and Aug. 3, 1943, Brooks MSS.

20. ESB to Charles V. W. Brooks, July 2, 1943, Brooks MSS.

21. ESB to Charles V. W. Brooks, Aug. 24, 1943, Brooks MSS.

22. ESB to Charles V. W. Brooks, July 2, Aug. 3, and Aug. 24, 1943, Brooks MSS.

23. ESB to Charles V. W. Brooks, July 2, Aug. 3, and Aug. 4, 1943, Brooks MSS.

24. Oliver K. Brooks to Charles V. W. Brooks, June 10, 1946, Brooks MSS.; ESB to Charles V. W. Brooks, June 19, 1946, Brooks MSS.; Henry Stimson to ESB, Aug. 1, 1946, Stimson MSS.

25. ESB to Charles V. W. Brooks, June 3, 1946, Brooks MSS.; Charles V. W. Brooks to Oliver K. Brooks, May 27, 1946, Brooks MSS.; *Brooks-Mumford Letters,* p. 299.

26. *Brooks-Mumford Letters,* p. 299; VWB to Ratcliffe, Sept. 16, 1946, Brooks MSS.; VWB, *Autobiography,* p. 561.

27. Gladys Brooks, *If Strangers Meet,* pp. 6–9; VWB, *Autobiography,* p. 229; Oliver K. Brooks to Charles V. W. Brooks, Nov. 22, 1946, Brooks MSS.; VWB to Finkelstein, Apr. 8, 1941, Brooks MSS.

28. Oliver K. Brooks to Charles V. W. Brooks, May 2, 1947, Brooks MSS.

29. Interview with Gladys Brooks, Mar. 1972; Gladys Brooks, *If Strangers Meet,* chaps. 1–3.

30. Interview with Mrs. Hamilton Basso, Mar. 1972; VWB, *Autobiography,* pp. 576, 465.

31. See, for instance, the files in the Brooks MSS. for Benjamin Appel, Margot Astrov, Irene Baird, Joran Birkeland, Paul Bishop, and C. L. Cleaves.

32. VWB to Hamilton Basso, July 28, 1943, courtesy of Mrs. Basso; Constance Rourke file, Brooks MSS.; VWB to Arvin, Mar. 2, 1941, Arvin MSS.

33. Box 41, Brooks MSS.

34. VWB, *On Literature Today,* pp. 15, 24–25; Farrell file, Brooks MSS.; Farrell, "The Frightened Philistines," *New Republic,* Dec. 4, 1944, p. 764; *Brooks-Mumford Letters,* p. 270.

35. VWB to George Russell, Jan. 8, 1932, Brooks MSS.; VWB to Benét, Dec. 31, 1940, Brooks MSS.

36. VWB to Howe, May 15, 1941, and Jan. 6, 1942, Howe MSS.; VWB to Walter Damrosch, Apr. 24, 1944, courtesy of the American Academy of Arts and Letters.

37. VWB to Howe, Oct. 4, 1943, and Mar. 21, 1951, Howe MSS.; Felicia Geffen to Brooks, Jan. 9, 1951, courtesy of the American Academy of Arts and Letters; Douglas Moore to Archibald MacLeish, June 24, 1953, copy in Brooks MSS.

38. Miller to VWB, Feb. 19, 1957, Brooks MSS.; Steinbeck to VWB, Nov. 13, 1953, Brooks MSS.

39. VWB to Howe, May 27, 1957, Howe MSS.

40. Mumford, "Mr. Beard and His 'Basic History,'" *Saturday Review,* 27 (Dec. 2, 1944), 27; *Brooks-Mumford Letters,* p. 273.

41. *Brooks-Mumford Letters,* pp. 317–22.

42. *Brooks-Mumford Letters,* pp. 322–27.

43. VWB to Henry A. Murray, "Sunday evening," courtesy of Professor Murray.

44. *Brooks-Mumford Letters,* pp. 328–30.

45. Ibid., pp. 333–34; *New York Times,* May 22, 1948, p. 16.

46. *Brooks-Mumford Letters,* pp. 345, 389; VWB to Felicia Geffen, July 5, 1954, courtesy of the American Academy of Arts and Letters.

47. *Brooks-Mumford Letters,* pp. 303–04.

48. Mary Colum, *Life and the Dream* (Garden City, N.Y.: Doubleday, 1947), p. 345.

49. *Brooks-Mumford Letters,* pp. 289–96, 237, 245, 289, 352.

50. VWB, *Oliver Allston*, p. 287; *Brooks-Mumford Letters*, pp. 365–66.

51. *Brooks-Mumford Letters*, pp. 369, 373.

52. Ibid., pp. 373–74.

53. Ibid., pp. 357, 293, 408; VWB, "Lewis Mumford: American Prophet," *Harper's Magazine*, 204 (June 1951), 50.

DISSOLUTION

1. Interview with Oliver K. Brooks, Dec. 1973; Oliver K. Brooks to Charles V. W. Brooks, May 2, 1947, Brooks MSS.

2. Gladys Brooks, *If Strangers Meet*, p. 23.

3. VWB to James Stern, Mar. 16, 1953, Brooks MSS.

4. Interview with Gladys Brooks, Mar. 1972.

5. VWB, *Autobiography*, p. 579.

6. Ibid., p. 579.

7. Gladys Brooks, *If Strangers Meet*, pp. 85–87, 112; *Brooks-Mumford Letters*, p. 342.

8. Interview with Gladys Brooks, Mar. 1972; VWB, *Autobiography*, p. 579.

9. VWB to Charles V. W. Brooks, Apr. 13 and Dec. 7, 1947, Brooks MSS.; Gladys Brooks, *If Strangers Meet*, p. 67.

10. VWB, "Recollections of Plainfield," in *Plainfield Public Library: A Record of the Seventieth Anniversary Celebration* (Plainfield, N.J.: privately printed, 1952); VWB, *Autobiography*, p. 13.

11. Gladys Brooks, *If Strangers Meet*, pp. 123–38; VWB, *Autobiography*, pp. 604–11.

12. Gladys Brooks, *If Strangers Meet*, pp. 128–38; VWB, *Autobiography*, pp. 604–11.

13. Gladys Brooks, *If Strangers Meet*, p. 125.

14. Ibid., pp. 149–55.

15. VWB, *Autobiography*, pp. 480–81; *Brooks-Mumford Letters*, p. 432.

16. Gladys Brooks, *If Strangers Meet*, pp. 193–207; *Brooks-Mumford Letters*, p. 394.

17. Gladys Brooks, *If Strangers Meet*, pp. 221–23, 233–36; *Brooks-Mumford Letters*, p. 402.

18. VWB, *Autobiography*, pp. 620–23.

19. *Brooks-Mumford Letters*, p. 404.

20. Gladys Brooks, *If Strangers Meet*, pp. 255–60; VWB to William McFee, Aug. 25, 1947, McFee MSS.; VWB to Allan Nevins, Dec. 2, 1959, Nevins MSS.; *Brooks-Mumford Letters*, p. 329.

21. VWB, *The Dream of Arcadia* (New York: Dutton, 1958), p. 263.

22. VWB to Ratcliffe, Jan. 11, 1953, Brooks MSS.

23. Leon Edel, "Under Skies Always Shining," p. 1.

24. VWB to Robert Spiller, Jan. 18, 1952, Brooks MSS.

25. VWB, *Howells: His Life and World* (New York: Dutton, 1959), pp. 187, 286.

26. VWB, *John Sloan*, p. 239; VWB to Howe, Aug. 15, 1955, Howe MSS.; VWB to Ratcliffe, May 9, 1955, Brooks MSS.; VWB, *Howells*, p. 287; VWB, *The Writer in America*, p. 175.

27. VWB to Kazin, Jan. 27, 1952, Brooks MSS. See also Kazin's review, "What Happened to the Nineteenth Century?" *New Yorker*, Jan. 6, 1952, p. 90.

28. VWB, *The Writer in America*, pp. 1–2, 19.

29. VWB, *Chilmark Miscellany* (New York: Dutton, 1947), p. 15; VWB, "Plastic Historian of an Age," *Saturday Review*, 34 (Dec. 1, 1951), 22.

30. VWB, *Chilmark Miscellany*, pp. 15–16; VWB to Dorothy Brewster, Feb. 23, 1957, Brooks MSS.

31. VWB, *The Writer in America*, pp. 9, 159.

32. VWB, "Journal," p. 103, Box 48, Brooks MSS.; VWB to Finkelstein, Apr. 17, 1931, Brooks MSS.; VWB to Ruth Stephan, May 5, 1954, Brooks MSS.; VWB to Peter Viereck, Apr. 2, 1950, Brooks MSS.

33. VWB, *The Writer in America*, pp. 183–88.

34. VWB, *Oliver Allston*, p. 270.

35. VWB, "Reflections on the Avant-Garde," *New York Times Book Review*, Dec. 30, 1956, pp. 1, 10–13.

36. Ibid., pp. 1, 10–13.

37. Ibid., p. 13.

38. Ibid., p. 13.

39. VWB, *Autobiography*, p. 637.

40. VWB, *The Writer in America*, pp. 193–94.

41. VWB, "Introduction," in Leo Stein, *Journey into the Self* (New York: Crown, 1950), p. xiv; VWB, "Preface," in Chiang Yee, *Silent Traveller in New York* (London: Methuen, 1950), p. x; VWB, *From a Writer's Notebook*, p. 125.

42. VWB, *The Writer in America*, pp. 100, 108.

43. VWB, *On Literature Today*; VWB, *From a Writer's Notebook*, p. 56; VWB, *The Writer in America*, pp. 63, 99–100; VWB, "Preface," in Chiang Yee, *Silent Traveller in New York*, p. x; Gladys Brooks, *If Strangers Meet*, p. 265.

44. VWB, *The Writer in America*, pp. 193, 89; VWB, "Reflections on the Avant-Garde," p. 13.

45. "Homage to Van Wyck Brooks," *Proceedings* of the American Academy of Arts and Letters (1962), pp. 145, 150.

46. Ibid., pp. 155, 143.

47. VWB to Ratcliffe, Oct. 31, 1955, Brooks MSS.

48. Kennedy to VWB, June 23, 1960, Brooks MSS.; VWB to Allan Nevins, Aug. 25, 1960, Nevins MSS.; John Saltonstall to VWB, Sept. 22, 1960, Brooks MSS.; *Brooks-Mumford Letters*, p. 425.

49. Gladys Brooks, *If Strangers Meet*, pp. 319–23; *New York World Telegraph and Sun*, May 5, 1962, p. 3.

50. VWB, "Introduction," in *Writers at Work: The Paris Review Interviews* (New York: Viking, 1963), pp. 1, 3.

51. VWB to Gregory, July 8, 1961, Brooks MSS.; VWB, *Fenollosa*, pp. 314–15; VWB, *Autobiography*, p. 284.

52. vwb, *Fenollosa,* p. 309.

53. vwb, *Autobiography,* p. 639; vwb to Ratcliffe, May 7, 1953, Brooks mss.; Gladys Brooks, *If Strangers Meet,* p. 31; *Brooks-Mumford Letters,* p. 411.

54. Gladys Brooks, *If Strangers Meet,* pp. 267–69; Wilson, *Upstate,* p. 183.

55. vwb, *Autobiography,* pp. 639, 642; Wilson, *Upstate,* p. 183.

56. Wilson, *Upstate,* pp. 183–86; Wilson, "Arvin's Longfellow and New York State Geology," *New Yorker,* Mar. 23, 1963, p. 174.

57. Wilson, *Upstate,* pp. 183–86.

58. vwb, *Autobiography,* pp. 638–40; vwb to Allan Nevins, Sept. 1, 1958, Nevins mss.

59. vwb, *Autobiography,* p. 640; Wilson, *Upstate,* p. 187; Gladys Brooks, *If Strangers Meet,* p. 269.

60. vwb to Arvin, July 12, 1941, Arvin mss.

61. Arvin to vwb, Sept. 28, 1948, and Feb. 14, 1954, Brooks mss.; Arvin quoted in Daniel Aaron's "Introduction" to Arvin, *American Pantheon* (New York: Delacorte, 1966), p. xv.

62. Gladys Brooks, *If Strangers Meet,* p. 54; vwb, *Autobiography,* p. 564.

63. *New York Times,* Sept. 4, 1960, p. 54; Sept. 6, 1960, p. 70; Sept. 8, 1960, p. 10; Sept. 9, 1960, p. 17; Arvin to vwb, Sept. 11, 1960, Brooks mss.

64. vwb to Arvin, Dec. 28, 1938, Arvin mss.; Arvin to vwb, Oct. 19, 1947, Brooks mss.

65. Arvin to vwb, Mar. 27, 1961, Brooks mss.; vwb to Arvin, Mar. 25, 1962, Arvin mss. The numerous introductions that Brooks "wrote" in his later years for reprints of American novels seldom involved a new act of composition. Usually, he copied a relevant passage out of *Makers and Finders.*

66. Arvin to vwb, May 27, 1962, Brooks mss.

67. *Brooks-Mumford Letters,* pp. 423, 416.

68. Ibid., pp. 191, 436–37.

69. Gladys Brooks, *If Strangers Meet,* pp. 329–30.

70. Gladys Brooks to Arvin, Feb. 9, 1963, Arvin mss.; Wilson, "Arvin's Longfellow," pp. 174–81.

71. Gladys Brooks, *If Strangers Meet,* pp. 330–31.

INDEX

Library of Congress Cataloging in Publication Data

Hoopes, James, 1944–

Van Wyck Brooks: in search of American culture.

Bibliography: p.

Includes index.

1. Brooks, Van Wyck, 1886–1963.

PS3503.R7297Z7   818'.5'209 [B]   76-8754

ISBN 0-87023-212-6